MAN'S QUEST FOR POLITICAL KNOWLEDGE

To Morgia

⌐ Preface

In conducting over many years a course on scope and methods in the department of political science at the University of Minnesota, I gathered a considerable amount of material on the study and teaching of politics. Not until my retirement in 1957 was I able, however, to devote full time to a systematic investigation of this subject. To supplement my own work, grants from the Ford Foundation and the Social Science Research Council made it possible for me to employ as research assistants from 1957 until 1960 a number of advanced graduate students from the departments of classics, German, and Romance languages, as well as political science. They undertook a search of the catalogue of the University of Minnesota Library and of the major bibliographies in such fields as political science, education, law, classics, history, and philology for books and articles that might contribute to my study. Each assistant worked primarily with publications in the language over which he had the greatest mastery. Every book and article in the preliminary bibliography of several thousand titles was examined for content. Even so, I soon became aware that I could not hope to find all the materials bearing on my subject before beginning to write the history of it that I felt was needed. I therefore ask that scholars who read this book will call my attention to any pertinent works that I may have overlooked, as well as to any misstatements or errors in judgment they may detect. I would like to have the record set straight and made as full as possible.

I want to express my appreciation to the following: the University of Minnesota, for direct and indirect assistance on this project, including invaluable library service; the Ford Foundation and the Social Science Research Council for their grants and support; my research assistants,

Santina (Mrs. Conrad R.) Bayerle, Ben Cochenet, Aliniece C. Crosby, Klaus Herrmann, Tom Jacobson, Phyllis King, Ruediger Moehle, Don Patterson, Donald Replogle, Herbert Sommer, Dean Swanson, Joseph Toft, and John Whiton; and Louise P. Olsen and Karla Hodgson for excellent work in typing the manuscript.

WILLIAM ANDERSON

Minneapolis, Minnesota
February 1964

ᔕ Contents

THE BACKGROUND AND THE BOOK

"In this subject as in others the best method of investigation is to study things in the process of development from the beginning." Aristotle's *Politics*, Book I, chapter 1

⤙ The Background and the Book

THE subject of politics has long been established as a college and university study in the United States. It appears under various titles such as Government (Harvard and elsewhere), Politics (Princeton), and, most commonly, Political Science. In secondary schools, where the elementary study of politics is also well established, course titles that emphasize the idea of citizenship are widely used. There is probably no important junior college, four-year college, or university in the entire United States that does not have the study of politics as a regular part of its curriculum. The numbers of students of college and graduate school level in political science courses run high in the hundreds of thousands each year, while the national professional organization of teachers in the field, the American Political Science Association, which is constantly growing, has over ten thousand members, of whom some thirty-five hundred or more are actively engaged in teaching.

Other countries in recent years have also seen considerable advances (influenced no doubt to some extent by the example of the United States) in political science as a college and university subject. A striking evidence of the increased interest around the world was the founding in 1949 of the International Political Science Association. By 1958 twenty-five nations had organizations of political scientists, most of them but recently established, that were affiliated with this association.

However, in the range of political science courses offered, in the numbers of teachers and students engaged with the subject, in the numbers of graduate and undergraduate degrees conferred, in the production of scholarly publications, in the many services that teachers of politics render to public bodies of all kinds—in all these respects the United

States has been and continues to be far and away the world's leader. To identify all the specific factors contributing to this intense American concern with the study and teaching of politics is probably impossible. But certainly one must begin with the circumstances of the nation's founding and growth and the manner of development of its educational system.

As American schoolbooks recite in detail, the founding fathers who landed at Plymouth in 1620 and those who came after them to settle up and down the Atlantic seaboard in thirteen colonies very early discovered that the British government to which they were nominally subject was too remote and too indifferent to their needs to be of much help to them. What they required from government they obtained mainly by their own exertions and through their own elected representatives in their respective colonies, but also through their town, borough, and county governments, with which they had almost daily contacts. When the United States became a separate nation in 1789, its Constitution declared sovereignty to be vested in the people. As the nation grew and its citizens multiplied, public interest in politics and government remained generally high, nourished by the frequent elections in which the voters chose most of their important officials, national, state, and local; by free discussion of national and state constitutions ("Every man his own constitutional lawyer"); by the efforts of the major political parties and the press and other media of communication to keep political issues before the public; by the widely held conception of government as a mechanism that can be improved by human manipulation.

At the same time, educational institutions and practices were being shaped, like the forms of government itself, by the varied needs of a free people. In the early years the examples of Oxford and Cambridge had dominated the thinking of American schoolmen, but their influence soon waned. In the liberating atmosphere of the New World American educators experimented broadly with their own educational ideas. The state governments, although beginning early in the nineteenth century to give substantial support to state colleges and universities, set down practically no regulations concerning college education generally. The national government had no direct power over education, had no national ministry of education or educational policy (and still has none). Local groups of citizens, church organizations, and other associations could establish schools and colleges almost without restriction and lay politics does not begin in 1900, or 1789, or 1620—dates of special American significance. In this as in other fields of intellectual inquiry, the foreshadowings of the American experience may be discerned in earlier ages—in fact, from the beginnings of recorded history in the West. Who were the men that first studied the different elements that go into modern American political science? When, where, how, and under what conditions did they work? Who studied political theory? public law? international relations? municipal government? When, where, and under what names did these subjects appear? When were they suppressed or dropped? When and how did they reappear? Were there any really political studies at all in the Dark Ages? under the feudal system? What efforts if any were made to teach citizenship or politics to the people? to the princes? How and by whom were men trained for the public service?

To my knowledge no one has attempted to answer these questions in any thorough and systematic way.[3] I believe such an investigation of political teaching and study through all the centuries, in all major Western civilizations, is long overdue.

One may ask, Why? What advantages are to be had from histories tracing the development of a field of knowledge? Aristotle, with the study of politics specifically in mind, wrote: "In this subject as in others the best method of investigation is to study things in the process of development from the beginning."[4] And he meant this study to encompass not only observation of actual things like animals, plants, and human societies, but reading and digesting whatever had been written about such things. He assigned to his assistants the exploration first of the history of each subject they were concerned with; they were then expected to carry on from where history left off. Many modern writers and scholars have held similar views. José Ortega y Gasset probably spoke the thought of many when he said: "To comprehend anything human, be it personal or collective, one must tell its history."[5] Harald Höffding said that "as we learn to know a man from his biography, so also we must be able to learn to know a science from its history."[6] W. P. D. Wightman, after commenting that modern scientific education "fails to give the sense of human continuity and all those intangible qualities which we express in the name culture," urged that history be taught "not to 'liberalize' science, but to understand it" and to reveal science as a struggle, "a struggle no less charged with humanistic value than the struggle for political liberty or national expression."[7] But best of all, I think, are some of the statements of George Sarton in his lectures on *The History of Science and the New Humanism,* where the humanistic values of the history of science are repeatedly stressed—and Sarton's vision was broad enough to include the humanities and the social sciences in his definition of science.[8]

It was with these values in mind that I undertook the present work. My approach is, I hope, suggested by my title: *Man's Quest for Political Knowledge.* My study was made and my work was written in what I consider to be humanistic terms. Beginning in prehistoric times under most primitive conditions, without letters, without tools or industries, without cities or civilization, the human species has gone forward (no doubt with many a slip backward or sideways) to develop arts and sciences and to gain increasing control over nature, though at uneven rates in different times and places. One part of this complex process has been to bring all the continents and islands under organized government and to advance self-government to the point where nearly all peoples will be in some degree self-governing before many years have passed. Long kept in ignorance and in some places led to believe that kings were gods and government over men was solely the concern of the gods, the mass of men only slowly—and with reluctance—recognized that they must accept the responsibility of governing themselves if they were to benefit from government. To do this they had to acquire a knowledge of politics and government, create political institutions, and build communities with defined boundaries, from the smallest of villages up to the great national states and empires and even to international organizations like the United Nations. In the history of human civilization these political advances—although as yet far from finished—have been among the most important of achievements, because they have required men to gain control over themselves, and to establish laws for themselves.

In using the phrase "man's quest" I have no illusions that all men have been eager to study politics or anxious to participate in political processes or in the reform and improvement thereof. Quite the contrary. I know that most men show a strong tendency to shun serious studies of any kind and to eschew politics if they can. Politics had a high repute among certain Greek writers, as the master art; but many others, ancient and modern, have looked down upon it. Even today the word is widely used in a pejorative sense, as if politics were primarily an evil.[9] Many forget or deny that politics (including government) is a necessity of communal organization, however evil it may be at times; and that progress toward just and honest government is essential to all advancement in civilization.

A sense for politics as a distinct and important part of all civilized living, and a realization of the possibility of improving political institutions and behavior, seem to come rather late in most individuals and in most societies. And yet here and there for brief intervals in ancient times, and increasingly in later eras, when the conditions were not unduly discouraging, a few individuals delved deeply into politics in the hope that from their studies men generally would gain the knowledge that gives them power to control and improve the political conditions and the governments under which they live. These students—at least many of them—were not motivated usually by the desire for personal power as rulers over others; rather, they were moved by the idea of spreading political education widely among the people in order to enable them to check the excesses of the governing authorities and to hold the latter responsible for their actions.

In these pages I have frequently used the terms "politics" and "study of politics." It is important to make it very clear what I mean by them, to define the concepts I understand them to identify.

Many writers have tried to define political science or the study of politics, but not so many have ventured to define what politics itself really is or is about. When they have attempted the latter, they have usually oversimplified, defining politics unitarily as the exercise of power over men or the authoritative allocation of values or the attainment of freedom or of justice. Clearly, power, values, freedom, and justice are involved in political processes, but no single concept can encompass all politics. No one factor can explain everything in a field composed of so many parts and presenting so many distinct facets and local variations.

In my view, "politics" is today a class name for a wide range of human activities relating to the establishment, organization, disorganization, and interrelations of communities, and to the formation and carrying out of community policies throughout the world. The communities concerned are of many types, from the most primitive to the most advanced. Some are small and others are large, some "sovereign" and others "nonsovereign." They range from pretty isolated primitive tribes or villages to mighty national states and empires. In a sense, all these communities form a single international community, although it is usually seriously divided. The activities concerned embrace all the "informal" acts of individuals, groups, and political parties in gaining power and authority in the community for themselves and also all the "formal" acts of governments and their officials in enacting and enforcing laws, defending themselves and the community against internal and external enemies, providing public services, and so on. Acts of violence are included among political acts as well as nonviolent ones, violation of the laws as well as obedience to them. The activities involved in political processes are indescribably numerous, varied, interconnected, and complex.

The elements of a political community are a land area, a population, and some sort of accepted community organization, however inchoate and rudimentary the latter may be. It is necessary for each politically organized community to have some powers, resources, and work to do, but it is not necessary for the organization to have exclusive or "sovereign" control over the territory it occupies. With a workable division of functions there can be small communities within larger ones, cities within states, and states within federal systems; and at each level in each area there can be a distinctive political life, organization, and group of public activities. The city will have one set of officials, the state another, and the nation a third, and each will have its own activities, resources, and problems, albeit there will be many contacts, interrelations, and sometimes conflicts among these different units.

My concept of politics is, therefore, one of a body of distinctly human phenomena—activities, organizations, institutions—as widespread throughout the earth as the human species itself, and as multifarious as the almost infinite differences among people, places, times, and conditions can make them. It includes all truly public affairs, community affairs, no matter how the publics and communities are organized; all their activities; and all their relations with each other, with smaller communities and groups existing within the larger units, and with their individual members. It includes formal, legal government as well as all informal acts that influence or are designed to gain control of government.

This concept of politics is probably not original with me, but I think it is one that I have developed in my own way as a result of my studies and background in the United States. I doubt that many writers of the past with whom I deal in this volume, as probable contributors in their

10

day to the study and teaching of politics—Greek philosophers and Sophists, Roman law teachers, and so on—held any such view. Some of the Greeks had very much broader ideas of politics. Many later writers, restricted in what they could do, dealt only with particular problems or aspects of the field, and were not led into wider empirical studies. While picking up and trying to weave together into a connected piece the many threads that these men produced, I have had to try to avoid attributing to them my own concept of politics as a whole. At the same time I have felt that if their work touched on what I conceive as politics, even if they would not have so regarded it, I was justified in considering it here.

As I use it, "study of politics" is another class name designating a wide range of human activities that are closely related to and overlapping upon but still distinguishable from the activities designated as politics. No distinction in these fields is of more practical utility than that between men called politicians and those who are students and teachers of politics. In a well-functioning political system both kinds of workers are necessary, and their cooperation with and understanding of each other are highly useful. A man may transfer from one class to the other, but he cannot easily and successfully be both at the same time.

English and American dictionaries agree that "to study" means to apply one's mind to the acquisition of knowledge. The study may be for any one of a number of purposes—for merely personal satisfaction, for vocational or professional, economic or political advantage, for the solution of personal or public problems, or for the advancement of human knowledge. Studies may range from simple cogitation and oral discussion (as in preliterate societies) to the perusal of written documents and printed works and direct observations of men and nature and finally to the much more systematic, logical, and mathematical endeavors characteristic of modern sciences.

In the field of politics, no level of study or learning should be omitted from its history. Even when the words "politics" and "government" are not used, there is indoctrination by parents, shamans, prophets, ministers, schoolteachers, and others, and possibly some reflection by the child, on what are at least potentially political matters—patriotism, respect for authority, and so on. In the analysis that follows I have not intended to exclude entirely any level of study or teaching, but for practical purposes I have found it impossible to give much attention to any studies carried out below the age level of adolescence; in more definite terms, I have not attempted to discuss work done with students younger than the ephebe (ages about 18 to 20) in ancient Greece or the high school student (say ages 14 to 18) in the United States. The point at which young people learn "the laws of the city" or take a first course in "civics" or citizenship marks more or less definitely the beginning of their formal study of politics. It is at this point that my investigations will begin; no part of the formal process of studying politics from adolescence on will be deliberately neglected.

It should be noted also that this work will not concentrate solely on the specialists called political scientists and their pupils. This class of scholar, now so numerous in the United States, is represented before the end of the nineteenth century by only a small number of professors in German and American universities, while none, I believe, had appeared in Great Britain, France, or other leading European or North or South American countries. For all practical purposes, political scientists are a rather recent class of scholarly specialists. But there have been students of various phases of politics for several thousand years. Writings on politics that make some contribution to the total body of knowledge about it have come from a long and varied list of scholars including historians (Thucydides, Polybius, Tacitus, Livy, among many), philosophers (Plato, Aristotle, Hume, Kant), theologians (St. Thomas Aquinas), lawyers and lawyer-statesmen (Cicero, Bodin, Alexander Hamilton, A. V. Dicey), Sophists (Isocrates), cameralists, statisticians, political economists (Adam Smith, John Stuart Mill), sociologists (Max Weber, R. M. MacIver), classicists (Ernest Barker), and many others.

Then, too, in the practical division of labor among academic disciplines some topics of the utmost importance to politics are not usually studied in political science departments but in departments of economics, sociology, law, and education. Almost all American universities, for example, assign such subjects as taxation, public finance, and fiscal policy to their departments of economics; yet there are very few subjects of more direct concern to politicians, legislators, and public administrators. I shall not be able to give a full account of any of these subjects, but I shall here and there consider them briefly.

Presently, every learned profession and every body of scholars interested in any aspect of human affairs (and which ones are not?) has its ideas about politics. Consequently, there have developed a number of hybrid or interdisciplinary studies affecting politics, such as political sociology, political psychology, political geography, and political ethics, not to neglect the older political history, constitutional history, and diplomatic history. These too will turn up herein from time to time.

In addition I do not intend to limit "study of politics" to what has been done by teachers or in educational institutions. Politics has been studied, openly or secretly, by governmental officials (in foreign affairs, defense affairs, public finance, public administration, and the like) from the most ancient times to the present. These studies within government have been, on the whole, but little publicized, and yet who can doubt that much of what has been so studied has entered into the general stream of political knowledge. Further, much study of politics takes place after the completion of a public career. Machiavelli is an example, as is Cicero. And so we have studies within governments and princely offices, in private homes and other places, by church, labor, business, and other organizations that have serious problems of relations with the political powers-that-be. In the United States, political parties and pressure groups are also becoming active in such study.

In fact, while politics may not be the central interest of a large proportion of any population, it is actually a common interest to some extent of every body of people who are sufficiently educated and alert to be aware of their political interests. Thus it happens that every organized segment of the population has its political specialists and advisers.

Articles that touch upon or even go deeply into political problems appear in almost every type of publication today: scientific, industrial, commercial, agricultural, educational, legal, religious, philosophical, literary, "popular." Modern journalists, publicists, columnists, and even cartoonists have made and continue to make important contributions. The novel, the short story, the drama, and poetry cannot be left out of account if the picture is to be complete. In short, if my time for research and writing had been unlimited, this history of the study of politics would have explored many areas that here can be little more than mentioned. The great masses of recent and current writings that are somewhat pertinent but in the main only peripheral to politics reveal how widespread in the United States is the interest in political affairs. It is important to know of this. On the other hand many of the investigations made and the materials published on politics by men and organizations to whom politics is only a secondary or minor interest are relatively unoriginal, superficial, and tendentious and can safely be passed over lightly.

Inevitably of course teachers and the formal teaching of politics will play a large role in the history that follows. Teachers have been the most productive of scholars, whether preparing material only for their own students or for a wider body of readers. Almost every endeavor to improve teaching materials opens new areas for investigation, and every presentation of new materials brings from students new questions for further study. The process is an endless one. It is the main generative process in the expansion of knowledge, as I see it, and conscientious, alert, studious teachers make constant contributions to man's knowledge in all fields.

In this history, I shall, then, seek out and pay special attention to the teachers of the various elements of knowledge that go to make up what I call political science. Will this therefore be a history of political science? In a limited sense, yes, but on the whole I think not. I see political science as, on the one hand, the great existent accumulation of observations, hypotheses, and generalizations about politics that all students of the field have made from ancient times to the present, and, on the other, as the continuous search by countless thousands of learners and teachers for more light and more truth in this broad field. Not everything in this ever-growing body of knowledge is "true"; not every item is important; and not every item is integrated or even consistent with every other item in it, any more than would be the case in biology, or chemistry, or geology, or economics. Nevertheless, it is the entire accumulation that makes up political science.

To write a complete history of political science would be, then, to put in its place every fact, hypothesis, generalization, and theory that has appeared throughout the centuries in the study of politics, and to describe the fate of each idea at the hands of later writers. This is, as a practical matter, impossible. My plan is more modest.

What I shall try to do is to discover, chronologically and by countries, (1) who were the more important men that studied one or another aspect of politics, indicating what each tried to do, what he taught, and what he wrote, thus providing something like an intellectual genealogy of the pioneers in the field; (2) what research methods men used in preparing their works on politics, and what types of writing they employed for conveying their thoughts and information; (3) when and how different parts of the subject were developed, under what names, and with what results; (4) how the subject developed in relation to cognate subjects, particularly those in the social sciences and humanities; and (5) how it rose to acceptance in universities, from the college level into the graduate schools, and how many of its professors developed the idea of a systematic and rigidly scientific science of politics. The influences and conditions under which the students of politics lived and worked—political and cultural conditions, church-state relations, the organization of higher education, the state of the sciences, the availability of books and libraries—will be important background at every stage. And finally there will be an attempt to establish a time dimension and some sense of developmental trends. I find a number of colleagues in the field who seem to think that everything is new today and that nothing in the past has any real significance. Some of these students also appear to hold that we are now in a position to escape the bonds of culture and take the great leap into a political science as timeless and culture-free as mathematics, physics, or astronomy. I disagree; and I think my findings here bear me out.

In defining what this work is intended to be, I want to make it entirely clear that it is not to be another history of political theories or of political utopias. Such works have their places in the total record of men's thought about politics, but their subjects are actually only a small part of the whole. Furthermore, the utopian schemes in particular marshal no evidence that describes any existing or past systems of government, and many books of political theory offer little more. They tend to take high ethical ground in the statement of what governments ought to be but offer little evidence of study on how to bring about the desired improvements.

Man's quest for political knowledge, and hence for the power to govern himself with human decency and dignity that goes with knowledge, is one of the most inspiring—though at times dispiriting—themes running through the history of civilization. I regret that my book could not have been written with that felicity and eloquence of style that would do it full justice. Too, in breaking new ground the work I offer here is unavoidably incomplete, and the evidence that I present is open to question as to its factual reliability, its pertinence to my theme, and its probative value for the interpretations I have put upon it. Other scholars retracing my steps and going beyond what I have done will doubtless find many points to correct and blanks to fill, for example in surveying materials on the Middle and Far East, to which I could pay little attention for the simple reason that my time and resources were too limited. Nevertheless, I believe that I have brought together a connected and reasonably substantial account of man's quest for political knowledge in the West that can be used as a foundation by others and that I have suggested insights, however subjective and debatable, that others may consider when rewriting the history I have attempted. This volume carries the story to approximately 600 A.D. A second volume is planned that will continue the account down to contemporary times.

I look upon improvement in the study and teaching of politics as probably more important to the welfare of mankind at this time of history than some of the current projects for the advancement of the physical sciences. I hope that this report of my researches will contribute in some measure to that end.

Part I

THREE ANCIENT LITERATE SOCIETIES OF THE NEAR EAST

ᴖ Introduction

Aɴᴄɪᴇɴᴛ men, both preliterate and literate, seem to have had rather
vague and fluid concepts in many fields. They were mostly inclined to
use only specific words for particular things. They knew about the king
and the judge, because these were definite persons, but one looks to
them almost in vain for a general word like "politics" or "government."
And even as concerns the king their ideas were, from our much later
point of view, ill defined. Was the king a man or a god, or both man and
god? Were his functions political or religious? These are the questions
of a modern man; they quite probably would have had no meaning to a
man in the earliest literate societies. What is the difference, he might
have asked. The king embodied or represented the whole nation in all
its interests and activities. For anyone else to attempt to define and de-
limit his powers would be to imply that there was some power higher
than his, and then the latter would presumably be king. And to separate
the religious from the political functions at the level of the kingship
would, in Egypt and Mesopotamia at least, have been inconceivable.[1]

Samuel, when protesting against the Israelites' demand for a king—
". . . now appoint for us a king to govern us like all the nations" (1
Sam. 8:5)—gave a distinctly Israelitish turn to his rebuke: "And when
you saw that Nahash the king of the Ammonites came against you, you
said to me, 'No, but a king shall reign over us,' when the Lord your God
was your king" (1 Sam. 12:12). This insistence that God is both God
and king, thus eliminating the need for an earthly human ruler or government, has echoed down through the ages, especially in Christian
writings about "Christ the King." But this is another matter. The point
I wish to make here is simply that one cannot read into the ancient texts

of the earliest societies the word meanings or the concepts that we employ today.

Another problem of similar nature that arises in the search for political studies among the early literate societies is the nature of the concept of law. Any American student who was industrious and hardy enough could take the published "laws" of his own state (that is, the compiled statutes and the digest of decisions of the state's highest courts) and the comparable publications for the United States government, all very bulky works that include the state and national constitutions, and could dig out a respectable descriptive summary of the legal or formal organization of his state and national governments. These works are shot through with materials on the structure, organization, powers, and procedures of the government and on the rights and duties of citizens. We read that in certain preliterate tribes young men were taught "the laws" of the tribe, and that in later societies "laws" of one sort or another existed. But do these "laws" cover the same ground as the laws an American student has at hand? Of course they do not. Studying the laws of these ancient societies might reveal little or nothing about their governments.

A related series of problems in formulating concepts and establishing clear definitions is linked with the development of human learning. Studies in a given field grow, expand, and change by the discoveries that men make within that field and by contacts with the men working in other areas who are also making discoveries and developing and expanding their fields internally. The interrelations between studies that began as apparently more or less separate and distinct subjects have become increasingly important in all branches of learning. At the same time new branches of study have over the centuries established their right to recognition as distinct entities with special aims and methods. Defining these fields more clearly does not completely detach them from one another, or from the older disciplines out of which they grew, but it does make necessary the establishment of new and more clearly understood relations between them. The point to be noted here is one already stressed in the first section of this book: that political study is not an isolated phenomenon in any time or place and in the context of ancient societies cannot be thought of as even an acknowledged division of intellectual activity. The three early civilizations dealt with in Part I, those of Egypt, Mesopotamia, and the Israelites, had somewhat different systems of government and administration, both local and central, and all had relations with other nations, so that experience of government as a human institution was widespread and continuous. Nevertheless, this experience was not greatly emphasized in the records that were left, and much of what is related is obscured by the theologies of the respective peoples. There were priests and prophets to present theology and some students of law to help write legal codes, but politics and government as a human contrivance humanly controlled received little separate attention.

In the next three chapters, then, the study of politics will be approached through theology and law. Occasionally the documents to be cited will yield glimpses of a humanistic and secular attitude toward politics. But for the most part the ancient records reveal how the realistic study of politics was severely retarded by the difficulties these peoples had in developing a clear concept of government as distinct from religion.

Chapter 1

﹏ Mesopotamia

T HE histories of Mesopotamia and ancient Egypt, the earliest known of the literate societies of the Near East, begin as they move out of the preliterate, prehistoric stage not later than the fourth millennium B.C. Their eras of greatest political and cultural importance relative to other peoples in the region reach a climax in the third and second millennia B.C. Their importance remains high even longer than this, however, and it begins to wane only when the Persians in the northeast and the Greeks in the northwest become powerful on the Near Eastern stage in the first millennium B.C. It is hard to realize that the period of greatness of ancient Mesopotamia and Egypt spans a time longer than the Christian era down to the 1960's. It is also difficult to grasp the fact that in the course of centuries Mesopotamia absorbed one new people after another—Akkadians, Gutians, Hittites, Assyrians, and others—without any fundamental changes or reverses in cultural development.

For a long time historians placed Egypt first in point of time, but important archaeological findings, especially of the present century, which have yielded documents and other materials that antedate earlier findings in Egypt, now give Mesopotamia a definite precedence in a number of respects.[1] In addition it has become clear that Egypt in early times was in contact with Sumer, the ancient southern portion of Mesopotamia, where literacy in the Near East began, and that Egypt to some extent was influenced by, and even borrowed certain cultural elements from, ancient Sumer.[2] Mesopotamia will, therefore, be considered first here, although it should be remembered that the eras of leadership of the two societies are essentially coterminous.

Geographically Mesopotamia was not, like Nile-valley Egypt, a sharply defined area protected by surrounding deserts and other natural obstacles to invasion. Mesopotamia lay open, as it were, and was easy of access from almost all directions. It consisted of the twin valleys of the Tigris and Euphrates. Beginning in the south, where these two rivers, now—but not in ancient times—joined into one, emptied into the Persian Gulf, Mesopotamia extended northward along the two rivers with some inclination to the west over fifteen hundred miles to where the headwaters of its rivers arise in the mountains of Asia Minor, now mainly in Turkey. There it almost reached the Mediterranean. In area Mesopotamia comprised most of present-day Iraq and parts of present-day Jordan and Syria. For the purposes of this chapter the term Mesopotamia is used in a somewhat enlarged sense as including also areas immediately to the north in Asia Minor and to the west of the two rivers that were at times under Mesopotamian or Babylonian hegemony, Babylonia being the name of the empire established by Hammurabi in southern Mesopotamia about 2100 B.C.

In dealing with the development of government and political studies in ancient Mesopotamia, I propose to summarize briefly what has been traced out by archaeologists, historians, linguists, and others, and then turn to the evidences of political ideas and studies that are presented by the numerous writings inscribed on clay tablets and to a smaller extent on stone. This will involve looking into epics, myths, proverbs, laws, and other literary remains. I shall, of course, be able to deal only with selected examples. Many of the ancient writings have not yet been published, but even so the literature on protoliterate and later literate Mesopotamia is already voluminous.

The Development of Political Institutions in Mesopotamia

In late preliterate times in Mesopotamia, roving bands were already settling down in somewhat scattered villages, which were becoming the political units of that period. The material basis for the village was the people's common occupancy and use of a locality or area of land, with its appurtenant physical resources. It was not primarily kinship or tribal bonds that held the villagers together in one unit. The bond of territorial attachment was reinforced, however, by the worship of common gods, some of general acceptance, but others local to the place. The higher gods represented the sky, the storms that raged over the earth, the earth itself, the waters, vegetation, and other phenomena, but each god had a name and the characteristics of a human being. The gods were supposed to be immortal, although in certain myths some were actually killed.

In the villages, community decisions were evidently made by assemblies of the people or at least by meetings of the elders. This early form of political organization, which carried over into the period of the city-states, has been designated as "primitive democracy."[3] In the gradual achievement of improvements in agriculture, irrigation, cattle breeding, weaving, the production of minerals, metal working, pottery making, and other hand industries, some villages surpassed others, becoming suppliers of goods to them. Urban characteristics developed—industrial, commercial, religious, and cultural. A number of villages became cities, as we would say, and the age of the city-states was at hand even before literacy was fully developed. Erech, Eridu, Ur, and Lagash are the names of some of the early ones in Sumer. Later and farther north came city-states like Nippur, Babylon, and Eshnunna.

With growth and maturity came new problems for the city-states. The settlements at first were scattered with unused land between them, but the ones that were growing needed more and more land to produce foods for themselves, and for other urban populations. As they pushed out toward each other, they came into conflict over boundaries. Inter-city wars followed. There were also internal problems attendant upon larger populations—problems of laws, courts, and law enforcement, of land ownership and business contracts. Then, too, water became increasingly important, as primitive irrigation systems in the bottom lands had to be extended to lands farther and farther back from the streams.

There followed several types of change in government. Internally, the delays in making necessary decisions in the assemblies of the people, and the disagreement and often bitterness attendant upon town-meeting government, became all too apparent to thoughtful and practical-minded local leaders. Even before literacy was achieved, it appears, a shift to kingship rule was in process. The most plausible explanation for the change seems to be that, with the increasing inability of primitive democracy to meet the multiplying and pressing needs of the community, the assembly in one place after another, when facing a serious military, food, or water crisis, turned to one of the more respected, wiser, but still vigorous elders, or to a younger man with an excellent military record, and gave him the powers of a dictator for the time being. If the dictator so appointed failed to meet his responsibilities, a different leader might be tried, or the city might lose its war with another city and become subject to its ruler. If the dictator succeeded, however, he would be well entrenched in power and skilled in governing so that it would be logical if not unavoidable to retain him in office. Indeed, the problems of the city would still be such as to call for one-man rule. From being a temporary dictator, he would become a king. Furthermore, men might reasonably think that the son of the king, already associated with him in his duties, should be his successor. Primitive men elsewhere have reasoned thus concerning the sons of their chiefs, while the chiefs themselves have not been slow to train their sons for rulership in order to enhance their chances of establishing a family dynasty.

For the people generally, or a majority of them, such a development from town-meeting government or primitive democracy would probably not be unwelcome. It would not only take a considerable responsibility off their shoulders and relieve them of irksome attendance at meetings, but also give them the promise of greater security. But to reinforce and better establish the idea of monarchical rule the Sumerians also developed, and the kings and priests joined them in propagating, the idea that kingship itself descended from heaven, and that the monarch was actually the choice of the gods.[4] This point will be dealt with again later. At any rate, even though primitive democracy lingered on to some extent, the institution of kingly government in the city-states was already in vogue in the protoliterate period of the Sumerian city-states, and it was then or later extended to city-states farther and farther north in Mesopotamia, if, indeed, it did not arise there equally early.

Another early internal development in the city-states was the setting up of a principal temple in each one, dedicated to the highest god or gods that were worshipped in that place, together with lesser temples for the worship of other and perhaps more local gods. As the king developed his own palace staff of civil servants, the priests in the temples developed theirs. Thus there were two centers of authority, the secular and the priestly, and two bodies of functions.[5] A certain amount of tension between palace and temple authorities resulted at times, but since the king had his authority from the gods, and was in some cases even worshipped as a god, he was nominally if not always actually the head of the priesthood and empowered to conduct the most important temple ceremonies. The dualism of church and state seems not to have disappeared, however, although the priests, as scribes, were among the most important upholders of the royal authority.

In the growing cities the functions of government like those of the temple called for more and more official attention. The duty of rulers and priests to serve the people and to promote their welfare was nowhere denied, but instead rather generally acknowledged and asserted. Each monarch boasted, in fact, of having protected the people from grafters, rich oppressors, and other malefactors. Courts composed of elders met regularly at the city gates to hear and to decide cases; land titles were registered; taxes were levied and collected; and many other functions of civil and military government were performed. All these activities, as well as the work of the temples, required methods of keeping accounts and records. Private businessmen also had great need of writing for their commercial contracts, and need of methods of accounting for goods and money delivered and received. Early and primitive ways of achieving these objectives gave way some time before 3000 B.C. to systems of writing and numeral notation sufficient for the purposes of state, church, and business. Records of various kinds were inscribed on smooth wet clay tablets, marked by distinctive cylinder seals pressed into the clay, and then dried and filed away for future reference. Whole libraries of such records on tablets have been recovered.[6]

To meet the continuing and often increasing demand for competent scribes and accountants, the principal temples in the larger cities opened schools for boys who hoped to do such work. In other places individual scribes conducted their own classes.[7] For each pupil this training must have taken a number of years. These advances made for greater certainty and regularity in public administration and gave the ruler and the people a substitute for human memory and oral repetition that was in fact immeasurably more retentive and expansible.

While these were some of the internal developments in the governments of the city-states, there were also external changes. When boundary disputes and disagreements over water rights arose between the cities,[8] arbitration alone could not meet the new situation. The simple fact was that many of the city-states were too small to cope with the growing need for irrigation over large areas of the river basins caused by population pressures on the food supply. There was as well the problem of invading hordes of alien men who descended upon the plains from the hills and mountains to the north and east. Against these invasions the city-states were too small and too disunited to provide adequate defenses. As a result here and there the king of one city or another in Sumer acquired hegemony over neighboring cities and provided a certain unity of leadership. In time, as the center of power in Mesopotamia shifted farther to the north, the areas and populations controlled by the kings became considerably larger. There were occasional local revolts, and new invasions by conquering tribes, but in general southern and central Mesopotamia remained united under one ruler or another for long periods. Irrigation works were extended and administered on a large scale, covering considerable areas of the twin valleys, while great ziggurats, noble temples, and other works were constructed and maintained.

Thus the age of independent city-states had been succeeded by that of empires, under the rulers of first one people and then another. Sargon was one of the earliest to gain extensive control in the area of the south (about 2340 B.C.), and Naram-Sin acquired great power a century later. The strength of these two and later rulers was concentrated in Sumer. Later came the empires centered in the more northerly cities. That of the Amorite Hammurabi of Babylonia in about the eighteenth century B.C. is one of the best known. Hammurabi was successful in consolidating his control over most of southern and central Mesopotamia and also in acquiring some control farther north. He became justly famous as an administrator and lawgiver. His dynasty lasted long, but it fell ultimately under the attacks of Hittites and Kassites from the north. Still Babylonia continued, though under new rulers, for some centuries. Later came Elamites, Aramaeans, Assyrians, Medes, and Persians to alter political geography, but it is not necessary for my purposes to follow these changes, because the essentials of Mesopotamian culture remained relatively unchanged even in decline.[9]

Religious Writings with Political Overtones

The foregoing brief sketch of the early political institutions and practices of Mesopotamia naturally suggests something about the political ideas and studies of the people as well. It is hard to imagine so complete a development of governments in city-states and over wider areas in Mesopotamia without leaders and scribes having given a great deal of thought and study to political problems. A separate examination of some of their writings may throw some additional light in this direction. The account cannot follow a strictly chronological course, but since there is reason to believe that myths, proverbs, and animal fables are, in origin, among the earliest of writings, I shall begin with some samples of these, and first take a principal myth of how chaos, fear, and tumult came to the realm of the gods, and how the restoration of order and quiet in heaven was brought about along with a change in the form of government from rule by the assembly of gods to practically absolute rule by a king.

The Mesopotamian myth-makers in creating their gods not only made them like human beings but also pictured them as confronted in their own heaven, world, or universe by problems of governmental organization, decision making, and executive action almost exactly like those that the Mesopotamian villages and cities were facing in their own time. According to an epic myth of creation, a universe with many gods existed before chaos developed in it, and then the need arose to restore order and quiet.[10] The highest god, An, Anu, or Anum, was appropriately the remote, serene, and static sky. The next one, just below him, was an active one, Enlil, the god of storms, who reigned and raged between the sky and the earth; he helped to keep the sky from falling on the earth. He was also the leader or king of the lesser gods. Besides two principal earth gods, one male and one female, there were a number of others, each associated with some physical phenomenon like salt water, sweet water, vegetation, and the like. These gods met in an assembly to decide questions just as the assemblies of the people in the primitive democracy of the cities and villages did. Tumult, violence, and chaos came about in the world of the gods when one goddess, Tiamat, became incensed against the rest because of some slight or threat to her. In anger she proceeded to bear monstrous serpents, dragons, mad dogs, and other vicious creatures, filling the world of the gods with them. These produced great tumult and fear, disturbed the general peace and quiet, and actually attacked the gods. The assembly proved to be disunited, given to much talk, and helpless when it came to action, even as the assemblies of men were in the villages and cities. Chaos took over.

One god after another, when asked by the assembled gods to attack and destroy Tiamat and her tumultuous brood of evil beasts, was struck with fear and indecision. Then the assembly turned to a vigorous and evidently younger god named Marduk to undertake the task of restoring order:

> "He whose [strength] is potent shall be [our] avenger,
> He who is keen in battle, Marduk, the hero!"[11]

Marduk accepted the task and promised quick results from his fight against Tiamat, but his terms were drastic:

> "Creator of the gods, destiny of the great gods,
> If I indeed, as your avenger,
> Am to vanquish Tiamat and save your lives,
> Set up the Assembly, proclaim supreme my destiny!
> When jointly in Ubshukinna [the assembly hall] you
>   have sat down rejoicing,
> Let my word, instead of you, determine the fates.
> Unalterable shall be what I may bring into being;
> Neither recalled nor changed shall be the command
>   of my lips."[12]

These were harsh conditions. Marduk in effect demanded the conferment upon him alone of all the power and all the decision-making authority of the world of the gods—to be exercised without recourse to the assembly. In effect the latter body was asked to abdicate, which it apparently did. Primitive democracy or town-meeting government among the gods was at an end, even as it was rapidly coming to be among men, first in the city-states of Sumer, and later in Mesopotamia as a whole.

But Marduk was not simply a great warrior god possessed of an overweening ambition for absolute personal power. He was also the guarantor of security, peace, and order for the gods. He was the one who made the dead to live and who knew the hearts of the gods. He was the "guardian of justice and law," and "the shepherd of the gods." On top of this he was a god of vegetation and agriculture, who made green things grow.[13] Here again we see in this myth about the gods the ideals of human government being expressed in Marduk's providing sustenance and justice for those whom he ruled. But these were gods; the creation of men was to come later.

Why did these ancient Mesopotamians deal with their own politics, government, and war under the guise of myths about the gods, instead of coming out with a straightforward account of human political organization and activities? To a modern reader the fiction and its disguise seem entirely transparent. The answer may be any one of a number or a combination of several explanations. For example, the scribes may have been doing merely the traditional thing in attributing everything to the gods from whom the kings were said to get their authority; or they may have feared to write about how their human kings had in fact gained power and established order, lest they cast doubt, through error in the account, upon the legitimacy, the authority, and the achievements of the king; or perhaps they were engaged in a clever bit of propaganda for the king by telling a story of human events, known to many, in the guise of a myth, thus providing for the actions of their rulers a divine precedent and a high ethical purpose. The people of the times were clearly accustomed to hearing and accepting myths from the learned men, the scribes and priests. Myths and proverbs constituted a large part of the literature of the times.

If the foregoing myth seems to deal only with the gods, there is also one which appears in several forms that relates to human kingship over men. Before there was such kingship, the myth held, there was primitive democracy or village and city rule by an assembly of the people. Then at some early time, before or after the flood, Enlil bethought himself to institute a king as shepherd of the people, and to provide him with the scepter of justice, a headband and crown, and other accouterments of office.[14]

In addition the myths indicate that the gods selected the one to be king over each human community. They did this by calling the name of the one so chosen and by fixing their gaze upon him. How the king's subjects were to know which person among them had been selected is not clear, but the kings themselves were not reserved about asserting their divine election. As Assurnasirpal II says in some verses that begin by telling of his humble birth in the mountains and his early ignorance of the gods,

> But thou, O Ishtar, fearsome mistress of the gods,
> Thou didst single me out with the glance of thine eyes;
>   thou didst desire to see me rule.
> Thou didst take me from among the mountains.
> Thou didst call me to be a shepherd of men.
> Thou didst grant me the scepter of justice.[15]

The general theory of kingship among the Mesopotamians was, therefore, one that included a divine creation of the institution of kingship itself; the giving by the gods of royal powers to a chosen human being in each city-state or other jurisdiction by the symbolism of conferring the scepter, the headband, and the rest; the actual selection, from time to time by the god or gods, of the person to be king, as evidenced to the recipient by the calling of his name and the glance of the god in his direction; and the rule of the king over the people as the servant, representative, or vicegerent of the gods, and not in his own right. The god or gods of the place in fact owned the city-state and its people, and were the true rulers, while the king himself was only a human tool of the gods and not himself a god. There were exceptional cases in which certain kings in Mesopotamia were worshipped as gods, but these were deviations from the normal pattern. The divine right of kings in Sumer, Babylonia, and the rest of Mesopotamia was clearly not like that in Egypt, where the pharaoh was himself recognized to be a god.[16]

These myths concerning divine and human kingship appear to have been part of the teaching or propaganda materials used by the ruling scribal and priestly classes when occasions arose to explain government or rulership to the people. No doubt the youths and young men in the schools for scribes and priests learned them and were prepared to repeat them for others. That there was any formal instruction for the people generally in matters of government is very doubtful.

If myths of the nature of those just summarized are as they seem to be, and if any myths hereafter discovered do not seriously contradict them, then clearly the literate people of ancient Mesopotamia had the gods deeply involved in human government, and they did not distinguish as modern men generally do between theology and politics. The gods took a hand directly in human politics to such an extent as to make inapplicable the concept of politics as a group of secular and strictly human activities.

These statements should not be taken to mean that people of that ancient time and place did not have any realistic ideas about politics, or any in which human behavioral patterns were not the basis of political interpretation. An animal fable of perhaps preliterate origin deals with a horse throwing off its rider (people revolting against their ruler). An old proverb concerns the difference in behavior between a king and a governor, to the discredit of the latter:

> You can have a lord, you can have a king,
> But the man to fear is the "governor"![17]

31

Further, the Mesopotamians worked out a gradation of rulers and their titles according to the extent of their domains and their respective ranks in the hierarchy of authority.[18] And while they did think of the gods as fighting to protect their own cities, they also believed that the gods helped those who helped themselves.

> The state weak in armaments—
> The enemy will not be driven from its gates.[19]

Myths, fables, and proverbs by no means exhaust the types of Mesopotamian writings that have political implications. Epics, bits of historical writing, laws, and the utterances of kings, as well as inscriptions prepared for them, all offer materials that reveal ideas about and a knowledge of politics. Again here I must confine myself to a few examples.

Gilgamesh was the name of a king of the city-state of Erech in Sumer in about 2800 B.C. whose deeds are recorded in several long poems of perhaps a thousand years later. The epic concerning his journey to the Land of the Living and his experiences there seems to have little concern with politics, but a poem about Gilgamesh and Agga is of considerable political interest.[20] Agga, the king of a nearby city named Kish, sent an ultimatum to Gilgamesh to yield to his demands or suffer the consequences. This obviously was a threat of war. Gilgamesh first summoned the elders, and asked them to approve resistance to these demands, but they refused. Then he summoned all the men of the city to an assembly and again demanded approval of his plan to resist the aggression. The assembly gave him the support he requested, but the city's defenses proved inadequate. An emissary sent out by Gilgamesh was cruelly crushed to death. After another emissary went out, Agga seems to have relented, Gilgamesh accepted Agga's supremacy, and Erech was saved from destruction.

This episode has been described as bringing to light "the first political 'congress' in man's recorded history" and also "the first bicameral congress."[21] While the relations between the council of the elders and the general assembly of the men of the city were not those of the two chambers of a modern bicameral congress, the description of the political procedures of an ancient city-state under threat of war is both interesting and enlightening. The fact that the account is in the form of a poem written many centuries after the event, and that it deals almost entirely with human affairs and contains only minor references to the gods, tells us something also about ancient Mesopotamian ideas of how political affairs should be recounted.

Other examples of early Mesopotamian writings on or closely related to politics exist in considerable numbers. Dating from about 2500 B.C. there is a historical account (possibly by a priest, because it is shot through with references to the gods) concerning a protracted struggle between the city-states of Lagash and Umma in southern Sumer over their rival claims to lands and water rights.[22] One settlement of the dispute after another is broken, with resultant strife, until a Sumerian overlord somehow compels both cities to accept a settlement dictated by him.

From about the same period there is a record on the usual clay tablets of a program of administrative reform and tax reduction in the city of Lagash after a long period of war, regimentation, governmental abuses, and burdensome taxation.[23] The old governor of the city had suppressed civil liberties, used public oxen to plow his own fields, and indulged in a number of other alleged abuses. A new governor, Urukagina by name, came into power with a platform of restoring liberties, reducing taxes, ending the oppression of the poor by the wealthy and powerful, and ridding the city of usurers, thieves, and murderers—a truly comprehensive program. The scribe who wrote the account tells how these reforms were put into effect. The whole account has a surprisingly modern sound.

Several related items are also of some interest. Edward Chiera reports that in some texts from the Hittite royal archives at Boghazköy in Asia Minor, which lies just to the north of Mesopotamia, "there is a surprisingly large number of well-preserved rituals telling what the various classes of officials and public servants should and should not do."[24] Here, too, we have what may be the first written constitution to be found anywhere. Established by a usurper of the crown, King Telepinus (about 1500 B.C.), who evidently felt the need to offer reforms in government, it lays down the rules for royal succession and the rights of the people and of the noblemen. It limits the power of the king, whose authority evidently was originally absolute. This constitution is preceded by a long preamble summarizing preceding history. The Boghazköy documents include also the annals of the various kings, copies of treaties, and other official records.

Law and Politics

Since Mesopotamia is, for the West, one of the two most important regions in which the earliest development of society from the preliterate to the literate stage of culture is well documented, Egypt being the other, it may be that its records will throw light upon both preliterate and early literate ideas about law. What were the "laws" of the ancient Mesopotamians? How much political and governmental content did they contain? Were they put forth in such a form and in such a way as to help the citizen, the member of the city-state or kingdom, to know his government? The most complete and most famous of the ancient law codes from this region is that of Hammurabi, whose code of Babylonian laws was published about 1710 B.C.[25] There were earlier laws and codes, however, and a word must first be said about them.

While some Mesopotamian records go back to perhaps as early as 2800 B.C., the earliest law code recovered up to now is variously dated from as late as 2050 B.C. to as early as 2408–2391 B.C.[26] This is the collection of laws promulgated by Ur-Nammu, ruler (by divine appointment) of Sumer and Ur, and founder of the Third Dynasty of Ur.[27] Most of the writing on the small tablet on which it was recorded has been destroyed. What remains legible on one side of the tablet begins with a prologue that tells, among other things, how the gods An and Enlil appointed the moon-god Nanna as ruler of Ur, and how he in turn appointed Ur-Nammu as his earthly representative to govern the city. Then there is a report by Ur-Nammu who states that, having first conquered some neighboring enemies and ensured the safety of Ur, he turned to reforming the city internally. He removed grafters and the "grabbers" of the people's cattle, established honest weights and measures, and looked out for the welfare of orphans, widows, and the poor people. So far this reads like a prototype of the re-election propaganda of certain American city mayors. On the other side of the tablet is what appears to have been a brief code of laws. Only a few sections are still legible, and these only in part. They deal with assaults with dangerous weapons, and state the punishments for such crimes. In short, it is the prologue, and not the code of laws that tells, however briefly, about the city government and about the politics of the gods in appointing Ur-Nammu.

Parts of other early codes have been found in sufficient numbers to reveal a pattern. The local kings who lend their names to the codes tend to propagandize for themselves about their appointment from on high and about having made justice prevail in their kingdoms. Codes earlier than that of Hammurabi include those of Bilalama of Eshnunna and Lipit-Ishtar, king of Sumer and Akkad.

The kings do not claim to have enacted new laws for their kingdoms, but rather indicate that they collected old laws, probably even some from preliterate times, that had not previously been written down and that may not previously have had the benefit of formal governmental enforcement. One thing that a king did in proclaiming the laws was to put behind them, either expressly or by implication, his own power of enforcement. This had the effect, among other things, of bringing the judicial courts that decided cases more fully within the governmental system.

As to contents, the codified laws show a considerable similarity, amounting in some cases even to identical phraseology. This is true not only of the Mesopotamian codes mentioned above, but also of the later Assyrian and Hittite codes. Nearly all of them fall within two categories, private civil law between individual persons and the law of crimes. They contain very little of what may be called public law or the law of governmental powers, functions, and activities. A few public officials are mentioned, but not to an extent sufficient to indicate their full powers and functions. There are no provisions concerning the organization and procedures of departments or the recruitment, training, and compensation of civil servants.

To clarify a little more the essentially private-law character of the early law codes, it would be well to indicate some of the main headings. G. R. Driver and John C. Miles, who base their masterly work on the Babylonian laws primarily on the laws of Hammurabi, comment on their contents under twelve headings.[28] The examples here offered in parentheses under each heading are but a few of many: Offenses and Crimes (false witness, thefts, stolen property); Land and Houses (tenants and workers on the land, trespass); Commercial Law (partnerships, agency, carriers of goods, slavery); Marriage (betrothal, dowry, dissolution, sex offenses); Inheritance (order of succession, rights of widow, daughters); Women of Religion (priestesses, votaress, lay-sister); Adoption and Wet-Nursing (rules of adoption, rescission of adoptive tie); Assault and Damage to Person or Property (assaults on men, on pregnant women); Agricultural Work and Offenses (hire of oxen, farm workers, the goring ox); Rates of Hire and Wages (wagons, boats, craftsmen, seasonal workers); Slaves (sale of slaves, purchase of slaves abroad); Courts and Punishments (judges, courts, punishment). These are in general subjects that one would expect to find dealt with in the courts of any country, whether primitive or advanced, and whether under a dictatorship or under popular control. They are common-law subjects, on the whole, and essentially of a private-law nature.

To say that the various rules embodied in the codes came from common-law sources is also to say that they probably originated in the decisions of judges and not from legislation as we know it today. Two reasons make this a justifiable conclusion. First, there is no record of distinct legislative bodies in the kingdoms and city-states of the times. Second, the form in which the laws are expressed clearly indicates that they could have originated in specific judicial decisions based on a definite statement of facts. The typical form of statement is "if a man" has done or does so and so, then certain legal consequences (recovery, fine, death, etc.) shall follow. Two examples from the code of Hammurabi, one with a criminal penalty, the other civil in nature, will illustrate the form: "22. If a man has committed robbery and is caught, that man shall be put to death." "233. If a builder has built a house for a man and does not make his work perfect and a wall bulges, that builder shall put that wall into sound condition at his own cost."[29] Although these laws are stated in generalized form as rules for the future, they are actually casuistic in form, not apodictic. The apodictic form of law, as found, for example, in the Decalogue, is simply that of a direct command coming from a higher being or from the state, saying "thou shalt" or "thou shalt not." The casuistic form says that in case you do so and so, you must expect certain consequences. This distinction is one used by various writers in the discussion of ancient laws.

It seems reasonable that a body of case law developed through many centuries in an extensive region where many states and peoples rose and fell would not be based upon constitutional rules or rules of government and citizenship that came and went with different states and regimes. There would be more uniformity and continuity in the everyday laws of human relations with which the judges everywhere were concerned. The rules laid down in the thousands of cases decided in the several fields of private law, both civil and criminal, could well become a common judicial currency that would be usable in any jurisdiction at almost any time. To codify these and to make them available to judges, counsel, and budding law students would be of great value in establishing justice and solidifying a regime. On the other hand, the rulers could have none but a negative interest in laying down and publishing the rules, if any, that restricted their own powers and freedom of government. This is, perhaps, at least in part, the reason why the early law codes contain so little public law, aside from the criminal law, which is in a sense public law, and why the Telepinus document mentioned above is so unusual among ancient records.

In addition to common or case law, however, the codes do include some provisions that arose out of royal decrees and ordinances. These represent an early form of legislation, usually on specific topics. Thus the laws of Hammurabi include the rules proclaimed by the monarch on the rates of hire for boats and wagons and on the wages of craftsmen and seasonal workers. These price- and wage-fixing decrees seem to be partly in the nature of findings by the monarch that certain rates of pay will meet the common-law requirements of what is just or reasonable, and that to demand more or pay less is unlawful. At the same time they represent substantive legislation on important economic relations, and are ancient forerunners of more comprehensive modern legislation in these fields.

The practical omission from these early codes of any public law, or laws on the organization, powers, and procedures of government, with the exception of the courts, is somewhat persuasive on the point that teaching young men the laws of the state or tribe is not necessarily teaching them anything about politics, government, or citizenship. It must have been true in many if not most primitive tribes as well as in the early literate societies that the great bulk of the law to be learned for living in the community was the law of private relations. If anything was taught about government under the guise of laws of the tribe, it must have been very limited. Knowledge of such matters was not necessarily secret or taboo in preliterate societies, although it was perhaps something of a mystery shared in by only the leading members; but certainly in many if not in most tribes there would have been but little encouragement given by the chiefs and elders to the young men to pry into such matters. Considerable variations from tribe to tribe must be assumed to have existed. In any case the law codes of the early literate Mesopotamian states show practically no transference of political knowledge from the primitive tribes to their successors, the earliest literate societies. The political part of the code in each case is the prologue in which each kingly lawgiver justifies his own power and policies.

To summarize the characteristics of the strictly Mesopotamian legal codes: They are all essentially secular, i.e., nonreligious, in their approach. They are not systematic statements of legal or juristic principles, but compilations of detached though related specific rules of law, mostly stated in casuistic form and devoted almost entirely to private-law relations. They do not contain much statutory material, and they are almost devoid of public-law principles. They contain no written constitutions, no provisions for the form and powers of government, no bills of rights. The only "branch of government" mentioned in them is that of the judiciary, and this but briefly. The organization and powers of the courts are not systematically described. In short, these codes of law were obviously not intended to serve as textbooks of government, but as guides for judges, litigants, and counsel, and perhaps as texts for students of the common law—just as most modern American "casebooks" for law students are based on the common law, not on statutes or even on the Constitution.

Many of the tablets of clay with legal contents that have turned up in excavations in ancient Mesopotamian centers have been found to be poorly written and ill arranged. In some instances they may have been rough copies hurriedly made by individuals for their own possibly temporary use, or they may have been defective tablets made by hired scribes that were inspected and rejected when the code or a full copy of it was being prepared. A more plausible explanation that has been put forward by competent authorities is that these defective tablets, or many of them, were copies of parts and sections of the codes, or of the common-law sources, that were inexpensively produced for law students or by them for their own use.[30] In some instances, perhaps in most, these students were probably at one and the same time learning the law and also learning to write or to write better, i.e., to be scribes. Anyone who has examined the notebooks of American college students will not be surprised that law students in ancient times made mistakes in copying. Ancient students who wrote on as heavy a material as a clay tablet, having memorized and recited their lessons, were probably happy to discard their tablets in the nearest convenient dump, where they would lie undisturbed for centuries, covered with dust, dirt, and debris.

Is it certain, then, that there were law schools in ancient Mesopotamia? The evidence is good that very much as in Egypt there were in Mesopotamian cities elementary schools, from about 2500 B.C. on, for teaching boys whose parents could afford the fees to write in cuneiform and so fit themselves to be scribes, civil servants, judges, or holders of other positions of rank and profit. Tablets inscribed with accounts of such schools have been found, and so have school "books" that consist of clay tablets carrying lists of words to be learned (such as the names of trees, animals, and cities), arithmetical tables, and literary items like poems.[31] Each school had its teacher ("school father") and some teachers had assistants ("big brothers") to prepare tablets for the pupils to copy, and to examine their work. The materials used in these schools for scribes, many examples of which have been recovered, apparently had no or practically no legal or political contents. But in addition the larger city-states had enough need for men who could read and write and who also knew the law to support classes or schools for the study of law. Men trained in law were needed in the courts, the administration, the diplomatic service, the army, the church, and commerce. The schools for scribes and those for priests provided sufficient precedents to give men the idea of schools for legal studies to replace the more expensive tutoring of one student at a time. These considerations, reinforced by the evidences already mentioned of considerable accumulations at some ancient sites of clay tablets carrying more or less defective legal inscriptions and sections from the codes, do not conclusively prove but do give strong support to the assumption that there was instruction in law in ancient Mesopotamia.

The evidence from the tablets presumably discarded by law students is that they studied sections of the common law as they appeared in legal documents, judicial decisions, and the codes of law. But did such instruction get beyond private law into fields of public law, or into the economic and administrative problems with which scribes and public servants should be familiar, and with which many law schools in the United States deal today? I do not know. The temple schools would probably do a little in the teaching of formal governmental organization and administration. Men with scribal ability taken into the monarch's service would presumably be taught by their superiors within the service what they needed to know about administrative organization and procedures and other things related to their specific duties. Private instructors would have enough to do teaching the private law of the land as it was developed and applied in the courts. As a matter of fact, for private teachers of law to engage in studies of constitutional and political questions in states under absolute monarchs, such as were typical of Mesopotamia in those ages, would have seemed impious and potentially revolutionary to the monarchs. Such studies were not encouraged and apparently were not even tolerated. Indeed, outside of Judah and Israel, as discussed in a later chapter, even public prophecy and the kinds of political discussions in which the prophets engaged were discouraged by the ruling powers.

If, then, the Mesopotamian law codes and such law teachers as there were stuck closely to problems of private law, was there any political significance to the codes? Had they any effects in the direction of inculcating political knowledge? I think the answers to both questions must be yes.

Clearly the monarchs under whose auspices and in whose names the codes were prepared and published had definite political objectives. The codes were means toward both improving and making more uniform the work of the courts. They would, therefore, if successful, help to unify the city-state, monarchy, or empire, reduce internal differences, and strengthen the hands of the rulers. This would be especially true in a put-together empire, composed of a number of diverse peoples and city-states, such as that over which Hammurabi ruled. It has indeed been said that a major objective of Hammurabi's code was to help unify his people and his empire by giving them one common set of legal rules. It is likely that various sections in the code were drawn from the laws of the different city-states that Hammurabi had combined into one empire.

In addition, the promulgation of a code gave the monarch an excellent opportunity to boast of his achievements for the people and to let them know who their master was. As already noted the code of Hammurabi was not the first to do this, but it must have been politically one of the most effective. As we have seen, its contents were almost entirely in the field of private common law. Not one of its nearly three hundred sections deals to any notable extent with the organization or powers of government. It was not planned as a popular textbook on government. Nevertheless, it is prefaced by an introductory statement in which Hammurabi enlarged upon his accomplishments for the people, and it is closed by a statement that starts off in the same vein but ends in a series of dire curses upon his opponents and enemies.

These opening and closing pronouncements constitute the political elements of the code. They were engraved, along with the legal sections, upon a diorite stela of somewhat conical or tapering shape, over seven feet high and over six feet around at the base.[32] Parts of the code inscribed on clay tablets have been found in other places, but the stela here described was recovered in 1901–1902 at Susa, ancient capital of Elam, now in Iran. There probably were other copies erected in other places. In any case, this stela contains the most complete and famous copy of the code yet recovered. At the top Hammurabi is pictured paying homage to the sun-god, Shamash, who is the god of justice, and receiving something from him. This massive pillar, showing the monarch associated with the god and putting forth the code of laws in the king's name, must have impressed the people deeply and at the same time have taught them all the king wanted them to know about his exalted position and power. The government was in his hands, and he had the support of the gods. That was all the people needed to know and in effect all that he told them, but the manner of his telling it is interesting.

What he said was that the great gods Anum, Enlil, and Marduk had called him, Hammurabi the shepherd, "the devout, god-fearing prince, to cause justice to prevail in the land, to destroy the wicked and the evil, that the strong might not oppress the weak . . ." and so on through a long series of vaunted claims of things done for the leading cities, for the shrines of the gods, for agriculturists, and against all enemies—all done by himself, "the perfect king . . . the beneficent shepherd . . . the king who is preeminent among kings," whose "ability has no equal," and more of the same.[33] He invoked blessings upon those who would heed his words and follow him, but baleful curses upon all who opposed him and on their kin. All this may not constitute a good example of the study and teaching of politics, but it is surely a moving and enduring piece of political propaganda, and at least the subject matter is in the realm of politics and government. As far as his subjects were concerned, this pronouncement effectively closed the door against any prying into the secrets of state.

Substantial portions of what appear to be law codes of the Assyrians and Hittites have also been recovered.[34] These are some centuries later than the code of Hammurabi, but probably a century or more earlier than the laws of Moses, which came during the Exodus in the latter half of the thirteenth century B.C. This difference in the antiquity of the several codes is rather interesting in view of the fact that all commentators seem to agree that the Mosaic laws, though later in time, are far more primitive and less thoroughly worked out than the other three in all cases where they deal with the same subjects.

Mesopotamian Contributions toward Political Studies

The law codes of Hammurabi and of the Assyrians and Hittites have considerable value as evidence of the prevailing attitude toward politics in ancient Mesopotamia. They have been cited and described mainly to get an answer to the question of whether learning the laws would enable men to learn anything about the governmental systems under which they lived. Except for the prologue and the epilogue to Hammurabi's code, and similar utterances in other codes, these ancient laws tell nothing of importance about government; and to read the prologue and the epilogue mentioned could hardly do anything to encourage anyone to study the Babylonian government, and would more likely serve as a strong deterrent. There is considerable other evidence on the monarchical and practically despotic forms of government in this region at that time, however; and this evidence reveals that effective systems of courts, public administration, taxation, and public works were developed and carried on. Some of them affected millions of people spread over wide areas, and lasted through crises and normal changes for centuries. As in Egypt, there must have been men in the administration, close to the king, giving constant study to problems of government, but they have left few if any direct records of their work as students of government. And there were no efforts to bring education and enlightenment to all the people; no systems of general public education; no programs of what we today would describe as education or training for citizenship, except perhaps through the priests and the temple rituals; no freedom of political utterance even for prophets such as the Israelites tolerated; no system of higher education for the general pursuit of studies in science, literature, the arts, philosophy, social problems, and humanities. Also, there came from these peoples no great treatises on history, on law, on science, on philosophy, not even on theology, or military science, or irrigation, or other practical interests, perhaps least of all on politics and government.[35] These peoples did not engage in theorizing or generalizing to any significant extent about law or government or society.

Lest I leave the impression that the Mesopotamians made no contributions toward the practice and study of government, let me state in conclusion some important contributions that I believe they made toward the beginnings in these fields.

First, the development of writing and the early uses and applications thereof in the field of government are exceedingly important. These developments made it possible in public affairs to substitute for faulty and debatable human memories written records of laws, treaties, judicial decisions, tax payments, and other public documents and transactions. Written records are not only indefinitely expansible, but they are also more certain and durable than unaided memories. By these means, too, history, with all its capacity for human enlightenment and instruction, became possible. History and historical records provide a now indispensable basis for the study of government and politics. And as Samuel Kramer and others have shown, actual historical documents were produced in early Mesopotamia.[36]

Second, Mesopotamians also brought about the enlargement of political units from villages to cities and later to units embracing a number of cities, villages, and intervening and adjacent lands. In short, they created political units capable of sustaining large-scale public services such as irrigation works for large river valleys, defenses against large-scale invasions, and the construction of ziggurats topped by noble temples. The fact that such enlargements in the scale of political units may have been brought about by violence and were justified as being the work of the gods hardly diminishes the importance of the achievements.

Third, these larger scale units, city-states and up, were provided with integrated governments under kings who could act on behalf of thousands and hundreds of thousands of people without the divisions and delays inherent in primitive democracy, although councils of elders and assemblies were still consulted at times. The kings, their viziers or prime ministers, and other responsible officers also organized and administered large-scale systems of defense, administration, irrigation, and other public services, including the collection and expenditure of public revenues through frequent censuses and otherwise. That they gave some sort of "in-service" training to their civil servants I cannot doubt.

Fourth, during the course of all these enlargements and systematizations of government, the monarchs insisted that they were servants of the gods to promote right and justice and to provide for the welfare of the people. While there were evidently many departures in practice from this standard, and justice was sometimes very harsh on the people, the principle that public office is a public trust for the people's welfare was maintained. When a usurper ousted an existing ruler, he seems to have done it in the name of the people and for their welfare. For this reason, apparently, the Hittite usurper Telepinus II, mentioned above, felt called upon, when taking office, to make a proclamation stating the framework of the government, outlining the rights of the people, and in effect presenting the essentials of a just constitution. Hammurabi and other kings also boasted of their services to the people in removing grafters from office, in protecting the poor from the rich, and in establishing right and justice. Here are at least some elements of a theory of justice, although stated in entirely practical terms. The very fact of the codification and publication of laws was also a step toward the ensuring of greater justice.

Finally, I think I sense in reading some of the Mesopotamian public documents a beginning of the separation of politics from theology and religion. While in general the kings profess to be acting for the gods who created kingship and who chose them as individuals to be kings, some of the royal documents seem to have hardly any religious overtones, and put little stress on the gods as decision-makers. Again the fact that they codify and publish the laws for all to see is, in part at least, a secularization of their attitude toward government. If the Greeks some centuries later went farther in this direction, the Egyptians and the Israelites in their several ways also took steps along the same road.

I believe, therefore, that the entire ancient Mesopotamian record, all of it that is available, should be studied very carefully for evidences of political inventions, discoveries, and thought, before the Greeks.

Chapter 2

〜 Egypt

GEOGRAPHICALLY ancient Egypt like the Egypt of modern times consisted primarily of the valley of the Nile, reaching from the Delta and
the Mediterranean Sea at the north upstream and southward to the
second cataract, or to about the twenty-second degree of north latitude.[1]
Egypt's political control also generally extended eastward to include
the Sinai Peninsula and the lands along the Gulf of Suez and the Red
Sea, and westward to some distance into the desert.

In this area there were many centuries of preliterate cultural development among a population composed of an aboriginal paleolithic stock,
the Hamites, and no doubt intermixtures of other peoples.[2] Agriculture
was established early and a village type of economy arose, first on the
higher lands where flooding was less likely, and later on the lower levels
near the river. Means of irrigation and of flood control were developed
so that more and more land could be cultivated and a larger population
supported. Many types of hand industry developed. A document of
about 1300 B.C. lists some sixteen different types of employment besides
that of the scribe,[3] and there is evidence of still others. But agriculture
continued to be the main occupation of the people, and big cities did
not develop to the extent that they did in Mesopotamia. There was a
class system without rigid castes. Many people were serfs, and most
were illiterate. There is much evidence to support the view that the
people were normally happy and relatively content with their lot
throughout ancient times.

The Development of Political Institutions in Egypt

From early times there was a recognized division of the Nile valley
between the upper (southern) and lower (northern) parts. What the

political units were in early preliterate times and what forms of government they had are not well known. There probably were a number of small units. Apparently kingship arose early as the form of government in parts of Egypt, contemporaneously with the so-called primitive democracy prevailing in parts of Mesopotamia. The kings who ruled the several parts of earliest Egypt seem to have been unchecked by any constitutions or assemblies. Strife developed here and there between such rulers, and some kings exerted strength sufficient to unite increasingly large areas and populations under their rule. About 3100 B.C. one ruler, called Menes and probably from the south, succeeded in bringing "the two lands," north and south, under his personal sway.[4] He assumed the double crown, the symbol of Egyptian unity. The concept and the ideal of a united Egypt were never thereafter lost, although actually in several periods of national weakness and trouble Egypt nearly fell again into two parts.

The conquest that united Egypt under one monarch also marked the beginning of the First Dynasty of rulers, i.e., of kings or pharaohs. Under this dynasty and the next two, there was a period of intensive organization of both the society and the government, when political and religious institutions and public services were established. From then on there were ups and downs in the nation's fortunes, and minor changes of many kinds, but the essential form of the government under a pharaoh or king-god endured through centuries that grew into millennia.

The durability that characterized the government was even more evident for the culture as a whole. The ancient Egyptian people had contacts with their neighbors in Mesopotamia, borrowed some ideas and culture traits from them, and were for a time under a sort of foreign rule, but their basic culture pattern survived all interruptions.[5] From 3100 B.C. to 525 B.C. the Egyptians saw twenty-six dynasties, one succeeding another on an average of once in a hundred years. At the end of this long period, when the Persians conquered them, Egypt was still Egypt in all its essential cultural attributes. This record hardly suggests a real cultural evolution, such as some writers have posited. An authoritative recent writer insists that "a basic conviction" of the Egyptians always was "that the universe is essentially static."[6]

Egypt's long history of little change in culture and institutions is no doubt attributable in part to its semi-isolated situation, and to the physical difficulties that confronted any potential invader. Its protections against internal disruption were also important, however. The general contentment of its people, the normal reliability of the land and the waters of the Nile in producing food in adequate amounts, the great convenience of the river for transporting troops, officials, and goods up and down, the general Egyptian feeling of superiority over Asiatics and desert nomads, the pride the people had in their great kings and their pyramids and monuments, and their worship of many common gods as well as local and personal ones—these suggest but probably do not exhaust the list of factors that held the people together and preserved their traditional culture.

Still there were times of trouble, when dissensions arose, when the central government weakened, when foreign conquerors invaded the land. One of these times, the First Intermediate Period, lasted from about 2300 or 2200 to 2050 B.C. The short durations of the five dynasties of this period suggest that it was a time of sharp interdynastic struggles and of weakness in central rule. It is known that at this time the administrators of the "nomes," or districts into which Egypt had long been divided, grew stronger and became feudally independent of central control. Some of the contemporary writings suggest also a condition of relative social disorder in which the poorer classes became demanding and obstreperous.

The admonitions of a prophet named Ipu-wer written in this period, and preserved in part in a papyrus manuscript of later date, present a political and social commentary on the times that is both searching and deeply pessimistic. "Why really," he says, ". . . Robbery is everywhere. . . . the Nile is in flood, (but) no one plows for himself . . . poor men have become the possessors of treasures. . . . nobles are in lamentation . . . The nomes are destroyed. Barbarians from outside have come to Egypt. . . . Gold is lacking. . . . laughter has disappeared . . . all maid-servants make free with their tongues. . . . (public) offices are open, and their reports are read. . . . the writings of the scribes of the mat [recorders of the grain harvest] have been removed. The grain-sustenance of Egypt is (now) a come-and-get-it. . . . the laws of the enclosure are put out-of-doors. Men actually walk on them in the highways. Poor men tear them up in the streets. . . . Behold now, it has come to a point where the land is despoiled of the kingship by a few irresponsible men. . . . Behold now, it has come to a point where (men) rebel against the uraeus [the serpent on the brow of the king, and thus the symbol of kingship], the . . . [here a symbol appeared in the original manuscript] of Re, which makes the Two Lands peaceful."[7] This is indeed a moving document, written by a perceptive and utterly discouraged observer of the then current political scene. It is by no means the only evidence of ancient Egyptian study of contemporary political conditions.

This period of disorder was ended by the accession to power of a dynasty of strong kings, the Twelfth Dynasty, who ruled for the next two hundred and fifty years (2050 to 1800 B.C.). This era is called the Middle Kingdom. Again social disorder and political weakness developed, however, and at this time internal weakness made possible the conquest of large parts of Egypt and at least partial domination of the rest by a mixed Asiatic people whose leaders, the Hyksos or Shepherd Kings, held sway over the land for over one hundred and fifty years (1730 to 1570 B.C.). These alien rulers were then driven out by the Egyptian people united under Amosis (Ah-mose I). He and his immediate successors in the Eighteenth Dynasty were content to rule Egypt within its old boundaries for over a century, but about 1465 B.C. they began a series of conquests, especially to the north and east in Asia, and thus ushered in a period of empire that lasted over three hundred years. (This period alone was almost as long as that from the first English settlements in North America in the early 1600's A.D. to the end of World War II in 1945.) Ceasing to be an empire about 1150 B.C. and reverting to its old boundaries, Egypt still remained an important independent nation for over six hundred years more, until it fell to its Persian conquerors about 525 B.C.[8]

I have presented this brief sketch of Egyptian political history as offering some evidence that for three thousand or more years before the Christian era the Egyptian people had a variety of political experiences. If only even the important movements and events in ancient times could be better known, these experiences would provide modern historians and students of politics with a wealth of materials for analysis.

Egyptian Steps toward Political Study

Through the long lapse of time and vicissitudes of life and climate, much of what the ancients put into writing has been lost. Modern men can judge of what the ancient Egyptians studied and thought only from the samples of their writings that have by chance survived. What they engraved on stone about their kings, their high officials, and their wars are among their products that have had the best chances to endure. Many writings that were committed to papyrus, the only important medium ordinarily available to poorer scribes in Egypt, have undoubtedly been destroyed or lost beyond recovery, although some have survived. The clay tablets of Mesopotamia had a better chance of survival, but it is to be presumed that large quantities of them have still not been recovered.

Studies and writings about the subject of government were limited from the outset by various factors in the culture and in the system of government. One of these factors was the dualistic nature of the ancient Egyptian kings and the resultant ambiguity about the nature of kingship and the kingly office.

In preliterate times in ancient Egypt men apparently saw or felt forces or spirits in all things around them—in the stones against which they stubbed their toes, in the trees that gave them shade and fruit, in the Nile, in the sun, in the stars, in birds and animals, in almost everything in man's environment.[9] Each thing had its spirit or force, in short its *ka*. Men began to personify these spirits; to give them names (and names were deemed very important, because they made things and forces into persons or, rather, gods comparable to, and in fact able to communicate with, human beings); to create myths about their deeds; and to form little rituals or sayings to be repeated in order to propitiate them, and keep them friendly. These verbal rituals were exceedingly important, because the gods were so very close at hand, and all had power to perform good or evil deeds affecting men. To the Egyptians it was not so much men as the gods who made decisions for better or for worse, decisions that affected human beings and communities; and gods permeated the entire human environment out to the farthest stars. Indeed the gods integrated men with their whole natural environment. And yet they were very much like men, although they had much greater power. It was in this kind of a mental world, a world peopled by both gods and men, that the ancient Egyptians lived and developed their beliefs. There was then no sharp, certainly no absolute, line of demarcation between men and gods in ancient Egyptian views of the universe. (The contemporary Mesopotamians were not much clearer on this point.) The Egyptian scribes and priests who left accounts about men and gods considered them sufficiently close together and alike so that they could join in the procreation of men who were also gods—creatures both man and god in one body. Some accounts had other versions, such as that the gods in heaven brought forth human beings whom they sent to earth to rule over men, or that the spirit or *ka* of a god like Horus entered into the body of an earthly man who was chosen by the gods to rule over such a people as the Egyptians. The minds of the Egyptians were sufficiently capacious, elastic, and undiscriminating to entertain without trouble a number of apparently different and even contradictory ideas on such a subject as this. They were not given to making precise and exclusive definitions. The important idea to the scribes and priests in working out a theory concerning their kings seems to have been that, although kings were human beings who carried on government on earth through other human beings (some of whom, like their own sons, would also have divine birth and qualities), they were also gods who had to be kept aloof from the people generally, shrouded in an aura of religious mystery. Furthermore, special arrangements had to be made through embalming, proper burial, and elaborate tombs and pyramids to provide for the eternal life of the departed god-king when his earthly body had died. As the earth was populated by men, so the heavens were filled with many gods, including those who had left a kingly life on earth to dwell and commune forever with other gods. The success of all these elaborate arrangements to stress the divine nature of the kings is perhaps best attested by the many centuries of quiet pharaonic rule over hundreds of thousands and later millions of illiterate Egyptians.

As long as and to the extent that this concept of the dual nature of the king-god was accepted, the modern Western distinction between religion and politics could have had little or no meaning to the Egyptians. As a divine being who condescended to give his time to ruling the people for their own good, the pharaoh had to be worshipped, and as an earthly ruler who was also a god he had to be obeyed. In the words of a father addressing advice to his children, about 1790 B.C.,

> Worship King Ni-maat-Re, living forever, within
>   your bodies
>   And associate with his majesty in your hearts. . . .
> Fight on behalf of his name,
>   And be scrupulous in the oath to him,
>   (That) ye may be free from a taint of disloyalty.[10]

Worship and loyalty clearly went hand in hand, if they were not one and the same thing.

This concept has been dignified by some as "political philosophy,"[11] and this characterization may be justified if one bears in mind that it introduces a modern distinction that the ancient Egyptians themselves apparently did not make. I find in the various translations of their writings no generic terms for "state" or "government" or "politics." The Egyptians knew concrete and specific things like Egypt, the Nile, the gods Horus and Re, grain and cattle, but were little given to general social science terms that might be applied to the cultures of various peoples. As a matter of fact, other nations or tribes of that time, like the "Asiatics," Libyans, and the Bedouins, which we today would think of as men in a less advanced state of civilization than the Egyptians but certainly as men, were looked down upon as quite inferior beings by the ancient Egyptians, who had a real god to rule them; and the Egyptians made no attempt to describe or analyze the systems under which these inferior beings lived.

What is more, since their king was a god and his rule was divinely ordained, he could do no wrong. It would have been impious for ordinary mortals to inquire into his government. The following "instruction" of a father, Ani, to his son at a considerably later date, possibly about the twelfth century B.C., appears to be relevant: ". . . Make offering to thy god, and beware of sins against him. Thou shouldst not inquire about his affairs [or "about his form of appearance"]. Be not (too) free with him during his procession. Do not approach him (too closely) to carry him. . . ."[12] If men felt that there were abuses in taxation or administration, these could be attributed to the lower officials, and appeals could be made up to the vizier and ultimately to the source of justice, the pharaoh himself.[13]

This matter of official abuses suggests another aspect of pharaonic rule and of the god-king theory. Pharaohs, officials, and scribes were agreed on the proposition that the god-king's true purpose in ruling men was to protect them and promote their well-being. He was the good shepherd, the herdsman, the protector of his people. He felt nothing but kindness toward them.

As early as the twenty-fifth century B.C. an aging vizier, Ptah-hotep, with the king's consent, wrote out some instructions for his son and potential successor in office. They were a mixture of rules for getting ahead in official standing and counsel of a higher ethical nature: "If thou art a leader commanding the affairs of the multitude, seek out for thyself every beneficial deed, until it may be that thy (own) affairs are without wrong. Justice is great, and its appropriateness is lasting . . . Wrongdoing has never brought its undertaking into port. . . . the strength of justice is that it lasts . . ."[14]

Such expressions in favor of justice and righteousness toward the people came also, and with even better grace, from the pharaohs themselves. One of the finest expressions of this attitude and one that is not so compromised by considerations of how to get ahead in life is to be found in the instruction that a king gave to his son and prospective successor, Meri-ka-Re, at the end of the twenty-second century B.C., a period of social confusion and turmoil. Along with some more cynical and brutal instructions this king said: "Copy thy fathers and thy ancestors. . . . Behold, their words remain in writing. . . . copy (their) wisdom. . . . Be not evil: patience is good. Make thy memorial to last through the love of thee. . . . God will be praised as (thy) reward . . . Respect the nobles and make thy people to prosper. . . . Advance thy great men, so that they may carry out thy laws. He who is rich does not show partiality in his (own) house. . . . Great is a great man [king?] when his great men are great. . . . Do justice whilst thou endurest upon earth. Quiet the weeper; do not oppress the widow; supplant no man in the property of his father; and impair no officials at their posts. Be on thy guard against punishing wrongfully. . . . Foster thy younger generation, that the residence city may love thee . . . Do not distinguish the son of a man [of high birth and position] from a poor man, (but) take to thyself a man because of the work of his hands. . . ."[15]

These instructions, even though presumably written out by a scribe, reveal that an ancient Egyptian king's sense of justice, of due process, and of public responsibility could find expression in words that are still heartwarming today. There is another side to his instructions to be mentioned later. Here it is enough to point out that ethics and politics as we define them and associate them today were brought together in the utterance of a head of state in Egypt over two thousand years before the Christian era. Although the gods were not all considered to be ethically motivated, this Egyptian king-god, as a result of his experience and thought, urged for himself and his successor a high standard of public morals and social responsibility. This was an important step in the development of an important phase of what I call the study of politics.[16]

In other directions, too, the early Egyptians took steps toward a study of politics and government. In the earliest dynasties an elaborate administrative system was built up by the kings and their officials.[17] The top administrator called the vizier, a man of princely rank and often one of the king's own family, was appointed by the king. In some instances there seem to have been two viziers, one for the south and another for the north. The vizier headed the central or highest judicial court as well as the administrative system. Central departments for irrigation and public works, for agriculture, for defense, and for taxation, with their respective department heads and civil servants, were under the vizier's supervision. The religious organization was kept separate under the king-god and a chief priest of the central temple at the place being used for the capital. All these elements of the central governmental and religious organization of the nation were developed during the earliest dynasties by the king in collaboration with his high priests and viziers. In time there were numerous central officials (a council of thirty is mentioned) who met with the vizier like a sort of cabinet. There was no parliament in the sense of a separately chosen legislative body. The final political decisions, though presumably based on the recommendations of the vizier and his council of officials, were made by the king.

Here obviously was a system of government that could be called an absolute monarchy. There was no written constitution to regulate the king's actions or limit his powers. There was no separately constituted supreme court to exercise any judicial control over the king's actions, and no appeal to a body of voters on government policy. As far as is known, there was not even a general code of laws to act as a restraint on royal action, although it is fairly well established that there were many judicial decisions and a considerable number of separate royal edicts or decrees. These must have been reduced to writing and kept in the office of the central administration for official guidance, along with a few treaties with outside powers. They were not posted for public inspection, however. When disorder came and developed into anarchy, as the Ipu-wer document quoted above clearly reveals, men who had known better times were shocked to find such records open to all, and even scattered about the streets for men to tramp upon.[18] Most of the "public records," as we would call them today, must have been considered the almost sacred as well as secret private records of the god-king and his top officials when the monarchy was strong.

It is clear that modern Western ideas of the political organization of mankind do not stand on all fours with ancient Egyptian concepts. The modern state is thought of as something historically developed by men, and as including all the people, rulers and ruled alike, other than aliens, within a defined territory, in a sort of corporate organization. In ancient Egypt, on the other hand, the political organization of mankind, or better say of Egypt, was something created once and for all time by the gods when the world was formed. The ruler, pharaoh or king, was considered a god, secluded, aloof, ruling human beings as a shepherd rules his sheep. If there was a "state," which is a modern concept, the king was probably it. He had no community of interest with his subjects, however kindly he felt toward them. His responsibility was to the gods, whom he would rejoin in time in a heavenly place to enjoy eternal life among them. Human beings could be forced to do his bidding, but they had no need and no responsibility to know about the laws or the government generally. There was no sense in a general publication of the laws for their benefit. The pharaoh's will was the law.[19]

In addition to an advanced elaboration of central government departments, the Egyptian administrative system included a division of the national territory into the districts called nomes for localized administration under centrally appointed officials of the national revenue system, irrigation works, and other services. Within each nome, rural villages and cities made up the lowest level of administrative units. The head officials of the nomes, called nomarchs, were either well-disposed men of some standing who were appointed by the king and vizier from among local residents of the nomes or, in the cases in which they were outsiders sent in to administer the nomes' affairs, became local magnates and tended to practice an almost feudal independence when the reins of central control became relaxed. Sons often succeeded their fathers in the office of nomarch. In any case the vested powers of the nomarchical families became a source of danger to national unity whenever the pharaoh and his vizier proved to be weak or inattentive.

To staff the principal offices in the nomes and the central departments, as well as in the temples, it was necessary that a corps of men be trained at least to read, write, and do arithmetic. The priests, in addition to performing religious rites, supervised the farms and the economic affairs of the church organization. The civil officials collected taxes, kept records (of censuses and taxes, irrigation and crops), and performed other administrative duties.

Learning the early pictographic and hieroglyphic systems of writing took much time, practice, and memorization. Later came alphabetical writing, which was somewhat simpler. The development of writing and of counting was a distinctly mundane and human achievement. It came from people, not from the gods. In its early stages at least it was in no sense planned, but as experience showed the benefits to be derived, both by the public and by individuals, it is evident that men put their minds to the development of simpler and better forms of writing words, and also of recording the numbers and quantities of things. The long-run result was to make possible the taking of censuses, the writing of laws and court decrees, and the production of historical records, rituals, epics and other stories, proverbs, instructions, and other "wisdom literature," and poems and songs. As in modern times, the language kept changing, so that then as now learning how to read the old documents, as well as how to prepare and read the current ones, took extra time.

Fathers who were scribes trained their own sons or adopted sons in writing, and the principal temple at the seat of government carried on a school for scribes.[20] Temples elsewhere probably also trained men to be scribes and priests. Nomarchs and other officials who trained their own sons in writing in order to have them succeed to their offices must have given them the words and concepts of their own official duties, thus providing the young men with the elements of an education in public administration.

The advantages of being a scribe were not so clearly evident to boys of the time as to make them all eager to go through the long and arduous training required. At least to some teachers it seemed necessary to cajole, persuade, and even threaten their students with severe punishment in order to get them to do their work. Several ancient writings have been found that satirize those who, like farmers and gardeners, workers in wood and stone, builders of walls and small buildings, launderers, and fishermen, worked with their hands under the commands of superiors, and ended each day weary, worn, dirty, and unrespected.[21] Such manual employments are contrasted with the work and the status of the scribe:

Behold, there is no profession free of a boss—except for the scribe: he is the boss.

But if thou knowest writing, then it will go better with thee than (in) these professions [i.e., manual occupations]. . . .

Behold, I have set thee on the way of god. The Renenut [harvest goddess, represented by a bird] of a scribe is on his shoulder on the day of his birth. He reaches the halls of the magistrates, when he has become a man. Behold, there is no scribe who lacks food, from the property of the House of the King—life, prosperity, health! Meskhenet [a goddess of birth and destiny] is (the source of) the scribe's welfare, he being set before the magistrates. His father and his mother praise god, he being set upon the way of the living.[22]

In short, the advice is: Become a competent scribe and so become an official, then behave well and your career is assured.[23]

Beyond this it is argued that if a scribe writes something of value, it will endure and preserve his fame even longer than pyramids. "A man is perished, his corpse is dust, all his relatives are come to the ground— (but) it is writing that makes him remembered in the mouth of a reciter. More effective is a book than the house of the builder or tombs in the West."[24]

At how early an age the young scribes from the temple schools, or those trained at home by fathers and other relatives who were scribes, began to work at the palace and the temple is not known. It is fairly well established, however, that boys and young men who could write were brought into administrative service in a sort of apprentice capacity to receive on-the-job training. The government departments were not large by modern American standards, and the lines of demarcation between them were not sharp and firm. It is likely, therefore, that grown boys in training would get opportunities to work under established officials on a number of different administrative tasks, perhaps copying tax lists, grain production records, letters to officials, and what not, and making and checking computations. This would amount, in effect, to an elementary in-service training in public administration. There were, of course, no universities or advanced academies engaged in studies of this nature. The apprenticeship and in-service types of training were accepted as being sufficient in professional fields like medicine and architecture as well as in the public services and in the mechanical trades.

There were also a number of things to read that probably got into the hands of many aspiring young scribes and civil administrators—writings that would give them some insight into political and administrative ethics and behavior, on how to achieve success and how to avoid dangers, on past political events and the claims of deceased pharaohs and high officials concerning their achievements. There is evidence that some of these writings were assigned to boys to copy when they were learning to write. To us these writings reveal some of the political thoughts and observations of the ancient Egyptian rulers and administrators. To the young men entering upon careers at that time they must have served to some extent as advice on what to do and what to avoid in order to succeed, and as starting points for their own observations and studies in administration.

The forms in which these ancient writings have come down to us are exceedingly varied. There were in a strict sense no writings to compare with modern textbooks or treatises on government and politics or with our somewhat standardized forms of periodical articles or book reviews. Such could hardly be expected. The book form in politics hardly began before the Greeks Plato and Aristotle, and the scholarly article not until after printing made periodicals possible. Besides, as mentioned earlier, an ancient Egyptian did not write books or articles critical or even descriptive of the government of a god over his people.

A leading volume of *Ancient Near Eastern Texts,* which includes much Egyptian material, classifies the documents under such headings as myths, epics, and legends; legal texts; historical texts; rituals and incantations; hymns and prayers; didactic and wisdom literature; songs, poems, and letters.[25] Most of the texts were found inscribed on stone in pyramids and tombs and, mainly at later dates, written on papyrus; a few were on other media. Although some of these literary forms seem hardly suitable for transmitting political facts and ideas, it is not safe to exclude any category a priori. Most useful for Egyptian political ideas and studies are the texts classified as didactic and wisdom literature (including "instructions"), historical texts, and myths, epics, and legends, but poems, rituals, and other forms of writing also yield something.

There is a category of writings related to politics and the study of politics that has come to be called the "prince literature" or "instructions for the prince." As the name indicates, such works are intended for sons who are likely to succeed their fathers as kings.[26] I have already quoted from the instruction prepared by an Egyptian king of about 2100 B.C. for his son Meri-ka-Re. The passages there condensed show the king's high sense of justice, righteousness, and responsibility as caretaker of his people. There is also another and more realistic side to the instruction. This says that some men are not to be trusted. A king must first of all look out for himself, be ever watchful, and take drastic action for self-protection:

[If] thou [findest a man . . .] . . . whose adherents are many in total . . . and he is gracious in the sight of his partisans . . . and he is excitable, a talker—remove him, kill [him], wipe out his name, [destroy] his faction, banish the memory of him and of his adherents who love him. The contentious man is a disturbance to citizens: he produces two factions among the youth. If thou findest that the citizens adhere to him . . . denounce him in the presence of the court, and remove [him]. He also is a traitor. A talker is an exciter of a city. Divert the multitude and suppress its heat. . . .[27]

Thus are budding politicians and popular leaders to be disposed of. But there is more:

Be a craftsman in speech, (so that) thou mayest be strong, (for) the tongue is a sword to [a man], and speech is more valorous than any fighting. . . . Protect thy frontier and build thy fortresses, (for) troops are of advantage to their lord. . . . make the offering-table flourish, increase the loaves, and add to the daily offerings. It is an advantage to him who does it. . . . A single day gives for eternity, and an hour effects accomplishment for the future. The god is aware of him who works for him. . . .[28]

Here and in other sections it is not right for the sake of right, but action for the sake of advantage that the king impresses upon his son. Defense both for the land and for the king is of the utmost importance.

What appears to be, and formally is, another instruction of a king to his son is that of King Amen-em-het of about 1960 B.C. It was obviously written by another person, however, for it describes how the king was murdered, and warns the son, Sen-Usert I, to beware of a similar fate:

Thou that hast appeared as a god, hearken to what I have to say to thee, that thou mayest be king of the land and ruler of the regions, that thou mayest achieve an overabundance of good.

Hold thyself apart from those subordinate to (thee), lest that should happen to whose terrors no attention has been given. Approach them not in thy loneliness. Fill not thy heart with a brother, nor know a friend. Create not for thyself intimates—there is no fulfillment thereby. (Even) when thou sleepest, guard thy heart thyself, because no man has adherents on the day of distress. . . . I gave to the destitute and brought up the orphan. I caused him who was nothing to reach (his goal), like him who was (somebody).

(But) it was he who ate my food that raised troops (against me) and he to whom I had given my hands that created terror thereby. They who were clothed in my fine linen looked upon me as (did) those who lacked (it). . . .[29]

The instruction goes on to describe how he was undone, while taking a rest, by members of his own guard. He had already planned, the document says, to turn the kingship over to his son (to whom he ostensibly writes) but had not told anyone. Now it is too late to give his son much instruction, but he does convey a little, as quoted above, along with some paragraphs of rather boastful appraisal of his own achievements in war, in the hunt, and in erecting a building for eternity. Whatever scribe wrote these instructions in the king's name was something of a student of human nature, perhaps one could say of human nature in politics.

Words of advice written by scribes and officials for the guidance of their sons and protégés about to enter upon official careers cover somewhat the same ground as the prince literature so far as ethics is concerned but include additional elements. The main purpose of such instructions was to ensure the personal success of young careerists but this does not mean that all the advice pointed toward purely selfish ends. One of the earliest of such instructions, from which a brief excerpt has already been given, was that of the aging vizier Ptah-hotep (about 2450 B.C.). Ostensibly composed for his son, its words of "wisdom" were so written as to have a wider application. First he emphasizes the importance of learning to speak well and thus "set an example for the children of officials." In a none-too-orderly manner he advises his son about marriage, love, and respect for his wife, the rearing of children, the evil of being greedy or covetous in divisions of property, and correct relations with his friends and their wives. While still young, and in the presence of a superior, he should show great humility and deference and not be aggressive, talkative, or noisy. "Laugh after he laughs, and it will be very pleasing to his heart . . ." The son should also be discreet and responsible in handling any official secrets and messages. With his own assistants he should be honest and see that they are satisfied. With those who come to his office Ptah-hotep recommends: ". . . be calm as thou listenest to the petitioner's speech. Do not rebuff him before he has swept out his body or before he has said that for which he came. A petitioner likes attention to his words better than the fulfilling of that for which he came. . . . a good hearing is a soothing of the heart."[30]

What is lacking in all the instructions from my point of view is an analysis of any of the technical problems of public administration. There is no discussion of administrative geography or organization, of procedures or of powers, of decision making or appeals, of revenues or expenditures, or of a number of other factors that the present-day student of public administration thinks important.

Egyptian Contributions toward Political Study

To sum it all up, it seems to me the evidence is conclusive that the literate men of ancient Egypt, the pharaohs, officials, scribes, and priests, studied politics and government more or less continuously. The evidences are to be found in the long history of the Egyptian government, which they developed and operated; in the numerous official documents they left; and in the extensive, unofficial literature produced by their learned men. Both their political actions and their political studies took place, of necessity, within the confines of the system of ideas and presuppositions that affected all they did. That system did not single out for study various groups of human activities under such captions as the modern Western world uses, namely, politics, economics, sociology, and religion, but lumped them all together. As John A. Wilson has put it: "Modern categories lead us to think in terms of the sacred and the secular; no such opposing purposes were possible in a society which long continued to be essentially sacred."[31]

Everything about Egypt and its people was integrated in its pharaoh, an absolute monarch who was both a great man and a god. As such he was just, omnicompetent, and fully responsible for everything affecting the people's welfare. Everything could and should be left to him and his advisers. His government was so personal that even the national capital moved with him from place to place. There was no need to bother the heads of the common people by educating them and informing them about the government and the laws. They would learn all they needed to know when called upon to pay taxes and render services.

The practical political achievements of the Egyptians have been described by many writers. These achievements included the following:

a complete system of government and administration organized at three levels—at the center for all Egypt, in the districts or nomes, and in the villages and cities; a system of judicial courts, which was integrated at the top with the government of the pharaoh and his vizier for appellate purposes; a religious organization, also headed by the pharaoh, directly under whom stood a high priest; a system of public taxes and corvées to supply the needs of the entire regime; tremendous monuments, pyramids, and tombs, public buildings, an irrigation system, and other works; and a series of nationwide public services for defense, agriculture, irrigation, and foreign relations.

To understand ancient Egyptian government at all, one has to pick up various scattered details and bare suggestions embedded in ancient writings on related subjects. Recent historians have done much to make the system reasonably understandable. The ancient Egyptians themselves produced, so far as I have been able to ascertain, no systematic accounts of the government of Egypt; no studies in comparative government (except perhaps in mythical accounts of the government of the gods—with whom else should Egypt be compared? the lowly Asiatics, or the Bedouins?); no treatises on constitutional law (there were no constitutional documents, no constitutional limitations on the pharaoh's powers, and no supreme court decisions against the government); no studies of international law or relations; no accounts of public administration, public finance, and public functions, of local government, or of the judicial system. Moreover, they compiled no comprehensive code of Egyptian law. There were instructions on how officials should behave, but no behavioral studies relating to the actions of kings, high officials, or minor bureaucrats, although some complaints against official abuses were put into writing. And, of course, there were no studies of elections or of voting behavior, since there was nothing of this kind to discuss.

Finally, what about political theory? The term "political philosophy" has been used in connection with the thought of the ancient Egyptians, and I think properly so. Egyptian political philosophy centered on the idea of a king who was a god, and upon whom the entire system of government was dependent. A theory that explains how a king who is both man and god came into being and gained power, how he operates, and to what ends, is just as much a political philosophy as one that deals with and tries to explain governments made and operated by men. But the two are obviously in different categories, and do little to explain or reinforce each other.

The ancient Egyptians developed no political theory of a secular, humanistic nature. It seems never to have occurred to them to try. They had no experience with human beings creating states, organizing governments, and struggling to govern themselves without the aid or intervention of the gods. Theirs was a god-centered system of government, and they knew no other.

Chapter 3

ꖶ The Israelites

T HE civilizations of Mesopotamia and Egypt discussed in Chapters 1 and 2 were basically Near Eastern if not Asiatic. Both reached their highest points culturally in the second millennium before the Christian era, and both continued to be important far down into the following millennium. They had military and cultural contacts with each other, and they suffered as well as benefited—but Mesopotamia more than Egypt—from the inroads of conquering peoples such as the Hittites, Assyrians, and Persians.

The next two cultures to be considered, that of the ancient Israelites in this chapter, and that of the ancient Greeks in Part II, reached their highest developments and made their greatest contributions to Western civilization much later, primarily in the last millennium B.C. They were practically contemporaneous. While the Greeks in various groups, Arcadians, Dorians, Achaeans, and others, were moving out of the north into Greece in about the thirteenth century B.C. and earlier, Moses in the south, probably preceded and not followed by Joshua in the center and north, was leading the tribes of Israel in the conquest of Palestine, to make secure their promised homeland there. Later, about 1000 B.C., while the Greeks were taking to the sea to conquer the nearby islands and to invade the Asiatic mainland in Ionia and Asia Minor, the Israelites not far away were fighting off the Philistine enemies and setting up their kingdom under Saul and, still later, David. In the centuries that followed, the Greeks were steadily building up their amazing culture in prose and poetry, in music and drama, in the graphic arts and architecture, in science and philosophy, while the Israelite priests, prophets, and scribes were developing their great national and religious literature in the many manuscripts that made them "the people of the book"—that is, the people of the Bible.

It is not too farfetched to think of Thales of Miletus, an early if not the first important Greek philosopher, making his studies in astronomy, mathematics, and natural philosophy at about the time that the Deuteronomist and his successor, the author of Leviticus, in about the time of the Babylonian captivity, were writing their respective books for what came to be the Pentateuch of the Old Testament. Centuries later, in about 460 B.C., Pericles in Athens was approximately contemporaneous with such Israelites as Ezra and Nehemiah. In the meantime, both peoples had faced the Persian armies, with different results, and toward the end of the fourth century B.C. both Greeks and Israelites succumbed to Alexander of Macedon. This was after the time of Plato but approximately during the period when Aristotle and his students were systematizing so much of human, and especially of Greek, knowledge, and also when the book of Job was being written.

The striking diversities in this passing comparison of pre-Christian Greeks and Israelites suggest much concerning the differences in outlook on life between these two superlatively gifted peoples and in their contributions to Western culture. Some of these differences will appear in what follows. Had these peoples been closer to each other in status, experience, outlook, and scale of values, there would have been no insuperable geographical obstacles to their having had many fruitful contacts with each other. The distance between Jerusalem and Athens is not over about nine hundred miles, and the island of Cyprus, which had a partially Greek population from early times, is even nearer to Jerusalem. The Greeks sailed throughout the entire eastern part of the Mediterranean, while groups of Israelites were present here and there from Egypt to Asia Minor.

The contacts of these two peoples in the pre-Christian era were, nevertheless, relatively limited. *Cruden's Complete Concordance*, 1949 edition, cites only three Old Testament references to Greece or the Greeks, and all three are relatively late. One is in Zechariah (9:13) where the reference is to the Greeks as the foes of the Israelites. This was probably written after Alexander's conquest of the Near East. A second is in Joel (3:6) where the author is pronouncing an execration upon the nations for the wrongs they have done to Israel. " 'What are you to me, O Tyre and Sidon, and all the regions of Philistia? . . . You have sold the people of Judah and Jerusalem to the Greeks, removing them far from their own border.'" There is good reason to believe that this passage is also postexilic, that is, after 538 B.C.[1] It is not clear what historic incidents the writer had in mind. In any case, both the foregoing references are probably fairly late, and neither passage suggests any Israelite love for the Greeks or any significant cultural exchanges between these two peoples. The third reference in Cruden is to a passage in the book of Daniel. Interpreting one of his own visions, Daniel says (8:21) that "the he-goat [he saw] is the king of Greece . . ." In my reading I have come upon one additional Old Testament reference to the Greeks in Daniel (11:2). In it the author says that a strong king of Persia "shall stir up all against the kingdom of Greece." While there is some disagreement about the date of this book it is generally thought to be after Alexander the Great's conquest of Asia, and it may be as late as the second century B.C.[2] Samuel R. Driver reports that Daniel's text includes several Greek words, one of which originated with Plato, another with Aristotle.[3] Such evidence contributes to the well-supported conclusion that the book bearing Daniel's name appeared late.

In ancient Greek literature I have found no comparable references to the Israelites. This does not preclude the possibility that such notices exist, but on the whole it seems safe to assume that there were no significant exchanges between the Israelites and the Greeks much before the time of Alexander the Great. After his conquests in Asia, however, and especially after both Greece and Palestine fell under Roman rule at a later date, the situation was greatly changed. Empires tend to promote freedom of internal migration over their entire areas, and to create common interests among the various subject peoples. Both the Greeks and the Israelites were peoples who were inclined to take advantage of such opportunities.

I have gone into this question of any possible cultural relations between the ancient Greeks and their contemporaries among the Israelites during the most productive period of both in order to assure myself that the evidence in the documents to be cited here is not misleading. That evidence seems to be conclusive that, so far as the study of politics is concerned, there were no significant borrowings whatever between these two peoples. Even though they were contemporaries, therefore, it is possible to deal with this aspect of their respective cultures before the time of Alexander the Great in separate analyses.

"The Book of the Israelites"

The Israelites have been known for centuries as "the people of the book," meaning, of course, their Bible, the "Book of Books." In contents if not entirely in order of parts, this is substantially the same work that Christians of today call the Old Testament. No people in history has had its religion, history, and politics so completely bound up and identified with any similar collection of writings for so long a time as the Israelites with their Bible. The Greeks with their multifarious writings are in this respect quite unlike the Israelites.

To call the Bible, that is, the Old Testament, a collection of writings or an anthology is essentially correct. It includes undoubtedly some of the best writing in all literature. It offers both prose and poetry, and its contents embrace such varied materials as traditions and myths, laws, history, genealogy, biography, stories of war and love, proverbs, prayers, works of praise, devotion, and denunciation, all in a wide variety of styles. How many men and women, over how many centuries and in how many places, had a hand in its writing, it would be impossible to say. It is the outstanding anthology in all literature, and since the invention of printing it has been the most widely published book of all. It serves two great religious communities of practically world-wide distribution—Jews and Christians. It has influenced the thinking, the actions, and the studies of countless scholars and of untold hundreds of millions of other people, in the field of politics as in many other areas.

Since the Bible is the principal source for any knowledge there is of political studies, such as they were, among the ancient Israelites, it is important to say at least a little more about its nature, its antiquity, and its contents. The Old Testament will here be the center of attention; the Christian New Testament will be discussed in a later chapter. Traditionally though not formally, the Old Testament is divided into three parts for purposes of analysis: The Law or Torah consists of the first five books, Genesis, Exodus, Leviticus, Numbers, and Deuteronomy (the Pentateuch), to which some writers add Joshua, to make six books (the Hexateuch). Actually there is a great deal of history, tradition, ritual, and other material in these books besides law. The Prophets come next, including the books from Joshua or Judges through Samuel, Kings, and the named prophets, both "major and minor," and both "former and latter." The Miscellaneous Writings or Hagiographa make up the third part. These include the books of Ruth, Psalms, Job, Proverbs, Ecclesiastes, Song of Songs (also called Song of Solomon), Lamentations, Daniel, Esther, Ezra, Nehemiah, and Chronicles. In any search for political ideas and studies, no one of these parts can be neglected; but they are not all of equal importance.

Although writing was known by the Israelites earlier, it is now doubted that any part of the present Old Testament was written much before the time of the United Kingdom under David and Solomon, or about 1005 to 925 B.C. Whatever happened earlier affecting the Israelites may have been in part written down, but it was more likely carried in oral tradition, in memory. When first reduced to writing the different manuscripts or "books" were undoubtedly separate. They were apparently written on easily portable but rather perishable materials like sheepskin, including its variant forms such as vellum and parchment. Unlike ancient Egyptian and Mesopotamian documents, the Hebrew Bible texts were not generally engraved on stone or on clay tablets baked to a durable hardness. Consequently, when the copies wore out and were replaced by new ones, errors crept in as well as deliberate changes by the copyists, despite efforts to prevent them.

Years that multiplied into centuries of use and of carriage here and there by a nomadic people, besides deliberate destruction by enemy forces, must have reaped a heavy toll of the earliest copies of what came later to be the books of the Bible. No substantially complete copy of the Old Testament in the Hebrew language has been found that is earlier than the ninth century A.D., but from that century made famous by Charlemagne and his successors have come a number of manuscript copies that are now in the archives of the Western world.[4] The discovery in about 1947–1948 of the first so-called Dead Sea Scrolls, and the subsequent successful search for more in the caves northeast of the Dead Sea, have made available a substantial portion of an Isaiah manuscript in Hebrew, along with many small fragments of other Old Testament books and other pre-Christian and later religious texts. These are variously dated by the experts from about 170 B.C. to about 68 A.D. These remnants represent, of course, but a small fraction of the Old Testament.[5] Fortunately there are also Greek translations. The earliest of these, the so-called Septuagint, exists in a number of copies that are dated by scholars from about the middle of the fourth century B.C., not long after the death of Alexander the Great, to considerably later periods.

How the "canon" of the Bible was determined, that is to say, how, when, where, and by whom it was decided what ancient Israelite writings should be put into a single, officially approved book, the Jewish Bible, and later into the Old Testament of the Christian Bible, and why it was decided to leave out certain other old Hebrew writings, are difficult problems into which I will not presume to enter.[6] While there are differences in some respects between the Jewish, Catholic, and Protestant canons, these are not important for my purposes. I propose to adhere rather closely to the text as translated from the Hebrew in the Revised Standard Version of the Bible.[7]

Not included in the Old Testament canon are a number of works of biblical and revelatory nature that are grouped together under the headings of Apocrypha and Pseudepigrapha.[8] The lists for these two collections overlap to some extent. When compared with the Old Testament works, most of these writings are relatively late (from 200 B.C. to 400 A.D., or thereabouts). Their authors were mainly Jewish, but some were Christians of various nationalities. Several of these works are of considerable interest in showing how more ancient ideas about politics persisted, though not without some changes, among later people of the Jewish faith. That a considerable interest in government persisted in some Hebrew circles, even though they were politically almost impotent under the Ptolemies and later under the Romans, is revealed in such works as *The Wisdom of Solomon, Ecclesiasticus, or The Wisdom of Jeshua, the Son of Sirach,* and *Maccabees.* I will quote from several of these books.

It is, then, out of the Old Testament, with some help from the Apocrypha and the Pseudepigrapha, that one must gather the principal evidences on any ancient Israelite interests in the study of politics and government. For many centuries the Bible was practically the only source for such a purpose, and the translations and interpretations were almost exclusively those of the "men of the cloth"—the Jewish rabbis and the Christian priests and ministers. These men were, indeed, for a long time, practically the only men of biblical learning, and they were looked up to by the illiterate majority as almost unquestionable authorities in other fields of knowledge, too.

A change began toward the end of the Middle Ages with the establishment of universities in western Europe. A little later came the Renaissance, with its revival of Greek and Latin classical learning; then the Reformation and the breaking of the one-church monopoly of biblical exegesis; and after that, or along with it, the invention and spread of printing with the great stimulus it provided for general public education and the printing and reading of the Bible and other books in the languages of the common people. Parallel to and supporting these developments came important discoveries in physical science, the exploration of new continents, and a new, more humanistic and secular attitude toward man's history, his politics, his economics, and his social life in general.

As humanistic and cultural interests advanced in Europe and the West generally, and as university scholars and the learned men of the different Christian denominations vied with each other in their attempts better to understand and interpret the Bible, a wealth of new information and insights developed concerning the ancient Israelites, their religion, and their society. Contributing to this mounting accumulation of new knowledge during the past several centuries have been the labors of archaeologists, philologists, linguists, epigraphers, historians, sociologists, jurists, and other groups of scholars. Although controversies remain over both important matters and minor details, many have been resolved, and the total advance toward a well-rounded and humanistic understanding of the ancient Israelites and their Bible is impressive.

Even so, much remains to be done. In the field to which this book is devoted, far less seems to have been written about the ancient Israelites than a scholar would wish to see. This chapter can be but a small beginning.

The Israelites: The People and Their Places and Government

The term "Hebrew" (Habiru, Apiru) originated in the Near East in ancient times as a general descriptive term for peoples who were nomads or wanderers.[9] It apparently had at first no ethnic or genetic connotation, but it became especially attached to and accepted by the people who were the central group in the Old Testament accounts, the same who evidently produced those accounts and who also came to be called Israel or the Israelites, and it clung to them after they had settled down in large part to an agricultural and village life. The writers of Genesis and other early books supplied the traditional genealogical accounts that served to bind the Hebrews together through the male line from Adam down to Noah and then through Shem to Terah and so on through Abraham, Isaac, and Jacob (who became Israel) to the twelve sons of Jacob whose names became those of the twelve tribes of Israel.

While intermarriage with Canaanites and other peoples among whom the ancient Hebrews lived was definitely frowned upon, even the biblical accounts reveal a number of examples of it. It is difficult to see how a people who moved about as much as the Hebrews did, and had to fight for a homeland occupied and surrounded by other peoples, could have avoided mixing with these others on a considerable scale. This had an effect on their political life as we are interested in it here. Equally important in this respect were the places in which they settled. Their movements from place to place, their separating from each other from time to time, their reuniting only to separate again, the captivity in which many of them lived for many years, and their several subjugations under the Assyrians, the Persians, and later under the Macedonians and then, well beyond the scope of this chapter, under the Romans—all these experiences had political implications for the Hebrews. At the least, they had innumerable opportunities to observe the governments of the other peoples among whom they lived, often as subordinates under alien rule.

Some of the principal places where they sojourned from time to time were "Ur of the Chaldeans," in Sumer on the lower Euphrates, near the head of the Persian Gulf; Haran or Harran in far northwestern Mesopotamia in what is now the southern edge of Turkey, between Carchemish and Nineveh; later in various parts of Canaan or Palestine, from Galilee south through Shechem, Samaria, Bethel, and Jerusalem to the Negeb; then some part of them in Egypt; and these later in the Sinai desert and so back again to southern Palestine. These movements took centuries of time and brought them into contact for long periods with many different peoples, both Semites and non-Semites. They learned among other things to appreciate those individuals and groups of other peoples who befriended them from time to time, and developed the idea of the equality of peoples without, however, yielding any of their fierce attachment to their own god and his law.

The families that moved with Terah, Abraham, and Lot from Ur of the Chaldeans to Haran were relatively small nomadic groups that apparently had no government other than that of the family patriarchs or elders. As they moved farther south into Palestine they came in touch with settled peoples such as the Canaanites who had city-states headed by kings as their primary political units, upon which were usually superimposed larger political units dominated by armed forces under oriental monarchs. Those Israelites who remained in Palestine, both east and west of the Jordan River, slowly accommodated themselves to settled living and the city-state type of organization. As they took over, by conquest or otherwise, one city-state after another, they developed their own type of city-state organization, one in which the elders continued to decide cases and to deliberate on community policies. However, a chief judge or prince gained ascendancy in many places, and he appears to have had or at least to have claimed in some cases the almost unlimited powers of the former monarchs whom the Israelites had ousted in taking over the place. The elders probably continued, however, to exercise considerable influence if not actual power.

Those Israelites who moved on into Egypt apparently continued to have a more primitive tribal, clan, or family type of local government by the elders. As they descended more and more into serfdom if not outright slavery under those later Egyptian kings "who knew not Joseph," their local communal organizations must have become limited in their powers to the deciding of cases involving religious and family matters within their own groups, plus some minor civil matters like the care of their own poor.

It seems evident that both in Palestine and in Egypt during the same centuries, but for somewhat different reasons, the Israelites' organization into tribes and clans began to weaken as it became less important. The city-state type of organization, with its territorial base and its diversity of peoples and religious groups under one rule, came to prevail generally among the Israelites of Palestine, whereas in Egypt the Israelite serfs and slaves had little to hold them together and apart from the slaves from other nations brought home from their wars by the conquering pharaohs. Nevertheless, tribal traditions remained, even though some tribes had become small and a few had practically disappeared as separate groups. How the Levites, the tribe of Levi, lost status as a tribe but acquired a sort of monopoly in the religious branch of the later Israelite state, will be recounted presently.

Up to the time of the Exodus neither the Israelites in Palestine nor those in Egypt had had national self-government in any territory that they could call entirely their own. But both branches had had at one time or another the experience of and the opportunity to observe at first hand not only the rulers and the governments of small-scale units like city-states, but also the large-scale monarchical governments of Egypt and western Asia. Their leaders could see great advantages to all Israelites in being united and strong, both politically and militarily. One of the great gains from such unity and strength would be the assurance that they could keep their own god, Yahweh, and their own religion, and be free from the temptation of worshipping other gods. For these purposes they needed complete control and sovereignty over a land of their own, and a land productive enough to meet the people's economic needs and large enough to be defensible against foreign enemies. It was to these ends that they developed the idea of a covenant with their god, Yahweh, that they were to acquire the land of Canaan in return for their complete obedience to him and his law. Religious zeal and political hopes and ambitions went hand in hand.

The two main groups of Hebrews remained fairly distinct for centuries, even though they joined together at one time in a united monarchy.[10] From about 1400 B.C. onward, various Hebrew tribes and related groups settled in central, northern, and eastern sections of Palestine. As they conquered and occupied one city-state after another they tended to urbanize and also to keep control over the surrounding countryside. These northern tribes and cities supported each other in wars against invaders and in the conquest of other places in their area. They came to be called Israelites, as distinguished from the tribes and groups to the south, who passed under the general name of Judah, or Judeans.

From about 1200 B.C. on, that is, after their Exodus from Egypt, the Judeans and the several tribes of Israelites that they absorbed or confederated with, the Levites, Simeonites, Kenites, and Calebites, came into control of southern Palestine and the Negeb.[11] The name Judah came to be attached not only to these people as one group, but also to the area they occupied. To some extent they too settled down in cities. They were for a time more aggressive and successful than their northern brethren, and for a while they gained ascendancy over them, despite the fact that Judah was less populous than Israel.

The two groups never really doubted their affinity. In the centuries of the consolidation of their control over Canaan they held religious festivals together, and representative elders from both groups got together at times in a general assembly, the *am ha-aretz*, to plan concerted action against their enemies, and no doubt for religious and other purposes. From about 1200 to about 1000 B.C. the northern and southern groups had an effective working coalition without any formal treaty, constitution, or unified national government.[12] The principal other people in the area, the Canaanites, who were somewhat more civilized, but devoted to other gods than Yahweh, were slowly overcome, but even before this process was completed, still another alien people, the Philistines, began to invade Palestine from the Mediterranean, while the people of Ammon continued to threaten from the east. The times were indeed critical, and national leadership was needed. Apparently out of the meetings of the elders, and to some extent out of successful military leadership, there arose without any formal designation or election certain widely respected leaders called "judges," men who "judged Israel." In this period of about two centuries a dozen or more of them attained nation-wide repute. Besides the military leaders, there was one (Eli) who was a priest, and two (Deborah and Samuel) who were prophets and seers.

As the pressure from the Philistines increased, and the Judeans and Israelites (having largely replaced the Canaanites in the control of the Palestine area) had to assume a greater responsibility for defending themselves and their territory, demands arose for a stronger national organization. Samuel, who was then the outstanding judge or leader in the nation, had already grown old in the service of his people. He had in fact already designated two of his sons to succeed him as "judges in Beersheba," in the Negeb. Acting as if Samuel really had the power to create and to pass on to some other person a sort of kingly power, the elders protested at once. They wanted a better leader or leaders to serve after Samuel, and they also desired some continuity of governmental authority through the times ahead. Specifically they asked Samuel to "appoint for us a king to govern us like all the nations" (1 Sam. 8:4–5). Samuel finally yielded to this demand, but with great reluctance, and with a harsh warning about what the people might expect from a king. I deal with this story more fully a little later.

Thereupon the kingship was established for a united Israel, with Saul as the first king. Then for almost a century, from 1020 to 925 B.C., union prevailed under three successive kings, Saul, David, and Solomon.[13] At the end of Solomon's reign the united kingdom fell apart. The northern kingdom, now called Israel, lasted for two centuries, from 922 to 723 B.C., when it fell to the Assyrians. Judah, the southern and smaller kingdom proved to be also the more viable. It endured from 922 to 586 B.C. Then Jerusalem finally fell, the Babylonian captivity began, and once more for a number of centuries the Hebrews (or Israelites) were without the benefits of their own national homeland and their own government.[14]

As a united kingdom, especially under David, Israel had developed great military strength, and had begun the organization of a strong central government. Solomon continued this work, but he also carried the kingdom into excesses of taxation, forced labor, wasteful expenditures on public buildings, disregard of the people's interests, and other extravagances of an oriental despot. All that Samuel had predicted about kings and what they would do to the people, and even more, came true under Solomon. Led by Jeroboam and others, apparently largely from the north, the people protested against the king's policies and the burdens imposed upon them. At Shechem, after his death, they appealed to Solomon's son and designated heir to the throne, Rehoboam, that he lighten the heavy yoke and the hard service that Solomon had placed upon them. Rejecting the conciliatory advice of the elders with whom he first consulted, and accepting that of the young men with whom he had grown up, Rehoboam answered the people with a harsh rejection, saying: " 'My father made your yoke heavy, but I will add to your yoke; my father chastised you with whips, but I will chastise you with scorpions' " (1 Kings 12:14). This action brought on the primarily northern revolt, and the splitting of the kingdom with secession of the north. Responding to the cry "To your tents, O Israel," the people of the north withdrew from the united kingdom and set up their own kingdom, called Israel, under Jeroboam I as their first king. Rehoboam continued to rule for some time as king of Judah, the southern kingdom.

So brief an account of the actual government of the ancient Hebrews is pitifully inadequate. It leaves out many things: the local judicial system (the elders sitting at the city gate); the national role of elders or leading citizens assembled in the *am ha-aretz* in relation to the judges and the kings and the leading officials; the distinctive roles of the priests and the prophets in the government; the relations of church and state; and other important matters. A really thorough work on the polity of the ancient Israelites would be of great value to the students of politics everywhere. While this is not the place for such a study, a little more probing into the evidences of ancient Israelite study of politics, even at the risk of some repetition of what has just been said, may help to illustrate what I have in mind.

The Political Knowledge and Ideas of the Israelites

It is generally agreed that the earliest Hebrews revealed by the records, let us say those who reportedly came up from Ur of the Chaldeans to Haran, were a nomadic or seminomadic, cattle- and sheep-raising people, who were culturally less advanced than the peoples with whom they came in touch in Palestine and Egypt, where there were organized governments in city-states and in larger units. Egypt certainly had a well-advanced governmental system when some of the Hebrews migrated to that country. They thus had opportunities, as I have already said, to learn from other peoples about governmental organization and administration in settled countries. When they began to settle down in the cities of Canaan, they also began to make some use of this knowledge, although they were slow to give up their tribal ways and their reliance upon the elders for all purposes except actual military operations. Before the people of the Exodus came up into Canaan from Sinai and the Negeb, however, there were incidents that raise questions about their knowledge of actual government. Let us begin with Moses in the Exodus.

After their long stay in Egypt, what did Moses and the other leaders of the multitude who left Egypt with them know about government? The tradition about Moses, as belatedly reported in Acts 7:22, is that "Moses was instructed in all the wisdom of the Egyptians." As far as putting into practice any knowledge of government is concerned this statement needs to be discounted a great deal. Whatever causes and considerations may be adduced to explain the fact—his concentration upon divine matters and the law; his revulsion against Egypt's political institutions resulting from Egyptian oppressions against the Hebrews; the many problems on his mind involved in just keeping his people alive and willing to go forward in the Sinai desert; his fear of entrusting any power to subordinates; or other factors—it is clear that Moses' wisdom did not carry over into the use of elementary rules of political organization. It took his father-in-law, Jethro (also called Reuel), a Midianite priest, the father of Zipporah, to teach Moses an elementary but important lesson in government.

The mixed people that Moses led out of their bondage in Egypt into the great hardships that they encountered in the Sinai peninsula before they reached the Promised Land had themselves had no collective experience of self-government, and no reason to desire any government at all. They had no national territory, little or no national unity, no common body of laws of their own, and no love for the laws or for the governmental system of Egypt, under which they had suffered. Moses, on the other hand, felt that he had a divine call to the leadership of the emigrating multitude, and he had his covenant with Yahweh that the land of Canaan was some day to be his people's home. He had also the prestige that resulted from his close relations with Yahweh and from his great initial success in getting the people out of Egypt.

Despite these advantages, Moses soon faced growing discontent and even a revolt that had to be put down. Most of the people still had faith in him, however, and his determination to bring them ultimately to the Promised Land remained strong. What his people needed before they could conquer and occupy the Promised Land was a combination of national unity and loyalty, an effective political and military organization, a body of laws, material resources, and other elements of national viability. To achieve all these objectives for Israel, Moses would indeed have needed all the wisdom of the Egyptians, and more; but for a time he was so weary and distraught that he seemed not to know what to do. Apparently this was his condition when his father-in-law, Jethro, "the priest of Midian," came to see him in the wilderness. This was before Moses had gone up into the mountain to receive the law. Here let Exodus 18:13–27, take up the account:

On the morrow Moses sat to judge the people, and the people stood about Moses from morning till evening. When Moses' father-in-law saw all that he was doing for the people, he said, "What is this that you are doing for the people? Why do you sit alone, and all the people stand about you from morning till evening?" And Moses said to his father-in-law, "Because the people come to me to inquire of God; when they have a dispute, they come to me and I decide between a man and his neighbor, and I make them know the statutes of God and his decisions." Moses' father-in-law said to him, "What you are doing is not good. You and the people with you will wear yourselves out, for the thing is too heavy for you; you are not able to perform it alone. Listen now to my voice; I will give you counsel, and God be with you! You shall represent the people before God, and bring their cases to God; and you shall teach them the statutes and the decisions, and make them know the way in which they must walk and what they must do. Moreover choose able men from all the people, such as fear God, men who are trustworthy and who hate a bribe; and place such men over the people as rulers of thousands, of hundreds, of fifties, and of tens. And let them judge the people at all times; every great matter they shall bring to you, but any small matter they shall decide themselves; so it will be easier for you, and they will bear the burden with you. If you do this, and God so commands you, then you will be able to endure, and all this people also will go to their place in peace."

So Moses gave heed to the voice of his father-in-law and did all that he had said. Moses chose able men out of all Israel, and made them heads over the people, rulers of thousands, of hundreds, of fifties, and of tens. And they judged the people at all times; hard cases they brought to Moses, but any small matter they decided themselves. Then Moses let his father-in-law depart, and he went his way to his own country.

Some fifty years ago Mayer Sulzberger, one of the few writers in English on ancient Hebrew government, described the Jethro idea of organization as "being military, pure and simple."[15] He contrasted the Jethro plan to its discredit with the "perfect scheme of organization" of peoples into tribes, clans, families, and individuals, arrangements presumably based upon kinship.[16] It is certainly true that military organizers have used units of tens, hundreds, thousands, and so on for organizing armed forces. It is also true that territorial units like towns, "hundreds," cities, and counties have been used for organizing both civil governments and military forces. As far as the Hebrews resting in Sinai after the Exodus are concerned, they were a mixed horde of people for whom any grouping by kinship would have been difficult and largely ineffective, while the territorial basis was unavailable because the people realized that they were only temporary sojourners in the Sinai peninsula.[17] Their aim was to reach Canaan before settling down permanently in a territory of their own, as promised them by the Lord.

On the other hand the Jethro proposal was clearly aimed at achieving better civil government, and especially the organization of a court system. The people were not at that time engaged in war with any important enemy, and the problem to which Jethro addressed himself was not that of military organization. He was trying to extricate Moses from the impossible task of being the sole adviser to all the people on both religious and secular matters, and the only judge to decide all their personal disputes and cases at law from the pettiest and most numerous to the most important and difficult. Jethro's proposal was simple and sensible. In the religious field Moses was merely to represent God before the people and to tell them their general duties under the divine laws. In the area of secular affairs he was to divide the people up into groups of ten and multiples thereof, and set up competent persons as rulers or judges at each level (tens, hundreds, thousands) so that small matters could be settled at the various levels according to their importance and difficulty. Thus only the biggest, most important, and most difficult cases would be brought to Moses for him to decide.

The use of a grouping system based on tens was by no means limited to military organization even among early peoples,[18] and it was clearly not so intended in the context of the Jethro story. Furthermore there is nothing in the words to indicate that the numbers used were anything but approximations to suggest the relative sizes of the groups. Nothing is said about what to do with remainders. It is significant, however, to see the relative sizes of the groups related to the importance of the cases to be decided at the respective levels. Someone had been doing some basic thinking on this important point in judicial and administrative organization.

At a considerably later date the authors of Deuteronomy substantially repeat and so tend to confirm the accuracy of what Moses is reported to have done in the Jethro episode (Deut. 1:9–18), but they make no mention of Jethro as the proposer of the plan of organization. It would have to be said that, if the Exodus account is accurate, the Jethro analysis of the defects or lack of governmental organization under Moses was one of the speediest governmental surveys on record, and that the resultant organization of local courts and administration, if it actually took place as reported, was startlingly swift and complete. Of course, the ideas on which this organization was based were not new even then; they were more or less "in the air" at that time in the Near East.

In a search for parallels, students of American history and government might think of the original organization of the colonial governments along the Atlantic seaboard of North America, and of the later formation of territorial and state governments from the Atlantic westward to the Pacific. There are important differences, of course, but the length of time required might be somewhat the same in both cases, and in both one has to deal with migratory populations preparing institutions to be used in a promised land.

It will be noticed that the Jethro plan of political organization did not touch the organization of the central government of the people that Moses was leading. The plan left Moses secure and unchallenged in his one-man control of all policies for the population as a whole, in both the spiritual and the secular or political realms. It made a slight beginning toward the separation of political from religious affairs, leaving Moses alone to represent God to the people, while giving the decision of most civil suits to his appointed magistrates or "rulers," subject to appeals extending finally up to him. For the rest it set forth the outline of a scheme of localized administrative organization based upon a delegation of powers from the center; the creation of several levels of local units or groups of people for administrative and judicial purposes (tens, hundreds, etc.); and the classification of civil business and cases at law according to importance and difficulty, for localized decision as far as possible. It also put emphasis upon ability and honesty for officials in the public service. Deuteronomy adds to this plan, among other items, the idea of central consultation with the local people concerned on the qualifications of those to be appointed as local administrators and judges.

The interest in these Old Testament passages lies in the evidence they give of studies of political and administrative organization among the ancient Hebrews and their neighbors at least as early as the writing of Exodus. This is nothing to be marveled at; Egyptians, Mesopotamians, Chinese, and other peoples provide as early or earlier evidences. What is worth mentioning is the tendency of later writers, both Jewish and Christian, to follow the lead of the priests, prophets, and other scribes who wrote the Old Testament books in emphasizing almost entirely the religious and ethical messages of the ancient books and to minimize the importance of, if not to ignore entirely, the political and administrative passages.

It is also of some interest to notice that the man who proposed a systematic plan of governmental organization for the Hebrews was not Moses himself, who had lived at the court of Pharaoh, but a relatively obscure priest of the Midianites, a man who was also a sheep raiser. He is identified as a Kenite, that is, as a member of a clan or tribe of Semites who were then friendly to the Israelites. To find such practical political knowledge in such a person suggests that either the priests made some study of government or this kind of information was fairly common and widespread, and in no sense a mystery, like some parts of religious and medical knowledge. I suspect that both were true to some extent. Yet Moses in the wilderness seemed to be unable to get himself out of his governmental predicament, or to give up his attempts to do everything himself, in both the religious and the political realms, for an increasing population.

Moses, the Law, and the Constitution

The mixed aggregation of people who took part in the Exodus had no body of laws that would be recognized by all. The laws of Egypt had been left behind as good riddance. There was a sort of covenant between the people and God, but this brief compact was more in the nature of a treaty than a code of laws. It could obviously not provide the needed principles, rules, and standards for the actions of private individuals, or for groups like families and clans, or for the judges and officials. A code of laws was needed.

It was soon after the Jethro episode that the people in their migration camped before the mountain in the wilderness of Sinai. Here Moses met with God, and received both a renewal of the covenant with God concerning Canaan and the gift of a body of laws, including the Commandments, that God ordered his people to obey as a condition for his fulfillment of the covenant. Apparently only the Ten Commandments, the Decalogue, were reduced to writing at that time and inscribed on the two tablets that Moses brought down from the mountain; but the rest of the Torah, or the Law, as far as its legal contents are concerned, presumably also came directly from God. It was supposed to be equally sacred, and beyond the power of the people to change. Just when it was written down is immaterial here, but it was obviously after Moses' descent from the mountain rendezvous with God.

At this point one senses an interesting and possibly significant change in the general historical account. The Jethro story is primarily a secular and public one, even though Moses, a prophet, and Jethro, a priest, are its main actors. Without any resort to God, these two men formed and reached the decision on governmental organization that is discussed above. In the making and the reception of the Law, on the other hand, the emphasis turns strongly the other way. God and the religio-ethical elements in the formation of the nascent Hebrew state come into the foreground. This is true despite the fact that numerous provisions of a secular legal nature, such provisions as civil courts normally apply to human affairs, are thickly interspersed among the more ethical, religious, and ritualistic provisions of the Law. A clear separation of the secular from the religious, the material from the spiritual and divine, in human affairs, was not visualized by the Old Testament writers generally, and certainly was not achieved in the making of the Law.

Indeed, the Law came to the people not as the legislation of their elected human representatives, or as the decisions of lay judges, arrived at in open forums after arguments from the several sides and the presentation of evidence, or even as the decree of a secular ruler announced in his own name. Instead it came as the words of an unseen God, sitting on high, and uttering his legislation with finality behind a curtain of great secrecy and mystery, and all obscured by clouds and smoke, thunder and lightning, and convulsions of the earth itself. And the laws came as the unexamined and unchangeable conditions of a covenant to which the people perforce had to consent, since there was no other choice, and no opportunity to debate or amend. This may have been Moses' own idea, a method he chose to put the fear of God and the threat of personal and national disaster behind the laws, as a means of making them permanently authoritative and binding. It necessarily forestalled any discussion of the justice of the laws, and any serious proposals to change them subsequently by mere human reason and choice.[19] Since obedience to these laws was a part of the price for the land and wealth of Canaan, upon which the people's lives were to depend, and since priests who knew the laws would inevitably be the interpreters of this essentially religious and ethical code, the field for popular discussion and secular choice in legal and political matters contained in the Law was also restricted within narrow bounds. The judges and elders who sat in the courts could decide questions of fact and of the application of the laws, but there was no room for a legislative body, no encouragement whatever for the people to make changes in public laws and policies.

In effect, the administrative and judicial organization and personnel provided for in Jethro's proposals had little to do outside of the judicial and military fields. The failure to make any institutional provisions for a central executive, pharaoh or king, or for any grand council of the nation to approve and modify laws left Israel without any effective system of central government throughout the period of the judges. The so-called judges themselves had no specific powers, and no written document in the nature of a constitution to refer to for their authority. Even the priesthood was not empowered by law to take any specific action other than to interpret, teach, preach, and try to enforce the Mosaic laws.

The general system that developed out of ensuing experience and practice may well be designated as a theocracy, since all the laws and the powers of government were supposed to come from God. The covenant with God was in a sense the nation's constitution. The judges and the priests interpreted the Law and the covenant, but only God could in theory relax or change its terms, and absolute obedience to the Law as given was the most important of the terms.

The numerous specific laws written into Exodus, and partly repeated in later books of the Pentateuch, do not clearly distinguish the constitutional provisions, as modern students designate those which provide for the organization, powers, and procedures of the government and its officials, from the provisions of law that apply primarily between private persons. Indeed, provisions of a constitutional or public-law nature are relatively few in the Torah.

Even when kingship was adopted later, in the time of Samuel and Saul, as the form of Israel's central government, no major effort was made to spell out the powers of the government and its officials, or the procedures they were to follow. Such a thing would have been contrary to ancient Near Eastern concepts of kingship. In Deuteronomy, however, a book that was probably written late in the seventh century B.C., when Israel had ceased to be a separate kingdom but Judah still had its independence under a monarch, the writers put in some sections that began a tradition of trying to regulate the kingly office. Let the text (17:14–20) speak for itself:

"When you come to the land which the Lord your God gives you, and you possess it and dwell in it, and then say, 'I will set a king over me, like all the nations that are round about me'; you may indeed set as king over you him whom the Lord your God will choose. One from among your brethren you shall set as king over you; you may not put a foreigner over you, who is not your brother. Only he must not multiply horses for himself, or cause the people to return to Egypt in order to multiply horses, since the Lord has said to you, 'You shall not return that way again.' And he shall not multiply wives for himself, lest his heart turn away; nor shall he greatly multiply for himself silver and gold.

"And when he sits on the throne of his kingdom, he shall write for himself in a book a copy of this law, from that which is in charge of the Levitical priests; and it shall be with him, and he shall read in it all the days of his life, that he may learn to fear the Lord his God, by keeping all the words of this law and these statutes, and doing them; that his heart may not be lifted up above his brethren, and that he may not turn aside from the commandment, either to the right hand or to the left; so that he may continue long in his kingdom, he and his children, in Israel."

The anachronisms in this curious passage are obvious. It was written late, yet it seems to anticipate events that occurred long before, including some of the delicts charged against Solomon. Had there been any such provisions in effect when Samuel faced the demand of the people for a king, he would almost certainly have quoted from them.

As it stands this passage has been called a "constitution."[20] Certainly it has some of the appearance and even some of the possible provisions of one. That the authors of Deuteronomy thought of it in such terms is most improbable, since the very concept of a constitution as it is understood today, and has been understood more or less for several centuries, did not exist in Israel in the seventh century B.C. Deuteronomy presents God, not the people, as the source of the powers of the king, of the choice of the man to serve as king, and of the restrictions upon the eligibility as well as upon the personal conduct of the king. The verses quoted are almost as much in the realm of religion as in that of human politics, and the restrictions upon the king's conduct relate more to his private life and his worship of God than to his actions as the ruler of the people. Nevertheless it is still true that here we have an early attempt to define the royal office and some of its duties, and these are some of the things that a constitution for a kingdom would include.

The ascription of all authority in the government of Israel to God, even to the selection of the king and the definition of his powers and duties, left the people politically in a cul-de-sac. Only by a revolution, a successful popular uprising, could any major change be achieved; and such an uprising would, in the circumstances, have to be denounced by the priests and other authorities as a breach of the covenant with God. Nevertheless, something of this kind happened, and a way was found to avoid its worst consequences.

Samuel and the Kingship

During the several centuries from Moses to Saul, political thinking and even action on the part of the people were not entirely lacking, but they were relatively ineffective. The tribes and clans were not well knit together; they were in constant struggle with their neighbors and even with each other; they lacked a strong and unified defense organization to fight off the almost constant threats of the larger powers such as Egypt, Babylonia, the Hittites, and the Assyrians. Their peoples suffered economic reverses, went off in pursuit of other gods and even idols, and fell into social disorder and corruption of morals. At least, so the biblical record seems to indicate. The people lacked formal institutions for anything like a true national government, and relied instead on the chance appearance of judges of uncertain authority to lead them in their various crises.[21] Samuel was the last of the great judges.

During this and later periods the prophets and other Israelite writers showed a progressive advance away from their earlier tribal concept of God, who was their source of law and their leader in battle, toward that of a single spiritual God for all mankind—a god of love and compassion, and of peace and security for all. They even showed a definite willingness to recognize the rights of non-Israelites to fair and friendly treatment in their communities.

The same degree of progressive advancement toward better organization of the government cannot be found among the political ideas of the prophets of this period. Just as Moses had apparently not sensed the need for a well-organized machinery of government, so the later prophets paid little or no attention to institutional and procedural measures that might help to ensure in practice the ideal of justice for which they pleaded. When the people demanded that a king be set up over them to replace the faltering and ineffective political leadership of the judges, certain prophets may have had a part in the agitation for the change, but the movement appears to have been of a popular and secular origin. That the priests had any important part in it is very doubtful. Evidently there were certain leaders among the elders who were thinking most seriously about the government of Israel, and who made the proposal to have a king, but their names are not recorded.

Several historians agree that a principal purpose of those who proposed the important institutional change that was involved in setting up a king was to strengthen the union of the tribes and its central government for defense against the Philistines and other enemies who were pressing them. This motivation is supported by the account in 1 Samuel 8, but there were other considerations as well:

When Samuel became old, he made his sons judges over Israel. . . . Yet his sons did not walk in his ways, but turned aside after gain; they took bribes and perverted justice.

Then all the elders of Israel gathered together and came to Samuel at Ramah, and said to him, "Behold, you are old and your sons do not walk in your ways; now appoint for us a king to govern us like all the nations." But the thing displeased Samuel when they said, "Give us a king to govern us." And Samuel prayed to the Lord. And the Lord said to Samuel, "Hearken to the voice of the people in all that they say to you; for they have not rejected you, but they have rejected me from being king over them. According to all the deeds which they have done to me, from the day I brought them up out of Egypt even to this day, forsaking me and serving other gods, so they are also doing to you. Now then, hearken to their voice; only, you shall solemnly warn them, and show them the ways of the king who shall reign over them."

So Samuel told all the words of the Lord to the people who were asking a king from him. He said, "These will be the ways of the king who will reign over you: he will take your sons and appoint them to his chariots and to be his horsemen, and to run before his chariots; and he will appoint for himself commanders of thousands and commanders of fifties, and some to plow his ground and to reap his harvest, and to make his implements of war and the equipment of his chariots. He will take your daughters to be perfumers and cooks and bakers. He will take the best of your fields and vineyards and olive orchards and give them to his servants. He will take the tenth of your grain and of your vineyards and give it to his officers and to his servants. He will take your menservants and maidservants, and the best of your cattle and your asses, and put them to his work. He will take the tenth of your flocks, and you shall be his slaves. And in that day you will cry out because of your king, whom you have chosen for yourselves; but the Lord will not answer in that day."

But the people refused to listen to the voice of Samuel; and they said, "No! but we will have a king over us, that we also may be like all the nations, and that our king may govern us and go out before us and fight our battles." And when Samuel had heard all the words of the people, he repeated them in the ears of the Lord. And the Lord said to Samuel, "Hearken to their voice, and make them a king." Samuel then said to the men of Israel, "Go every man to his city."

This chapter in 1 Samuel does not tell the whole story. In the following chapters Samuel meets and somehow recognizes the future king, Saul, a tall, handsome man of the tribe of Benjamin, as God had promised he would. Samuel dined him, annointed him, and in the name of the Lord declared him to be the prince over God's chosen people, Israel.

85

Then Samuel called all the tribes of Israel together. The tribe of Benjamin was chosen by the others to name the king, and it chose Saul. By this strange method of voting a sort of popular ratification of God's and Samuel's choice was obtained. The reluctant Saul was then dragged from a hiding place; Samuel proclaimed him to be the king chosen by the Lord; and all the people shouted, "'Long live the king!'" (1 Sam. 10:24).

"Then Samuel told the people the rights and duties of the kingship; and he wrote them in a book and laid it up before the Lord" (1 Sam. 10:25). Just what this writing contained is not recorded. It would be an important constitutional document to have. The biblical account suggests limitations on the powers of the king, but I find no evidence of their nature in 1 Samuel.

Saul and all the people returned to their homes (there was as yet no capital city), amid the mutterings of an undisclosed number of dissenters. Saul quickly found an opportunity to show his military ability in a successful campaign against some invading Ammonites. This much accomplished, some of Saul's supporters wanted to punish with death those who had grumbled against his being made king, but Saul would have none of such reprisals. "'Not a man shall be put to death this day, for today the Lord has wrought deliverance in Israel'" (1 Sam. 11:13). Thus he gave God the credit for his victory.

Samuel had yet one more task to do. Retiring as the judge of Israel, now that Saul had made good his right to be king, Samuel made his final accounting to the people for his long judgeship. The people who were assembled declared him innocent of any wrong, and Samuel called upon God to be his witness against them. Then he went on to recount Israel's history down to Saul's recent victory over the Ammonites, continuing as follows (1 Sam. 12:12–15):

"And when you saw that Nahash the king of the Ammonites came against you, you said to me, 'No, but a king shall reign over us,' when the Lord your God was your king. And now behold the king whom you have chosen, for whom you have asked; behold, the Lord has set a king over you. If you will fear the Lord and serve him and hearken to his voice and not rebel against the commandment of the Lord, and if both you and the king who reigns over you will follow the Lord your God, it will be well; but if you will not hearken to the voice of the Lord, but rebel against the commandment of the Lord, then the hand of the Lord will be against you and your king."

This is not the place to analyze the Israelite theory or theories of kingship. That has been done ably and interestingly in other places.[22] The main elements seem to be as follows: the Israelite and Judean kings like Saul, David, Solomon, Jeroboam, and Josiah were in a sense selected for the kingship by God, who had also approved the institution of kingship, but these and other kings were recognized as human beings and not reputed to be gods as the Egyptian pharaohs were; God himself was giving up his direct rule of the people and his leadership of their armies in battle, and becoming recognized more and more as an invisible, spiritual being, the creator and highest ruler of all men, and ultimately a god for all nations; but the people of Israel still were the chosen people of the Lord, who had a covenant directly with him which set them apart from other peoples and also put them into immediate relationship with God, and above their kings. Thus the Israelite and Judean kings, like the people themselves, were under the Law of God, or Torah, and yet that Law placed no specific constitutional limits upon the royal powers or powers of government as such.

Perhaps the important point for the history of the study of politics among the Israelites is that they had not a static but an evolving theory of kingship, and hence, to that extent, they had a dynamic if only partial theory of politics. However, since they never clearly separated religion and God from secular politics, they continued, as Samuel's last-quoted remarks reveal, to confuse the divine kingship of God over all mankind with the kingship of the local and human ruler who served under him. This is a confusion in the concept of kingship that arose again in the time of Christ and that still persists in some Christian sects.

The story of Samuel's appointment of Saul as king, given only in part above, is one of the early examples of the "prince literature" to which more attention must be given later. Clearly Samuel was a student of politics, among other things, as well as a judge and a teacher; and the Israelites were his somewhat reluctant pupils. Both his story and the earlier one of Moses and Jethro are reported in the Old Testament as actual political and historical occurrences, of which there are others in both the Old and the New Testaments. But the political knowledge and "wisdom" of the ancient Isaelites occurs also in other forms in their writings, of which I shall give only a few examples from their parables, "prince literature," psalms, and proverbs.

Other "Political" Writings

Jotham, the youngest son of Jerubbaal, who saved himself by hiding when his brother, Abimelech, had his seventy other brothers slain (Judges 9:5) in the crime of Shechem, gave a warning to the people of that city in the form of a parable about the king of the trees (Judges 9:7–15). This parable is capable of several interpretations, but as a warning to those who shirk their public responsibilities, whether in a kingdom or in a democracy, it is hard to surpass.

"Listen to me, you men of Shechem, that God may listen to you. The trees once went forth to anoint a king over them; and they said to the olive tree, 'Reign over us.' But the olive tree said to them, 'Shall I leave my fatness, by which gods and men are honored, and go to sway over the trees?' And the trees said to the fig tree, 'Come you, and reign over us.' But the fig tree said to them, 'Shall I leave my sweetness and my good fruit, and go to sway over the trees?' And the trees said to the vine, 'Come you, and reign over us.' But the vine said to them, 'Shall I leave my wine which cheers gods and men, and go to sway over the trees?' Then all the trees said to the bramble, 'Come you, and reign over us.' And the bramble said to the trees, 'If in good faith you are anointing me king over you, then come and take refuge in my shade; but if not, let fire come out of the bramble, and devour the cedars of Lebanon.' "

The author of this parable, whether Jotham or some other, knew that government is a necessity, and that if the best qualified persons decline to assume public office and responsibilities, there are always those "brambles" who will be glad to rule, and who will not be squeamish about using their powers for their own advantage and to punish their opponents. This is elementary political wisdom.

In the category of works written for the instruction of princes or kings, the Old Testament contains a number of scattered passages. These are mainly quite unlike the Egyptian documents that set forth instructions for future rulers and administrators. The Israelite instructions are in the main, if not entirely, highly religious and ethical or moralizing. They have little to tell the ruler about how to organize and administer a government (the Jethro story aside), or about how to get along with people, which the Egyptians stressed; but they have much to say about the ruler's duty to obey God's law and to pursue justice and righteousness.

Ezekiel, for example, condenses a great deal into one verse (45:9): " 'Thus says the Lord God: Enough, O princes of Israel! Put away violence and oppression, and execute justice and righteousness; cease your evictions of my people, says the Lord God.'" But he also has many other instructions for princes concerning honest weights and measures, fixed monetary values, proper division of the land, the taxes to which he is entitled, the building of the temple, the sacrifices he is to offer, and other matters.

Samuel's instructions to Saul, Nathan's denunciation of David, and various passages in Proverbs and other books fall in the same class. Even Psalms is not devoid of interest from this point of view. Among the Psalms I would refer especially to number 72 on kingship and justice; number 78 on the teaching of the Law to the children; number 82 on wickedness in high places; and number 83 on the conspiracy of the nations to destroy Israel. For political content and purpose, Psalm 72 is worthy to be quoted in part at this point. It is written in the form of a prayer to God:

> Give the king thy justice, O God,
>   and thy righteousness to the royal son!
> May he judge thy people with righteousness,
>   and thy poor with justice!
> Let the mountains bear prosperity for the people,
>   and the hills, in righteousness!
> May he defend the cause of the poor of the people,
>   give deliverance to the needy,
>   and crush the oppressor!

Proverbial wisdom was widespread throughout the ancient Near East. There are evidences of considerable copying by one people from another in this category of writing. It is clear that this form of wisdom ranked high, and that it was a sign of learning in any man to have many proverbs at the tip of his tongue. Modern scholarship puts a much lower valuation on this form of learning.

The book of Proverbs is much shorter than Psalms. Even so, its constant reiteration of words and phrases like "knowledge," "righteousness," "justice," "understanding," "fear of the Lord," and "avoidance of evil" makes it tedious reading. Its political content is limited, but not entirely lacking, and what there is is largely directed at princes. In 16:5–15, for example, the standards of kingly righteousness are set forth; in 24:23–25 the principle of judicial impartiality. In 25:2–9 there are some further words on kingship, and also some suggestions to individuals for making a humble and modest approach to great rulers and leaders. In 29 there are a number of suggestions on a commendable righteousness in rulers, similar to those in 16:5–15. Throughout Proverbs the emphasis is decidedly ethical, while the technical, legal, and fiscal problems facing the ruler receive little or no attention.

Ecclesiastes in its highly pessimistic way repeats in essence much of what is said in Proverbs in relation to government. See, for example, 3:16; 4:1, 13, 14; 5:8–9; 8:2–8; 9:13–18.

While the instructions that are directed primarily toward princes, other rulers, and public officials, including judges, would have application to any Israelite who happened to be placed in the position of a judge or administrator, like a tax gatherer, the Old Testament provides no important political instructions for the people in general. There is no shortage of religious, moral, and ritualistic instruction for the common people, however, and this is in keeping with the theocratic principle and the failure to make any clear distinction between religious and secular affairs. The secular political responsibilities of the people were so few, and their role in conducting the affairs of government was so small, that no special political instruction was needed for their purposes. They needed only to obey the Law to the letter, and if they did, then God would take care of them and of the nation.

The Priests and the Prophets

The fact that the Israelites consciously made various changes in their political institutions and practices is evidence enough that political studies, even if only in a broad and loose sense, were being made by some persons. Furthermore, the fact that political ideas were, to some extent, being recorded and transmitted to others is enough to warrant the assertion that there was some teaching or instruction in this area, however casual, informal, and lacking in organization it may have been.

Among the groups and classes of persons who must at one time or another have discussed the officials who ruled over them as a government and their policies, one must at least mention the elders in each family, clan, and tribe; the elders who sat at the city gates to decide cases at law; the more select group of elders who were summoned from time to time as the *am ha-aretz* to advise with the rulers of all Israel; the judges of pre-monarchical times; the later kings and their officials; and the priests and the prophets. To these the Rehoboam story (for which there is an earlier parallel in a Sumerian tale) adds another category, that of the young men—presumably the fighting men. For when the elders advised Rehoboam, the son and designated successor of Solomon, to accept the people's petition, and to lighten their burdens, Rehoboam turned to the young men, the warriors, who gave him the opposite advice. The results of his acceptance of the young men's advice, namely, the secession of more than half of his kingdom, were not such as to commend them for political astuteness.

The authorities appear to agree that the priests and the prophets were the two principal classes of students of public affairs, as they were also in religion and other fields. There must have been other classes, too, as mentioned above, who gave some thought to politics, but they were not primarily the teachers of the people, and they left relatively little of their thought in written form compared to that which came from the hands and minds of the priests and the prophets.

No one has been able to state a clear and invariable distinction between the priests and the prophets. Samuel was at one time a priest, then he became a judge of Israel, and he always had some of the characteristics of a prophet. Other priests also turned prophet. There were, however, some general distinctions between the two categories.

In primitive times in the Near East, as among other preliterate peoples, before there were any designated or official priests, there were shamans, medicine men, and various individuals of recognized spiritual and persuasive powers. Each tribe had its own god or gods. Judah had Yahweh as its tribal deity. In early times, under the elders and judges, and then later and more clearly under the kings, Judah developed an official group of men called priests to conduct the religious rituals and the sacrifices to Yahweh, and to teach the Yahweh religion to the people in their various places of abode or encampment. At the same time each father or head of a family presumably taught the children and young people under his control in both religious and secular matters. In the smaller groups the elders and heads of families had traditional authority, while the priests served communities larger than families and came to have authority above that of the heads of families.[23] Having responsibility primarily to maintain the status quo, both the heads of families and the priests tended to be conservative.

Parental authority, like that of the tribe and the later city-state, extended to both religious and secular-social matters, without any clear line of demarcation. The priests, on the other hand, were initially given official powers that related primarily to religious matters, that is, to the carrying out of the religious rituals and the burnt offerings as required by the Law. However, the line between religion and secular matters was not a sharp one, and once the priests and their helpers were in official positions in practically all communities, and were available for service, various secular matters closely related to religious services, such as the registration of births and deaths and the enforcement of sanitary and dietary regulations, also fell to them. Indeed, it is more than likely that in emergencies other secular duties were also delegated to the priests, who had some training and usually the ability to write. Thus they became engaged, to some extent, in public administration in various minor matters, and acquired familiarity with public problems.

It may be added, also, that in addition to the traditional authority they had, both the elders and heads of families and the priests received from those under them the respect and the moral authority that enure in traditional societies to "those who know." Greater experience and superior knowledge were theirs, although to a degree this is but another aspect of their traditional superiority.

Who, then, were these men that became priests in Israel? The phrases "Levite and priest" and "the Levites, the priests," occur in several places in the Old Testament. It appears that the Levites were originally a separate tribe like Judah, Simeon, and Benjamin.[24] At first they had their own god, Nahash, who was represented by a serpent, while Judah worshipped Yahweh. Living close to the Judeans in southern Canaan, the Levites evidently tried at one time to gain political supremacy in the region, but suffered defeat at the hands of Judah, and consequently became subordinate to it. When the lands of Canaan were divided among the tribes the Levites were denied a separate territory and sovereignty of their own. In recompense for this, and upon their accepting Yahweh as their god, they were assigned to priestly duties and the service of the temples. For these services they were paid according to the scale of offerings set forth in the Law. Judah thus acquired increased political authority as a tribe, while Levi, or the Levites, gave up tribal political independence for the status and the economic security of a preferred caste of priests and temple servants under Judah. The authority in religious affairs that they acquired they endeavored later, and with considerable success, to extend throughout all Israel. Yahweh thus became the most important god among all the tribes. That the Levites should be conservative upholders of the Law and of the political status quo is not a matter for great surprise. Their teaching consisted largely of reading and expounding the Law, that is, the Torah, to their congregations in their regular services.

The background for the prophets in primitive times is the same as that for the priests; they both hark back to the shamans, medicine men, performers of miracles, and spirited, eloquent speakers who have appeared rather generally in primitive societies. The priesthoods became distinct groups when they gained official status, developed an orthodox set of beliefs and rituals, and began to train selected young men in the beliefs, rituals, and mysteries of their calling. These younger men were selected and trained, of course, to become first the assistants and later the successors of their teachers. The prophets, on the other hand, were in general men who remained outside the priestly tradition or who departed from it.[25] They arose here and there, from time to time, among sheepherders, small farmers, and other social and economic groups, as men of special eloquence and ecstasy, each with his own moral message to transmit to his people as to what was wrong with their society, and as to what needed to be done for its improvement or salvation. In earliest times some of them posed also as seers, that is, not only as tellers of the future, but as intermediaries between God or gods and men, such as Samuel was believed to be in the story of Saul (1 Sam. 9:5–29; 10:1–27).

The prophets evidently received no formal or regular training, but after literacy became possible most of them who rose to fame learned how to write, and the best of them came to be recognized as among the most eloquent orators and the most effective writers of Israel in Old Testament times. Their numbers apparently waxed and waned, and are impossible to determine accurately. In some instances one or a few especially gifted and eloquent prophets drew to themselves a number of young followers, and they traveled together in groups, learning from each other and prophesying to any who would listen. These informal groups may perhaps be compared to the congregations and classes to whom the priests read and expounded the Torah in the temples, then and later.

In these groups of prophets and followers, one of which had Samuel as its leader, many biblical issues must have been discussed and debated, and the members must have learned much from each other. One prophet taught another, as Elija did Elisha. Throughout the period of the united monarchy prophecy gained considerable status; and later in the separate kingdoms of Judah and Israel the prophets, sometimes in large groups, were consulted by kings on public policy questions, including that of whether or not to engage in war. As they reveal in their writings, the prophets engaged in discussions on many current public issues.

Later on, prophecy changed considerably, moving away from miracle working and ecstatic or frenzied exhortations and toward a more literary, eloquent, and logical method of instruction and appeal. From about the eighth century B.C. on the prophets improved in literary quality while continuing their fervency in moral and religious discourses. They hammered away at the significance of God's covenant with Israel as his chosen people, which they interpreted as obligating the people not only to obey the sacred Law, but also, among other things, to do justice to each other and even to the foreigners living among them. Social justice became a dominant theme. Good deeds were put ahead of rituals and burnt offerings. The injustices of man to man were held to be transgressions against God and the covenant. The spirit of the Law was raised above the letter, and the dignity of man was proclaimed in increasingly stronger terms. Individual prophets revealed great courage in their denunciations of kings and officials for their sins against the people. Some of the prophets paid with their lives for their open accusations against the mighty, but prophecy continued, and was, on the whole, accepted by rulers and people alike.

In their preaching of social justice and individual righteousness the prophets set forth the ethical basis of all political and social relations as they saw them. Their approach to politics was essentially in moral or ethical terms. They were strongly against abuses of power and the practice of bribery. For the mechanics of governmental organization and procedure, on the other hand, they seem to have had little or no concern. This is probably one reason why they, and indeed the Israelites in general, are usually given very little credit for any beginnings in the field of political studies. Even when at an earlier time the leading elders among the Israelites demanded to have a king, so as to be governed as other peoples were, there is little or no evidence that the prophets took this side. Indeed, as noted above, Samuel, then the leading judge of Israel, and the outstanding seer and prophet of his time, argued strongly against the demand.

The lack of interest shown by the prophets in problems of governmental organization and in popular control over the government is consonant with their theory of rulership, whether under king or judge. They did not think of their rulers as responsible to the people, but only to God and the Law. Their argument was, in effect, that any injustice practiced by the rulers on their subjects was something for God to punish, even as the pursuit of false gods and the adoption of false religions by kings or people would be. There was, as we have seen, no attempt whatever to define the powers of the early judges over the people, and only a belated and limited effort to control the kings by any written document. The Law that applied to all was, in general, thought sufficient to curb the king.

In addition to stressing social justice and righteousness in government, the prophets and the priests showed some interest in international relations. In this field they were strongly against any political relations with Egypt. Having once been freed from Egypt, with the help of God, Israel was never to turn that way again. Even Babylon would be preferable.

One can sense in some of the prophetic writings a slight tendency, increasing with the passage of time, toward humanism and secularism in dealing with political problems. Justice in foreign relations, the more generous treatment of resident aliens, and social justice and righteousness in government are important examples of the subjects that came to be discussed in a secular manner. The changes in this direction come slowly and in a piecemeal rather than a general and systematic fashion, but they keep step with the slow movement toward monotheism. The early prophets insist, however, that the right of the people to just treatment from their rulers is not to be attributed to their own righteousness or freedom from sin. The prophets can be as savage in denouncing the shortcomings of the people as they are in castigating men in high places. There is little talk about the "dignity of man" in their pages. The moral mandate laid upon the rulers of Israel to be just and righteous comes from God. It is for the benefit of the people because they have been chosen of God from among all the nations as his own people, despite their many shortcomings, and he has made a special covenant with them.

The "God-centered" approach of the writers of the Old Testament books in all matters that concern Israel results in their failing to discuss adequately or at all a number of important public questions besides that of the organization and powers of the central government. One looks in vain for any statement defining a tribe, or stating the terms of the confederation agreement among the tribes, or showing how a man like Samuel became a judge of all Israel with extensive but undefined powers, or indicating what elders could participate in the *am ha-aretz*, or serve as judges at the city gates, and so on. The method by which Saul was elected king (the other tribes designating the tribe of Benjamin, and Benjamin nominating Saul) seems to be both casual and awkward, unless prior undescribed but successful informal caucusing had made the outcome a foregone conclusion. The brief sketch for or preface to a royal constitution set forth in Deuteronomy 17:14–20, as quoted above, illustrates the characteristic vagueness and inexplicitness of the Old Testament texts on the subject of government.

Since the ancient Israelites even in demanding a king did not spell out their constitutional principles in any legal or other secular manner, but were content to have an absolute, unlimited monarchy like the other nations near them, one is left with the impression that they did not really mark out the field of politics as something distinct from that of religion. The personal conduct and the policies of their rulers certainly were discussed by the prophets and other writers, but hardly in a way to distinguish their personal from their public and political actions. The authors of the biblical writings developed no distinct secular or humanistic vocabulary for the field of politics, nor, indeed, did they do so for those of economics, anthropology, sociology, and other social sciences as we know them today. All major decisions in human affairs came from God. The Law came from God. All Israel needed to do was to learn God's Law and obey it, and all would be well. Anything that any other nation or ruler did to harm Israel could be explained as God's use of these alien and unchosen peoples as instruments to punish the Israelites for their sins against the Law. And there was always enough sin in Israel, according to the priests and prophets, to explain any defeat or disaster that might befall them, no matter how catastrophic it might be. The thing to do was to find the persons guilty of the sins and punish them. It might be only a single obscure person in a tribe, and yet God's punishment of the whole tribe or people would explain the disaster.

It is interesting to read how this general attitude toward life and politics persisted among the Israelites long after the Greeks had begun to make politics into a secular and even a scientific study. In the work called *Ecclesiasticus, or The Wisdom of Jeshua, the Son of Sirach,* pro-

duced by a Jerusalemite about 180 B.C., the worldly minded author repeats almost the very words of the ancient priests and prophets.[26] Israel
is called God's "portion" or chosen people; his covenant with them is
described; the Law and their duty to obey it to the letter are outlined;
the duty to fear the Lord and to trust implicitly in Him is set forth. The
people are told that they must never investigate too closely things beyond their understanding, that mishaps and defeats are God's punishments for their sins; for "what is man?"—his "end is evil"; he lacks understanding, wisdom; he needs to be modest, soft-spoken in the presence of
those above him, yet able to "pour forth proverbs" as the highest form
of wisdom; and so on. All power is in God's hands, all decisions are his.
Jeshua says: "Authority over the earth is in the hands of the Lord, / And
in due time he will set over it one who will serve his purpose" (10:3-4).
"The Lord tears down the thrones of rulers, / And seats the humble-
minded in their places. / The Lord plucks up nations by the roots, / And
plants the lowly in their places" (10:14-15). "Fear the Lord and honor
the priest" (7:31). "No evil will befall the man who fears the Lord"
(33:1). "A man of understanding will trust in the Law, / And he trusts
the Law as he would a decision by the sacred lot" (33:3). "Divinations
and omens and dreams are folly / . . . Unless they are sent from the
Most High as a warning . . ." (34:5, 6). The author advises his readers
not to seek high office (7:4-7) because it might get them into trouble.
Those who are leaders of the people already, and "rulers of the assembly," he counsels against giving any power over themselves or over
their property to any relative or friend. In short, "In all that you do retain control . . ." (33:22).

As a subject people under the Ptolemies at this time, the second century B.C., the Israelites had at most only a low-level or secondary interest in government. Certainly they had little responsibility for it. Thus
several centuries after Protagoras, Plato, Aristotle, and several Greek
historians had begun to make politics, that is, the government of their
city-states, a secular and even scientific study, Jeshua says but little on
the subject, and that little is cast in a mold of religious thought that attributes nearly everything to God.

Ecclesiasticus is only one of a number of Israelite writings in the
last centuries before the Christian era, but in his general philosophical
and religious attitude its author seems to be fairly typical of his period.
It was not an attitude to encourage a clear-cut separation of the study

of politics from the study of religion, or even to stress the importance of politics in the secular and humanistic sense. After all, what had Israelites living under the rule of others to gain in any way from a concentration upon the study of politics? Rebellion was a possible way out of their state of political subordination, but hardly a study of the government and politics that they saw around them, any more than was the case with their forefathers in Egypt before the Exodus.

Part II

THE GREEKS OF ANCIENT TIMES

⸏ Introduction

IT IS generally accepted that the ancient Greeks were the principal if not the sole originators of the study of politics in the West. Why was it they and, so far as we know, not some other people who were the beginners in this intellectual activity? This is a double-barreled question, or, better, two different questions.

We have already seen in the earlier chapters that the conditions under which the several important non-Greek peoples lived were not right for the development of such a study. The ancient Egyptians, Mesopotamians, and Hebrews were, for one thing, subjected to the rulers of large-scale monarchies and empires, whose seats of power were remote from substantial numbers of the people. The Egyptians were dominated and mentally immobilized by a belief that their kings were gods, and the Hebrews by the belief that their potent but invisible god, Yahweh, was the maker of their laws and the real ruler of the people. These beliefs were perpetuated among the Egyptians by the priestly body of royal civil servants who were engaged in upholding the power of the pharaoh, while among the Hebrews the priests had a similar monopoly of the right to propagandize and educate the people about Yahweh's laws and government. For both peoples it was a profitless and dangerous impiety to question the legitimacy or the policies of the actual rulers. In Mesopotamia conditions were somewhat different but not such as to encourage subjects to pry into the affairs of state. Innate conservatism, ignorance of other governments than their own, or utter contempt for the institutions of such other peoples as they knew, and no doubt other factors, prevented these ancient peoples from developing any active inquiries, either comparative or analytical, into political affairs, although I have no doubt that there were individuals here and there who raised questions.

But even if such considerations explain why these other ancient people *did not* begin important studies of politics and government, they do not tell why the Greeks *did*. We need here to look at two sets of factors, the material and social conditions under which Greek civilization developed, and the attitudes and drives of the people themselves. These are, of course, intimately interrelated and interacting.

Over a long period before Homer various peoples from the north moved down into the area that is now called Greece. They found native populations that had long been there,[1] conquered them, and in the course of centuries amalgamated more or less completely with them. They also moved on as tribes, clans, and smaller colonizing groups down through the mainland, to Crete and the islands of the Aegean, to the eastern shore of the Aegean in what came to be called Ionia, and even to southern Italy and Sicily (Magna Graecia). Again they met and to some extent mixed with other peoples such as the Lydians. Thus the ancient Greeks, or Hellenes as they were often called, had mixed origins and were divided into various regional groups, but they spoke a reasonably common language and were basically one people. They emphasized this fact by calling all others barbarians.

The scattered settlements of the early Greeks developed into permanent villages—and in some cases grew into cities—to which the people developed strong attachments. Many settlements were built upon and around hills that could be and presently were fortified. From these defensible centers the people worked their farms and carried on their trade and cultural relations with similar Greek settlements nearby— and even far away, for there seems to have been considerable freedom of travel. There was no central government over them all; instead each village became a self-governing community. A number of the successful and favorably situated places became cities of considerable size, let us say of thousands and tens of thousands of inhabitants. The "citizens" of the place would of course be fewer than the total population, which included slaves, metics, and children.

The Greek word for such a city was *polis,* a term that originally meant fortress or fortified place and from which the English words "politics," "political," and "politician" are derived.[2] The term *polis* is usually rendered into English by the non-Greek hyphenated term "city-state." This translation is based on the idea that each such community was independent and wholly self-governing, like a modern state. In principle this was true, but in fact some of the larger cities dominated their smaller neighbors, either by force and conquest or by other means. Some like Athens and Sparta even built up little empires for themselves, though these were small compared to Persia in the fifth century B.C. and the empire of Alexander in the fourth.

How many of these city-states there came to be is not positively known. Diogenes Laertius, writing in the late second or early third century A.D., said that Aristotle described the constitutions of 158 of them in his lost work on constitutions.[3] This figure has become widely used, but is apparently not generally accepted as an index of the actual number of city-states.[4] It is not important to know exactly how many there were, but it would be well to have a reasonable estimate of the number of city-states and of their areas and populations in order to appreciate the physical milieu of Greek political studies.

Modern Greece, comprising the mainland and numerous islands, including large ones like Crete and Lesbos or Mytilene, has a land area of just under 52,000 square miles, which is, I believe, fairly close to the effective area of ancient Greece (with Magna Graecia excluded). This area is about the same as that of North Carolina, one of the fifty member states of the United States. As to population, it has been estimated that in 337 B.C., during the time of Aristotle, peninsular Greece had a population of about four millions, of whom over a third were slaves. In 1961 there were in the 48 conterminous American states more than 184,000,000 people, or an average of about 3,833,000 per state, which is probably about what peninsular Greece would have had in Socrates' time.

On the basis of these area and population figures, and with the fact that much of Greece is rugged terrain and incapable of supporting much population taken into account, some estimates concerning ancient Greek city-states can be made. If there were in the fifth or fourth century B.C. even 100 actual city-states in Greece, the average area would have been about 520 square miles (a little over one-half of a typical American county of recent years), including agricultural land as well as the central city; and the population, say in 337 B.C., would have averaged 40,000 per city-state. Actually the differences in population among the city-states (and in area as well, although all were small by modern standards) were considerable. With Sparta, Athens, Corinth, and a few others probably going to over 100,000 each, a number of others probably having over 20,000, and even more having around 10,000 (Aristotle's estimated minimum for "a well-ordered state" was 10,000 "citizens"), the population left over for the smaller 65 to 75 states to share would be sufficient only if many of them were very small.

My conclusion is then that the number of Greek city-states that were of sufficient area, population, or other importance to warrant a study of their political institutions and experiences was probably smaller than even the 158 supposedly examined by Aristotle.

Despite obvious differences in area, population, technological development, and other conditioning factors, there are many respects in which these ancient Greek city-states were much like the "open societies" of the West today—in Europe, the Americas, Asia, Australia, and elsewhere. In the larger ones there were a number of hand industries; considerable trade; some foreign commerce; a monetary system; accumulations of precious metals and other forms of wealth; artistic developments; some attention to education for the well-to-do; the beginnings of science and of philosophy; religious shrines, beliefs, and observances involving most of the people; military organizations; music, drama, and sports; and a great deal of rather free discussion of almost everything. Then, too, at some time before the eighth century B.C. the Greeks had become familiar with and somewhat skilled in writing and in keeping records. Political activities in the city-states from the sixth century B.C. on centered largely in the struggle of the unenfranchised classes against the entrenched power of the land-owning aristocracies for the right to participation in the decision of public questions. Interstate wars were mostly localized, but warfare was going on almost all the time in one part of Greece or another.

Such were in brief the conditions affecting the social, economic, and political life and activities of the Greek inhabitants of the city-states from the sixth century B.C. (and earlier) through the period of the greatest flowering of Greek political studies in the late fifth and all of the fourth century. While these conditions lasted the Greek student had within easy reach for observation and study a number of active, independent small states engaged in governing themselves, often warring with each other, and carrying out a considerable variety of political "experiments" or changes in forms, functions, and processes of government.

So extensive and yet compact a "laboratory" for the study of politics in all its phases had probably not existed anywhere on earth in all the previous development of mankind, at least in late preliterate and early literate time. Here were varied materials close at hand for comparative studies, historical accounts, intensive case studies, and philosophical-ethical studies of politics, such as would both delight and challenge the minds of inquiring men.

And the minds of the Greeks were of a highly inquiring nature. They were undoubtedly early stimulated by the encounters with peoples of long-established cultures different from their own which provided many opportunities for them to pick up novel ideas. It appears that it may have been these contacts with other cultures that helped to galvanize the early Greeks into the tremendous mental activity that they soon displayed.

At any rate when one turns from the ancient Israelites to the Greeks and their works, there is a sense of having been, intellectually speaking, transported to another world. The questions being raised are mostly different, and the answers and the ways of seeking answers almost entirely so. Century after century the ancient Hebrew preachers and writers, both priests and prophets, developed and reiterated the theme of Yahweh, i.e., God or the Lord, as the creator, the ruler, and the maker of the laws for men. These laws were higher than those of the rulers under whom the Israelites were forced to live when in captivity, indeed higher than any man-made laws. The priests and prophets emphasized the sinfulness of men in contrast with the righteousness of God, and the duty of all Israelites to atone for their sins by putting the worship of God and obedience to his laws ahead of everything else. The Hebrew Yahweh, though he sometimes was said to march with or before the people in battle, was actually a being of an entirely different and higher order, the creator not only of men but of all nature, too. While different Old Testament books present somewhat different views of God, and different names for him, he was always one and all powerful. This general attitude toward the governments of man and that of God turned the thoughts of the Israelites largely away from the study of human government and toward the contemplation of God. It left them, too, in no frame of mind to inquire into nature, the creation of God, and hence it limited greatly their contribution to the rise of natural science.

The ancient Greeks believed in the existence of gods or divine beings, but these were almost entirely different from the Hebrew Yahweh.[5] There was not just one god, but many of them, with different individual characteristics and different functions—gods of natural phenomena like woods, the sea, and springs; gods of places such as city-states; gods of wisdom, of music, and so on; and a pantheon of gods of more general scope, somewhat related to each other like members of one family, and headed at one time by Cronus but later by his son Zeus. There were gods who had in effect died, some through the violence of others. Some gods were male and others female, and they were sufficiently human so that male gods could cohabit with human females and have offspring by them. Their human qualities, including human weaknesses, showed up in many ways. Consequently the gods needed government just as men and women do. The gods had, therefore, a council or assembly to settle questions of divine policy, as well as to decide disputes among them. The oral traditions on this subject, and the works of Homer and other early writers, gave the Greek peoples ideas about government apparently derived from the gods.

Unlike the Hebrew Yahweh, the gods were not the creators of the world, but were themselves a part of it, and of nature. Thus they were close to the level of men and women, and could and did in some cases reveal themselves to human beings and give them counsel, as Athena appeared to Achilles when he was angry with Agamemnon. People set up shrines to their favorite gods, like the famous sanctuary at Delphi, which came into Apollo's possession. People high and low went to such shrines to lay their problems before the gods supposedly residing there, and to receive divine prophecy or counsel. A single god like Apollo could have shrines devoted to him in many places, so as to meet the needs of his followers near where they lived. It was not expected, therefore, that the god would always be present at any one shrine. Instead a priest or group of priests devoted to the particular god would be present at each shrine to act in place of the god.

This is certainly an inadequate summary of the nature of the Greek gods and their services to men but to go further into detail would carry this account far afield. The important point is that one can hardly understand the greatness of the Greek intellectual achievement in many fields of study from the seventh century B.C. onward without full awareness that in their minds the Greeks carried a great conglomeration of myths about their gods and what they did. In this mass of myths about gods and demons there were some superlatively wonderful, unnatural, and awful events and examples of divine behavior. For instance, there was the myth of the early great god, Cronus, who married his sister Rhea. When the children were born he seized and swallowed them, one by one, until she finally found a way to conceal and save her sixth child, Zeus. At an early age the latter overpowered Cronus, banished him, and ruled in his stead. Much of what was written by the Greeks beginning with Homer and Hesiod and continuing for centuries is shot through with such archaic and essentially preliterate materials. Call them religious or mythological or anything else, one cannot ignore their presence and influence in ancient Greek minds and writings.

Greek notions about government, justice (*diké*), culture, and education had their beginnings at a time when such mythological ideas partly filled the minds of the people. The presence of these ideas in great abundance may prove, as I think it does, that the ancient Greeks were a people of remarkably active and imaginative minds who were seeking for explanations of what happened around them. The wonder is that in a few centuries the leaders of Greek thought put behind them most of these mythical beliefs and went on to produce a great quantity of reasonably reliable information about man and his world, and to create philosophical systems that are still important to all mankind.[6] In the process of doing this they arrived at a more naturalistic and secular view of the world and of man himself, and discovered within their own minds previously unrealized capacities for advancing knowledge.

In connection with the early Greek study of politics I find two distinct but not entirely unrelated developments from the eighth or seventh century on to beyond the time of Alexander. One was within what might be called the religious area of thought and organizational activity, where adherence to ancient beliefs was the guiding principle and all else was incidental. The other came in the area of secular and political activity where problems and conditions were constantly changing and men had to use their minds freely and actively to find answers to their problems.

The former of these parallel lines of development is best illustrated by the history of the Delphic Oracle, the outstanding shrine to the god Phoebus Apollo. This center of worship and wisdom became, on a small scale, a sort of international meeting place where political questions as well as others were considered, but after a period of remarkable growth it fell on evil days, was several times almost destroyed, and in the end lost practically all its influence and prestige. Because what was done at this center has important implications for the study of politics, although it left no permanent deposit of political knowledge and ideas, and no written record of its own, Chapter 4 will be devoted to this oracle.

The other line of development began more uncertainly and casually, in the minds of one man here and another there, at different times. These were the men to whom the problems of government were more central and urgent than they were to the Delphic priests. Either they were men like Solon who were engaged directly in politics and government and who had to find solutions to problems; or they were primarily poets, scientists, and philosophers who, realizing the importance of politics, spoke and wrote on the subject to some extent. One of the most important things they did was to develop ideas about the best methods of increasing human knowledge generally by men's own efforts. Unlike the priests at Delphi these men left a trail of writings in which they expressed their own ideas. Thus they added to the stock of political information that became available to later men and generations, and laid a foundation for more systematic students like Plato and Aristotle to build upon. Out of the works of such men arises that long line of development, extending down to our own day, that has come to be known as the history of political theory, and the related field of the history of political institutions. The first chapter on the early secular developments in Greek political studies will follow that on the Delphic Oracle.

Chapter 4

⌇ The Delphic Oracle

Starting as a prehistoric settlement just north of the Gulf of Corinth in the district known as Phocis, with Boeotia on the east and Aetolia on the west, Delphi grew into an important city by the seventh century B.C., and continued so through the centuries of the greatness of Greece and on into Roman times, although it apparently never attained a population equal to that of places like Athens and Corinth at their largest, or any considerable commercial growth. Rather, its place in the Greek world was apparently due to its prominence as the seat of a religious organization called the "Delphic Amphictyony," or "dwellers round about" Delphi. This organization originally included, not city-states, but some twelve tribes—among them the Thessalians, Boeotians, Dorians, Ionians, Locrians, Phocians, and Dolopians—which suggests an early date for the formation of the Amphictyony.[1] The relatively small size of the population served by the organization throughout its history is underscored by the fact that such powerful city-states as Athens, Sparta, and Thebes never did become members. Indeed, through power politics and war the council of the Amphictyony was itself several times under the control of one or another of the more powerful Greek states. Of course along with them it finally succumbed to the Macedonians, and later to the Romans.

Nevertheless the Amphictyony had enough power and unity in its early days, first, to defeat the efforts of nearby villages or cities such as Crisa to tax and to interfere with road traffic into Delphi, and, then, to extend the area of Delphi at the expense of Crisa to the Gulf of Corinth, so that Delphi could be freely reached by sea. Though presumably a religious organization, the Amphictyony warred upon and largely destroyed Crisa for its interference with the freedom of access to the Delphic shrine. The intermixing here of politics and religion is but one of many examples of a confusion that makes difficult the writing of a history of the study of politics in early times.

The selection of Delphi as the shrine or cult center of the Amphicty-onic Council is not readily explained. Delphi was, however, fairly central in location. Further, archaeologists have found the remains of a very ancient shrine at this place, and it seems to have been a cult center more or less continuously from a time far back in the second millennium B.C. down through the rest of the pre-Christian and into the Christian era. According to an excellent recent work on the subject, the traditions describing how Apollo came to be the god of the Delphic shrine and the one who spoke through the Delphic Oracle are contradictory.[2] Suffice it to say here that Apollo became the god of the shrine in very early times, and that at some later time the members of the Amphictyony accepted him as such. Apollo himself was a god of uncertain origin, probably either northern or near eastern or Asiatic instead of Greek, but one who came to be considered by some "the most Greek of all gods."[3] One tradition is that Apollo searched long for a suitable shrine, found one at Delphi, and seized it for his own. Greek gods did this sort of thing.

Apollo was portrayed as having a beautiful body and a wide array of accomplishments, more perhaps than any other ancient god. This may have been in large part the basis for his widespread popularity. He appealed to different people for different reasons and for centuries he seems to have outshone other gods in the Mediterranean world. He was a god of music, archery, prophecy, medicine, flocks and herds, and a proponent of better codes of law, higher moral and religious principles, philosophy, and colonization. Justice and law and order would thus come within his purview, while terrifying and destructive phenomena like wars and storms were not attributable to him. Altogether he was a very pleasing god with something desirable to offer almost everyone, like a department store with many tempting goods on display.

The fact that he was so popular, so versatile, and so appealing may help to explain why the Amphictyonic Council was willing to accept his shrine at Delphi as its cult center and place of meeting. The further fact that the council would even go to war to protect freedom of access by all persons to his shrine and oracle at Delphi helped to make this sanctuary the most popular religious center of resort for a number of centuries for all the people from western Asia Minor, Mesopotamia, and the Aegean and Mediterranean world.

Delphi became, in fact, a sort of international free city, a place for travelers to see, and a point of meeting for statesmen and political leaders, for rich and poor, as well as for men of religion, throughout this whole region. Men went to it in search of political knowledge and advice as well as for other purposes. It came to have many side attractions —handsome buildings, works of sculpture by the hundreds, and many fine paintings also. Other attractions were added, like the Pythian games every four years that alternated with the Olympians. And for statesmen desiring to meet each other—to avert wars or to formulate treaties, to find out the plans and ideas and the strength and weaknesses of other states, to impress rivals with their own strength and wealth, and to carry out intrigues—there was no better place in those times. Within the area set aside for the temple to Apollo and close to it, a number of cities set up their own buildings, called "treasuries," where their own representatives could meet with others, and where some of their best sculptures, paintings, and other products could be shown. These buildings served some of the same purposes as the residences of foreign ambassadors and other envoys in such modern cities as Washington, D.C., London, and Paris.

But the central attraction of all was the temple to Apollo, a large columned building, with space for a number of activities. The main attraction in the temple was of course the place where the Oracle held forth, bringing to the true believers in Apollo the wisdom and the prophecies of the god himself. This had to be done through human intermediaries, to be sure; and as the modern believer in Christ accepts the words of his priest or minister, so did the pilgrims and inquirers then in similar situations accept the "Pythia," or priestess, and her utterances. People then did not expect to see Apollo in person at the temple any more than present-day Christians expect to see Christ in the flesh in their own churches. The priestess had divine authority to speak for Apollo, and the other priests the right to interpret her sayings, called "oracles." The Pythia was so important as Apollo's spokesman at Delphi that Apollo is often referred to as the Pythian Apollo.

The arrangements for the giving of oracles to the inquirers are clear enough in general outline but greatly deficient in details.[4] Oracles were given to both the high and the lowly, on personal as well as public problems. Some were in the form of prophecies about what would happen; others in the form of counsel on what to do; and no doubt there were other forms. The sanctuary from which prophecies and advice were given had originally been a deep hillside cavern from which supposedly prophetic vapors came forth. The Pythia had sat on a tripod before the cave entrance, while a priest had also been at hand. Presumably under the influence of the god or of the vapors, the Pythia had gone into a sort of trance or delirium, and in this condition uttered her replies. Later this ritual was moved to the temple. A question having been propounded, and the questioner being present (whether accompanied by others or not is not clear), the Pythia gave the answer in obscure, confusing, ambiguous, "oracular" language. When she was done speaking the priest interpreted her words in plainer, more understandable terms, but her oracle was the official statement. In early times the priest gave his explanation in poetic form, but later prose came to be accepted.

It has been said that the woman chosen to be Pythia was one of limited mental capacity, but I offer a layman's non-expert opinion that she was probably a woman of real intellect with a command of language, and an actress, too, who was well schooled by the priests to act her part in the framing of pseudo-answers that sounded mysterious and otherworldly enough to create a deep impression on the questioner.

At any rate it was the priest who formulated the real answer, and if the examples that have been preserved in the works of Herodotus and others are typical, the priests also engaged in obscure language and a certain amount of double-talk. If they did not commit themselves too clearly there was always the chance that a prophecy gone wrong could be re-explained later. An example of this sort is that of the oracle to Croesus, the wealthy ruler of Lydia, when he was contemplating a preventive war on Cyrus of Persia.[5] The first sentence of this oracle said that "Croesus, having crossed the Halys, will destroy a great empire." Croesus interpreted this to mean that the Persian empire would be destroyed, but it turned out to be his own. Later, with the facts before it, the Oracle pointed out Croesus' mistake in jumping to this conclusion. There is considerable evidence, in fact, that a number of Delphic oracles were thus re-explained in order to save the reputation of the Oracle.

112

The Croesus story provides an example as well of the weighty public affairs on which the Delphic Oracle was sometimes asked to prophesy or give advice. With so many important public figures coming to Delphi in the course of the centuries, Delphi became a sort of clearinghouse for important public information, like "a colossal modern intelligence bureau," as one writer has said, and whatever that may mean.[6] Its priests acquired a great reputation for learning and wisdom in many fields. This was a reputation they could not afford to lose, because their incomes and that of the Oracle as an institution depended so largely, if not almost entirely, on the gifts that were brought to it by sightseers and inquirers, and especially by those in public positions and of large means—gifts of money as well as of vessels made of precious metals and of many works of art. On the other hand, as long as the Oracle had a reputation for knowledge and foresight, the rulers of the day felt they must continue to go to it for advice. Lesser folk in large numbers also fell into this pattern of behavior.

To what extent the priests made any systematic study in the fields of public affairs on which they gave advice is not known. They left no writings as far as I can ascertain, and no library of manuscripts has been attributed to them. What they knew must have been largely of a current or recent nature, and was probably carried in their heads. Their prophecies had to cover many areas of interest, and those on public issues were probably much fewer in number, at least, than others, however great their individual importance.

Since it is only from the writings of others that evidence can be obtained, and these, coming from so ancient a time, are understandably incomplete and partly unreliable, one cannot be sure how widely the Oracle's prophecies and advice actually ranged. In private affairs almost every important area must have been touched upon—marriage, children, health, medicine, finances, work, religion, purification, rituals.[7] In public affairs the Delphic Oracle gave advice, and in some cases consent to actions, on such matters as sending out and establishing colonies, drawing up codes of law and individual laws, and constitutions and forms of government, and planning war and defense.

On the issue of colonization the Delphic record is fairly full and rather clear.[8] People here and there who felt they needed to emigrate to some new place—whose homes were threatened by the advancing armies of great powers like Persia or who were unemployed and living in over-crowded cities, or whose soil was poor and insufficiently productive—went to the Delphic Oracle for advice on whether and where to move. The priests evidently knew of places that offered good opportunities for agriculture and perhaps for trade, and gave advice accordingly. The motives for emigration and for colonizing in new places were basically economic, of course, and with these the Delphic Oracle had nothing to do. Furthermore it probably had little influence in directing the main streams of migration that went to the northern Aegean, the Bosporus, and adjacent places. But starting out to a new life in strange places, people felt that they needed some divine blessing and help on organizing their religious life so that they would not be out of touch with other worshippers in the same faith. It was probably for such purposes that the leaders in emigration movements went to the Delphic Oracle. Some of the colonies that went out with the Oracle's advice and blessing, like that at Cyrene in northern Africa, prospered very well. Others did not. Sending colonies to Sicily and places farther west in the Mediterranean was in some cases a mistake, because of the opposition of the Carthaginians who destroyed them. On balance, however, in spite of some colonizing failures, the Oracle had a good reputation for advice in this sort of undertaking, and its revenues were increased by the annual contributions of those that succeeded.

In the fields of war and defense also the Oracle's advice produced varying results. The case of Croesus' disastrous attack on the Persians has already been mentioned. To give a later example, the rulers of Athens about the middle of the fifth century B.C., standing in great fear of the Persians whose armies were about to descend upon them, sent to Apollo at Delphi for advice on the course to pursue.[9] The oracle this time was very clear: it advised the Greeks to desert Athens and to flee from the advancing Persians to the distant west in the Mediterranean. This advice the Athenians refused to follow: they decided to stand and fight. When by their own efforts the Greeks, led by Athens, defeated and drove back the Persians, the victors gained great confidence in their ability to decide human problems of policy by themselves, and to provide for their own self-government and defense secularly, without the aid (or hindrance?) of the gods. As a result the prestige of the Oracle went into a serious decline among other Greeks as well as among the Athenians, from which it never fully recovered. Sophocles' *Oedipus, King of Thebes* may have been written in part at least to try to revive the confidence of the Athenians in the Delphic Oracle.[10]

In the matter of the Oracle's approval of laws and constitutions the record is perhaps more mixed and uncertain than in other areas, but the tradition has at least some evidence to support activity in this field. A part of the tradition is that before Apollo took over the Delphic shrine, Themis, a goddess of justice and of law and order, had had a share in the Oracle.[11] In acquiring the shrine, Apollo presumably accepted these functions also. Indeed, this was but natural since, according to another myth, he already was a god of justice.[12]

Early peoples, including the Greeks, first looked upon law as a gift of the gods. The need of a god to enforce law and to mete out justice seemed to follow logically.[13] In time this attitude began to change, and perhaps among no people earlier than with the Greeks. Tyrtaeus, a Spartan poet who flourished about 630 B.C., wrote that, in response to a question from Lycurgus, a legendary ruler of Sparta, Apollo replied "from his rich shrine" as follows: "There shall govern the Council the Kings, honoured of the gods, to whose care is entrusted the lovely city of Sparta, and the Elders ripe in years, and after them the men of the people, giving obedience in turn to just decrees; and they shall speak fairly and act justly in all things, nor give any crooked counsel to this city. And upon the increase of the people shall follow victory and strength. Thus did Phoibos [Phoebus Apollo] make revelation to the city concerning these things."[14]

This is probably the earliest written outline of a constitution of government in the West. It reads as if Apollo dictated it, but there are differences of opinion as to what happened. Herodotus says that Lycurgus brought these constitutional ideas from Crete. Plato in the beginning of the *Laws* quotes Kleinias (Clinias), a man of Crete, as holding unquestioningly the view that a god instituted the laws of Crete.[15] Plutarch in his life of Lycurgus has the latter, after determining to reform the whole governmental and legal system of Sparta, go to Delphi "to consult Apollo there; which having done, and offered his sacrifice, he returned with that renowned oracle, in which he is called beloved of God, and rather God than man; that his prayers were heard, that his laws should be the best, and the commonwealth which observed them the most famous in the world." I take this to mean that Lycurgus, who was supposed to have traveled earlier to Crete and elsewhere to study laws and government, was really the author of the laws himself, but that he had received Apollo's approval of them at Delphi.[16]

There is evidence of another Delphic oracle in prose form, partly in "archaic Spartan diction," which outlines a few principles for a constitution or laws.[17] It commands establishment of a temple for Zeus and Athena; reorganization of the people on the basis of tribes; setting up of a senate of thirty appointed members, including kings; periodic meetings of the people to vote on legislative proposals. This appears to be a genuine ancient document, and while it is not closely related to the Tyrtaen poem or the Lycurgean oracle, it presents some additional evidence that the Delphic Oracle did engage in giving advice on constitutions and laws.

Supposing that something did happen similar to what Tyrtaeus, Plutarch, and Aristotle mention, that leaders in states like Sparta, and especially Sparta, did at an early date submit laws and constitutions to the Delphic Oracle for advice and approval or suggestions, it must have been believed that the Oracle had some special political knowledge and wisdom coming from Apollo and not available to others. At the same time this giving of advice is not a direct intervention by the god Apollo in the affairs of particular places. Presumably Lycurgus or any other inquirer at the shrine was free to reject the Oracle's advice, as the Athenians did nearly two centuries later in resisting the Persians.

There is also evidence of somewhat later date than the seventh century B.C. that the Delphic Oracle, i.e., the Pythia and the body of priests, was not without political bias. The Oracle had especially close relations with Sparta[18] and seems, in general, to have approved of its conservative if not reactionary institutions, while Sparta on the other hand did not fail to cultivate the Oracle. Athens with its secular, sophistic, and democratic institutions and political practices troubled the Delphic priests a great deal, and when tyrants arose on the ruins of democratic or aristocratic political systems—men who were potentially dangerous to their shrine's influence—they showed their deep displeasure with tyrants also. In short, they were not distinterested observers and students of the political life of the city-states. They were men of religion, representing and responsible for the welfare of their own institution and their cult, but seeking political support. Consequently the Delphic priests never attained very high rank as students of government and politics and were, in fact, destined to fade completely out of the political scene. On the other hand, certain of the men who flocked to Athens, along with natives of that city, rose to supreme heights as students of politics in the ancient world and left writings filled with ideas that were to survive the centuries and be of continuing value to men everywhere.

It may truly seem that the Delphic Oracle as an institution contributed very little. Its center of interest was, after all, predominantly in the cult or religion of Apollo. Other interests were subordinate to this, and merely ancillary. It had no direct responsibility in the field of politics. Even the Amphictyonic Council seldom consulted the Pythia or the priests in its work. It was, further, not a teaching institution organized to accumulate knowledge and to spread it generally among the people. No doubt it provided religious training and instruction for selected persons to serve as replacements for its Pythia and its priests, but as far as I can ascertain it held no classes for young people in any field of study. The Oracle was wrapped in secrecy, so that its mysteries would not leak out to the people and be attacked and possibly exposed. I find no evidence that it had any library worthy of the name, although there must have been manuscripts for novitiates to study and for the priests to use in refreshing their memories about the rituals and the mysteries. No doubt, too, there were records of events, of gifts to the Oracle, and of other information needed for the operation of the shrine. But these were not for the general public. As to research in an elementary sense there must have been some gathering of information from visitors to the shrine, and some recording of things learned about various places and peoples. Only thus could the Pythia and the priests be familiar with the vocabulary in various fields of study, and be informed sufficiently to give advice to travelers, to those sending out colonies, and to those asking about laws, government, health, agriculture, and what not. The oracles show a considerable range of current information about peoples, places, and myths. But I find no evidence of any attempts to put this information into written form, properly generalized for public use, or to draw any general principles from the materials, more than was needed to make up brief aphorisms like "Know thyself" and "Nothing too much."

The Delphic Oracle acquired great wealth and a set of handsome buildings, sculptures, and paintings. But "acquired" is the word, for it did not produce. Its architects and artists came from the outside. It left no great works of its own production, no books of religion or philosophy or history or law or literature. It made no scientific discoveries.

In summary, the Oracle's priests were apparently content to preserve their position as the heads of a major religious shrine, to increase its wealth and improve its physical equipment, and to extend its temporal influence. It had, no doubt, a certain ethical influence. A number of its oracles were based upon principles of justice, truth telling, and respect for others. One can hardly say, however, that it had much influence upon the moral conduct of the Greeks within its own area or on that of other peoples. Indeed its own priests are supposed if not absolutely proved to have been guilty of cupidity, while many of its oracles included elements of deliberate deception and confusion.

Why, then, deal with the Delphic Oracle at all in a history of the study of politics? I have discussed it primarily because I have wanted to get as far back into the beginning of political studies in the West as I could go—and the Delphic Oracle was there, along with other institutions and individuals. It was important in a number of ways, and there are not a few references to its counsel and its oracles on political questions, such as constitutions and forms of government, laws, colonization, and the setting up of new city-states, and issues of war and peace, along with references to its relations with the Amphictyonic Council, which some authorities have classed as an early example of confederal or federal government. Aside from this, it makes what might be called a negative contribution to my investigation. It demonstrates—in the nature of its organization, its objectives, and the conditions under which it worked—characteristics that may help explain why the scientific study of politics does not develop among some peoples, even when there is an interest in the subject and where some start is made. Its primarily religious or cultish objective; its secrecy; its attempts to preserve an air of mystery; its lack of interest in teaching or in writing and publication, or in building up a library and research center; its actual weakness in the face of the political forces with which it was surrounded; its equivocal moral position; its lack of real freedom to investigate, or of any desire to do so—these are some of the conditions that kept it, I believe, from making any real headway in the study of politics. Thus, by contrast, some light may be thrown on the optimum conditions for such study.

Chapter 5

⌐ Pre-Socratic Writers

THROUGH the centuries while the anonymous Pythias and priests in the Delphic Oracle were carrying on their counseling and prophesying, but leaving practically nothing in writing, another group of men were engaging in intellectual pursuits that produced for the study of politics results of immeasurable value to mankind. These men had names and biographies. Most of them showed a genuine interest in communicating their ideas and their knowledge to others. They left behind them written materials in which they stated what they knew or believed, not only about politics but about other matters. In thus initiating the production and accumulation of an enduring record from which each succeeding generation could benefit, Homer, Hesiod, Solon, and later writers in this succession helped to set in motion a fundamental educational process. They were, whether at first knowingly or not, generous teachers. With such persons one feels a certain affinity, through a common interest in the problems of humanity, that it is impossible to feel toward the nameless Pythias and priests at Delphi.

Some of these writers visited the Delphic Oracle, and even picked up and wrote out reports and purported oracles from the shrine, but the Oracle had little demonstrable influence upon their philosophical, historical, literary, scientific, or political ideas and works.

The basis for selection of persons to be included in the discussion here is somewhat different from that of the authors of three excellent, in fact indispensable, works on this period published in recent years. Kathleen Freeman (in her two volumes) and G. S. Kirk and J. E. Raven restrict themselves to those who might today be called philosophers or natural scientists.[1] (They were, it is true, considerably influenced by the selections previously made by the great German scholar Diels and were not trying to expand on his list.) I have cast a somewhat larger net in order to draw in men of many parts, like Solon, whose ideas and writings, in however fragmentary a form they survive, cast light on the development of the study of politics.

The centuries in which these men lived were times of numerous beginnings in many different fields of study.[2] The list of "firsts" from these centuries—the first philosopher, the first mathematician, the first geographer—is impressive if not practically astounding when one thinks of how relatively few the thinkers and writers were, and how little they had to work with in the way of such things as books and instruments, how primitive were their research methods, how little experience they had to draw on. To learn at all they had to travel, observe, question, and talk almost endlessly.

There were no shortcuts to learning in those times, not even a systematic division of the fields of study. Everything was relatively if not completely new. Since one man picked up this subject here and another one that one there, there is little continuity in the materials that have come down to us. From the scanty evidence at hand it appears that different writers arose in different places at different times and gave attention to different subjects or aspects of subjects and with decidedly different approaches to the nature of man and of the universe. A few writings of early times, like those of Homer and Hesiod, had considerable circulation, and with it some directing and unifying influence on later writers, but the works of philosopher-scientists like Thales that came later may not have been as widely circulated.

One thing is fairly certain, and that is that the everyday human problems of the *polis*, the city-state, received little attention in the writings of the learned men, Solon excepted. Most of what they wrote dealt with loftier and broader matters like the origin and nature of the earth and the universe, and the gods. Specific materials on government are scarce, but here and there it is possible to find a valuable clue to the actual conditions of the period and to political attitudes and approaches. These writings yield in addition materials that provide background and context for the study of politics. One learns from them something of how scientific attitudes and methods of study arose, and of how certain subjects related to politics—ethics, rhetoric, oratory, law, economics, civil liberties, education, for example—came upon the scene. Thus, when politics finally emerges as a distinct and important subject of study in its own right, various related subjects have already had some development, and are ready to give support to the new discipline.

It should be remembered that at the same time these developments were taking place in Ionia, Athens, and southern Italy, the Delphic Oracle of Apollo was prospering and had the continued support of some of the more backward city-states, including Sparta. Diversity was a prominent characteristic of attitudes and ideals during this period, and indeed until the unification under Philip of Macedon. But there was not just diversity; there were also antagonism, war, and mutual destruction, as exemplified by the long-continued enmity of the Spartans toward the Athenians. Not only did wars and slaughter arise out of interstate conflicts, but ruthless internal struggles erupted within states. The century and a half from the height of Solon's career, between 594 and 570 B.C., to the birth of Plato, about 429 B.C., would not seem, in retrospect, to have been a propitious time for progress in science, philosophy, culture, and general learning. Yet there were places where intellectual work could be done, like Miletus which was under Lydian protection for a long time and was also spared for a while at least from the Persians. And when the worst occurred, scholars often moved from a troubled spot to one more secure, and so their work could be carried on. Athens under several fairly moderate and cultured tyrants, and later under reasonably liberal and intelligent democratic rule, became such a place. By the end of the fifth century Athens was drawing to itself much of the best cultural and scientific leadership of all Greece. In the decades that followed Athens became the greatest center of productive scholarship and culture that the world had ever known.

But this is getting ahead of ourselves. The account in this chapter must begin at a much earlier period. We shall first look very briefly at two rather shadowy figures, and then turn to one of the greatest names in literature.

Orpheus and Musaeus

Orpheus, whose original habitat was near Mount Olympus, north of the Hellespont in what is usually called Thrace, was celebrated in ancient tradition as a wonderful singer and musician, especially with the lyre, and a promoter of rites and mysteries connected with the worship

121

of Dionysus.³ The stories about him are confused even on the point as to whether his parents were gods or humans. He was probably a Thracian king or leader of pre-Homeric times.

Writings offered by later sects like the Neoplatonists as Orphic in origin dealt with presumably religious matters like salvation, sacred robes, rituals, oracles, sacrifices, and astrology, not to forget theogony and power struggles among the gods. Orpheus was credited by his followers with being a teacher and the exponent of a code of correct conduct for men, in this world and the next. Nothing closer to a study of human government has been associated with his name—and this is understandable, for he probably lived in a period when tribal government was still prevalent in his region. Then too his later followers who attributed sayings or writings to him were themselves primarily interested in their religions and mysteries, and not in such mundane affairs as government.

Musaeus, reputed to have been a disciple of Orpheus, and hence also probably pre-Homeric, is credited with a number of writings, a gnomic saying that "art is ever far better than strength," and an oracle about a punishment to be visited on Athens because of "the baseness of their leaders."⁴ This oracle, which may be genuine, whether properly attributable to Musaeus or not, illustrates the early, and especially the early priestly, view that the gods interfere to punish men and cities for their misdeeds.

There is a certain amount of cosmogonical and cosmographical content in the thoughts and sayings of these two men, but gods and religious rites are far more important, while references to the secular affairs of human communities like tribes and city-states are almost entirely lacking. In this they are typical of their period. Beginning with Homer there is a shift—often slight—in interests toward greater concern with human affairs; it becomes more pronounced in Solon and those coming after him.

Homer

The two earliest and in some respects greatest works of the ancient Greek genius, the epic poems called the *Iliad* and the *Odyssey*, are generally attributed to a poet named Homer who probably wrote them about 900 B.C. on the Ionian island of Chios.⁵ The principal events recorded in the *Iliad* relate to a great Greek military expedition against

Troy, participated in by a number of city-states, to bring back Helen, the wife of a Spartan king, who had eloped with Paris. These events probably occurred several centuries before they were written down. The *Odyssey*, a later work, is taken up largely with the eventful but long-delayed return from the Trojan War of Odysseus, king of Ithaca, an island off the western coast of Greece. Perhaps even more than the *Iliad*, it is replete with incidental stories and myths, some of which had had wide circulation before Homer from western Europe to India.

Whatever may be the sources of the materials in these epics it is clear that the author was aware of some of the political facts of life in his own time and perhaps of those in earlier times. In its first few lines the *Iliad* speaks of "Atreides [Agamemnon] king of men and noble Achilles."[6] For the Trojan expedition, Achilles, a fearless warrior and lesser king, had joined forces with others under the leadership of Agamemnon, king of Mycenae, who also had hegemony over the rulers of some other city-states. According to Homer, Agamemnon, "greatest far of the Achaians," possessed a scepter of authority originally made by Hephaistos and given by him to Zeus, son of Cronus. From Zeus it had been handed down from king to king. Thus the scepter-bearing king could claim divine authority to rule stemming from Zeus. As Nestor put it, "'. . . no common honour pertaineth to a sceptred king to whom Zeus apportioneth glory.'"[7] Agamemnon stood on high, in a class by himself. But Homer mentions as well councils of elders, including lesser kings and nobles, and assemblies of all active men that were called at times to decide on major policies.

Thus the poet was aware of an already existing theory of kingship, and a kingly power tempered and restrained by a council and an assembly of the people.[8] How far back into the preliterate period of the Greeks this theory and its practice went it is futile to try to ascertain. Kingship seems entirely "natural" for any people in its primitive and protoliterate stages, and yet at some time in their past the Greeks and other peoples must have worked out its essentials, by experience and reason. In each city-state later men must also have modified its details (how big a council, who should be members of it, when to hold assemblies, what business to transact in each, and so on) from time to time, with the result that innumerable local and temporal variations came about in its practice.

That the principal unit of government among the ancient Greeks early came to be the city, or city-state, and not the tribe or clan is very clear. Peoples who did not have the *polis* with its settled population and defined boundaries were looked down upon by the Greeks even at this period. Homer mentions a number of cities in connection with the names of their rulers; but unfortunately for later students, he provides relatively little descriptive material about the government of the Greek city-states of his time and earlier.[9] It would indeed have been surprising if a writer with Homer's purposes had done so. He was a poet and a reporter of epic events, only incidentally a student of politics. The assembly of all the leaders and men called by Agamemnon to decide on the final attack on Troy, as Homer describes it, may have been typical of the assemblies of the city-states, or it may have been something agreed upon for miltary purposes only by the bands of warriors who joined in the campaign. The terms of the agreement among the participating kings, nobles, and city-states are not set forth, and neither are the powers that were vested in Agamemnon as supreme leader. There are passages in the *Iliad* that throw some light on the polity of Troy, and others in the *Odyssey*[10] that describe in some respects the organization of Ithaca, but in general Homer shows little curiosity about such matters, and his accounts of them are not systematic or complete. As descriptions of the organization of ancient Greek governments, therefore, the *Iliad* and the *Odyssey* leave a good deal to be desired.

In other respects, however, they reveal much. For one thing they set a high standard of public ethics, though in a rather unusual way. Emphasis is placed on *diké,* meaning right or justice as determined by human beings and secular authorities. On a somewhat higher level is *themis,* or right according to divine authority. Upholding this right is a solemn obligation resting upon all, but especially upon the great king, with his scepter symbolic of the power entrusted to him by the gods. But the king himself is not above criticism by others, as Achilles demonstrates when he denounces Agamemnon as a "folk-devouring king" for his grasping more than his share of the spoils of war.[11]

On the important point of the relations between men and gods in the making of important decisions, the first chapter of the *Iliad* is most revealing. Chryses, a priest of Apollo, comes to Agamemnon before Troy to try to ransom his daughter, Chryseis, who was seized in an earlier battle. Apollo is so angered by Agamemnon's refusal to release Chryseis

124

and by his surly remarks to Chryses that he shoots his arrows from afar into Agamemnon's ships, killing horses, dogs, and men alike so that "the pyres of the dead burnt continually . . ."[12] After nine days of this slaughter, against which there seems to be no defense, Achilles takes it on himself, at the suggestion of the goddess Hera, to call an assembly of the forces to consider abandoning the whole campaign. But first they consult an interpreter of dreams, one Kalchas, who, upon being assured of Achilles' protection, says that Apollo will never cease to punish the Greeks until Agamemnon releases Chryseis unconditionally to her father.

Agamemnon accepts this augury with bad grace, and not unconditionally. He will indeed release Chryseis in order to save his army but he demands of the assembly another "prize of honour forthwith, lest I alone of all the Argives be disprized . . ."[13] In a sharp exchange between him and Achilles, Agamemnon makes it clear that he will not scruple to enter Achilles' tent to take his concubine, Briseis, to replace Chryseis. Achilles threatens to withdraw his support from the expedition and to return home. More hot words follow between the two, and Achilles is so angered that he begins to draw his sword to kill Agamemnon.

The goddesses Hera and Athena are watching this encounter from heaven. At this crisis Hera, who loves both Agamemnon and Achilles, dispatches Athena to restrain Achilles. Almost instantly Athena, "to him only visible," stands beside Achilles and pulls at his hair. At once he recognizes her and asks why she has come. Her reply is: " 'I came from heaven to stay thine anger, if perchance thou wilt hearken to me, being sent forth of the white-armed goddess Hera, that loveth you twain alike and careth for you. Go to now, cease from strife . . .' " and she promises goodly gifts if he will yield. "And Achilles fleet of foot made answer and said to her: 'Goddess, needs must a man observe the saying of you twain, even though he be very wroth at heart; for so is the better way. Whosoever obeyeth the gods, to him they gladly hearken.' "[14] And so he returns his sword to its sheath, and follows the advice of Athena.

This important episode reveals much about Homer's ideas of the relations of the gods to men. The gods sit on high watching closely the actions of their favorites among men, and they stand ready to intervene at once in human affairs to avoid the destruction of those they love. Notice that Athena does not herself physically restrain Achilles' hand,

nor does she even give him an outright command not to kill Agamemnon. She reasons with him to do as she advises, "if perchance thou wilt
hearken to me," and she promises him good things if he will take her
advice. The choice is clearly to be his, and his own words show that he
yields out of considerations of policy, since it is "the better way" to
follow the wishes of the gods. The gods themselves are caught in something of a dilemma when human beings whom they love are about to
attack one another. These gods are, in effect, only a higher category of
beings than men, beings who are concerned with human affairs and who
intervene in such affairs when it is to their own interest.

There must have been at first only a few copies of Homer's two great
works available to the people. Rhapsodists, men who found remunerative employment in traveling about and reading or reciting poetry to
willing listeners, evidently took up the *Iliad* and the *Odyssey* at an early
but unknown date.[15] There was, indeed, a class of rhapsodists who came
to be called Homeridae or Homeristae, of whom at least some of the
earliest ones may have been from Homer's own immediate family or
close relatives. In time more and more copies became available and
were spread more widely throughout Greek communities and among
other peoples in adjacent lands. Indeed, Homer came to be regarded
as "the educator of Greece."[16] He was "required reading," everywhere
assigned by private tutors and public teachers to their students. His influence seemed not to diminish through the centuries but to spread and
grow, right down into modern times. Wherever Greek and Latin have
been studied, Homer's works have been known by countless students.

Later books like those of Plato, Aristotle, the Greek historians, and
others that came to occupy places alongside Homer's books had more
political content. Nevertheless, the elementary ideas about forms of
government that Homer conveyed and his accompanying moral teaching (about public right and justice, loyalty, patriotism, knightly excellence, and the free spirit of man) combined to make the *Iliad* and the
Odyssey excellent instruction in public duty and responsibility for all
who studied them. Although Homer probably had no specific intention
to teach about government, political knowledge and standards of public
decency and personal responsibility for the public welfare were introduced by Homer's works into the minds of both young and old while
they were seemingly reading great epic poetry for its history, its stories,
its style, and its entertaining qualities. The fact that he brought the gods

into his works as important advisers and decision-makers in political matters, and even had them reward or punish leaders for their political decisions, meant that he was very far from presenting a modern view of the study of politics. On the other hand he did not, like the Old Testament writers, make a divine being or beings the source of human government and laws. When compared with the Old Testament, Homer's works appear to be distinctly secular.

Hesiod

Hesiod, who probably lived in the eighth century B.C. though possibly earlier, also was a revered and famous poet, second only to Homer. One of his major works, *Theogony*, deals with the origins and genealogies of the gods, but another work, entitled *Works and Days*, has to do primarily with human problems.[17] Essentially a practical handbook of advice directed specifically to the author's brother—it lists the days that are best for planting, for reaping, and so on—it also discusses social problems. A competent classicist says that it contains "the earliest written record of the conscious application of human thinking to the problems of living together."[18]

It enters, indeed, into the problems of right conduct in human government. According to *Works and Days*, Zeus created successively four races of men before he created the one then living—the golden, the silver, the brazen, and "a godlike race of hero-men." Each of these in turn had vanished. The really golden age was apparently that of the fourth race, which included among others the heroes who had fought at Troy "for the rich-haired Helen's sake." When this race of heroes was gone Zeus created the men of Hesiod's time. A "race of iron," they did not "rest from labour and sorrow by day, and from perishing by night; and the gods shall lay sore trouble upon them. But, notwithstanding, even these shall have some good mingled with their evils." Their evil nature was shown by the dissensions between parents and children, irreverence toward the gods, ungratefulness, hardheartedness. The gods would soon forsake mankind, and for mortal men there would be no help against evil.[19]

In the field of politics and government Hesiod found that men relied too much on might and violence—"for might shall be their right: and one man will sack another's city"—and that rulers and judges abused their authority by taking bribes.[20] Deceit and perjury were also common failings. The old-time virtues of the age of the heroes had been lost. But Hesiod did not despair entirely of the possibility of improving government. He urged all men, including nobles and rulers, to observe justice and righteousness toward all men in public affairs, and to obey the law instead of taking the law into their own hands. Only by observance of law could the governments of cities be saved from anarchy. Thus Hesiod in effect developed the principle of government according to law, which is the basic principle of constitutionalism. Hesiod had nothing to offer on the organization of government or its modes of operation. He saw almost every political problem in terms of personal ethics and conduct, and looked to the actions of the gods or of Zeus alone to provide the people with good rulers. In line with the prevailing mythology of the times, Hesiod had Zeus wed Themis, goddess of justice and law and order. They had three daughters, the so-called Horae.[21] Starting as goddesses of order in nature, they became also guardians of the gates of heaven and superintendents of the moral life of men. The names of the three goddesses were Eunomia (Good Order), Diké (Justice), and Eiréné (Peace)—representing three of the great objectives imputed to human communities and to their political life. Thus we see mythology and early beliefs in the gods brought to the aid of the ancient Greeks in their gropings toward a human and secular basis, and a set of standards, for human government.

This is a far cry from modern secular attitudes and methods in the study of politics, for Hesiod still has the gods make the major decisions for men, yet one can see in his works some significant elements of secular and humanistic analysis of men's political behavior that appear again and again in later centuries. Hesiod clearly increases the emphasis upon human responsibility for the management and direction of human affairs, but the gods still play important parts.

From Hesiod to Solon

After the time when Hesiod flourished, there apparently came several centuries of confusion, disorder, and revolts in the Greek city-states. In the same period there was an increase in the numbers of states through colonization by Greeks in many places and their seizure of some cities already established by other peoples. The revolts that took place resulted in many a defeat for the aristocratic, landowning class of rulers by the unfranchised agricultural peasantry who were sometimes aided by the new merchant class and other underprivileged groups in the population. Following the uprisings there was a tendency to create a broader based, more democratic system of government, but this was in some cases preceded by a tyranny imposed by a powerful leader and his inner circle of supporters who had led the revolt against the ruling oligarchy of landowners.

In these troubled times the Greeks had many political experiences, with frequent opportunity to study rulers and forms of government and also to think about the basic principles of political life. As a result of the many revolutions and other changes a variety of political forms arose that provided rich material for comparative political study. But since the times were troubled, experiments had to be worked out for some time before men could settle down to analyzing and systematizing the results. It is a question too whether men were as yet prepared to think broadly and philosophically about government—they may well have been too much taken up with the local troubles and the issues of the day.

There were various writers in these centuries who were giving some study to problems of politics, although none attained the wide readership of Homer and Hesiod. Neither did any such writer concentrate on the study of and writing about politics as men understand that term today. A number of writers, perhaps a majority, probably were on the side of the landowning aristocracies, although the revolting elements also had their literate spokesmen. Unfortunately the materials touching on politics written in those days (say from the late eighth through the seventh and early sixth centuries B.C.) that have actually survived today are mostly fragments. The knowledge that modern scholars have of them has been derived mainly from the works of later Greek and Roman writers, who presumably had these ancient writings at hand; some of their versions of what the earlier men said are, for various reasons, to be viewed with suspicion. Such evidences as exist indicate that the men of this era who were thinking to some extent about problems of politics put their main emphasis, as Hesiod and Homer had done, on political ethics. "Justice," "righteousness," "nobility," "virtue," "truth" are words that occur frequently in the meager fragments of Greek writings that have survived.

It may be revealing to summarize the available evidence on a few men of this period.

Terpander of Lesbos lived in the early or middle part of the seventh century B.C. (c. 650 or 675).[22] Called the "earliest definite figure to appear in the history of Greek music,"[23] he was also a poet. Tradition has it that he was summoned to Sparta by the order of the Delphic Oracle, or at least at its suggestion, to help put down a disturbance among the people. That he was expected to do this by his musical ability alone is doubtful; he may have been supposed to possess some political wisdom or ability but what it was the record does not indicate. It may be that the young people of Sparta were demanding privileges in music and amusements enjoyed by young people in other city-states.

The story of Tyrtaeus, who may have been an Athenian, and who also lived at about the middle of the seventh century B.C., is similar in some ways to that of Terpander. It is also rather confusing.[24] According to one tradition, Sparta was at this time discouraged about the progress of its war against Messenia, so it sent to the Delphic Oracle for advice. The advice was to get an Athenian general. The man they got to help them was Tyrtaeus, who, according to another tradition, was a disgruntled lame schoolmaster in Athens. From there on the stories combine, and Tyrtaeus proved to be an excellent choice. By a combination of inspired military leadership and stirring elegiac poetry in praise of heroes who had died in war he aroused the patriotism and heroism of the Spartans, who went on to win the war.

In one passage of his writings Tyrtaeus claims there was an oracle from Delphi approving a Spartan constitution which provided for kings (there were usually two) at the head of the city-state's government; a body of elders; and an assembly of men to give approval to the decisions of the former. It will be recalled that Lycurgus is supposed to have received the Delphian Pythia's approval for a body of "laws" for Sparta, but Tyrtaeus does not mention him. The traditions on this entire subject are very confusing, but clearly Tyrtaeus was a man who, besides being a general, a preacher of patriotism or love for one's city, and a poet (which at that time meant almost any writer for popular edification, since nearly everyone who wrote did so in poetic form and was called a poet), was also a writer on laws and forms of government. But his importance is limited because he served Sparta almost exclusively, and Sparta became more and more isolated and ingrown, a peculiar, closed, repressive state, not one whose system of government appealed to liberally minded people. Tyrtaeus also looked to the Delphic Oracle, and perhaps through it to Apollo and the other gods, not to the people, for approval of his constitutional ideas. His emphasis on patriotism and the military virtues was at the expense of games and athletics, eloquence, and the other arts and studies that called for considerable knowledge. If he was originally an Athenian schoolmaster, he departed very far from the ideals of his early vocation.

Callinus of Ephesus, who flourished about the middle of the seventh century B.C., is credited with being the originator of the political and warlike elegy.[25] The Cimmerians were in his time threatening Ephesus. He apparently tried through his poetry to save the city by arousing the patriotism and fighting spirit of the Ephesian youths, whom he considered degenerate. Too little of his poetry remains for present-day examination to warrant any fair judgment on his knowledge of politics.

Pherecydes of Syros, who probably lived as early as the seventh century but may have been as late as the sixth, is worth mentioning for two reasons: he is said to have been the first Greek to write in prose, the form in which later nearly all political works were written; and the fragments left of his writings show him to have dealt to some extent with government among the gods.[26] Zeus as ruler banishes to the netherworld, the Tartarean part of the world, "any god who commits an act of lawlessness." Like Homer before him, Pherecydes obviously applies the knowledge he has of human government to explain the supposed government of the gods. This is an early anticipation of the practical uses of the study that modern students call comparative government. The principal works of this allegedly self-taught writer were in cosmogony, theogony, and theology. No work that is on a primarily political subject is attributed to him.

Epimenides of Crete probably flourished around 600 B.C. but may have been later. Strange things were told about him, such as that he slept in a cave for over fifty years and that he lived for over one hundred fifty years. There are reports of his having visited Athens on a mission of purification, and once having represented the Delphic Oracle on a mission. He was apparently a "religious teacher and wonder worker,"[27] probably connected with the Orphic cult. He is reported to have written a poem on theogony, or the genealogy of a certain group of gods. He also wrote a prose work called *Sacrifices and the Cretan Constitution*—

131

a most intriguing title, suggestive of the relations in ancient Crete between religion and politics or law.[28] None of his work survives, which may be specially regretted since the comments of such an essentially religious worker on Cretan politics in his time would be most interesting to read. While he apparently accepted certain myths as true, he denied others.

Solon

With Solon the city of Athens becomes the great center for developments in the political life of Greece. To these he contributed largely, not only as a distinguished writer but as a statesman as well.[29]

In 594 B.C. the aristocratic rulers of Athens were hard pressed by the debt-ridden farmers and other less fortunate citizens, and there was the danger of a revolutionary overthrow of the government. Both factions apparently recognized the high abilities of Solon, and they joined in electing him archon, or ruler. (He may have served again, considerably later, about 570.) In many cities under similar circumstances a leader so elected simply set aside the existing constitution and laws and ruled the city arbitrarily in the supposed interest of his fellow men but in not a few cases according to his own whim. Solon would not do this. An educated man of the middle or upper class, he had a decisive yet moderate disposition, strong ethical principles, and a great sense of public responsibility. He decreed the measures that he thought were necessary to unify a state torn by party strife and to alleviate the plight of the poor, but his principles favored moderation in legislation and the maintenance of constitutional government and of law and order. He found himself in a money and credit economy, with many small debtor farmers losing their lands and being forced into serfdom or slavery for nonpayment of debts. The government at the same time was in the hands of the landowning aristocratic class, some of whom were also money lenders. By ordering the cancellation of debts and forbidding future loans secured by the person of the borrower, he removed the main grievances that had led to disorder. His reforms, hard as they were on the landowners and money lenders, probably saved Athens from being wholly revolutionized and thus saved the dominant classes from complete destruction. In the political sphere he added a fourth class of citizens to the three already existing, endowing on the basis of income each class with a different degree of power in the government of the Athenian state.

The result was to give to the formerly unfranchised poorer elements the right to vote in the assembly and at elections, and to sit in the court of appeal; but the class system as such was only modified, not abolished. These measures did not satisfy the leaders of the poorer people and there was evidently much criticism that Solon had not gone far enough in his reforms. Some even wanted the land communized or divided up among the poor. Those formerly wealthy who had lost much by the cancellation of debts were equally dissatisfied.

Solon answered these criticisms in poems that apparently were widely circulated in his own day and were available to readers as late as Aristotle's time and beyond; long after his death they were still being used as texts for the education of Athenian youth. Only fragments survive but they reveal Solon as a student of politics in a truly modern sense, yet one who clung to earlier ethical principles.[30] Like Hesiod he insists on *eunomia,* or good order, and declares the loyalty of all to the state to be necessary for the welfare of all. He deplores the placing of supposed personal and party interests above those of the state, for this can only lead to disorder, even anarchy, which is harmful to all. He does not accept the idea that a tyrant can provide good government, nor does he countenance the killing off or banishing of a former ruling class by a revolutionary party. A common loyalty of individuals and classes to the state and operation of the government according to law under an established constitution are the essentials that he emphasizes. Freedom under law—freedom from subjection to any lawless tyrant or to any landowning or other class—is among the political ideals that he fosters.

As one turns from the works of Homer, Hesiod, and other such early writers to the poems of Solon and to such accounts of his work as that in Aristotle's *Constitution of Athens,* a great advance in political sophistication is apparent. How much of this is due to Aristotle's interpretation and how much to Solon's insight it is impossible to say, but clearly many modern problems of government were already present in the Athens of Solon's day and he approached the adjustment of class conflicts arising out of political and economic inequalities with confidence and practiced skill.

Solon became a great name among the Athenians, and indeed throughout the entire Greek world. His fame like his poems was widespread, as is evidenced by the number of later writers who mention him and quote his poems, almost always with approval. His poems constituted his textbook on politics. He definitely thought of himself as a teacher as well as a political leader. He commented in one of his poems: "These are the lessons which my heart bids me teach the Athenians . . ."[31] True, he did not engage in research in any modern sense, or organize any school or classes. He was, instead, an early example of the highly intelligent, practical man in politics, devoted to the welfare of the entire state, who was primarily a reformer compelled in carrying out this role to be also a student and teacher of politics. As such he is rightly to be regarded, I believe, as one of the most important Greeks of the pre-Socratic period, for in his poems he established a new point of view from which to observe men's political activities—a basically humanistic and secular point of view.

Solon was not necessarily the first to regard politics as man's business rather than the responsibility of a god or gods. Homer took a step or two in this direction, for example when he had Athena attempt to dissuade Achilles from personally attacking Agamemnon. In effect Homer was saying that even in momentous affairs men are to some extent free to make their own decisions. The goddess merely advised. In Hesiod's work too, while gods still play a leading if not deciding role, personal right living and industriousness are stressed as important to the course of man's fate. Some other even earlier thinkers whose writings have been lost may have recognized with some clarity man's role in the making of political decisions and the taking of political actions. But Solon is the earliest writer I have found whose words are clear on this point. The following is a significant example: "If on our city ruin comes, it will never be by the dispensation of Zeus and the purpose of the blessed immortal gods, so powerful is our great-hearted guardian, born of mighty sire, Pallas Athene, who holds over it her hands. It is the people themselves who in their folly seek to destroy our great city, prompted by desire for wealth; and their leaders, unjust of heart . . . Neither the sacred treasure nor that of the state do they spare in any wise, but they steal, each in his own corner, like men pillaging. They take no heed of the holy foundations of Justice . . ."[32]

The role of the gods in this situation, as the fragments of Solon's poems reveal it, is somewhat uncertain, but I interpret it in this manner: The gods of a city, like Athens' Athena, protect it in a general way, but they do not interfere to override the judgment of the people and their leaders or to punish them for specific actions. Even when the latter make mistakes and violate the laws or the principles of ethics and good government the gods refrain from action. They leave it to human beings to govern themselves, for better or for worse, but always hope that they will improve their ways.

"Not over single happenings, like a mortal, does he [Zeus] show himself swift to wrath; yet no man who has a sinful heart escapes his eye for ever; in the end without fail he is brought to light. But one man pays the penalty straightway, another at a later time; and if the offenders themselves escape . . . yet it [the penalty] comes without fail at another time; the innocent pay for those deeds, either the children or the generations that come after. We mortals, good and bad alike, think thus —each one has a good opinion of himself, before he comes to grief; then at once he begins to lament . . ."[33] Solon does not appear to be saying here that Zeus or the gods mete out various penalties and misfortunes to men, but that there is some sort of long-run law of compensation by which the follies and misdeeds of some men are somehow felt in time throughout the body politic, by few or many, by their descendants or others. Men as a whole are the authors of human suffering.

As Werner Jaeger has, I think, clearly demonstrated, Solon had the opportunity, which he seems to have used to good effect, to study the history of the governments of numerous Greek cities in Ionia, on the islands, and on mainland Greece.[34] He not only traveled abroad visiting rulers, but he also probably had foreign visitors in Athens. He learned how the cities had gone through certain cycles of change, including numerous experiences with tyranny. From these studies he reached the conclusion that, as in nature, so in human affairs there are certain laws of cause and effect. As quoted by Jaeger, Solon wrote: "From the clouds come snow and hail, thunder follows the lightning, and by powerful men the city is brought low and the demos in its ignorance comes into the power of a despot."[35]

Without making any formal classification, Solon put laws into three different categories. First there are the laws of physical nature which govern the sun, the stars, the earth, the wind, the storms. These are outside of man's control. Solon does not, indeed, sharply distinguish between the laws of nature and those of God. A storm that affects good men and bad alike is both, as it were, an act of Zeus or God and a phenomenon of nature.

Second there are the laws of human conduct, the inherent propensities of men to act in certain ways, and partly in arrogant, selfish, un-thinking ways. Such selfish actions bring injury upon the whole com-munity or state—"the public ill comes home to every single man . . ."[36] —because injustices set up reactions among the sufferers who then re-volt and destroy their oppressors. Unfortunately, Solon thinks, those who first suffer injustice and then revolt often go too far and bring themselves unwittingly under tyranny, so that their last condition is no better than their first. This suggests a sort of law of social compensation. But these man-made ills can be controlled and even prevented by men if they will recognize the importance of the well-being of the com-munity to each and every one, and put the public welfare—*eunomia* (order), *diké* (justice), and *eiréné* (peace)—ahead of personal desires.

That human propensities to act are not absolute laws of nature Solon illustrated in his own conduct by refusing to enrich himself unjustly and declining to become a tyrant when, as archon, he had ample op-portunity to do both. But he realized, too, that men vary greatly in in-dividual characteristics, as they reveal in their various employments, and that there is also such a thing as chance or fortuity in human ex-perience so that one prospers where another suffers loss. Men are not all equally capable of directing their lives and actions, nor are they all equally fortunate in what befalls them. Hence they need such help and protection from the community, and from each other, as can reasonably be provided.

Finally, then, there is the body of written laws that a people or its rulers adopt for the government of the city and for the regulation of in-terpersonal relations. These public laws, which are enforceable through public courts and officials, cover and regulate some parts of the second area or category of laws, the human propensities to act, but they never eliminate it and never cover the whole area of possible human actions. They are designed to promote order, justice, and peace, but they need to be observed and enforced adequately if they are to achieve these ends. Solon himself believed in moderation both in the extent and in the contents of such written laws, but in complete obedience by the people to those laws that existed. One of his principal themes was that "lawlessness brings innumerable ills to the state, but obedience to the law shows forth all things in order and harmony and at the same time sets shackles on the unjust."[37] Law observance and public law enforce-ment supplement each other.

136

While Solon left the gods outside of most of this discussion, and approached human problems of living together in essentially secular terms, he was far from being an atheist. He revered the gods sincerely, but he tried to teach the people that men were themselves responsible for the good government of their communities. Religion and politics he definitely distinguished if not separated. This was the great shift in point of view that made possible the development of the study of politics in its modern secular and humanistic form.

Thales and His Successors

Thales of Miletus, who flourished about 585 B.C., and hence was a contemporary of Solon, left no book of his own, and probably did not write one.[38] He is best known academically in modern times for his work in mathematics, in geometry, and in astronomy, and for his speculation that water is the basic or primordial stuff out of which earth, air, and all the other possible materials of the world came and to which they return. Aristotle called him the founder of philosophy, in the sense of natural philosophy. That he was a man of remarkable intelligence and industry is perhaps the least one can say in praise of him.

Thales' scientific work was not done in a vacuum; he was not a recluse scholar in a secluded library or laboratory. A leading citizen of Miletus, he took his citizenly duties seriously, as Solon did in Athens and yet also differently. Much of his work seems to have had practical purposes and to have been done in close consultation and collaboration with the authorities of the city. For example, he gave very considerable attention to the economic problems of Miletus. His city depended economically on navigation of the sea and on the production of agricultural products like olives. His studies of astronomy and meteorology had a direct bearing on the needs of both seafarers and farmers, and hence on the welfare of the city. The annual rise and fall of the Nile River, physical geography and soil conditions, and other practical subjects also attracted his interest.

The city had a very serious problem of defense, and Thales turned his attention to this very practical matter too. He saw the numerous small Greek city-states, completely independent of each other, stretched out along several hundred miles of a narrow coastal strip and on the adjacent islands, as incapable of adequate defense against the large Lydian and Persian forces then competing in the hinterland. He advised the Milesian authorities to unite with the other cities of Ionia in one federation, and if necessary to ally themselves with Cyrus, the Persian, against Croesus, the Lydian—to ally with the more distant potential enemy against the nearer one.[39] Given the strong feeling of particularism then prevalent among the Ionian city-states, this advice fell on deaf ears. But he had at least proposed a realistic political approach to the problem of defense. Had the will to try it been present, it might have worked. How different was this advice from that of the Delphic Oracle several centuries later which suggested the Athenians abandon their city and flee to the western end of the Mediterranean to escape the Persian menace of that time.

In the long run, however, what Thales did in the field of science was more important for modern politics and for the study of politics than any of his ventures into practical political advice. For Thales was moving toward a scientific attitude and method in dealing with natural phenomena that complemented and reinforced the secular and humanistic approach to political institutions and problems being developed at this same time by Solon.

Previously Greeks, Hebrews, and others had tended to ask, "Who made the world in the first place?" and to some extent, "Why does he make it change as it does?"[40] Now, as Philip Wheelwright has put it, Thales and his successors "began to ask questions in a new way."[41] They asked what it is that the world is made of, not who made it. They asked not why did he make it and with what purpose does he change it, but how does change take place in the what, the stuff of which things are made. Thales apparently spent no time in denying the existence of the anthropomorphic Greek gods, Zeus, Apollo, and the rest. He simply redefined them, saying that "all things are full of gods,"[42] meaning natural forces, as is so well illustrated by the magnet, which draws iron objects to itself and holds them. Thus in studying the forces of nature he was studying the gods.

To quote Wheelwright again, Thales "began the work of seeking for explanations of the natural world within the natural world itself. An understanding and formulation of the two questions—'what is basically real?' and 'How does change come about?'—is far more important, both for clarity of mind and in terms of subsequent influence, than any possible answers that can ever, then or now, be given to them."[43] Thales did, of course, get something from the Babylonians and the Egyptians, perhaps from others, but he took these data along with his own observations and "introduced the scientific way of arranging them, [and of] drawing from them generalizations, which could in turn be usefully applied."[44] Some of his answers proved to be wrong, but his method of seeking in nature the explanations of natural phenomena, though much improved upon in time, has never been abandoned.

The two Milesians Anaximander and Anaximenes were pupils, it is believed, and certainly successors of Thales.[45] They flourished about the middle of the sixth century B.C. Together with Thales they formed the nucleus of the Ionian school of natural philosophy. Since, unlike Thales, they seem to have had little or no interest in current politics and they left no records of any work in that field, they need detain us only briefly. Anaximander did, however, formulate some sort of analogy between the natural world and the political. One of the few sentences he left to posterity is revealing: "The Non-Limited is the original material of existing things; further, the source from which existing things derive their existence is also that to which they return at their destruction, according to necessity; for they give justice and make reparation to one another for their injustice, according to the arrangement of Time."[46]

Xenophanes

Xenophanes, born about 570 B.C. in Colophon near Ephesus in Ionia, is reported to have left there about 545 B.C., to have traveled extensively, and to have helped establish the colony and city-state of Elea in southwestern Italy. There he had something to do with starting the Eleatic school of philosophy, although Parmenides is recognized generally as its important founder. In contrast to the Ionian school of Thales and his successors, who looked to physical nature for answers to questions about the universe, and also to Heraclitus with his emphasis on perpetual change and flux, the Eleatics insisted on the universal unity and permanence of all being, "the all is One," and denied that men could through their senses arrive at the truth about the universe.[47]

Xenophanes' concentration upon the unity and stability of the universe and his insistence upon the unreliability of man's senses in attaining truth explain, perhaps, his failure to deal with specific and practically important segments of knowledge. Like the god he pictured, who "sees as a whole, thinks as a whole, and hears as a whole,"[48] and who without toil "sets everything in motion, by the thought of his mind," Xenophanes

139

took for his own the field of truth and wisdom as a whole, and did not emphasize or closely analyze any of its subdivisions. His work is, therefore, not a contribution to the study of politics, but rather a stepping aside from it into metaphysical contemplation, important as that may be for the history of philosophy. He did, however, play a part along with Heraclitus in clearing away the confusion in thinking inherent in the popular belief in a medley of anthropomorphic Greek gods who interfered directly in the affairs of men, a confusion that blocked acceptance of human responsibility for human affairs.

Indeed, Xenophanes did one thing more. He offered men hope. "Truly the gods have not revealed to mortals all things from the beginning; but mortals by long seeking discover what is better." But this promise was carefully qualified: "And as for certain truth, no man has seen it, nor will there ever be a man who knows about the gods and about all the things I mention. For if he succeeds to the full in saying what is completely true, he himself is nevertheless unaware of it; and Opinion (seeming) is fixed by fate upon all things."[49]

Heraclitus

Heraclitus of Ephesus (c. 535–475 B.C.), a man of aristocratic background and apparently good education, presents a strangely contradictory yet fascinating figure in the intellectual life of the century before Socrates. Many able writers have tried to understand him, and no two are fully agreed about his ideas.[50] He seemed to be against teachers and yet he himself was one, of a sort. He had little respect for men in general, and even tended to find something deficient in the ideas of every important writer before him—Homer and Hesiod, for example—and of such contemporaries as Pythagoras, Xenophanes, and Hecataeus. Yet, despite his contemptuous attitude, he wrote with the evident intention of encouraging people to become better informed and wiser.

He postulates something that he calls the *Logos*, perhaps definable as "the intelligible Law of the universe."[51] There is also human law (*Nomos*) which partakes of the *Logos* or divine universal law, "For all human laws are nourished by one, which is divine."[52] Men should follow this one, universal law, the *Logos*, even though most men cannot understand it. Not only that, but the man-made laws of the city, the *Nomos*, should also be obeyed and defended. "The people should fight for the Law (*Nomos*) as if for their city-wall."[53] They should obey this law even if it came from one man—a king or even a tyrant, perhaps? "To obey the will of one man is also Law (*political law, Nomos*)."[54]

The discussion of law at its two levels, divine and human, *Logos* and *Nomos*, brings us close to his strangely mixed attitude toward politics or the government of men in the *polis*. It is recorded that Heraclitus inherited the office of basileus, with religious or civil functions, in Ephesus, but refused to exercise it because he disliked the constitution of the city. Apparently at a later date he denounced the Ephesians (they "would do well to hang themselves, every adult man") because they had expelled one Hermodorus, the most valuable man among them, on the ground that they wanted no outstanding valuable men to outshine the rest of the Ephesians.[55]

Heraclitus is reported to have written a book "on nature."[56] Tradition, as written down by Diogenes Laertius and reported by Wheelwright, describes it as having been divided into three parts—on the universe, on statecraft, and on theology. Another modern author interprets the three parts as "metaphysical, political and theological."[57] There has been considerable discussion of what the book really dealt with, but in the absence of the document itself, who can say? Heraclitus apparently did not intend that people generally should read it, for he is said to have written it in an obscure, difficult style, like that of the Delphic Pythia, and to have deposited a copy in the temple of Artemis (Diana), goddess of the hunt and the torch-bearing goddess of "light by night."[58] The work was evidently seen by a number of persons, but no systematic or adequate summary of its contents has been preserved, if any was ever made. However, many of its more trenchant sentences were copied out by various readers, and of these about 120 fairly authenticated ones plus a few more doubtful ones are now available.[59] Many tend toward paradox: "That which is in opposition is in concert, and from things that differ comes the most beautiful harmony."[60] "The hidden harmony is stronger (*or*, 'better') than the visible."[61] The universe includes and is made up of all the opposites, and this is what seems to make it one universe.

From the fragments published in the standard works on Heraclitus one cannot discover evidence of a systematic study of politics. There is no description of the constitution of Ephesus or of any other city-state; no comparative study of constitutions and political institutions generally; nothing on international or intercity relations; no analysis of po-

141

litical processes like elections, legislation, or administration; no rounded-out political theory. What one reads of his suggests a man of strong antidemocratic leanings and a real distaste for politics, a man who withdraws into his study to write out acrid criticisms of people generally. Though some of his statements are highly quotable, very few of them could be meaningfully applied to the politics of self-governing peoples in the Western world today. Still, his ideas have some value for the study of politics. His notion of the constant flux and change in things, and of one thing seemingly turning into another, strongly suggests the need to study politics as a process of constant movement and conflict with resultant changes in institutions and laws. Likewise his concept of the one and the many being really the same thing suggests the well-known concept of "man and the state" or "man versus the state," a meaningful relationship in the study of politics. Finally, Heraclitus offered men some hope that by getting an education and pursuing proper methods they could advance their knowledge of themselves and of the universe, and also grow in wisdom, even though never attaining the complete wisdom and knowledge possessed by the gods. "The thinking faculty is common to all,"[62] he said. "All men have the capacity of knowing themselves and acting with moderation,"[63] but not all men do this. His own method in trying to understand the *Logos* or law by which the universe is ruled, Heraclitus explained, was that of "separating each thing according to its nature and explaining how it is made."[64] One must seek and follow the universal law, that which is common to all. To do this, and to acquire wisdom, one must inquire "into very many things indeed."[65] He said, "I searched into myself," apparently to test his own abilities. In this way he found that, for acquiring knowledge and wisdom, "The eyes are more exact witnesses than the ears."[66] Indeed eyes and ears are both bad witnesses for men who have "barbarian [i.e., uneducated] souls"[67] and in a more doubtful and possibly spurious statement he adds: "Education is another sun to those who are educated."[68]

Pythagoras and the Pythagoreans

Having given some attention to such an obscurantist institution as the Delphic Oracle, and a few pages to the obfuscations mixed with a little light that came from Heraclitus, I cannot neglect saying a few words about Pythagoras and his followers, the Pythagoreans.

Pythagoras was born in Samos at about the time when Solon was finishing up his constitutional and legal reforms in Athens, about 570 B.C. Probably an aristocrat of considerable means, he had strong political views and a great interest in intellectual speculation. An uprising of the commercial and industrial population having brought a tyrant, Polycrates, to power, Pythagoras left Samos about 530 B.C. and moved to Croton in southern Italy. At Croton he lectured for a time to the people generally, presenting his ideas on religion, philosophy, mathematics, and perhaps politics.[69] Then he changed his tactics, gave up his general public appearances, and restricted his teaching mainly to small select groups, although he did give summaries of his views to others. It is evident that he had found considerable support for his views among the more well-to-do Crotonians and that they preferred to keep him for themselves. Soon an organization or "society" of his followers was formed and not long after that this society came into control of the city government. For a number of years opposition to this oligarchical rule built up among the commercial and industrial classes. After Pythagoras himself moved on to another south Italian city, Metapontium, a savage revolt took place in Croton, with many Pythagoreans massacred by the revolutionists. The leader of the revolt, one Cylon, became the tyrant of the place. Members of the Pythagorean society, who were scattered around Magna Graecia, established a new headquarters at Rhegium for their religious-philosophical cult, and thereafter refrained from joint political activity. In short they ceased to be a "political club" of the usual kind.

It would be desirable, but unfortunately is not fully possible, to separate the ideas and activities of Pythagoras himself from those of his followers. He left nothing in writing, and in this respect many of his followers followed his example. There was evidently a rule of the society adjuring secrecy concerning their beliefs and rituals on all members. A few Pythagoreans did write and publish later, while Aristotle and others not members of the society also studied the Pythagoreans and wrote about them. Although the later developments of doctrines and practices undoubtedly differed in details from those of the founder of the cult, and may have come, in part at least, a century or more after his death, it seems best to discuss Pythagoras and the Pythagoreans in a single connected account. (A few later writers who were at least nominally Pythagoreans will also be touched upon later.)

Pythagoras had several principal lines of interest: mathematics (which was largely arithmetic, and in the hands of some of his followers turned into a sort of numerology); geometry as a branch of mathematics; religion, including beliefs about the soul and its transmigrations, dietary rules, rituals, etc., and politics. Looking for hidden harmonies, and for parallels, similarities, and analogies between the various fields of his interests, Pythagoras came up with some important truths in mathematics, in music, and in other areas. In religion, Pythagoras was considerably influenced by the Orphic cult. Sometimes he spoke of God in the singular, sometimes of gods. He developed a concept of the soul as something imprisoned in the body as a punishment for past sins which, on being released, might migrate into the body of a dog or other animal.

There is ample evidence that Pythagoras took a deep practical interest in political activities and policies, both before he left Samos and also during his stay at Croton. It is fairly clear that he chose Croton as a place to live because the political climate there suited him well. Whether during his early sermons or lectures to the general public at Croton he touched on politics is apparently unknown. As a newcomer to the city he probably refrained from discussing local political matters. His religious, philosophical, and mathematical interests must have provided enough material for these early talks. Later, when he had found his natural associates among the conservative and aristocratic leaders in Croton, he gave increased attention to politics although the extent and nature of his own actual political activity are open to question.[70] Certainly he played an important part in the development of the Pythagorean society, which had branches in a number of places.

The society's organization seems to have been based on a class system in accordance with the philosophy of the founder of the cult.[71] The "initiates," also called the "mathematicians," who apparently gave up their property to the society and lived in a somewhat communistic fashion, were the insiders, the elect, to whom all phases of the ideological system were communicated in full. They were or were to become the experts or professionals, to run the affairs of the society, and to administer the various public offices of the city. Pythagoras instructed them in small groups, more or less in private. It is not reported that he actually taught what we today call "public administration" as a separate subject, but he evidently did cover politics or government in a general sense. His classes met perhaps in the local gymnasium, a public place for meetings of various kinds and for wrestling contests and other athletic activities.

The society also had another class of members, the novitiates or *acusmatici*, the "hearers." These were taught the bare elements of the Pythagorean beliefs, the catechism, so to speak, but not the more advanced and intricate bases of the positions taken. These men could apparently hold minor positions in the society, and aspire to the rank of initiate and to higher offices in later years, but in the meantime they were not required to give up to the society their property or other sources of income.[72]

A basic philosophical tenet of the society was that "the foundation for human justice is the rule of the gods."[73] Man needs an authority that he fears and respects, so that he will not dare or desire to rebel against it. "The divinity is just such a power."[74] Since "God rules absolutely, in the universe,"[75] the only problem is to determine who should represent him on earth and tell the people what he wills for men to do. According to Pythagoras the choice is easy. Those men should rule "who are able to interpret . . . the will of the gods"[76] as expressed in the ancient laws. This means in practice not just the religious leaders, although they are important, but also those aristocrats of the old families that have in the past exercised power.

The rulers must uphold the old laws and usages, and for their acts in doing so they are not responsible to the people but only to God or the gods. They are, after all, serving the best interests of all the people, by keeping everything stable and harmonious; and they have the right to punish anyone who attempts to make any change in the laws. To be sure, the ruling aristocracy should be kind to the people insofar as possible and even help to educate (i.e., indoctrinate) them so that they will understand why the system is as it is and why it is the best possible. At the same time the rulers have and should exercise the right to punish all agitators and dissenters.

In short any change that would lessen entrenched power is dangerous because it will undermine the old laws and usages. Furthermore the opinions that circulate among the people on such a subject as the laws are worthless. There is no sense in trying to ascertain public opinion.

One can readily understand why the aristocratic rulers of Croton so completely embraced Pythagoras and the comforting doctrines that he and his followers worked out to defend the status quo. What is harder to comprehend is how, with aristocracies toppling under democratic onslaughts in one Greek city-state after another, they could be so blind as to think that their city could avoid making the changes to which Athens and other cities had been forced to yield.

It is clear enough, I think, why the Pythagoreans made no significant contribution to the advancement of the study of politics. They could not or at least did not separate religion from politics. They apparently never tried to put that study upon a human and secular basis. They put God or the gods (I am not sure which is meant) in the seat of power over men's affairs, and permitted no questions to be raised about the self-appointed earthly representatives who pretended to act for the gods in governing and punishing men. They made no serious effort to study the revolutions and the constitutional and political changes that were taking place all around them in order to learn from the experience of others. Pythagoras apparently did not believe that the sort of revolution that had driven him out of Samos could happen in Croton. He was not a true social scientist or political scientist.

This judgment of mine goes directly contrary to a curious statement made by the Syrian mystic Iamblichus (c. 250–325 A.D.) but which may stem from a writing of Aristoxenus (of about Aristotle's time, say 375 to 310 B.C.). This begins: "Generally they say that he [Pythagoras] is also the originator of the whole science of politics, having stated that nothing which exists is pure but that earth partakes of fire and fire of water and wind of these and these of wind, and furthermore, good partakes of evil, just of unjust," and so on until Pythagoras puts together "three lines to represent the constitution," the familiar right-angled triangle whose sides measure three, four, and five units respectively.[77] Here in one short passage we find cited two examples of the sort of speculative tour de force of which Pythagoras was capable. He indulged in numerous interesting analogies. Almost everything could, by a sufficient stretch of the imagination, be compared to almost anything else. Here the constitution of a state is compared to the group of supposed physical components of the earth and to a mere geometric figure, empty of all content. This is interesting early speculation about politics before a clear-cut differentiation of the fields of study had been made but it is hardly to be called political science.[78]

Although it would be fruitless to compare Pythagoras with the Delphic Pythia, it may be noted in passing that both practiced a similar secretiveness and "economy of truth" toward men in general while favoring the existing aristocratic rulers against the multitude.

Politics and Education in Ancient Greek Culture

To end the present chapter with the arch-conservative Pythagoreans would be likely to leave the reader with a distorted view of Greek progress and potentialities in the study of politics in the period down to about 450 B.C. The Pythagoreans were a particularly backward-looking sect, a minority trying to rule the people without their consent—and they were driven out of one place after another by the rising forces that demanded greater popular control of the government. That the weight of Greek opinion was on the side of the more liberal political developments seems rather clearly demonstrated by the fifth-century list of Seven Sages (or Seven Wise Men), who were widely accepted throughout the Greek world as representative of the people's best leadership.[79] Of the seven men in the usual list (the same men were not always included) six were notable for their political services, and mostly on the popular side: (1) Thales of Miletus, later better known as a scientist-philosopher, who in various ways served well the popular government of his city; (2) Pittacus of Mytilene, statesman and military leader, who helped to overthrow a local tyrant and to establish a republican form of government for the city; (3) Solon of Athens, lawgiver and reformer of the constitution, who refused to become a tyrant; (4) Cleobulus of Lindus, who led a popular political movement and then ruled his city as a tyrant for a time; (5) Chilon of Sparta, who is said to have founded the office of ephor for that city and to have increased the strictness of Spartan military and civic training (not exactly on the democratic side!), and (6) Periander of Corinth, who made himself tyrant after a revolt against the aristocracy but proved to be a forward-looking statesman, builder, and leader in both war and peace, a colonizer, and a promoter of prosperity. Less is known about the last man in the usual list, Bias of Priene, but he also showed political interests. He wrote a poem telling how to make Ionia prosperous, and when the Persian invasion was imminent he is said to have advised the Ionians to migrate westward to Sardinia and to establish there a single Pan-Ionian city.[80]

Perhaps the single most important evidence of the direction of Greek development in this period is to be found in their increasing recognition of the need for education in preparing the leaders of the people for the task of government, and the transformation of this idea into that of educating all the people for self-government.[81] As a wise Englishman put it a century ago, when the suffrage was being extended to the working classes, "We must educate our masters."[82]

As early as Homer (perhaps even earlier) the Ionian Greeks already had definite ideas about the importance and nature of education. Chiron appears as a teacher of Achilles, as well as of a number of others. He covered the skills and arts of war, the hunt, horsemanship, playing the lyre, even medicine. Achilles had another teacher also, Phoenix, who had him in charge when Achilles was but a small boy. This sort of education, where one learned and skilled man would devote much of his time to tutoring a single boy, was obviously possible only in the wealthiest circles. But Homer, by giving such attention as he did to this teacher-pupil relationship, spread the idea of education widely among the Greeks as his works gained more and more readers. Other men, even the poor, could begin to dream that their boys, too, might become educated. The intellectual side of education, especially such elementary skills as reading and writing, receives no specific attention in Homer. Neither does training for the task of being a ruler, a political leader. For Homer's purposes it was enough that Achilles was taught the knightly code of ethical excellence and the military and other skills that he would need. After all he was still rather young, and it was for his father, Peleus, whom Achilles would succeed, to teach him about rulership. But eloquence he was taught, and mention of this in Homer's *Iliad* gave early recognition to its importance for rulers. Indeed, Homer's epics in themselves revealed to all intelligent readers and hearers how great a power over men's actions there can be in eloquent poetic expression.

In Sparta the course of cultural development, including education, was outside the main Greek stream. Its rulers, faced with threats to their authority, turned Sparta into a closed society, a garrison state. The chief educational effort was to turn all able-bodied boys seven and older into soldiers. A Dorian Sophist of about 400 B.C. reported that "The Lacedaemonians consider it a bad thing for children to learn music and reading and writing, whereas the Ionians think it is shocking if they do not know these things."[83]

Athens followed the Ionian lead, not that of Sparta. The Athenians began in about the middle of the sixth century to give up their former official emphasis on military education and to turn to training in athletics and in sports.[84] Wrestling was given special emphasis, but other sports recognized in the Olympic games were also included in the training. At times of special danger to the state, military training was revived, as illustrated by the two-year program of compulsory military training for the ephebes, the eighteen- to twenty-year-olds, a program that lasted for a long time. But the trend at Athens was toward de-emphasizing military training.

In the early period it was almost entirely the young aristocrats of Athens, the sons of the old families of wealthy landowners, for whom education was provided. Without a program of regular activities and physical education these young unemployed persons might easily have become mere idlers. On the other hand there was no regular program of military or physical training for slaves, serfs, the free sons of free workers, or those of the merchant metics—they had various employments to keep them busy and out of mischief. In time, however, from the reforms of Solon on, merchants and others who could afford it, and who were now becoming important in the government of the city, began to seek education for their sons also. To increase their influence and power they needed a kind of education somewhat different from that provided by the landowning aristocrats for their sons. They needed less of athletic training, and more training in skills that would increase their political power and influence and improve their economic position. They needed adeptness in writing and reading, eloquence in public councils, and a knowledge of law and government. They began also to have money enough to buy education for their sons.

In response to their needs new classes of teachers arose, the *grammatists* or teachers of reading, writing, and arithmetic, who served primarily the younger boys, and the so-called *sophists*, who dealt more with adolescents and young men. Some of the latter became so famous as teachers that young aristocrats as well as others flocked to their lectures. In the new situation created by the enfranchisement of the non-aristocratic classes, the aristocrats needed every assistance they could get to maintain their once-unchallenged leadership.

Education had become an increasingly important part of Greek life in the city-states that were moving toward democracy in politics, and beginnings were being made that looked toward new and important developments in the study and teaching of politics. That Athens, one of the principal leaders in the democratization of Greek politics since at least as early as the time of Solon, should also become the first great center of education and of political studies is hardly to be wondered at.

Chapter 6

↩ Socrates' Contemporaries

T HE second half of the fifth century B.C., from 450 to 400, covers practically all the adult life of Socrates. During these years and on through the fifty that followed there flourished in Greece as varied and productive a group of great intellectuals as any country ever produced in an equal period, at least down to recent times. There had been significant beginnings before 450, just as there were important tasks of finishing up and rounding out the work after 350, but the golden age of Greece, intellectually and culturally, was undoubtedly the century from 450 to 350 B.C.

In the 450 to 400 period two great historians emerged, Herodotus and Thucydides, while near its end another, Xenophon, was getting a start. Similarly in the drama there were Sophocles and Euripides, and toward the end of the period Aristophanes was maturing and beginning his writing. The important school of teachers that came to be known as the Sophists was in its heyday, with Protagoras, Gorgias, Prodicus, Thrasymachus, Hippias, Antiphon, and Critias the leaders. The philosophers Zeno, Empedocles, Philolaus, Anaxagoras, and Democritus; the greatest early Greek physician, Hippocrates; one of the most able and eloquent of statesmen, Pericles—these also fall largely within this period. And all these, be it remembered, in addition to Socrates, who was just nineteen in 450 B.C., and lived but one year beyond 400. Later, from 400 to about 350 B.C., Plato and Isocrates dominate the scene. But before the end of Plato's career his student Aristotle arises to challenge him. Great names all in the history of Western civilization. And almost all contributed in some measure to the development of political studies.

The title of this chapter implies the very great importance of Socrates in this era: he was the key figure. This is no less true for the study of politics than for other subject matters, even though he left nothing of his own in writing. But while Socrates may rightly be regarded as a focal figure, it should not be assumed that Greek thought and studies in this period developed in a centralized and closely unified way. Rather there was what might be called a series of dialectical movements. Once individual Ionian Greeks began to expound their ideas publicly, and especially when they put them into writing, they provoked others who thought differently to reply, which in turn led still others to enter the debate in order to present their own distinctive views. Since there was no monopoly of learning in any priestly or other class, and no rules of holy writing to keep the debate within bounds, new and conflicting ideas sprang up on every hand. The intellectual life of the Greeks and of the West thus began like an uncontrolled and unpredictable debate in which one idea was constantly giving rise to another and different idea. These movements cannot be sharply defined in time or place, and hence in the discussion that follows there can be no strict chronological sequence. A certain amount of backing up and jumping forward will be inevitable.

The "Nature Philosophers" of Socrates' Time

By 450 B.C. the cosmological speculations that began with Thales and continued through Anaximander and others had apparently done more to confuse than to enlighten men.[1] Was the world basically composed of only one material or of many? Also, did it originate from one primordial material such as air, or water, or earth, or fire, or from a combination of them and possibly others? Was it static or in constant flux? Since no generally satisfactory answers had been found to resolve the confusion, men of scientific and philosophical bent began to turn away from such cogitations to other problems that might be easier to solve.[2] The resultant variety of speculations about nature between 450 and 400 B.C. is not easy to summarize briefly, and indeed a complete review is hardly appropriate in the present study. The aim here will be to emphasize studies closely related in subject matter to politics and, in addition, to note any advances in scientific outlook and methods of study that contribute something to methods for studying politics. Because they seem closer to Socrates' contemporaries than to the Pre-Socratics, two philosophers who actually lived and worked before 450 B.C.—Alcmaeon and Parmenides—will be included in the discussion that follows.

ALCMAEON

Alcmaeon of Croton, prominent from about 500 B.C. on, had medical training and showed considerable knowledge of the human body and of animals.[3] He stressed the balance of opposites in people as well as in nature generally, a theory that he may have derived from Pythagoras. In his speculations he introduced a comparative method, comparing men with animals as well as with the gods, and individual health with that of society or the *polis*. He said "the majority of human affairs are in pairs,"[4] presumably like sweet-bitter, good-bad, great-small. Apparently he thought that in the body politic as in the body of man health consisted in a proper balance (*isonomia*) between the opposing elements in each pair of factors, while ill-health or disease resulted from the excessive dominance (*monarchia*) of one over the other in a pair. His terminology suggests a definite interest on his part in politics as well as a real familiarity with that field. The records do not suggest, however, that he ever wrote anything directly on the government of the city-states, or that he made any special study of politics.

Alcmaeon's studies concerning the brain and sensory perception have led to his being called "the founder of empirical psychology."[5] Sensations were carried to the brain, he said, where the "governing faculty" by means of thought "somehow fitted together" the impulses that were received, and thus interpreted their meaning to the mind. His use of a semipolitical terminology in this connection reveals that he may have anticipated the move to join politics to psychology that has had so much support in the West since 1900.

THE ELEATICS

Parmenides of Elea, born about 515–510 B.C., was in his prime about 470 B.C., when Socrates was born.[6] (Later, when visiting in Athens, Parmenides at age sixty-five met the young Socrates.) One of his teachers apparently was Xenophanes, whose views he did not accept. He was influenced by a Pythagorean named Ameinias. Zeno, a somewhat younger man, was closely associated with him in the fragmentary reports about their lives and beliefs; they were the principal members of the so-called Eleatic school of philosophy.

Parmenides' philosophical views are presented in his poem *On Nature*. Through the words of a goddess, he asserts that only *what is* can be, or can be understood. What *is not* cannot be or be discussed. It is nothing. However, the senses cannot be trusted to reveal to us *what is*. They bring to men only illusions, false opinions, including the erroneous view that there is constant change in things. Man's mind is capable, however, of conceiving reality, and what his mind sees (i.e., what Parmenides finds) is something that is "incapable of development, imperishable, immutable, unbounded, and indivisible."[7] It is always one and the same; ideas of plurality and change, such as those of Heraclitus, are simply wrong. All phenomena and all apparent changes therein that appear to the senses are mere delusions.

That a man who developed and held such metaphysical ideas should have been in any serious way either interested or active in politics would seem unlikely. Nevertheless, Parmenides was apparently deeply involved with the government of Elea. Plutarch, who is in substance corroborated in this by both Diogenes Laertius and Strabo, reports that "Parmenides set his own state in order with such admirable laws that the government yearly swears its citizens to abide by the laws of Parmenides."[8] A very interesting political device! Despite this testimony to the excellence of his laws and government, I find it difficult to credit him with importantly advancing political study, in either content or methods. He was no Solon. Had his views prevailed in the minds of men there would have been little or no incentive for them to use their eyes, ears, and other sense organs in studies of physical phenomena, of nature, of individual human activities, or of society and government.

Zeno of Elea, who was active about 450 B.C., was a student of Parmenides' and was also associated with him in the government of Elea.[9] It would seem safe to assume that Zeno must have learned something about government from his mentor, but no work mentioned as having come from Zeno appears to have been on any branch of politics.

His major contribution seems to have been the development of a method of deducing from any statement two plausible but opposite conclusions in order to invalidate it. Aristotle later called this the dialectic method, and he credited Zeno with being its originator. The utter artificiality and absurdity of some of Zeno's arguments is well illustrated by his proposition that if a tortoise were given some head start, even fleet-footed Achilles would never be able to overtake him in a race. Like some other propositions attributed to Zeno, this one seems to have been made up by him or someone else for the mere purpose of argument. A simple experiment of pitting any good runner against a tortoise would have been enough to destroy Zeno's argument, but of course that would have meant resorting to human observation for proof, and, by Zeno's definition, the human senses cannot be trusted. The obvious weaknesses of some of his propositions do not, however, invalidate the dialectical method of analysis he proposed. When properly used and checked by observation, it has had and still has usefulness in reasoning about and trying to clarify propositions in various fields of study, including politics.

Melissus of Samos, who worked about 440 B.C., is spoken of as the last of the Eleatic school of philosophy.[10] Diogenes Laertius described him as a pupil of Parmenides, a statesman, and an admiral of the Samian navy in a war against Athens.

It is interesting to find the tradition of political activity among the Eleatics, and at the same time to note how they almost completely ignored the mundane subject of politics in their writings. This was as true of Melissus as of his predecessors. Politics being something one could apprehend through the senses, it was evidently forever doomed to remain in the realm of mere opinion, not that of truth; and hence it was not worthy of serious study. It was something you could practice without serious investigation, a field, indeed, in which even study by others could not help your practice. Fortunately, others of this time believed that searching with the senses among the phenomena of life could yield some truth, if not absolute truth. These men, rather than the Eleatics, would be the ones to enlarge significantly the study of politics.

ANAXAGORAS

Anaxagoras was originally of Clazomenae, north of Ephesus in Ionia.[11] Having a strong distaste for business and public affairs as a young man, he gave up his inherited wealth and family position, together with the political responsibilities in Clazomenae that these entailed, and migrated to Athens sometime before 460 B.C. in order to pursue the life of abstract thought and natural philosophy in which he had become deeply interested. At Athens, where he apparently devoted several decades to his studies and teaching, he had several outstanding students including Euripides, Archelaus, and the great statesman Pericles, "his chief pupil and protector," according to Kathleen Freeman.[12] He also had some association with Democritus. If he hoped to escape from politics by his move to Athens, he ultimately failed. Perhaps it was his friendship with Pericles that got him into trouble. At any rate, some of Pericles' opponents impeached Anaxagoras before the assembly for impiety and apparently also for disloyalty to Athens, defined as Medism or pro-Persianism. Pericles defended him with some success, but prudence required his withdrawal from Athens. He moved to Lampsacus on the Hellespont and started another "school." It was there that he died in 428 B.C., about the time of Plato's birth.

In his studies at Athens and elsewhere he dealt largely with the nature of the physical universe. He speculated that the physical elements are divided into infinitely small particles, but are infinite in their totality, and that they perdure, time without end, forever and ever, mixing with and separating from each other, constantly changing their aggregate forms, but never diminishing or disappearing. He also postulated a second category or entity that gives life, form, and direction to the physical material of which the universe consists. This separate thing which is also everywhere, and in everything, but not of it, he called *nous*, which is translatable as "mind," some might even say "soul," or a universal power of a mental and nonmaterial nature, which organizes everything material, sets it in motion, and controls its actions. Whether this *nous* is strictly nonmaterial, or is just a different kind of material that can coexist in the same space with material entities, has been much debated.[13] But whatever Anaxagoras may have intended to imply the nature of *nous* to be he indicated that all living things have some portion of it within themselves, and in human beings it rises to higher levels than in other living things. The *nous* within any human being is stimulated to action by things from the outside that are opposed in some way to what is within the human body, or that are apprehended, seen, or felt by the body or organ as being strikingly or even painfully different from itself. "All perception is accompanied by pain" is one of Anaxagoras' statements, the pain being caused by the collision of opposites, "for unlikes when they meet cause distress."[14] How reliable are the sense perceptions of men thus obtained for establishing dependable knowledge? Anaxagoras seems to say that the sense perceptions of men differ considerably from and are superior to those of other animals. Even the sense perceptions of men, however, as Kathleen Freeman has summarized his views, "cannot judge of exact truth . . . But the senses are not entirely

155

misleading; their evidence must be used in order to arrive at the truth: to see the invisible, we must use the visible."[15]

All this has little or nothing to do directly with the study of politics. But indirectly at least there is a connection, and an important one. We see Anaxagoras here trying to keep open the door that Parmenides, for example, had virtually closed—the door to human observation of things and events and to the use of men's perceptions or sense experiences as a means of moving forward toward the attainment of truth and knowledge.

It does not appear from anything that remains of the book that Anaxagoras wrote, and which once apparently sold widely at one drachma per copy, that he ever dealt specifically with the study of politics. Although he was closely associated with a great political leader in a turbulently active democracy, Anaxagoras' early aversion to participation in politics evidently did not abate. He seems to have declined even to enter a discussion of it. Perhaps he was prudent not to try to write about political matters.

At the same time political movements seriously affected his life; he could not ignore the subject of politics entirely. By the analogies or metaphors he used, he revealed that the subjects of government and politics were indeed not wholly banished from his thoughts. *Nous* is "the ruler element" in the universe. It is a sort of monarch that relies only and absolutely on itself. It is "an infinite and autocratic being," not mixed with any other element that might check its power. It does not operate like an ordinary monarch by commands, like the God of the Bible, but by exerting its own pressure directly. It is the most powerful thing in the world, a thing of sovereign nature, "that rules out of an original plenitude of power of its own, an autocratic being." It is not truly omnipotent, but it is all-knowing, and the most powerful thing in the world. It knows what can be done, and can do whatever it wills. These statements read like a description of an absolute and omnipotent monarch, and suggest that the writer was secretly in favor of government by such an all-knowing, all-powerful ruler.[16]

EMPEDOCLES

Empedocles of Acragas in Sicily, who was writing about 450 B.C., held certain views in common with Anaxagoras, but on others differed widely.[17] Like Anaxagoras he left aside in his studies most of mathematics and astronomy but otherwise covered an exceedingly wide range. He is said to have combined "the roles of philosopher, scientist, poet, orator, and statesman with those of mystagogue, miracle-worker, healer, and claimant to divine honours . . ."[18] He has also been called "the only native citizen of a Dorian state who plays an important part in the history of philosophy."[19] Furthermore, Aristotle credited him with being the inventor of rhetoric, and Galen called him the founder of the Italian school of medicine.[20] His was a brilliant but somewhat mixed and confusing record.

As for politics, he was an active leader in the public life of Acragas but left no work devoted to that subject, and only a few statements that relate directly to it. The records about his political position are few and the traditions somewhat contradictory. Like Solon he appears to have been a man of the aristocracy with democratic sympathies, but unlike Solon he seems to have had a distaste for politics, and he apparently declined to hold public office. The evidence concerning his political views and activities comes mainly from sources other than his own writings. In the latter I find the statement that "it is of great concern to the lower orders to mistrust the powerful,"[21] but very little else that relates to politics. The numerous fragments that remain deal with the gods and with God, who is mind; the continuing competition of love and hate; metaphysical propositions such as that something cannot come out of nothing, and that nothing that exists ever ceases; and many somewhat disconnected utterances about the anatomies and physiology of men and animals.

In the fields of epistemology and scientific method he left a number of rather optimistic sayings. Although men have only limited means "scattered throughout their limbs" for grasping knowledge, and cannot expect to be able to grasp "the Whole," if they "observe with every means" in their possession, and do not arbitrarily put sight ahead of hearing or other means of sense perception, they will learn much, and "learning will increase [their] understanding."[22] He observed also that all living things "have intelligence, by the will of Fortune" and that "The intelligence of Man grows towards the material that is present."[23] These were not really new or advanced thoughts, even for their time, but they do place Empedocles on the side of those who believed in the possibility of science, perhaps even of a science of politics.

157

ARCHELAUS AND LEUCIPPUS

Archelaus of Athens (450 B.C.) had studied under Anaxagoras and he in turn had Socrates as one of his students in the field of physical science or speculation.[24] Practically nothing remains of any work of his, but he is reported to have written on physics along Anaxagorean lines. He had ideas on the origin of the human species and the rise of civilization, but no evidence has survived of his studies, if any, in politics. His biological studies led him, however, to one interesting if elementary conclusion: that notions of right and wrong come not from nature but from man-made customs and conventions. The importance of this for the legislative role of the state is obvious.

Leucippus of Miletus, who flourished about 440–430 B.C., also worked primarily in the field of physical science, cosmology, the structure of matter, and so on.[25] He is credited with originating and Democritus with further developing the atomic theory of matter, but both should probably have about equal credit. On politics Leucippus seems to have had nothing to contribute.

Men like Archelaus and Leucippus—and they were not alone in this —show a tendency toward specialization in the field of physical speculation. At the same time, in the absence of suitable instrumental means of observing and measuring nature, and with what we can see as a lack of usable mathematical and statistical methods of analyzing the data they obtained from observation, they seem to be approaching a sort of dead end in their field. They go round and round the same problems without making sure advances. The time was almost at hand when men would demand new and different approaches to the study of reality, approaches that would have more meaning in the lives of men and cities. Socrates was already on the scene. He and others like him would raise ethics and politics to the high levels of philosophical debate while physical speculation, having more or less run its course, would recede into the background. The wide range of interests of the next philosopher to be discussed make him something of an exception, but even so he stood more at the end of an old line than at the beginning of a new one.

DEMOCRITUS

Democritus of Abdera in Thrace was born a little after Socrates, in about 460 B.C.[26] Son of a wealthy and high-placed Thracian aristocrat, and a student of Leucippus, Democritus devoted some years to travel and study abroad, and then returned to Abdera, poorer but better informed, to devote the rest of his life to study, teaching, and writing. Hippocrates, the famous Greek physician, and Protagoras, the great Sophist, are mentioned as having come under his tutelage, but he apparently did not advertise himself as a teacher. He took no significant part in public life.

He has been called "the most learned Greek before Aristotle."[27] He was certainly a polymath and the producer of a large number of writings covering many subjects. Those fragments of his work known today have been classified and analyzed in a recent volume under the major headings of metaphysics, cosmology and meteorology, biology, sense perception, ethics, education, and politics, but there are also contributions listed under mathematics, music, painting, military tactics, agriculture, sacred writings, research, logic, legal causes, and other special topics.[28] Aristotle found this universal genius so absorbing that he wrote a special book covering some parts of Democritus' ideas and gave him considerable praise.

Democritus is perhaps best known for his scientific view, no doubt partly derived from Leucippus, that "all phenomena could be explained" in terms of "combinations of atoms and space" or "atoms and the void," as the atomic theory of Democritus is usually summarized.[29]

Along with his many other interests, Democritus was a student of politics and of the related subjects of ethics, education, scientific methods, and economics.[30] There is a surprisingly modern tendency in much that he wrote in these fields. What he said must have appealed to, gained acceptance by, and affected the thinking of many scholarly men of his own and later generations. Although no major work of his has survived in its entirety, a surprisingly large number of fragments of his writings have been preserved in the writings of others, giving evidence that he was widely read in his own time and after his death.[31] Through his writings he was a teacher in fact though not so professed by himself.

Finding man to be living in a universe composed simply of physical atoms and the void, he recognized that man could not truly know the "reality" of things. He was "severed from reality." Nevertheless he had a soul in his body, which was different from the physical atoms, and was something in the nature of a reasoning faculty. Also he had powers of sense perception, through the wise use of which he could gain better knowledge of the world, even though the senses were to some extent unreliable and could only form his opinions about reality. To gain better control of himself and his surroundings, man needed education, the development of his powers of perception and of reason. He also needed the *polis,* the city or community in which he lived. As Democritus said: "One must give the highest importance to affairs of the State, that it may be well run; one must not pursue quarrels contrary to right, nor acquire a power contrary to the common good. The well-run State is the greatest protection, and contains all in itself; when this is safe, all is safe; when this is destroyed, all is destroyed."[32] Although "Rule belongs by nature to the stronger,"[33] it is better to be governed by men of ability and good will. "When base men enter upon office, the more unworthy they are, the more neglectful, and they are filled with folly and recklessness."[34] Only the most deserving should be given public offices. Officials deserve no special commendation for intelligent and right conduct in office; they are "elected not to make mistakes but to do things well."[35] In short he outlines in elementary terms a system of public organization based upon democracy, education, freedom of speech, and the election of public officials; harmony between social classes; and the need of men to do justice to each other in order to promote happiness, mutual good will, and the maximum safety for the city and its inhabitants.

Democritus advances no profound political theories; makes no detailed historical or comparative study of constitutions or systems of government; and does not appear to have looked beyond the city-state as a unit of government toward any federations or other large entities. If the subject matter in the entire body of his writings is proportionally represented in the fragments that have been preserved, then clearly politics was not a primary interest with him. Also, he wrote no major work specifically on politics and government; he started no school for the teaching of politics; and he left behind no devoted followers to propagate his political teachings. Nevertheless, he seems to me to be an important enough man in the history of the Greek study of politics to deserve a thorough modern study of his contributions in this field, a work that I have not had time to undertake.

SOME LATE PYTHAGOREANS

Before turning to groups of writers representing new and rather dynamic intellectual interests, I should add a brief note on a few late representatives of another waning movement in the field of philosophy: the Pythagoreans Philolaus of Croton and Tarentum, who was at the height of his activity about 425 B.C., and his pupils Eurytus (about 400 B.C.) and Archytas (about 380 B.C.).[36] All three were interested in the study of numbers, to which certain of them evidently attributed a mystic power. They had other scientific as well as metaphysical interests in common also.

Less is known about Eurytus than about the other two, in fact very little. His attention was concentrated upon metaphysics and some problems of numbers. Nothing suggests any real interest in politics. Philolaus, on the other hand, seems to have had such an interest, and one story is that he was put to death for advocating the establishment of a tyranny at Tarentum. In writing his one book, giving an account of Pythagoreanism, he departed from the old rule of secrecy long observed by the members of the society. Of the three Archytas was the most active in politics. He was a popular leader in Tarentum "under the democratic constitution,"[37] and was also elected general of that city and head of a confederacy of Greek cities in Magna Graecia. He was voted autocratic powers but did not abuse them. He knew Plato well, and influenced both his thinking and his actions. His range of interests was broad enough to include studies in biology and in the methods of acquiring knowledge.[38] He stressed the importance of personal effort for the discovery of truth as distinct from merely learning from others, and the employment of correct methods in research. He also emphasized the utility of reason "as a force towards social amelioration: it checks strife, increases harmony, gives equality and justice, and banishes greed. Rich give to poor, poor receive from rich, in a desire to achieve this 'equality' or fairness. A correct 'calculation' of consequences prevents the commission of crime."[39] His general approach to the problems of man and knowledge appears to have been as secular and as free from religious slanting as Solon's.

The Sophists

The group known as the Sophists is another example of the diversity in Greek intellectual life of the fifth and fourth centuries B.C.[40] The Sophists offered themselves as teachers of an assortment of what we would today call liberal arts courses. No two of the Sophists gave the same instruction, and yet there was considerable similarity in their programs. They appealed primarily to young men, of about what we today would call college age, who already knew how to read and write, but who lacked maturity in such skills as speech, dialectic, debate, and oratory. It was assumed these skills were needed, under the democratic conditions that were coming into being, by men who wanted to get ahead in the life and politics of their several city-states.

Democracy was indeed on the march. The aristocratic families who had ruled their tribes and clans in migratory times found themselves outnumbered in the growing populations of the cities, which were firmly establishing themselves as the principal units of government. By exerting pressures that often went as far as open revolt, the commercial and working classes were becoming enfranchised and beginning to dominate the cities. Young aristocrats as well as young men of the newly enfranchised classes, some of whom had considerable means, stood ready to pay for any instruction that would help them gain influence in the rising popular assemblies and in the courts or win election to public offices. Such occupations as engineering, business, or scientific agriculture, as we know them today, were practically nonexistent. The important outlets for talents were in public leadership and service, in the closely related military and naval services, in teaching, and in literary work such as poetry, drama, and oratory. For all these purposes men needed skill in the arts of speech, writing, and persuasion, and some knowledge of public affairs. Most of the Sophists concentrated their teaching in the fields of grammar (the form of language), rhetoric (the form of oratory), and dialectic (the form of thought)—in short, in a group of related *technés* that would encourage clear, effective, and persuasive thought and speech. What they taught in addition, where they put their emphasis, and the methods they employed were the main factors, aside from personality, of course, that differentiated one Sophist from another.

It is not surprising that Socrates himself should have been taken for a Sophist and lampooned as such by Aristophanes.[41] After all he was a public teacher; he ridiculed the studies of the nature philosophers and pointed out the confusion into which they had fallen; and he, like the Sophists, turned his attention to the problems of the Greek people. But in important respects he was different from them and reacted against them. Sophists were significantly limited in outlook and knowledge: they were not deep-searching scholars; they strove too much for immediate effects and results; their students did not turn out to be great scholars or scientists, nor was it intended that they should; their knowledge, being based largely on opinion, was inadequate; and their reasoning certainly left much to be desired. Socrates, if we may trust Plato in this matter, became one of their keenest critics, and Plato himself, sometime before 390 B.C., began a series of attacks upon them that helped to give them the bad name from which we get such disparaging words as "sophistry" and "sophism." (Basically, of course, the word "sophist" meant "wise man" or a man who knows.) By early in the fourth century most of the Sophists had run their course. What they contributed directly to the study of politics was not great, but they were among the first after Solon to move in the direction of such a study, even though they did not develop the concept of a science of politics.

There are four principal though not equally important sources of information about the Sophists, none of whose major works have survived intact into modern times: the collection of Plato's dialogues and miscellaneous writings, undoubtedly the first in importance; the brief treatment of the Sophists in Xenophon's writings, especially in the *Memorabilia*; the considerable body of fragments, generally well authenticated, of the Sophist writings, mostly preserved as quotations in the writings of later authors; and, finally, the things said about the Sophists by other ancient writers who did not pretend to quote them directly.

It was characteristic of Plato to build his writings largely out of words and ideas that he attributed to others. The dialogue form he used so extensively gave him the opportunity to control his materials to his own ends. He chose the participants, he reported what they said and how they phrased it, he could easily disparage or poke fun at those with whom he disagreed or whom he disliked and place in a favorable light the speakers and ideas he preferred. Because Plato's writings have been so influential in creating the Western image of the Sophists, it is well to look into his reporting about them a little deeper.

It is clear that Plato as a young man had been most impressed by Socrates and his ideas. This led to a personal devotion to Socrates that seems to have been almost an obsession, as revealed throughout the dialogues in which Socrates appears and in what Plato wrote after Socrates' death. But if Plato was strongly attracted to Socrates, he was repelled by the Sophists. There was something almost morbid and perverse about his attitude toward them, as if he were looking at something essentially so evil that he could not take his mind off it. He came back to the subject time and again. Five of his dialogues carry the names of leading Sophists: Protagoras, Gorgias, Critias, and Hippias (two dialogues, Lesser and Greater Hippias). There is also a dialogue called simply *Sophist*, while other Sophists (Prodicus and Thrasymachus, for example) appear as participants in certain dialogues. The amount of attention that he gave to them is, of course, some evidence of their importance in his time; and however much he may have fallen short of presenting an objective picture of their true views, we owe him a great debt for the information he preserved. Nevertheless his bias should be kept in mind. It should be specially noted that the interlocutors whom Plato presents in the dialogues in which Socrates carries the main burden of the questioning are all unequal in ability to Socrates. The best of them, even Protagoras in the dialogue of that name, do not appear to be prepared to stand up under the persistent cross-examination to which Socrates subjects them—and when they consent to discuss a matter on the basis of the sometimes far-fetched analogies that he proposes, they are soon lost.

Xenophon's treatment of the Sophists is much briefer and less detailed than that of Plato. While he is not as keen as Plato, he is usually honest and clear. When he and Plato agree in substance, the evidence can be taken as reasonably conclusive.[42]

The fragments that have been preserved from the writings and reported sayings of the Sophists have been assembled in English translation by Kathleen Freeman in her *Ancilla to the Pre-Socratic Philosophers* and have been thoroughly analyzed and commented upon in her *Companion to Diels,* and in Mario Untersteiner's *The Sophists.* The comments of later writers in ancient times on the Sophists, along with an extensive bibliography of modern writings about them, are gathered together in Untersteiner's work. I do not pretend to have covered thoroughly this extensive literature.

PROTAGORAS

Protagoras of Abdera (c. 480 to 410 B.C.) evidently came from a family of some means though not of the nobility.[43] At least he did not have the aristocratic prejudice against accepting money for teaching. Who his teachers were is uncertain. Anaxagoras, who would have been some ten to fifteen years older, is mentioned, and so is Democritus, but the latter would have been impossible unless he was born some thirty or more years earlier than the date usually assigned for his birth (460 B.C.). Protagoras had some contact with the Persian Magi, who probably helped to raise doubts in his mind about the gods. Certain it is, however, that Protagoras did a great deal of reading in many fields and that he made up his own mind about many important questions.

At about the age of thirty he began his career as a teacher, traveling about the Greek world giving his lectures. He was a man of eloquence and impressive personality. His fame spread throughout Greece, and he met and talked with important leaders like Pericles. He became so noted for his political knowledge that Pericles is reported to have employed him to draw up the constitution for Thurii, one of the colonies of the expanding Greek empire. He also attracted many students who were able to pay high fees; thus he amassed a considerable fortune.

In his teaching Protagoras evidently directed his attention not to the masses but to their leaders—the aristocrats and the other wealthy people,[44] who wished to learn how to guide their cities effectively through the political storms that threatened their own security and position.

As to his writings, the evidence has been differently interpreted. The list given in Kathleen Freeman's *Companion to Diels* is a full one, but Untersteiner thinks that a number of the items listed there were not separate pieces but parts or chapters of a principal work called *Antilogies* or *Contradictory Arguments*.[45] He believes that the *Antilogies* consisted of four parts: "(1) On the Gods; (2) On Being; (3) On the Laws and all problems which concern the world of the *polis*; (4) On the Arts."[46] At any rate the titles in Freeman include *Truth, On the Gods, On Being, Mathematics, On the Original Social Structure, On Ambition, On Virtues, On the Errors of Mankind, On Constitution (Politeia)*; there were also works on rhetoric and education.

These titles reveal Protagoras' wide range of interests, and also show his emphasis on human problems as distinct from those of the physical universe. The few actual fragments of his works that remain reveal mainly secular and humanistic interests, and these fall largely within the range of ethics, politics, rhetoric, and education.

His work on the *politeia* is said to have been "the first work to bear as its title the word made famous by Plato's *Republic*."[47] That the word comes from *polis*, the term for a city, is evident, but it is not clear whether it actually meant in Protagoras' time merely the "constitution" of the city, in our present-day sense, as it is sometimes translated. It seems reasonable to think that the book dealt with the city or *polis* as a whole, in all its then important aspects, including its political organization, to be sure, but not to the exclusion of many other factors—its territory, population, layout, popular customs, economics, and what not. As Sinclair has pointed out: "[The Greeks] early found that civilised society rests on three bases—maintenance of adequate subsistence, character . . . of the people, and political institutions or constitution (*politeia*). We tend to separate the study of these three into Economics, Ethics and Politics, but Greek thinkers kept them together. The study of behaviour and of goods and supplies were as much part of *politike* as questions of forms of government."[48]

That Protagoras was an agnostic in religious matters is well borne out by a major quotation that presumably comes from his work *On the Gods*: "About the gods, I am not able to know whether they exist or do not exist, nor what they are like in form; for the factors preventing knowledge are many: the obscurity of the subject, and the shortness of human life."[49] Here Protagoras is in effect saying that life is too short for him to get to the bottom of this subject, and I think it is a fair inference that he is dismissing this subject without prejudice so as to be able to concentrate on some others that he knows something about. Thus interpreted this quotation fits in well with another major statement of his: "Of all things the measure is Man, of the things that are, that they are, and of the things that are not, that they are not."[50] Here Protagoras takes his stand on the side of humanity and asserts man's prime importance in the world. Whatever the "physicists" or nature philosophers might say about the importance of knowing the physical universe, or the men of religion might believe and preach about the gods, mankind came first for Protagoras and the other things were important only as they contributed to the well-being of man. This was the only measure that Protagoras as a man could apply, and there was no one else but men like him to do any measuring. Protagoras' own attention would therefore be concentrated on mankind.

There has been much discussion of the question whether in this statement Protagoras did not make every individual man the sole judge of his own welfare, and thus open the door to complete anarchy.[51] There is practically nothing in what is known about the rest of Protagoras' teaching to warrant this interpretation. He believed in the city-state, in the need to have political leadership and government to guide and rule the state, and in education to form the minds and characters of the young so as to ensure acceptance of such community organization. He held no ultra-individualistic ideas.

There is also implicit in Protagoras' ideas an answer to those writers who believed that all nature was so elusive, changing, and deceptive, and man's senses so unreliable that it was impossible for men to learn, i.e., come to know, anything through the use of their eyes, ears, and other sense organs. Protagoras, a man who was trying to teach others to be leaders in their cities and who certainly wanted his students to believe what they heard from him, could hardly have held such a negative attitude concerning man's ability to learn.

He clearly recognized some of the problems of learning and of teaching. "Teaching needs endowment and practice. Learning must begin in youth." And again, "Education does not take root in the soul unless one goes deep." Eloquence was, he believed, one of the most important qualifications of the teacher, but it was difficult to attain.[52] What actual subject matter Protagoras expounded to his students is not fully known. In the *Protagoras* Plato seems to lead up to this question but in the colloquy that follows the matter of subjects to be studied is quickly dropped when Socrates persists in shifting the discussion to the question of whether virtue can be taught. However, a brief summary of the dialogue may be worthwhile at this point.[53]

Young Hippocrates had asked Socrates to help him arrange to have Protagoras become his teacher. Socrates chided the youth for being willing to entrust his soul (mind?) to the instruction of a man whom he did not know and about whose teaching he had no clear ideas. Did he wish to become a Sophist (i.e., paid teacher) like Protagoras? Hippocrates admitted he would be ashamed to do so, but seemed to think he could get a gentleman's sort of liberal education from a man like Protagoras, "one who has knowledge of wise things" and can make clever speakers.[54] Socrates was not satisfied. In what things was he wise? On what subjects did he make clever speakers? Didn't Hippocrates realize a teacher like Protagoras might have an adverse effect on his soul? For what a man learns is what "nourishes a soul," said Socrates.[55] And so it was agreed that Socrates would ask Protagoras some questions about what he really taught.

Protagoras responded to Socrates' questions by telling Hippocrates

167

that every day under his tutelage he would become a better man. Unsatisfied with this, Socrates broke in to ask "better at what?" Protagoras answered Socrates clearly and directly. Unlike other teachers who insisted on teaching young men special subjects like arithmetic, astronomy, and music, he would make the subject of his teaching "the proper care of his personal affairs, so that he may best manage his own household, and also of the state's affairs, so as to become a real power in the city, both as speaker and man of action."

Do I follow you? said I [Socrates]. I take you to be describing the art of politics, and promising to make men good citizens.

That, said he [Protagoras], is exactly what I profess to do.

Then it is a truly splendid accomplishment that you have mastered, said I [Socrates], if indeed you have mastered it. . . . The fact is, I did not think this was something that could be taught . . .[56]

Socrates continued to insist on his point, and in the process made unconcealed gibes at the democratic system of Athenian government. When the Athenian assembly wanted ships built it called in specialists in naval design, he said, but when questions of government came before it every member of the assembly, no matter what his calling—blacksmith or shoemaker, merchant or shipowner, rich or poor—gave advice without pointing to anyone who had taught him in this field. Said Socrates, "The reason must be that they do not think this is a subject that can be taught."[57] Moreover, Pericles gave his boys the best education available "in everything that depends on teaching, but in his own special kind of wisdom [i.e., politics and government] he neither trains them himself nor hands them over to any other instructor . . ." He could give other examples, too, he said, of excellent men who never made their own sons or "anyone else better." "With these facts in mind, Protagoras," said Socrates, "I do not believe that virtue can be taught."[58] Because Athenian assemblymen acted as if they didn't believe teaching was possible in Protagoras' field, and because Pericles and other leaders acted as if they didn't believe it either, therefore Protagoras must be wrong in trying to teach it. The weakness in Socrates' line of argument is obvious.

I find it hard to believe that Socrates would have made such an argument on the basis of such inadequate evidence. On the other hand the line of reasoning used against Protagoras' method of instruction and its content does give a sort of collateral support to Plato's own and different idea on how to instruct rulers and political leaders. When Plato had the task of instructing young Dionysius of Syracuse on how to rule his city, he tried to "form his soul" or mind by putting him through a course in mathematics, because mathematics is the science of numbers and because Plato accepted the Pythagorean proposition that numbers are the basic elements in what exists. This Plato believed was the better way to educate rulers. In short he was opposed to direct instruction in the arts or *technés* of government and politics.

In any case, the lines were drawn between Protagoras and Socrates-Plato and the debate went on from there. Protagoras presented an interesting pseudo-historical parable beginning with creation in which the lower animals got the better deal while man who came last was "naked, unshod, unbedded and unarmed" (recall Hobbes' later characterization of earliest man!). Somewhat remorseful because of this oversight, the gods stole things from each other to help man get started, but when cities replaced more primitive forms of social organization, men still lacked "the art of politics." Good government then became necessary and again the gods came to the aid of man: "Zeus therefore, fearing the total destruction of our race, sent Hermes to impart to men the qualities of respect for others and a sense of justice, so as to bring order into our cities and create a bond of friendship and union." But Hermes wanted to know whether the political virtues of justice and respect for their fellows should be given, like medical knowledge, to only a few experts, or to all the people. "To all," said Zeus. "Let all have their share. There could never be cities if only a few shared in these virtues, as in the arts." All who proved incapable of acquiring these two virtues were to be put to death. Thus by divine decree the groundwork was laid for popular education and participation in government, and for governments to make and enforce laws that would correct the natural deficiencies of man. In short, with divine sanction, men could make laws in their several cities that would have superiority over the laws of nature.[59] The gods in their remorse over having made men so weak and helpless in effect set aside or subordinated the laws of nature to the laws made by men for their own cities, wherever men, having learned to do justice to each other, made appropriate laws of their own. Protagoras in this respect stood out in opposition to other Sophists, Hippias and Antiphon, for example, both of whom gave higher force to the laws of nature and deplored the man-made laws of the cities that countervened natural laws. According to Protagoras, then, all men were to share in the responsibility for achieving good government, but still they had to learn how to provide good government through experience, reflection, and instruction.

In the translations from the Greek, the word "virtue" has come to be used as a shorthand expression for Protagoras' statement as to what he was trying to teach, and even for Socrates' own revision of that statement to include "the art of politics" and how "to make men good citizens." I think few today would say that "virtue" is identical with these other expressions. "Virtue" is an exceedingly broad term and concept. It covers morality, integrity, uprightness, in all the affairs of life. Protagoras had made it very clear, I think, that in addition to teaching young men how to manage their own affairs, he instructed them also in managing "the state's affairs" and in becoming public leaders. He agreed with Socrates that he was "promising to make men good citizens," but all this was far from saying that he was trying to make men good or virtuous in all respects.

Following Werner Jaeger, a leading authority on ancient Greek education and ideals, I believe that the word that is involved here is *areté*.[60] This word had a history of changing and expanding meaning. Basically it signifies excellence. In early tribal and aristocratic days this meant primarily valor and skill in war, in hunting, and in athletics. Later knowledge and proficiency in intellectual, musical, and artistic lines were included as well.[61] When the city-state or *polis* became the prevalent political unit, and the democratic movements for popular control of the affairs of the *polis* became widespread and successful, the meaning of the word expanded to embrace skill or excellence in the affairs of the *polis*. Jaeger insists that it was political *areté* that Protagoras was trying to teach.[62] It was not *areté* in the broad sense that might include excellence in athletics or in music or in any one of a number of other types of activity, or virtue generally, but the kind of *areté* that made a man capable of being a leader in, and a good manager of, the affairs of the state.

Just what the full content of Protagoras' teaching was will probably never be known. But he seems actually to have been much like a modern American college teacher of government and politics, who gives some attention to the responsibilities and opportunities of the citizen in politics, but also goes into problems of governmental powers, organization, and activities. Protagoras taught other subjects in addition, to be sure—grammar, rhetoric, and debate—but these were also intended to train his students in the skills necessary to success in public affairs.

I find no evidence that he went into any special fields like international relations or political theory; or that he grasped the concept of a science of politics applicable to all members of the human race throughout the world and at all times. But in conceiving and establishing the idea that politics in a practical sense can be taught and can be learned to some extent through teaching, he surpassed, I believe, all earlier Greeks.

GORGIAS

Gorgias of Leontini in Sicily (c. 480–380 B.C.) was the second of the more notable Sophists.[63] He was reported to have been a pupil of Empedocles. Among his own students, at one time or another, were said to have been Isocrates of Athens, whose case seems to be certain, Menon of Thessaly, Aristippus, Critias, Thucydides, and a number of others who also became well known.[64] He influenced the style of writing not only of his pupils, but of some of his other associates as well. As a student and teacher of politics he was not nearly as important as Protagoras; the emphasis of his studies and teaching was mainly in other directions.

In an early venture into the field of philosophy, in a work on "being" or on "nature," he is reported to have asserted the nihilistic doctrine that "nothing exists," but "If anything exists, it is incomprehensible," and so on.[65] If followed through, this meant a denial of knowledge, and therefore of the teachability of knowledge and of virtue or anything else. The work may have been merely a youthful exercise in pessimism. At any rate this doctrine evidently did not affect his own activities seriously, for he kept on trying to teach people and to influence the conduct of men and of states as if they existed and were, in fact, important to themselves and to others.

As a young man and on into middle age he evidently developed unusual persuasive abilities. His arts were those of rhetoric and full-blown oratory—that is, of long, involved, yet balanced speeches that swayed men to his point of view. He disliked the courtroom or forensic type of speaking, with its dialectic, its questions and answers, and other interruptions. He also disliked holding public office and exercising public responsibility, but his powers of persuasion were so outstanding that the rulers of Leontini wanted him to represent them on an embassy to

Athens, and he was induced to go there, about 427 B.C. His part of the mission was performed successfully.

Aside from his philosophical book on being or on nature, his writings consisted of a number of orations and a work on rhetoric, "one of the earliest textbooks" in this field.[66] His method of teaching rhetoric included the assignment to his students of speeches to be memorized, but little more than this is known about that aspect of his work.

One political subject to which he devoted some time and effort, and on which he wrote an important oration, the Olympian, was the need for concord and some sort of union among the Greek city-states, so that they could stand united against powerful foreign enemies like the Persians. His pupil Isocrates carried on this propaganda after him, equally in vain. The rest of his orations, the encomiums on Helen, on Palamedes, on Achilles, and on the Eleans, the funeral oration, and the Pythian oration, none of which have survived, were apparently show pieces that he used on special occasions, and were not intended to change anyone's views, especially not on political questions. It is evident that he avoided political topics as much as he could.

HIPPIAS

Hippias of Elis (a city lying near the western tip of the Peloponnesus) was another contemporary of Socrates who is classed as a Sophist and about whose life less is known than one would desire.[67] The dates of his birth and death are uncertain. If he was indeed present, as Plato says, at the discussion described in the Protagoras, which took place about 432 B.C., and if he in fact sat "on the seat of honor" on that occasion,[68] he must have been a mature man, born thirty or more years earlier (say 462–472 B.C.). A recent authority says, however, that he was born about 443 B.C.[69] He was still active in 399 B.C., when Socrates died, and possibly lived on to 390. According to the usual accounts, Hippias claimed to have made more money than any two other Sophists. He traveled extensively and lectured or delivered orations wherever he was invited to do so. He also represented Elis officially on trips to other states. There is a reasonable belief that he had democratic leanings. He had one unusual specialty for a Sophist, mathematics. In that subject he is credited with having made an important invention or discovery, that of the quadratrix, a special type of curve that is useful in trisecting a triangle. He apparently thought it would be helpful in squaring the circle. This is one of the bits of evidence that reveal the breadth of his interests and knowledge.[70] He seems to have had a remarkable memory and a tremendous fund of information in all phases of language and speech, Greek literature, painting, sculpture, early history, anthropology, astronomy, and other fields. His oratorical display of such diverse knowledge must have dazzled his audiences (as indeed did the ability he showed in making his clothes and other personal effects!). He was undoubtedly an impressive orator. But he did not come off as well in the quick give-and-take of debate, at least as pictured by Plato.

In Plato's two dialogues that bear Hippias' name, the *Lesser Hippias* and the *Greater Hippias*,[71] he is shown up by Plato as a very vain and boastful man who is no match for Socrates in a battle of wits. In the first he argues that it is better to do wrong unintentionally than intentionally while Socrates takes the other side, no doubt with tongue in cheek. After a short time Hippias sees what a trap has been set for him in the argument. He flatly rejects the conclusion toward which Socrates has been leading him, namely, that the man, if there be such a one, "who voluntarily does wrong and disgraceful things . . . will be the good man."[72] Socrates admits that he, an ordinary man, cannot accept this conclusion either, but he remarks how strange it is that a wise man like Hippias should have been led so far along the road toward the wrong conclusion.

The *Greater Hippias* is a more extended dialogue between Hippias and Socrates, mainly on the subject of "what is the nature of beauty." Socrates here pretends throughout not to be speaking his own mind, insisting that he is merely repeating questions raised by a third person. Otherwise the plot is the same. Hippias is led along a devious path by Socrates which seems to lead to the conclusion that "the good cannot be beautiful, nor beauty good" since it was agreed that beauty and goodness are not identical with each other.[73] At this point Hippias rebels again, and this time he really loses his temper. He says Socrates has been indulging in pettyfogging arguments, which are no more than "the scrapings and shavings of argument, cut up into little bits."[74] To this denunciation he adds: "What is both beautiful and most precious is the ability to produce an eloquent and beautiful speech to a law court or a council meeting or any other official body whom you are addressing, to convince your audience, and to depart with the greatest of all prizes, your own salvation and that of your friends and property."[75]

These two dialogues, though relatively insignificant as compared with the longer and more famous Platonic dialogues, are important in being among the most useful sources of information about Hippias. Some of the facts about him shine through the pall of doubt about his character and intelligence that Plato contrives to create.

A recent thorough re-examination of the life and works of Hippias by a highly competent scholar, Mario Untersteiner, has added to the materials available for study of this Sophist. Untersteiner concludes that Hippias himself was a voluminous writer. It is evident that he wrote for pay many orations or "epideictic" speeches. One of these, called *The Trojan,* was in the nature of a collection of moral and practical precepts written as if coming from Nestor for the guidance of a young man or of young men generally. To these mostly lost speeches and the fragments, Untersteiner feels there must be added, as almost certainly coming from Hippias, portions of the *Dissoi Logoi* (Twofold Arguments); the display piece of oratory known as the *Anonymus Iamblichi;* "a chapter of Thucydides, (III, 84)"; and "a considerable part of the Prooemium to the *Characters* of Theophrastus."[76] I believe that Untersteiner has made out an excellent case, based on internal evidence, style, and other factors, for crediting Hippias with the authorship of these works. I will therefore summarize here the evidence they reveal of political studies.

Hippias, says Untersteiner, directed his studies along lines that he thought would help the men engaged in politics, an objective that a modern political scientist would naturally applaud. He found the faculty of speech so important to the orator and political leader that he made special study of it. Beginning with words, the indispensable units of speech, he worked intensively, but not by the Socratic method, to discover their precise meanings and proper uses. From this point he went into the sense experiences that words convey and on into the formation of more general concepts.

In human affairs he found the concept of justice to be one of the most important to analyze. Justice, he found, is "that edict of nature which is valid for all," and which is revealed in unwritten law. Unfortunately the laws made by men in their city-states varied from place to place and were full of contradictions. The laws made by men were, consequently, not the same as the law of nature, but in fact often contrary to nature's laws. He felt, therefore, that men had to look beyond the laws made by their own rulers and their own cities to something more general. He favored something far more cosmopolitan than the laws of the various city-states. Did he, perhaps, believe that the larger the political unit, the more nearly its laws would have to conform to the laws of nature?

As I understand him from Untersteiner's analysis, he recognized that the kind of cosmopolitanism with extreme individual self-rule that he had in mind might lead to an anarchic state. This would hardly do, even if it helped to make men more versatile as they became more self-dependent. His remedies pointed in several directions: toward a great expansion of the body of knowledge available to men, something practically encyclopedic; toward a spreading of this knowledge more generally among all men through education; and, since knowledge can be used for bad as well as good ends, toward the formulation and the inculcation into men of standards of ethics, of right conduct as distinguished from wrong. He recognized that there is good as well as bad in men, but this has to be faced. Virtue can be taught, he believed, and he was in favor of teaching it. Virtue in this case must have meant political virtue, the kind of virtue that is appropriate to life in the *polis*, where men have to live together.

This is an inadequate summary of what Untersteiner has said concerning the views of Hippias, but I hope it shows that Hippias was a fairly important student of politics in the theoretical rather than descriptive and historical sense.

CRITIAS

Critias of Athens was born sometime about 480 B.C.[77] He came from a wealthy and aristocratic family that had connections with Solon in earlier times and later with Plato. As a young man he developed a strongly antidemocratic attitude, which meant that he was both pro-aristocratic and pro-Spartan. He engaged in several oligarchical efforts to overthrow the democracy of Athens, and was several times exiled. Late in his life when Sparta defeated Athens and ruled the city for a short time, the Spartans approved him to be one of the five ephors to rule the city in Sparta's interests. He served later as one of the Thirty Tyrants. He was very nearly a full-time politician on the side of the oligarchy, but was capable also of turning against his fellow oligarchs and siding with the democrats. Some of the evidence against him comes from unfriendly sources, but enough of it seems to be sufficiently well verified to warrant describing him as an unscrupulous and vengeful man, whose burning

175

hatred of the Athenian democracy led him to violent and disloyal conduct. Yet such was his political shrewdness and luck that he could bound back into power from one defeat and exile after another.

In his late youth or early manhood he attached himself to Socrates, as Xenophon wryly says (in Kathleen Freeman's paraphrase), "to attain to superiority over his companions and train himself for a political career,"[78] or, in Untersteiner's words, also based on Xenophon, "in order to learn the art of expert government."[79] This is one of the few cases of written evidence to the effect that Socrates was considered to be like the Sophists and was recognized as in some respects a teacher of politics and government. Critias, however, quit Socrates when he thought he had learned what he needed, and much later, when in power, he acted against Socrates and the Sophists by having inserted in the laws of Athens a "prohibition of instruction in the art of argument."[80] Thus the former student paid his sardonic respects to his old teacher.

Why Critias should be listed among the Sophists as he seems to be I do not know. He was not by vocation a teacher in the usual sense, but a man devoted to practical politics. If he did any teaching in a broad sense it must have been for strictly partisan purposes. And as an aristocrat he presumably would not have committed the sin of taking pay for his teaching. On the other hand he was a student of law and government, and wrote some works in these fields. He worked on the revision of the laws of Athens; wrote on constitutions in both verse and prose, in which he dealt especially with the constitutions of Sparta and Thessaly; and wrote some model political speeches, or introductions to such speeches, entitled *Preludes to Public [Political?] Orations* or *Prooemia for Political Speeches.*[81] In these works (which are no longer extant except in small fragments) we may have some early examples of the comparative study of constitutions—even if not from a strictly unbiased point of view.

Had Critias been a more able and popular writer, more of his early essays into political studies might well have been preserved.

THE TWO ANTIPHONS

There were two men named Antiphon who were of some importance in the intellectual and political life of Greece in the second half of the fifth century B.C.

"Antiphon the Sophist" was an Athenian who is described as having been "a rhetorician, seer, and interpreter of dreams."[82] He is also said to have started as a sort of mental healer and later to have turned to the teaching of rhetoric. What famous pupils he had is not known, whereas "Antiphon the Orator" seems to have had several, to be noted later. He is not reported to have been active in politics, as the orator was.

The works produced by Antiphon the Sophist, of which, with one exception, only small fragments remain, included a substantial book *On Truth*, which represented his attempt to find the relationship between appearances and reality, and the smaller works *On Concord, The Statesman (Politicus)* or *Discourse on the State*, and *On the Interpretation of Dreams*.[83] Some of the writings usually assigned to Antiphon the Orator are also attributed by certain scholars to Antiphon the Sophist.

In the work *On Truth* Antiphon apparently probed into some of the basic problems of knowledge, of how men from sense experiences can arrive at reliable knowledge.[84] When he moves into some of the areas with more obvious political interest, he finds concord to be one of the most important factors in society, and justice, so important to concord, to consist in obedience to the laws of the state. But here he encounters a basic problem—the conflict between the law of nature, or *physis,* and the law called *nomos* made by men for their particular states. The majority of the laws made by men are contrary to or at least discordant with those of nature, an evil situation to him. But he is not completely pessimistic. Education can accomplish much in achieving concord both internally, in home and in state, and externally. Factional divisions within the state, such as those resulting from inequalities in wealth, are deplored; but they can be overcome in part at least by neighborly kindness. Presumably this is one way in which nature's laws and those of men can be better harmonized, although I do not find that he says this specifically.

If these thoughts are not very deep or original, they at least reveal the level of study and thinking of a man who is listed as one of the more important late fifth-century Sophists. If more of his writings were available we would have a better basis for judging his thought on its merits. That he wrote on politics and the state is a matter of some importance, but too little is left of his work in this field to warrant analysis here.

Antiphon the Orator, who "was also a politician and leader of the oligarchic party"[85] and apparently a trial lawyer too, came from Rhamnus in Attica, not far from Athens. He became famous as a writer of orations for others to deliver. Some orations he delivered himself; hence his fame. He also seems to have done some teaching. Both Thucydides and Socrates are said to have been his pupils.[86] He developed a number of series of speeches for courtroom delivery—for the prosecution, for the defense, the prosecutor's reply, and the concluding argument of the defense.[87] Thus he must have made some study of one branch of government, the judicial.

THRASYMACHUS

Thrasymachus, who was a citizen of Chalcedon, a Greek city on the Bosporus opposite Byzantium, was in his prime about 430 to 400 B.C., but the exact dates of his life seem to be in doubt.[88] He is widely known for his statement as given in Plato's *Republic* that "the just," or as we would say, justice, "is nothing else than the advantage of the stronger,"[89] and for his strong defense of this proposition. What he meant, of course, was not any ideal justice but what any party in power called justice, which was always composed of laws and policies that promoted its own party interests. Thrasymachus was primarily interested in the techniques of rhetoric and oratory and made some contributions in this field.

Untersteiner calls attention to a recent minor controversy in Europe as to whether Thrasymachus was a real Sophist.[90] One writer insisted that Thrasymachus was not a Sophist because he put so much stress on mere oratory and eloquence. Others called him a Sophist "because he studied the essential nature of the state." Still others took equivocal positions, one saying that he fell short of being a true Sophist because he was not clearly "a teacher of virtue." These are interesting sidelights on what the controversialists in this case considered a Sophist to be. Clearly some of them would equate "Sophist" with "student of politics" or with "teacher of virtue," probably meaning, as with Jaeger, teacher of "political virtue."

Of the many writings that Thrasymachus is supposed to have left only a few fragments survive.[91] These point to discussions of political questions and the problem of justice. In one sentence he harks back to Solon, almost paraphrasing him: "The gods do not see human affairs; otherwise they would not have overlooked the greatest of all blessings among mankind, Justice—for we see mankind not using this virtue."[92] In another passage: "When the worst results [of misgovernment] are not the work of Heaven or Fate but of our administrators, then it is necessary to speak."[93]

PRODICUS

Prodicus of Ceos, a Greek island southeast of Attica, was probably born about 460 B.C.; and he lived on past the time of Socrates' death in 399 B.C.[94] He is generally classed as a Sophist and he followed a fairly normal pattern of activity for that class of Greek scholars. He went on embassies for Ceos, especially to Athens; men paid to hear him give displays of oratorical skill; he delivered lectures to young men desirous of learning; and he carried on various studies and wrote works about them. Among the men who may have been his pupils, or who at least heard some of his lectures, the following may be listed: Euripides, Isocrates, Theramenes, Thrasymachus, and, somewhat doubtfully, Xenophon. Socrates, Callias, and others also heard him lecture. One of his specialties in studies was the correct definition and use of words, a branch of learning to which he seems to have devoted much time and in which he both attained considerable fame and contributed some ideas to Socrates and others.

He also wrote various works. Untersteiner believes that a major work of his called *Hours* consisted of various parts (listed by some as separate books) on such subjects as nature and the nature of man.[95] Like Solon and other writers after him, Prodicus put man and his nature and needs at the center of his studies, but he did not ignore the gods. The latter, according to Prodicus, helped to get man started on his own course of learning or discovery, a course which brought man from the natural or *physis* state to that of social and political organization, where there was *nomos,* or law made by men. Thus Prodicus develops a myth of the origin and social development of mankind, beginning with fairly close relations between men and gods, but moving on toward a stage in which man is more independent and makes his own laws within the limits set by *physis* or nature. Beyond this limit he can in fact never go.

In the field of ethics Prodicus took the view that certain things, wealth, for example, are not good or bad in themselves but in accordance with the use men make of them. Men have to make their own choices between good and evil, and can do so, as he illustrates in a myth called *The Choice of Heracles* or *Heracles at the Crossroads,* wherein the young Heracles must choose to follow one of two women, Vice or Virtue.

He chooses to follow Virtue although she shows him the harder way. Virtue is teachable, he comes to learn. Did Prodicus mean here political virtue, or *areté*? To a considerable extent, I think, he did. Of the Sophists he said that they occupied a position halfway between the philosopher and the statesman, and so combined the virtues of both.[96] Though it involved hard work and difficult decisions, men in this profession could therefore, be truly virtuous, i.e., excellent or skilled in governmental services, and so presumably could other men.

Writers and Writings on Political History

There is material of historical value in ancient Egyptian, Mesopotamian, and other Near Eastern inscriptions and papyrus remains. But this is generally, so to speak, raw material, like lists and dates of rulers. History as I understand it is essentially a written account, both factual and interpretative, chronologically arranged, that traces out the developments in some chosen area, from the beginning or from some chosen point in time. I consider political history to be one of the most important branches of study for both history and politics. While most general histories of peoples, nations, states, and cities unavoidably pay considerable attention to political problems and events, there are also many histories that emphasize the political almost to the exclusion of the religious, cultural, economic, and other phases. But the various facets and activities of life in communities are usually so closely interrelated that a sharp differentiation of political from other aspects is not possible. General history is itself always to a great extent a contribution to the study of politics.[97]

Possessed of active and inquisitive minds, and a deep secular and humanistic interest in themselves and other peoples, the Greeks began early to prepare prose genealogies, chronologies, lists of rulers, and "histories" of things that happened, especially during the rise of Persian power and its pressure on the Greek cities of Ionia.[98] A semimythical Cadmus wrote about Miletus, and Eugeon (Euagon) about Samos. These pre-Socratic beginnings clearly foreshadowed the rise of true history, but so little remains of what such men wrote that not much can be said about them. Later writers classed them as logographers, which signifies little more than "prose writers" or "chroniclers." These men were unwittingly, perhaps, preparing materials necessary for the writing of history, but they are not generally considered to have been historians in the full sense.

Hecataeus of Miletus, who was born about 550 B.C., was active in the political affairs of his city, giving counsel on important matters. The titles of his reported writings, one on the geography of the earth, and one on Greek fables, do not suggest any political writings, but John B. Bury believes that his geographical work included something on the monarchies of Assyria, Media, and Persia. Any study of these monarchies could hardly fail to contain political material. In any case, however, Bury credits Hecataeus with having initiated the composition of "modern" history.[99] He certainly took a critical and skeptical view of what he called the "ridiculous" stories of other writers about early Greece. His attitude toward human affairs was also, like that of Solon, a secular one; he did not seek or expect to find divine or supernatural causes of events in the human realm.

While Hecataeus was in some sense the "initiator" of the modern historical attitude, Herodotus is generally called the "father of history."[100] For our purposes it is not important which one of these men, or whether both together, should be credited with starting modern history on its course; but in the study of politics Herodotus is the larger figure.

HERODOTUS

Herodotus was born at Halicarnassus in Asia Minor between about 490 and 480 B.C. and died about 424 B.C. at Thurii.[101] He came of a noble family, received a good education, and traveled widely. He was also well acquainted with the literature of his time. At Halicarnassus he got into political controversies, with unfortunate results, but at Athens and other places where he lived and lectured he was generally well received. His great work, *The History*, in nine books, is the oldest extant substantial work of history in the Greek language, and still one of the most interesting and informative. And it presents evidence of approaches to the study of politics by a fertile Greek mind of the fifth century B.C.

It is important to remember that as yet no major student had devoted himself to writing about politics in any systematic or comprehensive way. Homer and Hesiod had mentioned government and had discussed the actions of rulers as they were influenced by the gods. Solon had clear ideas but wrote far too little. The philosophers had touched the field of politics in various ways, partly with an ethical approach. The

Sophists, too, had recognized the importance of politics, but in their studies and teaching had gone off mainly into auxiliary studies like grammar, rhetoric, dialectic, and oratory as important aids and skills for men who wanted to influence people and so succeed in public affairs. A number of short works had been written on constitutions, on the *polis*, and on particular city-states. These had undoubtedly entered into the streams of Greek thought, with some cumulative effect in shifting the attention of informed people from mythology, religion, nature, and personal affairs at least a little toward politics. In the general background of course, there were two discouragingly widespread ideas that stood in the way of a direct study of politics—the notion that *areté*, or excellence, meaning essentially public virtue or political *areté*, was something that could not be taught, and the notion that in the search for knowledge men could not trust their senses. But at some point there arose the unpretentious idea of writing out in prose for practical use simple lists of rulers and of winners in the Olympic games, chronologies of events, geographical descriptions of cities and other places, and accounts of the origins of city-states. Herodotus seized upon this idea and turned it into something big. Living at the eastern edge of the Greek world, close to the nations of the East, he conceived the grand design of writing an account or history of the two worlds, that of Asia Minor and western Asia and that of the Greeks, in contact and in conflict with the East, basing it on his own observations, conversations, reading, and reflections.

One of the greatest attractions of *The History* seems to me to be the great variety of subjects to be found within its pages. Popular tales and myths, geography of strange places, religious practices, ethnology of foreign peoples, biography, popular customs and manners, military ruses and naval maneuvers, agriculture and grazing, gold washing and coinage systems, and numerous stories of military campaigns and battles—these suggest the wide variety of fare that Herodotus provides in his history. And throughout its panorama runs the stuff of politics, high and low. Lydia, Persia, Scythia, Libya, the Ionian cities, Sparta, and Athens are in a constant seesaw of maneuvering and warfare; making agreements and breaking them; suffering internal revolutions and the assassination of rulers; invading and repelling invasions. Recurrently in Herodotus, great kingdoms and small are involved in struggles almost

to the death, because military might and stratagems and battles were
in the long run accepted as almost the only way to settle the conflicts
that arose. In this setting Herodotus presents an illuminating commentary on the domestic and international politics of his time. International relations without international organization and the consequences
of such international anarchy are well presented. In the many little statements that are made about the governments of Lydia, Persia, and the
several Greek city-states, there is implicit a comparison of these governments with each other. Tyranny, kingship, double kingship, councils, assemblies of nobles, officials of various titles—all are mentioned and discussed in various passages.

One of the longest and most interesting passages on government is
that in Book III, entitled "Thalia," where the leading Persian conspirators who led the revolt against the Magus, the earless usurper of the
crown, discuss the question of what form of government they should
set up in Persia.[102] Speeches were made by different conspirators on behalf of democracy, oligarchy, and monarchy, and the majority voted
for monarchy. Back of these speeches there evidently lay some study
and reflection as well as experience on the part of Herodotus and earlier
Greeks. Herodotus also describes how, when Darius brought about his
own election as king of the Persian monarchy, he divided the empire
up into twenty satrapies, each including certain "nations," not always
contiguous ones.[103] Over each he set a governor, and for each he established the amount of tribute it was expected to pay him annually. This
is one of the earliest accounts of administrative organization and districts.

In short, scattered throughout *The History* are materials on political
questions, on international relations, on nations and city-states and their
governments, on political parties and conspiracies, on the theory of the
best form of government, on public administration and finances, on the
lust for political power and the effect of such power on its holders, on
war as an instrument of national policy, on the relations among politics,
economics, and religion. Without these materials the work would be
obviously incomplete. Herodotus was, then, one of the earliest writers
on political history, and a very important one. For later students it is unfortunate that his work in this area was not more penetrating and systematic.

Herodotus was not in all respects as secular as Solon in his attitude toward politics. He had some belief in divine intervention in human affairs, and in divine vengeance on those who failed in morality.[104] He did not fully separate politics from religion. But he helped to start a new wave of humanistic studies in the field of history, and he considered politics and government in nearly all that he wrote. It remained for others to define the subject matter of politics more precisely and to bring it out more clearly into the open for intensive study.

THUCYDIDES

Thucydides was born in Athens about 471 B.C., some ten or more years later than Herodotus. Of an aristocratic Athenian family, he was well educated and prepared for a life of public service. His teachers are said to have included Antiphon the Orator, Gorgias, the famous Sophist and rhetorician, and the philosopher Anaxagoras. He evidently engaged in public activities in Athens for many years; in 421 B.C. he was commander of an Athenian fleet engaged in the fighting against the Spartans in the Peloponnesian War. This operation did not go well, and Thucydides was convicted of treason and banished from Athens. He then moved to Thrace where he had property in gold mines.

Even before his banishment, Thucydides had turned his thoughts toward writing the history of the Peloponnesian War, which he believed held fateful implications for the Greeks. To quote the words at the very beginning of his work, he says of himself (unless someone else supplied this statement): "Thucydides, an Athenian, wrote the history of the war between the Peloponnesians and the Athenians, beginning at the moment that it broke out, and believing that it would be a great war, and more worthy of relation than any that had preceded it."[105] Banishment with its relief from official duties in Athens gave him the necessary leisure to pursue this scholarly undertaking. He traveled when and where he could; he interviewed; he thought; and he wrote. These activities went on for ten years after he left Athens. In 411 B.C., when he died at the age of about sixty, he left an unfinished work which has come to be known as the *History of the Peloponnesian War*. Others, notably Xenophon and Theopompus, took up the story where he left off.

The Peloponnesian War covers some twenty-one years of almost continuous warfare, from 431 to 411 B.C. It is made up of accounts of military and naval battles and campaigns, political discussions and speeches, interstate negotiations and agreements, and internal crises and politics within Athens and within the Peloponnesian group of states.

Unlike the best modern historians, Thucydides did not list the places he visited, the people he interviewed, the documents he studied, or other sources of information he utilized. It is only by historical detective work that scholars have been able to piece together considerable parts of the background of Thucydides' work. But the fact that he does not usually reveal his sources or the authorities he consulted does not mean that his work has been held in suspicion. On the contrary, wherever it has been found possible to check his findings of fact and his conclusions, they have generally stood up very well. The book is compact, tight, and well reasoned. Unlike the discursive *History* of Herodotus, with all its wealth of interesting but unrelated matter, Thucydides' book contains little extraneous material.[106] His critical judgment, too, is outstanding. On the whole, Thucydides has been recognized as probably the ablest critical historian of ancient times and "the father of historical method."[107]

These statements must, however, be read against the background of certain conditions affecting Thucydides and his work. He dealt with Athens and its rivals while they were subject to the stress of wartime conditions. Three factors were identified by Thucydides as of major importance at this time for Athens (and it was from the Athenian point of view that he wrote): economic resources (about which he wrote very little), military might, and political strength, both internally and externally. It is understandable that under the pressures of a long-drawn-out and highly dangerous war, Thucydides would discuss the political-military fortunes of Athens with primary emphasis on these "power" factors and with little attention to other factors that are politically important in peacetime, such as the distribution of wealth and tax burdens (not just economic resources), rights of political participation, and various ethical, religious, educational, and cultural matters. Still, this is a limitation on his work in terms of general political history.

Thucydides' political philosophy was another conditioning influence that should be noted. He seemed almost to adopt the viewpoint of the philosophers of nature and to look upon the events in human society as controlled by natural laws beyond the power of men to change. All man can do is study these forces and adjust himself to their operations. This is not exactly the same thing as saying that political virtue cannot be taught, but it is a similar doctrine. Events move on to their fateful conclusions because men are what they are, individually and in communities. Thucydides apparently thought that he reported events simply and impartially, but his philosophy must at least have had some influence on his choices of events to record and on the importance he attached to them.

At the same time, considering his background of experience in Athenian politics, I must question whether he truly believed that the laws of human behavior in politics are utterly inexorable. Surely Thucydides did not believe that it made no difference who led and ruled a city. There were the examples of Solon and Pericles to balance those of Cleon and Alcibiades. He unquestionably did believe that there are laws of human behavior that are practically inexorable if certain things are done under certain conditions. Given like conditions and policies, history does repeat itself.[108] But his own experience must have shown him that conditions change, and also that men do have choices in politics—choices of leaders and choices among policies. If he did not believe that men have some degree of control over their actions, why did he write the book he did? I think he must have wanted to teach men some of the facts of politics and the ways of politicians, as well as the consequences of pursuing various public policies, so that men could be better advised tomorrow and in the future than they were yesterday. I think he really did believe that, to some extent at least, "political virtue" could be taught and learned for the benefit of mankind.

One feature of his book that has come under considerable criticism is the series of speeches that are interspersed throughout the text. These speeches contain a wide range of contributions to political thought, including even those of unscrupulous men like Cleon and Alcibiades.[109] About these speeches Thucydides says: "With reference to the speeches in this history, some were delivered before the war began, others while it was going on; some I heard myself, others I got from various quarters; it was in all cases difficult to carry them word for word in one's memory, so my habit has been to make the speakers say what was in my opinion demanded of them by the various occasions, of course adhering as closely as possible to the general sense of what they really said."[110] This, it seems to me, is an honest and proper statement, and it puts every careful reader on his guard against any misconstruction. That the speeches are all in Thucydides' own style is generally admitted, and is a fact not to be deplored, since Thucydides had a terse and clear style. It means, of course, that the thought is also to some extent that of Thucydides, even where he is trying to state views with which he has no sympathy.

To summarize Thucydides' contributions to political studies: We have to recognize the limitations in scope of *The Peloponnesian War*; he does not go extensively into questions of comparative government, constitutional law, public administration, legislation, and other divisions of the field that are today considered important. He did bring into his work one subject that had received but little attention before from the Greek writers on politics: "international" or (then) interstate relations (since the separate city-states were hardly nations). Treaties, conferences and negotiations between representatives of different city-states, alliances, war, and related interstate matters are dealt with in several places. In this Thucydides was an important innovator. Later Greek writers like Isocrates also took up this subject, but Plato and even Aristotle gave surprisingly little attention to it.

In methodology, Thucydides had sound advice for all scholars dealing with human affairs, not only for political scientists: "And with reference to the narrative of events, far from permitting myself to derive it from the first source that came to hand, I did not even trust my own impressions, but it rests partly on what I saw myself, partly on what others saw for me, the accuracy of the report being always tried by the most severe and detailed tests possible. My conclusions have cost me some labour from the want of coincidence between accounts of the same occurrences by different eye-witnesses, arising sometimes from imperfect memory, sometimes from undue partiality for one side or the other. The absence of romance in my history will, I fear, detract somewhat from its interest; but if it be judged useful by those inquirers who desire an exact knowledge of the past as an aid to the interpretation of the future, which in the course of human things must resemble if it does not reflect it, I shall be content. In fine, I have written my work, not as an essay which is to win the applause of the moment, but as a possession for all time."[111] (There is here a strong implied criticism of Herodotus.) Finally, as I see it, in collecting the speeches of many men, *The Peloponnesian War* was the first book of readings on political theories and problems in any language (if we except the much briefer "collection" by Herodotus, who reproduced in his *History* the statements of three different speakers on three different forms of government).

In his own time Thucydides' work, not surprisingly, had little circulation or influence. He painted no rosy picture, offered no real hope to man. But his book would prove itself in the long run—across many miles and many centuries it would reach untold numbers of Western readers.

Four Dramatists

One would not ordinarily turn to the writers of plays for evidences of the study and teaching of politics, but for Greece of the fifth century B.C., when the classification of studies into different categories was just being developed, and when there were strictly speaking no "specialists" in political writing (though Thucydides came close to being one), one cannot afford to ignore any substantial body of materials that might shed light on the political thinking of men of that period.[112] Playwrights when they dealt with current human affairs could hardly avoid the subject of domestic politics and such related subjects as war and international relations. Further, the theater in those days when there were no newspapers, radio, or television was clearly an important means for conveying political as well as other ideas to the people. The theater was in effect an important institution for political teaching, indoctrination, and criticism for any playwrights who chose to use it as such. It was by no means a mere place of amusement.[113] Others have gone rather thoroughly into some aspects of the political orientation of the Greek theater;[114] there is room for an extended analysis of the political content of all the famous Greek plays and of the use of theatrical productions for political education and propaganda. Here I can only call attention to certain evidence in plays of the four best known of Greek dramatists that bears on my special topic.

AESCHYLUS

Aeschylus (525 or 524 to 456 B.C.) was born at Eleusis near Athens.[115] Eleusis was the center of annual dramatizations of the Eleusinian Mysteries, having to do with the yearly decay and revival of vegetation as well as with human death and resurrection. Aeschylus' family was of the Athenian aristocracy, and he was early engaged in aiding in the defense of Athens against the Persians. His military service brought him public fame, but when the Persian menace had been dispelled, he took to brooding over the gods and fate and man, and to writing poems and

188

tragedies to express his thoughts and feelings. Between 499 and 458 B.C., he produced some eighty, possibly as many as ninety, plays, of which some seven tragedies remain: the *Suppliants*, the *Persians, Seven against Thebes, Prometheus Bound* of the Prometheus trilogy, *Agamemnon, Choëphoroe,* and *Eumenides*—the last three dealing with Orestes, a son of Agamemnon and Clytemnestra, and hence called collectively the *Oresteia.*

All through the plays one finds solemn religious sentiments and overtones, with much contemplation of the gods and of the hereafter. The dramatis personae in *Prometheus Bound* and the *Oresteia* come mainly out of Homer, and are gods and demigods, or at least mythical beings with godlike characteristics. They also, however, have human characteristics and problems. Among the latter are rivalries for kingship and other struggles for political power.

The other plays concern human beings. In the *Persians* the old men and women of Persia, headed by the queen mother and sole ruler, Atossa, are waiting in the council chamber for word of the fateful battle of Xerxes against the Greeks at Salamis. When the news of the disastrous Persian defeat arrives, great lamentations are heard, and with the arrival of the defeated Xerxes, recriminations follow. For the Greeks however, the battle had been a glorious victory and the play undoubtedly stimulated the Athenians' feeling of loyalty toward their city—it may have been for this patriotic purpose that Aeschylus produced it. But if it was political and patriotic poetry, it was also probably the first historical drama in the Western world.

Sinclair believes that Herodotus' *History* and Aeschylus' *Persians* would make a better introduction to Greek political thought than Plato's *Republic.*[116] But the *Persians* is not the only play by Aeschylus that contains political ideas and materials. In the *Suppliants,* for example, an apparent conflict between a man-made law and one presumably derived from the gods evokes a discussion about divine versus human laws, and how divine law gives liberty without anarchy. In the *Eumenides* an argument is made for government by the middle class over other systems. It is clear that Aeschylus, despite his strongly religious feelings about government, law, and justice, could also appreciate and utilize more secular arguments on political subjects. In this respect he stood fairly close to Solon.[117]

SOPHOCLES

Sophocles (c. 496 or 495 to 406 or 405 B.C.) like Aeschylus was born near Athens, of wealthy and aristocratic parents, and like him he took part in military and other public affairs in Athens including service on missions abroad for the state.[118] In his military career he rose to become a general, but was too easygoing and pleasure-loving to please the military-political leader Pericles. Included among his public services was membership on a "commission of preliminary investigation" to consider the desirability of giving Athens an oligarchical type of constitution[119] —the earliest constitutional study commission to come to my attention. His special interest, however, was in music and drama.

He began as a young man to write poems and plays, and is credited with having written many of both. In the annual competition for best dramas, he defeated the considerably older Aeschylus at least once. As in the case of Aeschylus, only seven of his plays remain. The extant tragedies of Sophocles are *Oedipus Rex* (sometimes called *Oedipus, King of Thebes*); *Antigone*; *Electra*; *Oedipus at Colonos*; the *Trachiniae*; the *Ajax*; and the *Philoctetes*. Of these the *Antigone* is probably the most political; it will be the only tragedy of his I will cite.[120]

The plot is simple and completely tragic. Oedipus, the blind, deposed, and exiled king of Thebes, puts a curse on his two sons Polynices and Eteocles for not having helped him. These two kill each other during a struggle by Polynices to gain the crown of Thebes for himself. Creon, who is governing Thebes as regent, permits the body of Eteocles, who was not anti-Creon, to be buried on Theban soil; but he forbids anyone to bury Polynices. Despite this decree, Antigone, one of Polynices' sisters, goes out secretly and covers it with soil, and when soldiers uncover it, she is caught trying to bury it again. Creon first decrees her death, but later orders her locked up in a vault of stone never to come out again. Creon's son Haemon, Antigone's fiancé, tries to kill his father with a sword; failing this, he commits suicide. Eurydice, wife of Creon and mother of Haemon, learning of her son's death and having previously lost another son, also commits suicide. Creon is left alone, full of remorse, his life utterly shattered.

Let me fill out this framework by quoting some passages with political overtones. An early chorus recounts the assault of Polynices and his foreign cohorts on Thebes, and their defeat by Creon's forces with the elimination of both Polynices and Eteocles as aspirants for the crown. And so Creon comes:

> Crowned by these new and strange events, he comes—
> By will of heav'n our new-created king,
> What counsel pondering?
> Who by his sovereign will hath now convoked,
> In solemn conference to meet,
> The elders of the state;
> Obedient to whose summons, we are here.[121]

As nearest of blood to Oedipus and his two dead sons, Creon claims the power

> To wield alone the scepter and the realm.
> There is no way to know of any man
> The spirit and the wisdom and the will,
> Till he stands proved, ruler and lawgiver.[122]

He says a king should seek good counsel, speak his mind courageously, put the public interest ahead of the claims of friendship, and treat every enemy of the state as his own enemy, because the state alone "brings us safe." "So for the good of Thebes her laws I frame."[123]

Then follows his proclamation against the burial of Polynices, with the penalty of death for anyone who disobeys. The chorus, representing the elders and the people, meekly submits. A sentinel then comes to report Antigone's violation of Creon's degree. Creon is infuriated. The chorus suggests that perhaps the gods had ordered the burial, but Creon will have none of this. He denounces the elders for bringing the gods into the affair, and also declaims against those murmurers in the city, the makers of public opinion against him, who "with stubborn necks unbent, and hearts disloyal," have been bribed, as he says, to oppose his one-man rule.[124] Gold is the root of evil. He will not rest until the perpetrator of the burial is found, and if not found, there will be death for those who fail to find the culprit. The picture of a fearful, mistrustful, angry, perhaps mentally unbalanced, tyrant is clearly drawn.

The chorus here sings of man as the most wonderful of the wonders of the world. They relate how he wearies the gods, captures and dominates birds and beasts,

> Language withal he learnt,
> And Thought that as the wind is free,
> And aptitudes of civic life . . .

But he is as restless as he is resourceful:

> So soaring far past hope,
> The wise inventiveness of man
> Finds diverse issues, good and ill:
> If from their course he wrests
> The firm foundations of the state,
> Laws, and the justice he is sworn to keep—
> High in the city, cityless, I deem him,
> Dealing with baseness: overbold . . .[125]

Clearly the chorus is saying that anarchy will not do, nor should men tamper with the foundations of state and justice, even if it means submitting to the rule of one man. Absolute obedience is necessary.

Antigone is then brought to face Creon. She does not deny her deed in burying Polynices, but defends it as a righteous act according to divine law.

> *Creon.* And didst thou dare to disobey the law?
> *Antigone.* Nowise from Zeus, me thought, this edict came,
> Nor Justice, that abides among the gods
> In Hades, who ordained these laws for men.
> Nor did I deem *thine* edicts of such force
> That they, a mortal's bidding, should o'erride
> Unwritten laws, eternal in the heavens.[126]

Creon will not hear of this divine law, nor will he be defied by a mere woman. If he gives in to Antigone who has boldly violated his decree

> I surely am the woman, she the man,
> If she defies my power and I submit.[127]

Haemon comes in to plead with his father not to punish Antigone, to be reasonable, and to consider public opinion. Creon becomes, if anything, more unyielding than before. He has the power, and he will not take instruction from others or brook disobedience. "Shall Thebes prescribe to me how I must govern?"[128]

> The worst of evils is to disobey.
> Cities by this are ruined, homes of men
> Made desolate by this . . .
> > We must defend
> The government and order of the state,
> And not be governed by a wilful girl.[129]

There is much more, but these quotations are enough to show Sophocles' superb handling of a complex theoretical, legal, and political situation with its various interrelated aspects. That he was an able student of politics and that he was trying to teach something about government and politics, and especially about absolute monarchs of dubious legitimacy, can hardly be doubted.

EURIPIDES

Euripides (c. 485–480 to 406 or 405 B.C.) was born on the island of Salamis near Cyprus at just about the time of the great naval battle there. He apparently was educated and spent much of his life at Athens, but moved late in life to the north and died in Macedonia.[130] His education is said to have included instruction from Protagoras and Prodicus; his associates included some of the best thinkers and students of all time, like Anaxagoras, Protagoras, and Socrates. Obviously he was a man of means as well as of outstanding intellect. He followed public affairs closely but, not being an Athenian citizen, he took no direct part in Athens' political life. His domestic life was not happy, and he became something of a scholarly recluse, devoted to his books and his writings.

As a writer, he was highly productive. In addition to a number of poems, he is said to have produced some seventy-five or more plays (up to ninety-two, according to one estimate). He was not as successful as Aeschylus, for example, in winning first prizes in the drama competitions. On the other hand, his plays must have been well liked by many, and widely copied, since eighteen of them have survived.

Aristophanes in *The Frogs* has sport with both Aeschylus and Euripides by staging a postmortem debate between their spirits in the lower regions, a debate that Aeschylus wins. The question is which was the better craftsman in writing plays and so entitled to sit beside Pluto at dinner in the underworld assembly hall. In the debate each of the two wraiths quotes from and ridicules the plays of the other to the enjoyment of their fellow spirits. Aeschylus is adjudged the winner by the assembled spirits, but Euripides seems well content with the points he has scored. Defending his "democratic way" against Aeschylus' demand to know "the points for which a noble poet our praise obtains," Euripides replies:

> For his ready wit, and his counsels sage,
> and because the citizen folk he trains
> To be better townsmen and worthier men.[131]

Euripides' realism, in describing people including leaders as he actually saw them in a period of considerable decay in morals, militated against early popularity for him. Aeschylus berates him in *The Frogs* for his realism and for the sordid facts he brought out about his characters, a thing that Aeschylus would not do. For, said Aeschylus,

> . . . we, the poets, are teachers of men.
> We are BOUND things honest and pure to speak.[132]

Clearly Euripides was an early realist in the appraisal of men and their motives in politics as in other walks of life (if Aristophanes' words can be trusted).

No one of Euripides' plays is strictly political, as one might expect from a writer not directly engaged in the activities of politics, but there are incidental discussions of, or references to, important political questions here and there. Some of the points discussed in the plays are these: that the laws of men should not go against the laws of nature (*Hyppolytus*); that men should be legally and politically equal, whether they are called slave or free, since the difference between them is really only one of the words used (*Ion*); that the sexes should be equal also (*Medea*); that what holds cities together is the interchange of services and advantages among men (*Phoenissae* and *Suppliants*) and faithful observance of the laws (*Suppliants*). In other plays questions are raised as to whether monarchy (tyranny?) or democracy is to be preferred, and whether government by the middle class is not best. In addition, Euripides gives an example of political education, or education of the prince on how to govern. In the *Suppliants* Aithra, the mother of Theseus, teaches him how to rule, basing her teaching on the theory that it is good observance and enforcement of the laws that makes cities strong.

ARISTOPHANES

Aristophanes was born in Athens, the son of a naturalized citizen. The year of his birth is in considerable doubt, with opinions on it ranging from about 455 to as late as 444 B.C.[133] If the latter date is correct, he produced his first play at the age of seventeen (427 B.C.), which is unlikely but not impossible. From then on he averaged about one new play a year until his death in about 385 B.C. The total number of his plays has been estimated to be as high as fifty-four, and even the more cautious scholars credit him with over forty, of which eleven are extant.

Little is known about his education or his teachers. Politically he seems to have leaned toward the conservative if not aristocratic side, but he took full advantage of the prevailing democratic freedom of speech and writing to lampoon all and sundry, notably in the fields of politics and teaching.

Aristophanes is identified with the late Old Comedy in Greek drama. Of the plays in this class, in time admitted to the drama competitions, it has been said that "The subject-matter *par excellence* . . . is personal invective, mainly against political characters and individuals otherwise notorious. The politicians attacked were, as a rule, those of the popular party, such as Pericles, Cleon, Hyperbolus . . ."[134] But poets, philosophers, and musicians were also ridiculed. It is perhaps not surprising, in view of the great political activity in Athens in the fifth century, that a number of Aristophanes' early plays had in the main political motifs, and that the political element was not wholly absent from any of them. In addition, there were attacks, largely farcical it is true and designed to provoke a mocking sort of laughter, upon schools, teachers, scientists, philosophers, and even other dramatists like Aeschylus and Euripides. In general there was an antidemocratic and antiintellectual bias in his plays.

One of the earliest of Aristophanes' plays, *The Babylonians,* was a thinly disguised political attack upon Cleon, the violent and unscrupulous Athenian leader who succeeded Pericles. *The Knights,* a later comedy, was also aimed at Cleon. *The Acharnians* called for peace in the Peloponnesian War, a theme that was repeated a few years later in *The Peace,* and again in *Lysistrata,* which presents a "women's conspiracy to bring about peace." Several other plays dealt with various activities and ideas of women that Aristophanes did not like. One of these, *The Ecclesiazusae,* or *The National Assembly of Women,* ridicules the idea of restoring Athens to its former condition by constitutional revision. Other plays, too, *The Wasps* and *The Birds,* for example, have important political aspects, while one of the most famous, *The Clouds,* is an attack upon the Sophists, in which Socrates is ridiculed as the leading example of that class of teachers.

How much of what Aristophanes put into his plays can be taken seriously as expressing his own views, which he intended to get before the public for political or educational effect, it is impossible to say. I think it cannot be challenged that through his plays he was in fact a teacher in the field of current politics, in the sense that political writers for modern newspapers and periodicals, political and news commentators on radio and television, and the writers of popular books and plays on politics are. He was limited to the one principal medium, his comedies. The literate could obtain and read handwritten copies of these, while both the literate and the nonliterate could see and hear them as presented on the stage. Considering how many of his plays have survived, many copies of them must have been made; and it is altogether likely that he had a wide following of readers and playgoers. The great powers he developed early in life as a poet and dramatist, and his remarkable insight into human character, were reinforced by unusual courage and a willingness to face dangers to himself in order to present his message. His lampooning of political leaders like the notorious Cleon got him into trouble with the law, but with general public support he contrived to carry on his attacks on leading personages in politics for many years. He must be acknowledged to have been a hard-hitting and influential political propagandist.

At the same time it must be recognized that he saw no need in his chosen medium to stick closely to the facts. In some instances, as in his classing of Socrates with the Sophists, I have a feeling that he did not see the real differences; if he did, he must have lumped Socrates with the Sophists for reasons of his own. Aristophanes, then, carries poetic license so far that he can hardly be trusted as a historical source except in the most general sense, such as that there was a man named Socrates, that Athenian democracy under Cleon was clearly on the downgrade after the days of Pericles, and that there were schools whose arguments for and against certain propositions were presented and discussed.

Having said this much, I hasten to add that for the study and teaching of politics Aristophanes was nevertheless a very important figure, and one who is still well deserving of a substantial monographic study under some such title as "Aristophanes as a Student and Teacher of Politics." However misleading many of his particular statements may be, the record shows the outstanding role he gave to comedy in political discussions. As Jaeger well says: "More and more comedy assumed the function of expressing all kinds of public criticism. Not content with passing judgment on 'political affairs' in the narrow sense of the phrase, it discussed politics in the full Greek sense—that is, all questions of universal interest to the community."[135]

The objects of its criticisms, and this is especially true of Aristophanes' works, ranged from individual leaders and separate political acts up through the system of government, to interstate relations, the educational system of the state, and other public concerns. Everything of a public nature was "brought to judgment in the theater before the whole Athenian people" by comedies written by dramatists like Aristophanes.

One should say, perhaps, *especially* by Aristophanes, because he was by far the leading writer in comedy during a most important period of Athenian history. Following the death of Pericles, when such leaders as Cleon came to power, the beginnings of the decline of Athenian leadership in Greek politics and culture were soon evident. By his courage, his persistence over a long period of years, his great poetic ability, and his broad yet incisive view of all that concerned the welfare and the culture of Athens, Aristophanes kept alive freedom of speech and thought in the discussion of the political problems of his city through a long and trying period. And he made the theater an important rival of the assembly as a forum for the discussion of Athenian politics and political personalities.

A Statesman

It would seem to follow almost as a matter of course that a ruler of men should be to some extent a student of government; yet such have been the varieties of men in a position to rule, and of the conditions under which they attained and held power, that one cannot be sure. There have been imbeciles and madmen among rulers, as well as men of great intellectual powers, learning, and wise judgment. The information available concerning the ancient Greek rulers is too meager to permit any firm generalizations about their studies. But Solon, already discussed, and Pericles stand out as well-informed and competent rulers.

Pericles of Athens (490–429 B.C.) was an important enough leader and ruler in the minds of later students to justify the use of his name for an entire era, "The Age of Pericles"—a phrase that summons up a picture of the golden age of Greece. A member of the famous aristocratic family called the Alcmaeonidae, and the son of a distinguished Athenian leader, he was educated by, among others, Zeno the Eleatic and Anaxagoras. The latter remained a friend of Pericles, along with Sophocles and other famous men. By the age of twenty-seven Pericles was already a leader in Athenian politics. He held also for a time the highest military office in Athens, but as a rule, he relied mainly upon his ability to lead the popular assembly. In this capacity he was for a long time perhaps the most important teacher of politics among the Athenians if not in the entire Greek nation.

Unfortunately, although he left an impressive record of achievements in Athenian politics, both domestic and foreign—a record, it must be noted, that is clouded by what historical hindsight can point out as serious mistakes—he left no writings of consequence of his own. Consequently, we are dependent primarily upon his contemporary Thucydides for versions of several of his speeches, and secondarily upon accounts of Xenophon and other later writers.

Thucydides preserves in his history summaries of three of Pericles' speeches. While, as already noted, the words of such summaries are Thucydides' rather than the orator's, they presumably reflect his general thought. Taken along with the historical records of Pericles' political acts and laws, they provide an invaluable insight into the man's political thoughts and deeds. What he had learned and what he tried to teach others about politics are probably well reflected in these speeches.

Regrettably, there is a modern tendency to pay attention almost entirely to his funeral oration, which in Thucydides' work is his second speech, and to neglect the other two. His first address[136] was a masterly albeit unduly optimistic survey of the geographic, economic, and naval-military position of Athens as against the Peloponnesians; it was possibly too pessimistic about the impossibility of getting any concessions whatever from the Peloponnesians on the basis of which war might be avoided. There is little political theory in this address, but a good deal of sound political-military analysis, such as modern men have come to expect from a "Pertinax" (André Géraud of World War I), a Walter Lippmann, and other political commentators of that stature who in the present century certainly deserve high places among the students and teachers of politics.

Pericles' third speech[137] came after Attica had been twice invaded by the Peloponnesians, with great losses to the Athenian cause, and after the plague had settled itself upon them with devastating effects. Temporarily very unpopular because things had gone so badly, Pericles summoned the assembly and addressed its members with great frankness. He did not mince words. On important matters of war policy they had not followed his advice, and the disasters suffered had been partly due to these deviations, and partly to the plague. His analysis of the situation, and his warning as to what total surrender to the Peloponnesians would mean, had their effect. He was re-elected—but did not live long enough to help bring about any real turn in the tide of war in favor of Athens.

His funeral oration, delivered for the men lost in the first year of the war, is, by general agreement, one of the most masterly and enlightened political speeches of all time.[138] Its statement of the Athenian democratic and cultural ideals is probably very nearly as he made it. Thucydides, having adopted a position on Athenian government similar to that of Pericles, would have had little or no reason to distort the meaning of what he said.

Pericles stood in spirit very close to Solon. He put the responsibility for the good government and security of Athens directly upon the people. He did not expect the gods to intervene to help them, or promise that they would. Thus, he taught them the lesson of individual and collective responsibility for their own welfare. Furthermore, by his enlightened cultural policies, and the improvements in the people's conditions of life and in the beauty of their city that he helped to bring about, he taught them also what great benefits a democracy could achieve for itself by following a moderate and liberal policy.

By precept and example this active political and military leader was one of the greatest teachers of the virtues and benefits of intelligent self-government that the world has ever seen. That he made mistakes in his policies concerning war and imperialism, mistakes that possibly could have been avoided, must, unfortunately, be recorded on the debit side.

An Ancient City Planner

Hippodamus, a native of Miletus, was probably born about 475 B.C. He apparently spent much of his life at Athens.[139] He is mentioned as a Sophist in some writings, and also as an architect and city planner. His connection with the Sophists is not wholly clear, since he does not seem to have put himself forward as a teacher, or to have made a career of teaching.[140] He is remembered especially for his work in Pericles' time as the city planner of the harbor town for Athens, called the Piraeus, and as a planner or architect also in the building of Thurii on the boot of southern Italy about 444 B.C. and of Rhodes on the island of the same name in about 408 B.C. He used a rectangular layout of streets and

199

blocks, and has sometimes been credited with being the originator of that idea; but apparently it was in use long before his time.[141]

He combined an interest in the physical planning of cities with a concern for the proper size of the city's population and the form of its government. It may have been his interest in the best form of government for a city-state that led to his being classed as a Sophist, because the Sophists did teach something, however little, about governmental organization in connection with their efforts to train men for citizenship, and for participation in public affairs.

Most students of politics know of Hippodamus primarily from a passage in Aristotle's *Politics*, the gist of which for present purposes is this: "Hippodamus, the son of Euryphon, a native of Miletus . . . was the first person not a statesman who made enquiries about the best form of government."[142] The sentence indicates that Aristotle believed Hippodamus was not a statesman, i.e., not a *politicus*, political leader, or man devoted mainly to the government of the *polis*; that some statesmen (unnamed) had made inquiries concerning the best form of government; that Hippodamus had also done so; and that he was the first non-statesman to do so. The idea that Hippodamus was not a statesman is supported negatively at least by the lack of any records that he served as one. But just what his major role in life really was is not very clear. There probably were long intervals of time before he engaged in public planning, and between assignments of such work; what did he do then? The assumption made by Aristotle that statesmen (politicians, public rulers, high officials) had made inquiries about the best form of government is one that I have made from the outset of this work, but in support of which I find little concrete evidence. Aristotle's implication that after Hippodamus other non-statesmen had made inquiries about the best form of government raises an interesting question: Who were the specific men he had in mind? Unfortunately no positive answer is possible.

The nature of the studies made by Hippodamus is suggested by Aristotle's summary of Hippodamus' plan of government and laws for an ideal city.[143] This is our best source in the absence of the original text, even though Aristotle was somewhat biased against the plan. It does not appear that Hippodamus made a careful comparative study of various city governments in order to see how they functioned and what results they produced. Instead he worked with a supposedly ideal number of citizens, ten thousand in all, divided into three classes (artisans, husbandmen, and armed defenders of the state); land was also divided into three parts (one sacred, one public, and one private); and lawsuits were classified into three groups, based on insult, injury, and homicide. He laid down rules concerning lawsuits, public care for the children of deceased soldiers and sailors, the election of judges by a three-class system of voting, and the duty of magistrates to watch over the interests of the public, strangers, and orphans. One specific proposal which has received considerable praise is that there should be a single high court for judicial appeals.

Clearly Hippodamus made a fetish of numbers—round numbers like 10,000, and the number three. The available evidence does not make clear why he thought 10,000 would be better than 5000 or 20,000, or how he related the size of the population to, for example, problems of defense against other cities, or against the Persians or anyone else. The stress upon these numbers points to a possible belief in numerology or the magic power of numbers as such, and this in turn has overtones of Pythagoreanism. One might reasonably conclude on the basis of what is known about Hippodamus that he was not a careful empirical student of politics. If all that he wrote were available, and not just Aristotle's summary, one might be compelled to reach a different conclusion.

As to the place of Hippodamus in the history of the study of politics, it is necessary, again, to rely on Aristotle, whose statement is a precise one and was evidently worked out with care. Aristotle does not say that Hippodamus was the first non-statesman to consider questions of public policy. Obviously Thales, for example, considered carefully the need for union among the Greek city-states to strengthen their defense against the Persians. Neither does Aristotle say that Hippodamus was the first Greek non-statesman to become a full-time student and teacher of government—a statement that could not have stood up against the obvious facts concerning Hippodamus' professional work in city planning and architecture. What he does call attention to is the beginning of a functional differentiation under which study of the best form of government is not left entirely to the professional politicians. The ancient Greeks did not, I believe, visualize and certainly did not realize in practice the differentiation of functions as a result of which there is today a class of professional students and teachers of politics who are not active in politics and who are not engaged in any other profession as Hippodamus was. At most, Hippodamus' venture into the study of governmental structure and of the best form of government was that of an inspired and educated amateur of whom (Aristotle notwithstanding) there may have been a number of earlier examples, just as there have been numerous examples in modern times.

Chapter 7

↶ Socrates and Political Education

Socrates (469–399 b.c.), the great but enigmatic Athenian teacher and moral leader, was nearing twenty years of age when the Greeks won their great deliverance from the Persian menace. He was about twenty-five when Pericles came to power; twenty-six when Sophocles' *Antigone* was first performed; thirty-one when Phidias' statue of Athena was dedicated and Euripides' *Alcestis* was first performed; thirty-seven when the Parthenon was completed; thirty-nine when Pericles delivered his great funeral oration; and so on through a series of memorable dates. But he also lived to see the plague wreak havoc on the Athenian population; to observe the Athenian empire disintegrating and fading away during the disastrous Peloponnesian War; and to behold Athens itself being humbled in the dust of complete defeat and loss of empire a few years before his death. In fact, he watched Athens experience not merely disasters of war, with great losses in population and in financial and other resources, but also debilitating internal strife between the extreme democrats under such leaders as Cleon and the aristocratic elements who struggled on in an effort to save themselves and the old aristocratic system of government. One marvels at the fact that Athenians like Socrates and his contemporaries could carry on their work with such equanimity as most of them seemed to show through those troubled times.

Scholars will probably never cease to regret that the sources of information about Socrates and his contemporaries are so inadequate and, in the case of Socrates himself, so suspect. Plato's writings as they concern Socrates are under suspicion for one set of reasons, and Xenophon's for another, while Aristophanes' hints and statements in *The Clouds* are still more dubious. And these three provide nearly all the direct information there is. I shall not here try to pass judgment on the specific points at issue in the recent works on "the Socratic problem." For my purposes this is not necessary—my aim is not to try to settle this problem but to present Socrates as a link in the chain of the Greek development of the study and teaching of politics. It is enough to indicate that I follow in the main the judgments of Alfred E. Taylor and Werner Jaeger that Xenophon is to be given more credence than other writers have usually attributed to him, and that where Plato and Xenophon can be shown to be in substantial agreement there is little need for further questioning.[1]

Socrates' fame is based not upon his writings, for he left none, but upon his outstanding character and a number of his acts and achievements that need only be mentioned to be appreciated. He led the way in helping to shift the attention of the Greeks away from the study of the physical phenomena of the universe, in which they were making but little progress, to the study of the problems of mankind. In this Socrates emphasized the supreme importance of cultivating the human soul. Indeed he is credited with the creation of the very concept of the soul.[2] His concept of the soul in effect equates it with the human intelligence, or, as some would say, the mind, which can be improved only through the deepening, widening, and perfecting of human knowledge. He also equated wisdom or knowledge with goodness (areté, or excellence): he believed that with knowledge men would not do wrong but would strive for right action, and he gave both an ethical and a technical meaning to goodness. In support of his ideas about perfecting the human soul through increased knowledge and wisdom, he developed what is known as "the Socratic method" of acquiring, inculcating, and spreading human knowledge (i.e., teaching). Finally, he demonstrated in his own life—and death—what the soul's mastery over the body can achieve in the way of supreme self-control, simple living, rugged courage, and devotion to ideals.

Christians have often called attention to certain similarities between the life of Christ and that of Socrates, who lived and died four hundred years earlier than Christ. The religious background of Socrates' life was, of course, fundamentally different from that of Jesus. Neither Socrates nor his followers pretended that he was a son of God or that he was going to prepare a place for them with God in heaven. In taking the hemlock Socrates was showing his loyalty to the state and to the law, two major instruments of human well-being on earth in which he strongly believed. In a sense it was for his ideals of life in a Greek *polis* that he died.

There is an understandable tendency in the literature about Socrates to idealize the man. It is well to remember, however, that he was a man of his times, and the social practices of his day in Athens were not all such as would win commendation in modern America. His obvious neglect of his wife and family while he engaged in discussions in the streets or in the gymnasiums, and his failure to support the emancipation of women and the elevation of their status generally, are only two of the counts that might be made against him if one applies anachronistic modern standards. Such not so admirable features of his life should not be glossed over, but they in no way invalidate his very great positive achievements. It is these with which we are concerned here.

The Mission of Socrates

Socrates began life as the son of a stonecutter, a "statuary" or maker of statues. If he actually tried this type of work himself, as has been suggested, he soon found it not to his liking. He then turned to the study of natural science or, as it was then, a speculative sort of "natural philosophy." At this stage he was associated for some years as a pupil with Archelaus, who himself had been a student in the same field under Anaxagoras. He acquired a good foundation in the subject but was not satisfied with it. At that time there were rival schools of natural philosophers who held almost diametrically opposed views: one that everything was static and unchanging, the other that everything was changing and in flux. To resolve such conflicts in theory there were then very few methods and practically no instruments of identification or measurement that could be used with any confidence. When he finally turned his back on this field of study, he is said to have remarked that men should pursue physical inquiries only far enough to make simple practical applications of their knowledge, such as measuring off a field.

Just when Socrates began to shift to a lifetime mission in a new field, the study of the problems of men living in communities, is not known, but it probably was before he was thirty, or at about that age, when he developed the practice of going almost daily to one of the several gymnasiums in Athens. There with other young men and older boys, stripped for exercise like the rest, he engaged in the various kinds of physical exercises and athletic contests that were then popular. When the rest periods came, he engaged his companions in discussions on various subjects, some no doubt chosen by himself, for he seems to have had a dominating personality. In this way he became an important leader and teacher. He must have been one of those who helped to turn these centers of gymnastic exercises into places where talk and learning at least supplemented the physical exertions. After leaving the gymnasium, Socrates spent some time in the afternoons and evenings loitering about where people gathered together, on the streets, in the markets, and elsewhere, and carried on his question-and-answer discussions with all and sundry. Apparently these discussions went beyond the physical sciences that he had been studying into questions involving religion, ethics, and the varied problems of men in the city. (It should be noted that Socrates always had some belief in the existence of gods or spirits outside of man who had some influence on men's lives. He himself often felt the presence of a spirit or, as some say, a "daemon," who advised him what to do and not to do in various crises, large and small. Even during his military service, when he made a splendid record for loyalty, courage, and efficiency as a fighter, this spirit voice was sometimes his guide.) His keenness and his persistence in developing his ideas, and his critical method of trying to arrive at clear definitions and sound generalizations, began to gain him something more than local fame. The years were passing, however, and he had still not fully realized his mission in life, when an event of some importance brought things to a head for him.

Some time about 434 B.C., near his thirty-fifth birthday,[3] Chaerephon of Sphettus in Attica, "an enthusiastic disciple of Socrates," as the *Oxford Classical Dictionary* describes him,[4] visited the Delphic Oracle and put to the Pythia this question: Was any man wiser than Socrates? The answer of the Pythia was that there was no one wiser. There are other and stronger versions of what she said, one being that "Of all men Socrates is wisest." The latter version is, of course, an extremely sweeping utterance, since it precludes any man being even equal in wisdom to Socrates. Socrates took seriously the Delphic Oracle's apparent praise of his wisdom. As Plato reports in *The Apology*,[5] written after Socrates' death but put in what are supposed to be Socrates' own words, he had been much surprised (some thirty-five years earlier) when he heard of the Delphic utterance praising his wisdom. Being somewhat skeptical, he decided to assure himself of the facts, and to explore the meaning of the oracle. Thereupon he undertook to make one of the first (if not the very first) oral interview surveys ever reported. He went about Athens, from man to man, starting with the politicians (men in the government of the city), then going to the poets (in a sense the more advanced educators of the people), and finally to the skilled workmen of the city, asking them one by one certain questions to see if they by their responses could prove themselves wiser than he. He naturally aroused a great deal of resentment among those he interviewed because the bystanders applauded him and thus confirmed his little victories over those questioned, to their humiliation. But since he was not trying to make friends or to influence people favorably, he persisted with his survey, interviewing until he was satisfied that the weight of evidence was sufficient (how many he interviewed is not on record). He concluded that no man interviewed had showed himself any wiser than Socrates. By implication at least Socrates seemed to lay claim to knowledge that belied his own probably ironical, self-contradictory, or at least illogical and unsupported statement in another connection that "he nothing knew save that he nothing knew," or words to that effect. Of course, Socrates' survey technique left much to be desired from a modern scientific point of view. He alone set the questions, decided what the answers should be, selected those to be interviewed, and then decided whether the answers received were right or wrong. And he had a personal interest in the outcome.

But what about the words of the Delphic Oracle which had started him on his inquiry? Did his questioning of a number of Athenians prove them to be true or not? Was he the wisest of men, or was he wiser than or at least as wise as any other Athenian? Socrates refused to make any of these claims. The statement of the Delphic Pythia proved only, he said, "that real wisdom is the property of God, and this oracle is his way of telling us that human wisdom has little or no value."[6] Indeed, "in respect of wisdom" the wisest of men "is really worthless."[7] In this way he confessed his own ignorance along with that of all other human beings, at the same time acknowledging the Delphic Oracle as the voice of God. This conclusion of his fits in better with his own philosophy (of which it is a part) than with the actual words of the Pythia. In short, he had decided that the oracle did not mean what it seemed to say, which was, of course, not an unusual reaction to the cryptic utterances pronounced at Delphi; the Pythia, he said, merely used his name as an example for men in general. But how could these conclusions about God be derived from the interviews he conducted with the politicians and other citizens of Athens as he went on his questioning rounds? The conclusions seem to be nothing more than the characteristic Socratic ideas with which he started.

But his discovery and admission of his own ignorance, and of the comparable ignorance of all other men, apparently helped to bring about the great turning point in his life. He felt more clearly than ever before the call to devote his life to philosophy as it concerned the lives of men. What had begun some years earlier in a tentative and uncertain way now became a full-time life mission. Men needed to be convinced of their own ignorance and inadequacies before a start could be made toward any improvement in their knowledge and wisdom—and after that they needed to be taught.

The "natural philosophy" to which Socrates had previously given much attention was now more fully than ever relegated to second place. Socrates also pushed aside to a large extent consideration of problems concerning man's physical well-being (having solved them for himself largely by his simple fare and hardy mode of life), as well as those connected with the material things that most men value so highly—money, goods, and land. What was left for Socrates' consideration, then, was man as a being with a soul, a spiritually controlled sort of being, though housed in a physical body and dependent upon a physical environment. The doctrine he developed is not easy to grasp, and cannot be adequately stated in brief form. It seems to me to have two sides: the cognitive and intellective, having to do with man's knowledge and understanding, and the ethical or moral, having to do especially with his attitudes and actions vis-à-vis the gods, the state or community of men, and other individual men. These two sides are closely if not inseparably related. Socrates argues that it is more ethical to do anything with knowledge of what one is doing and its effects on others than to act without knowledge. Man should rise to the level of completely intelligent action. To happen to do good by chance when one is acting without knowledge of what one is doing, or of its probable consequences, is no credit to man.[8] States also need to know what they are about when they act.[9] Consequently the improvement of the soul must come through the cultivation of it, and it was to this end of education or culture, as we would say, that Socrates developed his distinctive methods of education and carried on his one-man crusade to elevate the human soul or mind.

Socrates' Methods of Studying and Teaching

Socrates is generally credited with having developed a method of study that was more or less original with him, and an improvement over previous ways of studying human affairs. This method starts with the proposition that mere opinion, based upon unexamined traditions and popular beliefs by which most people are satisfied to live, is not the sort of true knowledge that is needed for the highest development of man's soul or mind. Opinion is an inferior sort of knowledge above which the soul must arise to the true knowledge that leads to goodness. To be sure of having true knowledge, men need to doubt every proposition until it has been tested and found to be reliable.

What men had put into writing was no more to be trusted than oral traditions and opinions.[10] Although, and perhaps partly because, he read a great deal himself, Socrates knew that in the works on natural philosophy, for example, there was much mere opinion, and that men differed sharply in their opinions. Not only did books perpetuate errors; they also encouraged the lazy habit of accepting what was written in books as necessarily true, and hence led to the belief, as revealed by the naive young man Euthydemus, that if one had a good library he had knowledge within his grasp. In Socrates' view of learning, knowledge had to be a living thing in a man's soul or mind. How to produce this was the next question.

In rejecting natural philosophy as a field of study, although he seems to have kept some interest in the human body, in medicine, and in analogies between the human body and the *polis* or state,[11] Socrates also practically gave up direct observation and inspection of things as a means of acquiring true knowledge. The hopeless contradictions between one man's view and another's concerning the nature of the physical earth and the universe apparently led him to drop this method of gaining knowledge. Although he certainly was observant of men and governments, it was not he but historians like Herodotus, Xenophon, and especially Thucydides who were studying human affairs by the direct observation of men's actions, by interviews with them, and by the reading and criticism of their works in the same subject. Outside of Athens, Socrates apparently made no direct observations, and he said little directly about what he saw inside it, although the actions of men like Alcibiades, Cleon, Critias, and Socrates' principal accuser, Meletus, were not entirely ignored by him, nor was the tendency of men to multiply material things, which he deplored.

But if one avoids or at least holds to a minimum one's direct observations in the study of human affairs in cities like Athens, how does one gain the knowledge that leads to wisdom and to ultimate goodness or excellence? And how does one acquire it in such a way as to embed it firmly in and thus improve the soul or mind? Socrates believed the solution lay in an oral question-and-answer, dialectic, or discussion method by which a number of men (at least two and preferably more) direct their attention to some question or proposition that is in dispute. If a thing cannot be effectively studied directly, propositions concerning it that are put forward by various persons who have come together in a group, as in the gymnasium, can be put to the test of debate to determine how well they will hold up. Any such discussion concerning human affairs must, however, first establish agreement among the discussants on what is being discussed. A working definition, even if not a highly refined and polished one, must first be found. What is justice? What is law? What is excellence, virtue, or *areté*? These are not physical things like trees or stones or water or a distant star that can be easily identified, but mental constructs, conceptual things that must be stated in words and about which there can be many differences of opinion that must be cleared away before helpful discussion can begin.

The Socratic method, so called, with its emphasis on making working definitions and defensible general propositions, has been extremely useful to later scholars in philosophy, history, politics, ethics, and other fields. Unfortunately, Socrates' failure to write down his definitions and his generalizations, to make comparisons between his views and those of others, has left later scholars unsure of what he really knew and said. In practice I find few modern scholars in political science, for example, quoting his definitions or his generalizations. They quote Plato as a rule, instead. Socrates did not do the scholarly work that he might have done, therefore, to provide continuity for the development of study in such a subject as politics.

As I have already mentioned, in Plato's reporting of discussions between Socrates and others in the *Dialogues,* weaknesses of the Socratic method become apparent. The discussants were always unevenly matched; some of them said little but "yes, yes, yes" to anything Socrates stated. Socratic remarks that read today like mere ironies or teasing nonsense went unchallenged, leaving Socrates free to charge ahead on any course he chose. The analogies that he introduced were in some instances rather farfetched, such as that in the *Protagoras* between virtue and a human face, and more confusing than helpful. The speakers seldom stopped to set down in precise language the definitions on which they had agreed (if they *had* agreed), or the conclusions about a question they had reached. The *Protagoras* is a good example. As Plato, and Xenophon too, report the discussions there are many loose ends. In fact very few of the dialogues presented by Plato seem to me to come to any clear conclusion.

Socrates as a Teacher of Political Virtue

Through his many years as a teacher, and he clearly was one of the greatest of all time, Socrates did not like to be called a teacher—perhaps because that in his day would have implied being a Sophist, one who took money for his services.[12] He did not have "pupils" or "students" under him but, in his own terminology, "associates" and "companions" who met him on a supposedly equal footing. How effective this pose was in attracting men to study with him is not known. Protagoras, Gorgias, Hippias, and others who lectured seem to have had fully as many, and they exacted pay for their teaching. They also spoke to large crowds, but I find no report that Socrates lectured at all.

That his "associates" were not always men of high ideals and virtue is well known. He consorted with all classes of men.[13] Critias, later one of the Thirty Tyrants, and Alcibiades, a notoriously unscrupulous politician on the democratic side, both had close personal relations with him. Both participated in his discussion groups but afterwards left him.[14] In these cases, Socrates learned from sad experience that it is indeed impossible to teach political virtue or excellence to some men. Although this might be taken as evidence supporting his assertion to Protagoras that political virtue could not be taught at all, I am not convinced that Socrates really held this view. I believe his statement can be put down as the tactic of a devil's advocate—intended to provoke Protagoras into making his best possible defense of Socrates' own position. The fact that Socrates claimed to have tried to reform such men as Critias and Alcibiades would indicate that he considered it his function to teach political virtue.

The evidence on Socrates as a teacher of politics, including political virtue, is very considerable. Xenophon in the *Memorabilia* has this to say: "His own conversation was ever of human things. The problems he discussed were, What is godly, what is ungodly; what is beautiful, what is ugly; what is just, what is unjust; what is prudence, what is madness; what is courage, what is cowardice; what is a state, what is a statesman; what is government, and what is a governor;—these and others like them, of which the knowledge made a 'gentleman' . . ."[15] Socrates discussed (according to Xenophon) such questions as what a law is and whether one must obey the decrees laid down by a tyrant;[16] what the various forms of government are, distinguishing kingship under law from despotism, aristocracy, plutocracy, and democracy;[17] what the functions of citizens are;[18] what is expected of a good ruler;[19] why states need to know their own strengths and weaknesses vis-à-vis other states;[20] and why obedience to law and civil concord are the highest civic virtues.[21] There is much more in Xenophon's work that is of importance for illustrating Socrates' handling of political problems; and on the whole, Xenophon seems to have done a good if not actually inspired job of reporting.

Discussing the "kind of political education" Socrates gave, Jaeger goes on to raise a different though related question: "But the crux of the problem is this: why did Socrates himself take no part in political life, but give others a political education?"[22] Thus stated the question is somewhat misleading. Athens was an advanced democracy at the time, and any citizen under its laws could be called on by lot or otherwise to perform political duties, including military and judicial services. Socrates was, in fact, drawn into both and distinguished himself in both as a man of intelligence and courage. He did not, however, make a career of political leadership, and for this he had a sound reason. In Xenophon's version, Antiphon asked Socrates: " 'How can you suppose that you make politicians of others, when you yourself avoid politics even if you understand them?' 'How now, Antiphon?' he retorted, 'should I play a more important part in politics by engaging in them alone or by taking pains to turn out as many competent politicians as possible?' "[23] Today, of course, this reasoning is still pertinent; and teachers of other subjects—economics, medicine, agriculture, and so on

—might give similar answers to the question of why they do not engage in business, medical practice, or farming, but instead go on studying and teaching these subjects to others.

But if Socrates did not undertake a full-time career in the practice of politics, and preferred instead to teach the subject to others, his incidental contacts with practical politics showed that, by example, he could teach also how ethically minded politicians ought to behave. As one of a panel of citizen judges called upon to condemn certain men to death contrary to law, he stood as a rock against conviction. And when he himself was first indicted and then condemned to death by the Athenians—really because he was politically objectionable to the rulers of the day,[24] and not for the religious and moral reasons stated in the indictment—he showed such respect for the state and the law, and for the right of the people to condemn him even though for bad reasons and contrary to their own law, as should have taught the citizens the highest loyalty to the state and shamed the rulers into reversing the decision before he drank the hemlock. Unfortunately, even the Athenians at that time could not appreciate such high-minded citizenship.

Socrates did not study and teach only politics. Among the other aspects of human culture that concerned him in his teaching were religion and ethics. Socrates was a deeply religious man who had great respect for God, to whom he frequently referred in his talks. God alone had true virtue and wisdom. The ethics that Socrates taught was not, however, an ethics of monotheism and personal conduct such as the Hebrews were developing and putting into the Ten Commandments some centuries before Christ. For example, Socrates seems to have been little concerned with such problems of sex relations as pederasty, adultery, prostitution, or coveting another man's wife, or, indeed, with covetousness in general. There was, on the other hand, much in Socrates' teaching on the ethics of justice and observance of the laws, which are essentially matters of political ethics. Thus, his ethics was very close to politics, and Werner Jaeger seems to be well supported in his contention that *areté* as used in the ancient Greek texts meant not virtue in a broad and general sense but political virtue, that is, the excellence suitable to ancient Greek dwellers in cities. Modern students of politics and students of ethics, then, both have claims on Socrates as a revered predecessor.

Chapter 8

↘ Plato and Anti-Politics

THE facts of Plato's life are in general well established and widely known.[1] He was born about 428 or 427 B.C. of respectable and wealthy Athenian parents, who on one side could trace their lineage back to Solon's family. As a boy, Plato evidently had good tutors in reading, writing, mathematics, and other subjects. He early fell under the influence of Socrates and became a devoted follower. One can imagine him in the gymnasium with other boys and young men while Socrates was holding his thought-provoking question-and-answer discussions. Being of the aristocracy, he was not gainfully employed. He no doubt did considerable reading and studying, but it is not known who his tutors were in the ephebic range of studies, except for one Kratylus and then Theodorus of Cyrene in mathematics. Socrates certainly loomed large among his unofficial teachers.

At the age of twenty-four, he was urged by the reactionary, antidemocratic party to which some of his relatives belonged to become one of their active members. He had decided to make a career of politics, and he apparently began to work with the aristocrats, but the violent and illegal acts of the reactionaries turned him against them. In the meantime, things were going from bad to worse for Athens in the Peloponnesian War, and the ruling radical democratic politicians were looking for scapegoats to sacrifice in order to cover up their own failures. Socrates was chosen the victim, and in 399 B.C., when Plato was about twenty-nine, Socrates, under sentence of death, drank the hemlock and died. The disrespect for law and the cynicism shown by the democratic leaders in Socrates' case so incensed and embittered Plato that he turned against all Athenian politics and politicians, both aristocratic and demo-

214

cratic, and gave up any further thought of a political career. He was, indeed, one of the earliest writers to spread the impression that the practice of politics is an evil business.

His friendship for Socrates made it unsafe for him to remain in Athens, or at least so he seems to have thought, and he was not the kind to stay in the face of risk. With several other Athenians, he took temporary refuge with a friendly ruler in Megara. In the following years he must have been back in Athens from time to time, using that city as his base; but he also traveled extensively. He later wrote with some familiarity of Egypt, Persia, Italy, and Sicily, and mentioned definite trips to the latter two. About 388 B.C., in Italy and Sicily and especially in Syracuse, he became thoroughly disgusted with the sensuality of the people of his general class, but he also met one kindred spirit, Dion, who was related to the then ruler, Dionysius I. Plato also met Archytas of Tarentum, the Pythagorean, whose ideas had considerable influence with him. No doubt he learned much and wrote some things in these years soon after Socrates' death.

When Plato was about forty, say in 387 or 386 B.C., he returned in safety to Attica and there, just outside Athens proper, he established a school for young men which came to be known as the Academy. From then on, Plato's principal occupation was the conduct of this school.

Over the years Plato gained a considerable reputation as the head of the Academy and as a teacher. About 366 B.C. Dion of Syracuse, supported by Archytas, and evidently with the consent of the new ruler, Dionysius II, invited Plato to Syracuse to tutor the young king in the art of government, or, shall we say, in the philosophy needed for his post. Apparently Plato and his friends had in mind a grand experiment in turning a presumably willing and able young man into an ideal philosophical ruler. But the mission failed and Plato returned to Athens and the Academy.[2] Some years later, in 361 B.C., when Plato was about sixty-six years old, he was back in Syracuse on the same mission with the same pupil. Again he failed.

Between and after these experiments Plato continued to serve his Academy and to carry on his writing until death overtook him at the age of eighty, in 348 B.C. Besides the numerous dialogues and the epistles, he left two works which, though both in the dialogue form, are recognized as being of a different stature and nature. These are *The Republic,* his greatest single work, dating probably from about the time he founded the Academy or soon after, and *The Laws,* which he wrote in his old age.

Despite the comparative wealth of his writings that survive, Plato remains an enigmatic figure; and his work is frequently puzzling and hard to classify. One must always question whether the views being expressed in the dialogues are those of Socrates or of Plato himself. At the least there is an ambivalence and inconsistency if not actual self-contradiction in the words put in the mouth of Socrates. Then too both were men of diverse moods. Sometimes they seem to be just joking, or speaking teasingly or sarcastically, and trying to provoke the interlocutor into a careless statement; at other times, even in the same dialogue, they seem to be deadly serious. Finally, it must be noted that Plato changed some of his views as he advanced in years, so that one is uncertain whether the younger or the older writer was the "real" Plato. Definite years cannot be assigned to these shifts; they may well have come rather gradually and unobtrusively.

All these factors make difficult the assessment of Plato in any such investigation as this. It has to be recognized that here was a man of powerful intellect and tremendous mental activity. The sheer mass effect of all his writings on Western thought has been greater than that achieved by any single writer who preceded him. And among those who love theory for its own sake, his is still a potent voice in every major field that he touched. My final evaluation of his contributions to the study and teaching of politics perhaps gives him a somewhat lower place in this area than his admirers can accept. But I would emphasize that I am not attempting to judge—or even describe systematically—his very important contributions to philosophy, to the theory of education, and to certain other fields that were dear to his heart. I hope that my reading has made me sufficiently familiar with these aspects of his thought to hold them in proper perspective while I consider him in relation to the specific problem to which this volume is devoted. But they—and Plato's standing in the history of Western culture as a whole—are not my primary concern here.

Plato's Approach to Politics

At least a partial key to Plato's attitude toward politics is, I believe, to be found in the clash between the high ideals of his youth and early manhood and the disillusioning experience he had first in observing

Athenian politics and later in both observing and participating in politics in Syracuse. He was no historian or sociologist with a long-run and relativistic view of life; for him a sorry example or two were enough to prove his case against politics in an "open society." Many centuries later, Robert Browning in discussing "the real problem" said:

> The common problem, yours, mine, every one's,
> Is not to fancy what were fair in life
> Provided it could be,—but, finding first
> What may be, then find how to make it fair
> Up to our means—a very different thing![3]

Plato had no such outlook. He was no realist in the usual sense. Nothing would satisfy him but a complete overturn of the existing unprincipled practices in politics.

It must be understood that for Plato "politics" had a very broad meaning. He believed that it encompassed the total life of men in communities—religious, cultural, educational, and economic activities, as well as official and unofficial acts directly connected with the operations of government. *Polis* denoted the entire community in all its facets. We are no doubt justified in calling *The Republic* a work on politics if we take the term in this comprehensive sense. In proposing therein his ideal society Plato gives attention, to be sure, to the "philosopher-king" and to the basic principles under which the republic would be ruled; but he also concerns himself with the family, the rearing and education of children, religion, the contents of poems and myths, defense, law enforcement—everything he deemed important to the good life or excellence (*areté*) of the community. Plato did not for the most part even make a distinction between public and private—justice, courage, piety, wisdom, temperance were needed in both personal and community life for the general good of the *polis*.

To achieve true excellence in individuals and communities it was essential, Plato felt, that the soul—the nonmaterial, spiritual, or mental part of each man and woman—be developed to the point where each person would know what is best in life and would be prepared to pursue and defend it. Material things, except to the extent needed for a Spartan sort of existence and for defense against enemies from without, would be firmly subordinated. (That he had Sparta in mind as a model to some extent is fairly clear, but the Spartans did not encourage intellectual interests in the way that Plato did.) Plato did not, in his program for the ideal republic, advocate greater economic production or the more ample distribution of commercial goods in order to raise material living standards. What was needed instead was emphasis on "tendance of the soul," the intellectual and spiritual development of the individual.

To this end Plato envisioned a system of *paideia*, that is, of education and culture, that would extend from infancy into maturity—but the later stages were to be for a few men only.[4] Only those destined to rule or to teach potential rulers would go on to the higher education that Plato himself was concerned to provide at the Academy. For the rest, the masses of men and the "guardians" (the next higher class in Plato's ideal society), education was to be at a low level and carefully controlled so that no "wrong" or dangerous thoughts could easily enter into their minds. They were to be indoctrinated with myths designed to justify the regime under which they lived and to encourage their unquestioning support. In line with this Plato sets forth in *The Republic* myths and analogies obviously intended to be taken seriously by lesser men. At one point he contrives "one of those opportune falsehoods . . . one noble lie . . ." (also characterized as a fiction) about the fashioning of men down in the earth and the way they come out composed of various proportions of the metals.[5] Using Socrates as his spokesman, Plato writes:

. . . While all of you in the city are brothers, we will say in our tale, yet God in fashioning those of you who are fitted to hold rule mingled gold in their generation, for which reason they are the most precious—but in the helpers silver, and iron and brass in the farmers and other craftsmen. And as you are all akin, though for the most part you will breed after your kinds, it may sometimes happen that a golden father would beget a silver son and that a golden offspring would come from a silver sire and that the rest would in like manner be born of one another. So that the first and chief injunction that the god lays upon the rulers is that of nothing else are they to be such careful guardians and so intently observant as of the intermixture of these metals in the souls of their offspring, and if sons are born to them with an infusion of brass or iron they shall by no means give way to pity in their treatment of them, but shall assign to each the status due to his nature and thrust them out among the artisans or the farmers. And again, if from these are born sons with unexpected gold or silver in their composition they shall honor such and bid them go up higher, some to the office of guardian, some to the assistantship, alleging that there is an oracle that the state shall then be overthrown when the man of iron or brass is its guardian. Do you see any way of getting them to believe this tale?[6]

There is in Plato much emphasis on truth, and yet he deliberately concocts lies or "myths" to be used in imposing thought control on the great majority of the people. This is strictly of a piece with his plan to censor large portions of the works of Homer and other ancient writings in order that no troublesome questions might be raised by the people about the worship of the gods. Truth, in fact, is to be the special preserve of the rulers. They are to determine what the people must believe. Evidently Plato's study of politics in Athens and elsewhere had led him to the conclusion that the great mass of the people could not be trusted to make correct political decisions on any important matter, and hence must be kept forever in a condition of pupilage to their rulers and betters. I prefer to think that it was his fear of the people more than misanthropism that led him to this proposal. But perhaps fear and hate were not far apart in this case.

At any rate, government was to be the sole preserve of a tiny ruling class—selfless, Olympian, all-wise men. They would know the absolute necessity for the firm exercise of power and when called upon would use that power without pity. But they would not relish the possession of political power at all and would gladly turn it over to others of their group in order to return to their studies. These were to be a totally different breed of men from politicians of the kind Plato had seen about him. They were to be philosophers and their education was to center about mathematics, ethics, and the enduring ideas of which the universe is composed. Plato did not consider special training in politics, or political science, or public administration desirable for them. His program at the Academy was actually intended to wean men generally away from "politics," that is, from the struggle for control of governmental machinery, and to purge them of political ambitions.

In this sense Plato was anti-politics. In saying this I do not mean at all that he was an anarchist or wanted to abolish government itself. On the contrary, he wanted to make government stronger, more stable, more effective, more just, and more virtuous generally. He wanted fundamental reforms in the society and in the constitution that would wipe out the evils of unofficial politics and the party struggle that he had seen in Athens under both aristocratic and democratic regimes and later in Syracuse. He believed his system of rule by philosopher-kings would eliminate these evils by making it possible for the official government to carry on its activities independently of popular control and without regard to popular protests, and still in the interests of the community as a whole as he conceived them.

The Philosophical Basis for Plato's Political Ideas

In order to create an appropriate background for his revolutionary proposals concerning government, Plato developed a new framework of ideas and concepts, far removed from practical and even theoretical politics. If he could get people to accept his fundamental ideas, his political proposals were more likely to find support. At least, this is my interpretation of his work.

There were a number of influences on Plato's philosophical ideas, none of which can be adequately evaluated. There were his early teachers, of whom Socrates was pre-eminent. There were schools of thought like the Pythagorean, which had much influence on him, and the Chaldean or Babylonian, which he came upon in his travels and which influenced him considerably less. There were his own studies in medicine and biology, which led to his drawing from these fields numerous analogies, comparisons, and contrasts for his writings on politics. But Plato was clearly a man of vigorous and independent mind, who took nothing from anyone without carefully working it into his own system of thought.

For example, Socrates had directed most of the discussions in which he took part away from the problems of the physical or material phenomena of the universe into moral and ethical fields, into the area of the soul or mind, where one could contemplate noble and admirable things and the moral acts of man. Plato followed Socrates here—but he went much farther than his teacher. Indeed he tried to create a world of pure ideas or forms.

In addition to Socrates, Plato had come upon men in various places (Dion, Archytas, and others) who were concerned with the same general ethical problems of virtue, justice, piety, and the rest that he was. He saw something trans-national, even worldwide, in these problems. Men everywhere were groping toward an understanding of them. It could not be that ordinary men, whose intellects he held in considerable contempt, were the authors of the noble if vague ideas that were circulating. There must be a higher source, one higher even than the ordinary Greek gods, for Olympian though they were, they also had many failings. He pictured "forms" or "ideas" as coming from some transcendent source that ruled over gods as well as men, and as having existed from time immemorial. Carrying the thought one stage further, Plato postulated that each such transcendent idea (virtue, justice, piety, moderation, in the ethical field; beauty and others in other nonmaterial fields) was a real entity, not a merely transient or apparent material thing. Besides these and most troublesome to explain are the ideal forms of physical things, both living and non-living. Each is an eternal, ever-present, unchanging entity, nonmaterial in nature, or perhaps composed of some material entirely different from that of which the earth is made. Thus there is an everlasting world of forms or ideas, co-existing and in contact with, but separate from, the changing, decaying physical things of the world. As the physical phenomena of the world are related to, and even enter into and include the human body, so the ideas or forms are related to the soul or mind of man. The ideas or forms are prior to men in all respects, and they are self-subsistent. They do not need man, but by study and concentration man comes to know that he needs them. All that men can do is to try to apprehend them, then to understand them, and so to permit them to enter into and to "form" their souls or minds. This applies clearly to men's ethical ideas and to their actions vis-à-vis each other in communities. The differences among men in comprehending and defining these "forms" are the result of human error and insufficiency. The ideas or forms are always there in their own completeness and perfection for men to aspire to, and to bring into their souls and lives.

To gain for themselves a thorough knowledge of the forms, men must turn away from the ephemeral, unstable, changing, and utterly confusing facts of the material life, both human and nonhuman—political facts as well as others—to a life of quiet but earnest discussion and contemplation. Reason was to be relied on, not the observation of facts and events. The nonmaterial ideas and forms were not visible to the eye, or detectable by the other senses, but at best the human senses are untrustworthy, and the things they observe are changing and deceptive. As the *Stranger* puts it in Plato's *Statesman*:

. . . Likenesses which the senses can grasp are available in nature to those real existents which are in themselves easy to understand, so that when someone asks for an account of these existents one has no trouble at all—one can simply indicate the sensible likeness [tree, or dog, or couch, for example] and dispense with any account in words. But to the highest and most important class of existents [qualities like justice, virtue, and piety, for example], there are no corresponding visible resemblances, no work of nature clear for all to look upon. In these cases nothing visible can be pointed out to satisfy the inquiring mind: the instructor cannot cause the inquirer to perceive something with one or other of his senses and so make him really satisfied that he understands the thing under discussion. Therefore, we must train ourselves to give and to understand a *rational* account of every existent thing. For the existents which have no visible embodiment, the existents which are of highest value and chief importance, are demonstrable only by reason and are not to be apprehended by any other means. All our present discussions have the aim of training us to apprehend this highest class of existents.[7]

The technical method by which men would come to know the great truths was for Plato that of recollection. Here we must return to Plato's emphasis on the soul. Under the influence of Orphic and Pythagorean concepts, but without merely accepting and combining them, Plato, following Socrates but again going much farther, placed the immortal and intellectual part of man in the human soul and emphasized the necessity of cultivating it. In Plato's view, the immortal soul was never really happy in any human body, but nevertheless needed such a body for its habitation on earth. Moving out of a dying body in order to be reborn, as it were, in a new and living one by the process known as transmigration of souls, the soul forgot what it had learned in its previous incarnations and had to start learning over again. But this learning process was not a difficult one. The soul or mind could regain the knowledge it had forgotten by the simple process of recollecting one thing, and then the other things would come easily. To quote a passage from the *Meno*: "Thus the soul, since it is immortal and has been born many times, and has seen all things both here and in the other world, has learned everything that is. So we need not be surprised if it can recall the knowledge of virtue or anything else which, as we see, it once possessed. All nature is akin, and the soul has learned everything, so that when a man has recalled a single piece of knowledge—*learned* it, in ordinary language—there is no reason why he should not find out all the rest, if he keeps a stout heart and does not grow weary of the search, for seeking and learning are in fact nothing but recollection."[8]

This attitude toward learning colors much of what Plato thinks and writes. Since the principle of recollection that he postulates is as important for his political studies as for those in any other field, it is necessary to examine rather closely his demonstration of the principle in the *Meno.*

In the *Meno* Plato again uses Socrates as his chief questioner, and Socrates as usual dominates the interchange. In this case a timid Greek boy slave belonging to Meno is used as the redoubtable Socrates' foil in an attempt to prove that all so-called learning "is in fact nothing but recollection" from a previous incarnation of the soul. It is admitted that the boy has been "born and bred in the house," but Socrates assumes that the boy's mind is practically a blank. Socrates proceeds to draw in the sand at his feet, where the boy can see it, a square divided into four smaller squares and then goes on to ask him a series of questions about it in which he uses some twelve or more different terms (figure, square, four sides, equal, lines, go through, middle, larger, direction, area, etc.) without stopping to define them. At the outset the boy's answer to the long and leading questions is simply "Yes." As the questions become more difficult, some of the boy's answers are incorrect, whereupon Socrates pauses and asks other questions until the boy sees his error. Only then does Socrates direct his questions into new ground.

Later Meno in answer to a series of questions from Socrates says that no one had taught the boy any of the things drawn from him in the colloquy. From this Socrates concludes that it is "immediately clear that he possessed and had learned them during some other period . . . that his soul has been forever in a state of knowledge . . . and if the truth about reality is always in our soul, the soul must be immortal." Meno says he thinks Socrates is right, to which Socrates replies, "I think I am," although he says he wouldn't like to take an oath that the whole story is true.[9]

The entire performance is most unconvincing and most unscientific. Nothing was done to establish first what the slave already knew or how he learned it; Socrates did act as a teacher in the dialogue despite his denials; and the conclusion about the immortality of the soul and the perpetuity of what was known in previous incarnations is quite unwarranted by anything that was developed during the exchange between Socrates and the slave.

That the soul in its previous incarnations had "learned everything" is even more difficult to accept. The implication is, of course, that knowl-

edge is complete and finished, even from ancient times. There is nothing new to be learned, ever. For the human soul it is only a matter of
recollecting what was learned in earlier incarnations.

The recovery of this forgotten knowledge was not, of course, un-
opposed. The soul had to struggle for mastery over the body, which
was always filled with sensuous desires and evil passions. To be successful in gaining mastery over the body, according to Socrates, the soul
had to use a rational and dialectical method instead of a scientific one.
It was not useful to gather new evidence; the only way to philosophical
knowledge was that which Socrates had employed—the logical analysis
of ideas and concepts, by the question-and-answer method, reinforced
and corrected by reason. By this intellectual and rational method the
individual soul could gain a thorough knowledge of the immutable
forms or ideas, achieve mastery over the body, and so be on the way to
that perfect result, the philosophical power of rulership over others.

Before concluding this brief survey of the more or less abstract aspects
of Plato's thought, we must give some consideration to his attitudes on
religion. He was insistent on the point that the gods did not create ideas
or forms, but he did have a god or demiurge create the world. One
of his main attacks was against those scientists and philosophers
who had the world and indeed the entire universe come into being
by chance, and who denied that any directing mind brought about the
creation. These men seemed to find no purpose in the universe as such,
and attributed purpose only to those creatures who had minds or souls,
that is, human beings. These same men found governments, laws, and
constitutions to be nothing more than agreements or conventions, created by the arts of men for their own convenience. Their approach
tended to put the responsibility for good government directly on men
and on men alone. They also turned the creation myth upside down by
saying that men had created gods in their own image. This revealed
what Plato considered to be the first error of these impious physicists,
namely the atheistic idea that the gods do not exist at all.

He attacked this notion along with two others that were espoused by
various men in his time. The second was "that the gods exist but take no
thought for the affairs of men," and the third "that the gods can easily
be placated by prayer and sacrifice."[10] The crucial one in this trio for
the study of politics is the second. This is equivalent to Solon's position.
He had recognized the existence of gods, but kept them out of human

affairs. Government, social policies, personal virtue, etc., were strictly human responsibilities, for which men could expect no aid and no interference from on high, from the gods.

Plato is, however, more prolix, more repetitive than Solon, and his position is not easy to understand. He sometimes speaks of God or god in the singular, as if there were but one. At other times he speaks of "the gods." He seemed to have in mind two classes of deities. One is the class of ancient Olympian gods who were by tradition definite beings much like humans, and who could, therefore, consort with and marry human beings, and in the case of male gods have children by human females. To these gods Plato showed considerable indifference, although he seems to have concluded that they should not be undermined in the faith of the people but left as the objects of popular belief. On the other hand, he built up an argument for "the deity or divinity of sun and moon, planets and earth" and the stars.[11] These were the "visible gods, and the greatest, most worshipful, and clear-sighted of them all,"[12] although below them were ranked various invisible "daemons and the creatures of the air" and underworld, to whom it was also important to pray. These astral deities were apparently for the upper and ruling class to know and worship.

In any event, the gods do not really love men, but they do their duty —and what they do is always and only for the good (*Republic*, 379b). Homer was wrong in charging them with sinful and evil deeds. Yet, in carrying out their duties, the gods do care for men, as a doctor cares for his patients (*The Laws*, 905d,e). And they can be called upon to help in human affairs, though not bribed by sacrifices. In the *Phaedo* it appears that a god looks after his creatures and their possessions. Elsewhere in his writings, too, Plato seems to hope for divine help to assist rulers in avoiding troubles. Though man has a soul or mind, he reveals more evil than good tendencies; but for this the gods who created him are not responsible. They get credit for the good in man but no blame for the evil—apparently very much in line with the Old Testament story of creation and the fall of man. The gods themselves can see and comprehend the ideal "forms" by which man should guide himself through life, but they did not in creating men give them a clear vision of right and wrong.[13] Nevertheless man, though created deficient by a god who wills only the good and moved about by the gods like a piece in a game of drafts, becomes in *The Laws* entirely responsible for his own goodness and well-being.

It must be admitted that in this aspect of his thought, Plato is somewhat less than clear or consistent. As for the Platonic philosophical system as a whole, if one accepts its presuppositions—the existence of immutable and eternal forms or ideas; the dualism of body and soul in the human being; the propositions that "body equals evil" and "soul or mind equals good"; and the rest—one can admire the skill with which Plato worked out the consequences. That his scheme of thought was, in a modern sense, unscientific is, I think, not debatable. It excluded any real search for new knowledge through the use of the senses and the general powers of human observation; it made history in effect useless; it gave into the hands of the first discoverer of the "ideas," namely, Plato, great authority over the minds of all his followers and believers. Plato himself was probably not unaware of these conclusions.

There is much more to his system, but enough has probably been said to suggest its implications for the study of politics, whether current or historical. All the answers that men needed to their questions were to be drawn by the consummate philosopher from the Platonic forms or ideas. This was in effect just to recall past knowledge, since the forms or ideas were from everlasting to everlasting, without beginning and without end. As there is back of every man-made couch or house the universal idea or form of a couch or of a house, similarly, one supposes, there hovers back of every man-made *polis* or state the true *polis*, the ideal or true form of community and of government.[14] Men make many efforts to realize this ideal form, no doubt, but in practice they fall so far short of it that Plato could not approve any existent form. That is why he, who felt himself to be so superior to most men and so much nearer to the gods, wrote *The Republic,* in order to set forth the ideal form. *The Laws,* which he put together late in life, was an incomplete attempt to describe a more workable, second-best form of government and body of laws—a sort of limited return to the world of actualities.

About all this, one question disturbs me more than any other. How did the philosopher, the Socrates or the Plato, come by his perfect knowledge of everything? Was there someone who before him knew everything, who could and did ask all the questions and who had all the answers? For Plato it might have been Socrates, although Plato's term of study under him was far short of the ideal thirty years. But who was before Socrates? Who was the questioner before him who knew everything and who aroused in him a recollection of all knowledge? And who before him, and before him? The theory that once the slave boy had received his start toward recollection all knowledge would come flooding back into his mind, automatically, complete and perfect, will not do. We hear no more of the slave boy. Furthermore, Plato himself insisted that most men, those of brass and iron, were incapable of becoming philosophers and hence were unfit to share in the power of government. They did not have and could not acquire or recollect the necessary knowledge.

A *reductio ad absurdum* in this case must appear to be a little crude, but how can one resist thinking that Plato was perhaps, in his own judgment, the first philosopher who, with some assistance from Socrates, really had recollected all knowledge? He certainly recognized no one else in his own time, and speaks of no predecessor, as his equal. Yet he affected to turn out from his Academy philosophers fit to be rulers, and tried seriously to turn a young king into a philosopher.

The Academy

Physically the Academy appears to have been a garden or grove outside and to the northwest of Athens proper. It was near a gymnasium of the kind that Socrates had frequented, and near also the suburban home or country house of Plato. Here, away from the politics and the bustle of the city, in about 387 B.C., Plato (no doubt with the aid and cooperation of others) set up the school, institution, society, or corporation (whatever it was) that came in a short time to be called the Academy (the word derived from the name of the military hero Academus; the grove had been called after him). And there apparently it stayed, through some nine centuries of time and many changes in its nature, functions, and personnel. It was finally abolished by Roman imperial decree in 529 A.D. No modern university has yet had so long a life.[15]

Placed about the grounds were altars to various gods—Eros the god of love, Prometheus, Athena, and others. Thus the place had the appearance of a religious center, as indeed it was to some extent, as the following description of its legal basis indicates: "[The Academy was] a legal corporate entity. To it belonged the land and possessions, not to Plato and his heirs. For this reason we find no mention of this in Plato's testament. According to Attic law, the institution was formally a cult

227

organization, so that one could say that the owner was the deity whose cult the members formed."[16]

The location of the Academy outside of Athens proper may have been dictated by necessities such as the lack of proper buildings and other facilities in the city. One may speculate that there must have been other reasons as well. Those who established the Fabian Society in London and the New School for Social Research in New York chose in-city locations for their headquarters, where the everyday problems of the people could be seen at first hand, and where the clashes between political parties and between social philosophers were ever present. Not so with Plato. He may have felt still somewhat uncertain about his safety in Athens, especially if he headed a school of active young men who tended to get into politics on the spot. Aside from that consideration, the city's hurly-burly of activities, social conflicts, and currents of thought at the very doorstep of the school would have been very upsetting to the sort of studies and teaching he had in mind. Socrates liked that sort of life and thrived on it, but not Plato. Since he aimed to turn his students' minds away from the confusing and ever-changing problems of current life, and toward the eternal truths, unaffected by men's opinions, he needed a place more conducive to contemplation. In this respect the location in a suburb of Athens was a sort of compromise. A spot even more remote from the city might have been ideally better. But Athens was Plato's home, the place where his friends and his property were, and a great center to which men came from all parts of Greece.

We are here interested in this institution as it was during the almost forty years of Plato's leadership in it, from about 387 to 348 B.C. It was to a great extent a "thinking house," a place for quiet, rational contemplation of broad ethical, religious, and aesthetic ideas, though not to the exclusion of such political ideas as justice and law. To some extent it seems to have been like a chapter of a society similar to the Pythagoreans, but with a turn toward dialectical discussions in which topics of mutual interest, primarily philosophical, ethical, and political, were discussed by a question-and-answer method led by two, three, or more chosen interlocutors.

Then, too, it had some of the characteristics of a small modern college or "academy." It consisted of one respected leader (Plato at first) who was the principal teacher and organizer; a group of younger assistants or associates of the head of the school who assisted in the teaching and research, and in such duties as building up and operating the library; and a larger number of young men who were the pupils or students, although ready to step in to help as they became more learned and skillful.

In addition to these aspects and functions, the Academy also became a center for some kinds of research and for practical public service. Research was done in mathematics, for example, in geography, and in the description and classification of plants. As the fame of the Academy spread, and men came to it as students from Greek communities lying in all directions, and returned to their homes again from time to time, appeals were made to its members for help in the drafting of sets of laws for new colonies and in the revision of the laws of established city-states. These requests were met to some extent, either by sending a man out to the place, or by doing some of the drafting at the Academy.

Now Plato approved strongly of mathematical studies, and was not averse to helping out in the drafting of laws for Greek communities. His final (or almost final) writing was devoted to *The Laws*. But he poked fun at the attempt to classify plants and other living things. To me this indicates, as other evidence does too, that he was not in complete command of all the work of the Academy staff. There was a flexibility about the institution that made it possible for individuals and small groups to develop their own specialties even if these were not fully in accord with Plato's general ideas. Even his nephew, Speusippus, took up empirical studies in biology, and showed little interest in the transcendent ideas, yet he stayed on in the Academy and became its head when Plato died. As far as I can ascertain, there was no direct supervision by Plato, or by any of his successors as head of the institution, of the instruction that was being given. Also, there is no evidence that any diplomas or certificates were granted.

It appears, too, that there was no fixed length of time in which men could get anything like a "degree." Plato's ideal course of education and conditioning to turn out a finished "philosopher" fit to be a ruler was thirty years, from about age twenty to age fifty. By then a man would not only have completely absorbed and accepted Plato's forms or ideas, but would also have given up any juvenile ambitions he might once have held to be a politician. The life of contemplation would be so ingrained into him by that time that he could be the perfectly selfless philosopher-king. He would be a man who could be trusted to govern all alone, and strictly in accordance with philosophy or wisdom, unimpeded by any laws.

Whether any actual "courses" (in the modern sense) were given at all is unknown. That "subjects" or "fields" like mathematics were studied is well established. (The fact that mathematics in the broadest sense has come to have, in modern times, an indispensable role in the practice of government as well as in the study of politics has only the remotest connection with Plato's reasons for making the subject so important in his "curriculum." To him it represented mind-training and the purest sort of reasoning for "forming" the minds or souls of philosophers. Its practical uses seem to have meant very little to him.) Of the specific subjects that have been mentioned as being taught in the Academy we may name these, following John Burnet's list: arithmetic, astronomy, plane geometry, solid geometry, harmonics, and dialectic.[17] This is obviously a very limited curriculum, and one composed mainly of propaedeutic subjects, i.e., those given to beginners. It offers no clue to the fact that members of the institution and students who had gone beyond the propaedeutic level were carrying on studies in geography, botany, law, philosophy, religion, and probably other subjects. There were several levels of study. Some men like Aristotle and Speusippus who came in as young men stayed in residence more or less for fifteen, twenty, or more years. After their first few years some of them helped out with teaching. Other men, Dion of Syracuse, for example, came in as mature or middle-aged men, but usually had other things to do and so remained for only short periods. Plato probably participated in teaching primarily for the more mature students.

Plato and those who helped him to plan the propaedeutic studies were evidently opposed to offering courses such as the Sophists gave in oratory and rhetoric and to discussions of current political problems as carried on in Isocrates' school in Athens at that time. Also there is no record of any courses in any physical or biological science or medicine or any of what we call the social studies such as history, economics, politics or government, sociology, or law. It is only in the reports on studies being carried on more or less independently by members of the staff that one finds mention of a few of these subjects.

Many writers have tried to characterize the Academy as a whole in a single word or in a phrase or two. It is not surprising that, like the blind men ranged around an elephant and trying to describe it from the feel of the parts they could touch—its tusks, its ears, its trunk, its legs, its sides, and its tail—they have come up with different results. I have made no attempt to gather all these characterizations together, but a sample of quotations may be illuminating:

[The Academy was a] University or college with a fixed domicile and a constitution . . . the direct progenitor of the medieval and modern university.[18]

[It was] the first European university.[19]

[It was] the first university of the world.[20]

[It was a] preparatory school for men going into public life.[21]

[It was] an institution for training rulers and legislators [and] no mere lecture hall [but] an institute for scientific research.[22]

[It was] a school of legislation [among other things].[23]

. . . the Academy was a school not only of philosophy but also of political science: it was a seminary that provided councillors and law-givers for republics and reigning sovereigns . . .[24]

[It was] a higher school of philosophy and politics.[25]

[It was] a philosophical school.[26]

[It was] primarily a school of political science, and therefore also a law school.[27]

[It was] a cult organization [formally, at least].[28]

[It] had some resemblance to the old brotherhood of Pythagoras: it had a religious basis and its activities were part of a cult of the Muses.[29]

Its only prototype was the Pythagorean order in Southern Italy [and it was "perhaps" connected with that institution].[30]

That the Academy was a community of teachers and disciples united by Eros is apparent.[31]

In other descriptions one finds these phrases: "a center of research," "a mystic cult," "a school of political science."[32] For the considerable discrepancies among these brief appraisals of the Academy I take no responsibility.

It seems to me that the sensible way to look at the Academy is as a society and institution that went through various stages of change, development, and finally atrophy and decay; and whose functions and operations changed with changes in personnel, with the demands put upon it, and with the variations in the conditions under which its members worked. It was at all times in some sense a center of study and learn-

231

ing, but it did not spring full-panoplied from the brow of Plato, as in the myth Athena did from the brow of Zeus. Neither was Plato the whole of the Academy. And at any moment in its history men both inside and outside it might well have disagreed as to just what it was.

The general idea of the Academy and of its propaedeutic studies in mathematics, astronomy, dialectic, and the rest was most likely that of Plato, and he was its first head and leader. But at the age of forty, after intermittent absences from Athens, and probably before he had won wide acclaim for his writings, he was probably not in a position to impose a rigid plan on those whom he recruited to cooperate with him, though his intellectual ability could certainly win support for a project to counteract the influence of the Sophist teachers, the school of Isocrates, and other such projects then afoot in the field of learning. A full-fledged plan for anything like a modern college or university, with which some modern writers compare the Academy, was unquestionably beyond his powers.

Just what Plato's role was in the Academy is not wholly clear. Modern scholars differ considerably on this point. Ernest Barker takes the generally accepted view that Plato did much lecturing. He says that "The lectures which he [Plato] delivered in the Academy, both on mathematics and other branches of science, and on the final studies of logic and metaphysics, to which science was intended to serve as a propaedeutic, must have engaged the bulk of Plato's thought and leisure in the last forty years of his life."[33] This idea of a heavy and long-continued load of lecturing for Plato has been attacked and certainly weakened if not completely undermined by recent research. Professor Harold F. Cherniss says there is little evidence to support this view, and that there are important considerations against it.[34] There is but one ancient reference to a lecture by Plato—by Aristoxenus, a pupil of Aristotle's in the late fourth century B.C.—and even this reference has only dubious support. If Plato did lecture, in the modern sense, and for so long a time, it is indeed surprising that no single lecture of his should have survived, while apparently all his dialogues have. Lecturing was a practice of Sophists, but of them and their teachings Plato did not approve. In his major writings he used the dialogue form, but never used himself either as principal speaker or as interlocutor.

A further word should be said about the dialogues themselves. Socrates' concern was with oral discourse, with questions and answers from men gathered together. Only from such discussions did Socrates think that men could improve their knowledge and their conduct, and thus their minds or souls, and so make for better communities. To Plato this seemed to be the right procedure for learning. He too had little faith in writing, or in the reading of what others had written. But when he had students in the Academy coming and going, and there was not enough time for him to go over every subject orally with each new arrival, he yielded to necessity to the extent of writing out the Socratic dialogues that seemed most important, and having copies of them made available as parts of a collection that became the library of the Academy. In clinging to the dialogue form, and refusing to write what would have been the equivalent of a modern prose textbook, he seems to have shown a humility concerning his own powers and a recognition of the fallibility of human knowledge—even his own!—that are not in accordance with one's usual impression of him. His apparent humility appears to have been to a large extent a pose.

Except when on his trips to Syracuse, Plato was probably at the Academy much of the time, or available at his home nearby. He must have participated in many discussions, advised students, suggested topics for study, criticized their products, and consulted with other members of the staff and society. Visitors also must have taken some time. That he had much administrative work to do is doubtful.

As to Plato's teaching of politics, certain statements can be made with confidence. He did not, as we have seen, favor such instruction for the people generally, not even for the guardians. He preferred to have their thoughts controlled completely by the select and very small class of philosophers who were to rule the city. His program of propaedeutic studies, even for those taken into the Academy, began as far as possible from the subject of politics. Citizenship training in any modern sense was not for them. History, government, economics, public administration, jury service, and other such practical subjects were not on Plato's recommended list for any category of the people. Gymnastics, military skills, music, and mathematics were acceptable, however. Even the philosophers were to be started on their long training and indoctrination as far as possible from subjects that were directly concerned with government: with the exception of law the latter were never really reached in the teaching work of the Academy. What Plato did in his own writing of the dialogues was in a different category. In those works, of course, the evils of politics were brought out, along with enough other political matter to make the evils well understood.

As to studying existing constitutions or governmental systems, or teaching politics on the basis of such empirical data, Plato expressly denies interest in such inquiries. In *Epistle VII* he says he once considered ways of reforming existing constitutions, but he "finally saw clearly in regard to all states now existing that without exception their system of government is bad" and there was no hope of improvement until philosophers held political authority. It took Aristotle to discover values in studying and teaching about actual governments.

It might be asked, however, whether one should not look at the later lives and achievements of students at the Academy to find proof of its —and therefore Plato's—influence on their political activities. This is at best a doubtful test of an institution's character, and even more doubtful as applied to an individual. One factor to keep ever in mind is that, as contrasted with the influence of a single private tutor upon one or a few students over a period of years, the influence of one teacher on any student in an institution where there are several engaged in teaching is modified by the influences of other instructors and fellow students. In the case of Plato at the Academy we must remember that he was the head of the institution, somewhat austere and aloof, and relatively busy with his writing and other activities. One doubts that he had very close relations with the younger students at all.

Nevertheless, on the theory that Plato was the Academy and the Academy was Plato, Plutarch listed some of the Academy's students in Plato's days as proof of his great influence, and recent scholars have carried forward this idea. Henri I. Marrou, for example, has added some names to Plutarch's list.[35] Marrou's complete list, alphabetized and with some information added, is as follows:

1. *Aristonymos,* identified as "lawgiver of Megalopolis," in the Peloponnesus.

2. *Aristotle of Stagira,* who apparently studied for a time and then taught in the Academy, and left Plato and the Academy in disgust, to start his own school later, the Lyceum.

3. *Callipus,* apparently of Syracuse, conspirator, and murderer of Plato's friend, Dion of Syracuse.

4. *Chabrias,* an Athenian, professional soldier and general.

5. *Chion,* opponent of Clearchus in Pontus.

6. *Clearchus,* tyrant of Heraclea in Pontus.

7. *Coriscus,* shared with Erastos rule of Assos on Gulf of Adramyttium, facing south toward Lesbos.

8. *Dion of Syracuse,* Plato's friend of long standing; later a successful conspirator against Dionysius II; murdered by Callipus (above). While exiled from Syracuse, he lived near the Academy for some years.

9. *Erastos,* ruled Assos along with Coriscus (see above).

10. *Eudoxus of Cnidos,* mathematician and astronomer, student under Archytas; stayed for a while in Athens (c. 385 B.C.); heard Plato.

11. *Euphraios of Macedonia,* adviser to ruler of Macedonia; later leader of democratic independence movement in his native city of Oreos in Euboea.

12. *Heraclides of Heraclea,* in Pontus; pupil at Academy under Speusippus and later Plato; in charge of Academy during Plato's third Syracusan venture (361–360 B.C.); failed of election to headship after Speusippus' death in 339; opened his own school in Heraclea; wrote in many fields: philosophy, mathematics, music, grammar, history, politics (on constitutions).

13. *Hermeias,* enlightened tyrant of Atarneus in Mysia (opposite Lesbos); had been student at Academy but never met Plato; friend of Aristotle, Xenocrates, Theophrastus; Aristotle married his niece.

14. *Menedemus of Pyrrha.* No important evidence on him.

15. *Phocion,* onetime successful Athenian general and statesman (see Plutarch on him).

16. *Phormion of Elis.* No important evidence on him.

17. *Python of Thrace,* who had some acquaintance with Heraclides. No important evidence found.

18. *Speusippus of Athens,* nephew of Plato; associated with him in Academy and on one trip to Syracuse; head of Academy after Plato (347–339 B.C.); switched to empirical research in biology; wrote also on mathematics and ethics.

19. *Xenocrates of Chalcedon,* disciple of Plato; head of Academy after Speusippus (339–314 B.C.); in philosophy tried to restate Plato's ideas; also wrote on the gods and daemons in relation to heavenly bodies, like later Neoplatonists.

This is the best list I have come upon. What can one make of it as evidence of Plato's success as an educator? Or as a student and teacher of politics? The list shows that men came to the Academy from many different Greek communities, and that on returning to their several cities, they engaged in military and political activities in about the proportions that one would expect men of the aristocracy to do, whether they had attended the Academy or not. The most famous of them in later times, men who made their careers in learning and teaching (Aristotle, Eudoxus, Heraclides, Speusippus) did not follow the Platonic "line" concerning "forms" or ideas, while Xenocrates who apparently tried to do so veered off into studies of daemons in relation to the stars. Of those who engaged in politics one was Plato's early friend, Dion, who overthrew his nephew's regime in Syracuse and was later murdered by another former Academy student, Callipus; another, Euphraios, led an un-Platonic democratic uprising in Oreos, and five others (Chion, Clearchus, Coriscus, Erastos, Hermeias) were ordinary tyrants or rulers, or opponents thereof, in their several cities. Then there were two successful military leaders (Chabrias and Phocion, both of Athens) and one "lawgiver" (Aristonymos). There are also three (Menedemus, Phormion, and Python) about whose careers there is insufficient evidence to indicate what they did.

I do not doubt that a more thorough study of available materials than I have been able to make would yield additional names and records of men who attended the Academy in Plato's time. On the basis of the sample before me, I am quite unimpressed by Plato's achievements in "forming the souls" of the Academy's students, in persuading them to follow the path of pure reason and dissuading them from going into empirical and scientific studies, in indoctrinating them with his peculiar views on the real existence of forms or ideas, or in providing them with political knowledge and wisdom.

That the Academy produced no philosopher who, following his training there, became a philosopher-king in the Platonic sense is obvious. It was the by-products of the Academy in other and mostly in quite un-Platonic directions that made it an important and long-enduring institution.

The Experiment in Making a King into a Philosopher

Plato's longest and most sustained efforts in the study and teaching of his peculiar type of politics, or anti-politics as I call it, were devoted to his students in the Academy. But most of the young men who came to the Academy could not spend the length of time required for the full course of studies and indoctrination that Plato had in mind for forming their souls for "true" statesmanship, and it was not certain, as a practical matter, how any who might become philosophers in the highest sense could achieve elevation to kingly office. An alternative and much quicker method of developing a philosopher-king seemed to offer itself at Syracuse. On the death of Dionysius I in 367 or 366, he was succeeded as tyrant of the city by his son, Dionysius II, who was already, no doubt, strongly addicted to the life of the court. Nevertheless, Dion, brother-in-law to Dionysius I and a friend of Plato's, persuaded Dionysius to bring the famous Athenian teacher and philosopher to Syracuse and to accept instruction from him. Plato was then nearly sixty years of age, his pupil thirty. For several centuries the more enlightened rulers of Greek city-states had, for prestige and other purposes, made it a practice to keep leading "wise men," scholars and teachers, at their courts; and young Dionysius must have been pleased with his success in attracting so famous a man as Plato to Syracuse.

But Dion and Plato had in mind serious instruction for Dionysius, not a mere show of culture. Plato seems to have looked upon this opportunity as a dispensation of the gods. He began at once to introduce Dionysius to the mysteries of mathematics, especially arithmetic and geometry, as the prelude to a long period of "forming the soul" or mind of Dionysius. The coterie of young military men, civil servants, and courtiers around Dionysius must have looked on with dismay. The social life of the court was going to be disrupted. Tongues began to wag. The austere Dion, in personality something like Plato himself, and already disliked at court, became the target of adverse criticisms. He was to blame for bringing in Plato. He must have some ulterior motive—no doubt to deflect Dionysius into philosophy while Dion took over the rulership of Syracuse. Dion was, after all, not really a member of the ruling faction at court. Soon even Dionysius turned against him and had him expelled from the city.

Thus Plato's principal supporter at the court of Syracuse was removed, and Plato himself, still valuable to the court as a cultural asset, if only for publicity and prestige purposes, was left behind as a semi-prisoner of Dionysius. In that situation he could do little or nothing to help his friend, the banished Dion, or even to "form the mind" of Dionysius. Indeed, he was little more than a pawn held by one side in the political struggle for the control of Syracuse that was then going on. Dionysius continued to show some interest in philosophical studies and mathematics, but outside events affecting Syracuse were moving too fast for him to have much time for intellectual matters. A developing war with Carthage, to which Dionysius needed to give great attention and in which he also needed the support of all factions in Syracuse, led him to release Plato to return to Athens, and to promise to bring back both Dion and Plato after the war was over.

Things did not turn out as promised, or as Plato expected. In 362 B.C., though the promises concerning reconciliation with Dion had not yet been kept, Plato was persuaded by Dion and other friends to accept another invitation from Dionysius to come to Syracuse. He arrived there early in 361 to find the strife between Dionysius and Dion worse than ever. The young tyrant was confiscating all of Dion's property, and he was soon so at outs with Plato, probably for his friendship with Dion, that Plato was kept under house arrest until, by a sort of ruse engineered by Archytas, he was smuggled out of the city and thus enabled to return to Athens.

By now, however, Plato was so fully entangled in the struggle between the rival Syracusan factions of Dion and Dionysius that other members of the Academy were drawn into it. At a time when Dionysius was absent from Syracuse, Dion returned to the city with a force of friends and supporters, seized power, and proceeded to rule the city. It was a member of the Academy, Callipus, who in 354 B.C. murdered Dion and threw Syracuse again into civil strife.

Almost any modern student of politics, knowing of the constant pressures on a ruler for daily decisions in public affairs and for participation in social affairs, of the insecurity a tyrant with a dubious claim to his position feels, and of his fairly natural belief that because he is the ruler he knows how to rule, would say that the Dionysius experiment was doomed to failure from the start. If in addition Plato's method and the content of his teaching are considered—a course designed not to teach a man about government (that dirty business) but to make a king wish not to be a king, not to get any satisfaction from his position or his power, to do the work of governing only as a matter of duty that takes him away from his real interest in the beauties of mathematics, the "forms," philosophy, and the higher things—it would seem abundantly clear that no plan could have been more unrealistic.

PLATO AND ANTI-POLITICS

Plato's Continuing Importance to Political Studies

Although Plato's efforts to prepare men to become philosopher-kings in the Academy, and to make a king over into a philosopher at Syracuse, failed completely, and he could not even bend his associates in the Academy to his anti-empirical and rationalist methods of thinking and studying, the work that he at first deplored having to do at all has lived on in the literature of philosophy and in the study of politics. I refer, of course, to the dialogues, treatises, and epistles that he—reluctantly it may well be—wrote down as convenient aids for use in the Academy. These reveal that at least in the early years he did observe and reflect upon politics as actually practiced, both in Athens and abroad. He later decided, of course, that everything in current politics in his day was inherently bad and not worth perpetuating or even studying any further. His attention swung over almost completely to the—to him ideal—system of rule that he set forth in *The Republic*, and later to the less ideal but as he thought more practical scheme in *The Laws*. These are, of course, Utopian and semi-Utopian plans that have little to do with reality. On the other hand, these works and many of the other dialogues provide numerous incidental comments on government and political problems—for example Plato's analysis of the various forms of government, which is one of the first in the ancient literature, and his excellent analysis of the Spartan polity. Later students of political theory have, of course, made a good deal of some of these passages in Plato, but there is still, it seems to me, much room for an excellent monograph on the relatively more empirical materials in Plato by a scientific student of politics and government. It is, I think, to be regretted that Plato sailed off on the wings of his Utopian schemes instead of applying his outstanding critical intelligence to realistic political analyses.

ᴐ Plato's Contemporaries

W HEN surveying the important eras of the study of politics, it will not do to consider only the greatest luminaries, the truly Olympian figures, such as Plato and Aristotle were in Greece in the fourth century B.C. Just as government and politics affect people of all levels of wealth, power, and ability, so men of all levels of ability, including those with something less than the very best minds, may make important contributions to the study of politics. They may have had practical experiences and opportunities for close-up observations that enable them to see the importance of things overlooked or undervalued by others, and thus serve as useful correctives even to the work of the Olympians. It seems to me, indeed, that in the long-run dialectic of scholarship in the study of politics, as indeed in the social sciences and the natural sciences generally, students not in all respects of the first rank have made important contributions.

Isocrates, Xenophon, and Demosthenes did not write any systematic political theories, or set forth any ideal republics. But in their several and quite different ways they studied politics as it fell under their observation and wrote their respective pieces of political advice and accounts of what they observed for the information of others. Essentially they were not systematizers and theorists; they were rather practical-minded and perhaps somewhat pedestrian and limited men. But each one had something worthwhile to say, and said it well enough so that his contemporaries and successors preserved substantial portions of his written works.

Isocrates

If one had to select a single ancient Greek scholar as the one who in his day most nearly corresponded to a typical American college or university teacher of political science of recent years, I suppose Isocrates would have to be designated instead of either Plato (certainly) or Aristotle.[1] The latter would be excluded despite the greatness of his writings in politics and ethics because he covered such a wide range of subjects—in natural science, in metaphysics, in rhetoric, and in other fields—that no American political scientist could really match him. One can hardly say that Aristotle was even primarily a political scientist. Isocrates clung more closely to the subjects of politics and ethics, disdained the field of natural science, and attempted no great work in philosophy although he professed a certain practical philosophy. His works and studies in education, rhetoric, and oratory were largely supportive of his primary interest in training men for public affairs or politics. The comparison between ancient Greece and the United States today should not be pressed beyond reason. There are fundamental differences between the conditions then in Greece and those in the United States in recent times. What Isocrates did in the study of politics was deeply influenced by the problems of his day and time. He did not even pretend to consider politics in the broadest sense.

Isocrates was born in Athens in 436 B.C., eight years earlier than Plato and about six or seven earlier than Xenophon. His parents were well established and they gave the boy a good education. He evidently had considerable inquisitiveness and wide-ranging interests; he early became acquainted with the different varieties of "philosophy" or wisdom then flourishing in Athens.[2] Two teachers of different schools had special influence on him. One was Gorgias of Leontini, the Chalcidian colony in Sicily. Gorgias was a complete skeptic about proving the existence of anything. In his reaction against the work of the nature-philosophers, he swung over to the development and teaching of a flowery, ornamental style in rhetoric and oratory; he wanted the latter to equal or outrank poetry for beauty and effect. Isocrates learned much from Gorgias about style in writing but did not really copy him. A second influence on Isocrates was that of Socrates. The latter mentions Isocrates in Plato's *Phaedrus* as a young friend of great natural abilities, especially in literary composition, who might become dissatisfied with being merely a skillful writer and strive to do greater things. "For that mind of his, Phae-drus, contains an innate tincture of philosophy."[3] Isocrates also had some training in law, probably under a third teacher. Neither Gorgias nor Socrates would have been likely to teach him this subject.

After his family lost most of its fortune when he was a young man, Isocrates needed to work for his living. Making use of his training in law and rhetoric, he spent some years writing forensic or law court speeches for others. These dealt primarily with private controversies.[4] Later he became ashamed of this work, and tried to have this episode in his life forgotten. He wanted a higher purpose and a nobler and wider arena for his lifework. But he still had to support himself. Although he was deeply concerned with political matters and had ability as a writer, he reasoned that his voice and delivery were inadequate for success in politics. Further he was disgusted with Athenian rough-and-tumble politics. At the same time he had become greatly disappointed with the intellectuals who went by the name of philosophers or Sophists. In his judgment the latter merely taught men certain tricks of speech to gain their ends; their work reflected no moral standards. Plato, on the other hand, was taking his followers completely out of the struggle for more ethical and more effective and sensible government by leading them over an endless detour through mathematics, astronomy, and dialectic: they never would, Isocrates believed, find the absolute and final truth they claimed to be seeking, nor would they get back to the practical problems of Athens and other Greek cities.

Isocrates therefore created his own middle way that would keep him close to politics but not in it, that would enable him to make some con-tribution toward improving the political lives of the Athenians, and indeed of all Greeks. To this end he opened a school to educate young men for political careers. He planned that his school would stress ethical standards and motivations in the public interest; that the actual subject matter of government and politics would be taught; that the best at-tainable knowledge would be acceptable for practical guidance in rec-ommending public policies until better knowledge became available; and that rhetoric, or how to organize, write, and deliver effective speeches on public or political questions, would be the principal meth-od used in providing instruction and training for politics.

The result was to be a number of young men who would enter politics in Athens, or in the other Greek cities from which they came, equipped with training as speakers and writers, with high ideals of public service, and with practical knowledge about government. His school competed for students and popularity not only with the Sophist teachers but also with Plato's Academy. It had considerable success in attracting and holding able students, and may have had a larger enrollment than Plato's school. A number of men who studied politics under him are known to have had subsequent political careers of some distinction. In his *Antidosis* he mentions by name nine of his former students; of these his favorite was probably Timotheus, who became a famous Athenian general.[5]

I have not found it easy to ascertain just what political content received emphasis in Isocrates' teaching. He did not publish and probably did not organize a formal curriculum in the modern sense. His remaining works do present some evidence, however. He wrote no general treatise on actual politics or on political theory. That would have been out of line with his method of teaching politics under the guise of rhetoric and oratory. As the poem was the form and the vehicle for Solon's political ideas, and the Socratic dialogue served the same purpose for Plato, so the public speech or oration form—a forerunner of the modern political article or pamphlet, each a complete unit in itself— served Isocrates' dual purpose of teaching politics and public speaking. It is known that, like a modern political pamphleteer, Isocrates wrote out his speeches in part to educate the leaders of Athens and other Greek cities, and to influence them in the making of public policy. But it is most unlikely that he would have written so many orations on public questions without presenting the same subject matter to his students. These speeches must have been at least "recommended reading" for them. Some of Isocrates' extant letters, which are nine in number, also contain political matter, mostly advice to various rulers.

Of the twenty-one speeches now extant, six are of the forensic type, prepared for use in private-law cases. These are least important for present purposes. Political content does not make up all the remaining fifteen speeches to the exclusion of other matter, but it dominates several of them, and even those that seem to be on nonpolitical subjects cannot be wholly ignored. For example, the encomium to Helen, who was involved in bringing on the Trojan War, contains near its beginning, in some paragraphs on Theseus, a neat discussion of the fears and miseries that afflict tyrannical rulers, and of what Theseus did as a ruler

243

to try to satisfy the people under him. The works that are primarily political in content, arranged in alphabetical order, are the *Archidamus*, the *Areopagiticus*, the *Panathenaicus*, the *Panegyricus*, *On the Peace*, the *Address to Philip*, and the *Plataicus*. These need to be read as a group to get at Isocrates' political ideas.

Pan-Hellenism was a major theme in his writings. Isocrates pleaded urgently for an end to the senseless and destructive wars of Greek against Greek and for some sort of union of the city-states that could make an effective defense against powerful foreign enemies. He was concerned especially about the Persian menace. When he became convinced that voluntary political union among the city-states was unattainable he turned his hopes to Philip of Macedon who had been extending his power ever more widely throughout the north. Philip was a Greek-speaking ruler of a mixed but partly Greek people. One of his forebears, Alexander I, in the early fifth century B.C. had begun to enter Greek politics and to introduce Greek culture into his realm. The process continued under later rulers of Macedon, and when Philip came along in the fourth century he seemed almost like a Greek monarch. Isocrates saw the conquering Philip as a man who could unite the Greeks, by force if necessary. To Isocrates the sacrifice of the sovereignty of the separate city-states and the loss of popular control over the government in cities like Athens (for which in any case he had little love) seemed a small price to pay for peace between the city-states and the promise of a strong defense against the Persians.

In supporting Philip in the unification of Greece by force, Isocrates clearly did not fully visualize the consequences. Philip and Alexander did not stop with uniting the Greeks under their rule. Instead they (and especially Alexander) went on to conquer other adjacent peoples and then widened their horizons to include parts of Asia, Africa, and the Mediterranean region. If Alexander had not died young, he might well have carried his conquests still further in several directions. Had Isocrates lived to see what happened under Alexander he might well have asked himself whether he was right in backing Philip as the one to unify Greece. But he died in the year of Philip's defeat of the Athenians and Boeotians at Chaeronea, 338 B.C.

The internal government and policies of Athens also received considerable attention from Isocrates in his writings and presumably in his teaching. He dealt not only with the type of constitution then in effect, but also with the political activities that affected its operation. He was disappointed with the democratic system and its leadership, and himself favored a monarchical form of organization. But he refrained from starting any local reform movement, and must have been discreet in his adverse criticisms, for there is no evidence of his getting into trouble with the city authorities.

Three orations deal with practical ethics, or the relations and duties of a man (a) to the gods, (b) to his community, friends, and relations, and (c) to himself. These are entitled *To Demonicus, To Nicocles,* and *Nicocles or the Cyprians.* Their interest here lies partly in the relationship shown between ethics and politics, but more particularly in the practical instruction given to the prince (*To Nicocles*) on how to govern, and to the people (*Nicocles or the Cyprians*) on their duties toward the ruler. Even in *To Demonicus* there is some discussion of how this young man should comport himself if ever vested with public office.

These orations make some contribution, therefore, to the earliest Greek literature on the education of the prince, a somewhat varied type of political writing that comes down through Machiavelli's *Prince* to modern times. There is a modicum of this sort of advice also in some of his letters.[6]

But the works for which Isocrates has become most famous are those on educational theory and practice generally. Many writers have spoken of him as the greatest teacher or the most illustrious educator in ancient Greece.[7] He did not reject completely the ideas of those, like Plato, who used the dialectical method of writing and teaching or who emphasized the value of mathematics and astronomy in education. He recognized that these methods and studies helped to sharpen the wits and improve the retentive powers of the minds of young students. At the same time, he felt that they had little practical value in the lives of men, and insisted that other subjects, primarily ethics and politics, were most important for mature men.

His principal writings in this field are *Against the Sophists* and *Antidosis.* The former attacks those "who profess to teach political discourse" but "have no interest whatever in the truth."[8] These men promise to turn their students into clever orators who "will not overlook any of the possibilities which a subject affords" but without paying any attention "either to the practical experience or to the native ability of the student." In short these men "not having taken [the] trouble to examine into the nature of each kind of knowledge . . ." act as if instruction in "political discourse" is as easy as teaching the letters of the alphabet.[9] Verbal cleverness and an impressive style of speaking are not enough. The subject matter must also be thoroughly learned. The orator must speak "in a manner worthy of his subject" and his discourse must have "the qualities of fitness for the occasion, propriety of style, and originality of treatment . . ." No warmed-over speeches made by others will do. A man must know his subject, and also know how to make up his own speeches for every public occasion.

Thus *Against the Sophists* hits mainly those charlatans engaged in teaching who taught merely clever tricks of speech to win points against others, and who had little or no regard for the truth, for ethics, or for sound politics. Both this work and the *Antidosis* contain passages, however, that appear to be aimed at Plato and his philosophical followers who engaged in speculations that in Isocrates' judgment had little or no value for practical living. The term "Sophist" was thus applied by Isocrates to a wide range of professors of knowledge and wisdom who did not see eye to eye with him.

The tremendous influence that Isocrates has had on educational theory and practice down into modern times deserves, and has elsewhere received, a great deal of attention.[10] It is hardly appropriate for the present study, however, for me to go into it, except to say that I think Isocrates realized better than most of his contemporaries the need for education and the advancement of learning to make better government possible.

Before leaving Isocrates, I do wish to raise one question: Did he have any consistent body of political doctrines that could be reasonably called a political theory? Modern historians of political thought have been all but unanimous in paying little attention to him. One of the most recent writers on Greek political thought has concluded that Isocrates' work can never hold a high place because "first, it is largely second-hand and derivative; second, it is very much attached to the time, place and situation which the author at the moment has in mind. He has ideas about politics rather than political ideas." His proposals for Hellenic unity, for example, are "not based on a political principle of general application." In short, "We do not find political principles [in Isocrates' works] because he himself did not set out in search of them, but only of the right way to deal with a situation."[11]

These statements are, in general, well warranted. Isocrates did not formulate a set of general political principles; that would not have been in accordance with his method of teaching. It does not follow that he did not have such principles. He obviously did have, and in the main he remained loyal to them, and consistent in what he did. He held firmly to the need for high ethical standards in government and politics; he believed in the education of the people up to the limits of their abilities as desirable for better government; and he showed the need for larger units of government for defense and security. As to the forms and procedures of government, he also had ideas, which, though they seem to be rather pedestrian, do provide a practical and realistic basis for government anywhere and at any time.

The modern author cited just above compares Isocrates very unfavorably with Plato.[12] I take a contrary view, at least so far as the specific subject at hand is concerned. Plato rejected the whole category of human politicians as evil, along with all the facts of politics and the crying needs of humanity. Isocrates accepted politics as necessary to the welfare of mankind on earth, and politicians as a necessary vocational group. He believed in educating the politicians in what they needed to know practically, here and now, on the basis of experience and historical evidence. In short, Isocrates came so much nearer to being a modern political scientist, and social scientist, than Plato ever did that there is hardly any basis for comparison. And yet even Isocrates hardly advanced to the level of foreseeing anything like a science of society or politics.

Xenophon

Xenophon was born into a well-to-do Athenian family about 430 or 429 B.C. He evidently had a good education, but who his teachers were is unknown. He had some early contact with Socrates, and remembered him with respect. As a young man seeking adventure, he participated as a mercenary in military operations in Asia on behalf of Cyrus of Persia, along with other Greek mercenaries from Athens, Sparta, and other cities. Later he served Sparta under Agesilaus and perhaps under other Spartan military leaders. He may even have fought with the Spartans at Chaeronea in 394 B.C. against the Thebans, who were then allied with the Athenians. His most famous military exploit was his part in leading the ten thousand Greek soldiers of Cyrus' army in their retreat from the scene of their Asiatic defeat to the Black Sea and home to Greece. (The *Anabasis,* his account of this military experience, written some years later, is undoubtedly his most famous work.) His services for Sparta led to his banishment from Athens, with loss of its citizenship. From the Spartans, on the other hand, he received as a reward for his services an estate that they had seized in war. He lived on this rural estate in the northwestern Peloponnesus for a number of years and there he wrote some of his major works. He evidently visited Athens between 360 and 355 B.C. during a period of peace between it and Sparta, and did some writing there, where the sources of information were better. (It was at this time that he produced a short work on the finances of Athens, the *Ways and Means,* one of the earliest works still extant on public finance.) But he was already over seventy years of age, too old to change much, and he remained a Spartan at heart. He died at Corinth about 354 B.C.

Thus Xenophon was a contemporary of both Plato and Isocrates, but his contacts with them must have been very limited. He was born a little later than Isocrates and a little before Plato, but he lived longer than Plato by about ten years, and not as long as Isocrates by about twenty years.

In losing his Athenian citizenship, and being banished from that city, Xenophon forfeited opportunities he might otherwise have had to engage in, or to observe at first hand, its politics, or even to participate as Isocrates and Plato did in its literary and educational life. He had, in fact, as a young man, developed a low opinion of Athenian democratic politics, and had become an admirer of the Spartan oligarchical system. But being a foreigner, and not a member of the Spartan ruling class, he could not participate in Sparta's politics. Neither could he observe it closely, since he lived in the country; he had to rely upon the writings and the oral accounts of others for his political information. These deprivations do not seem to have diminished his interest in politics; perhaps in some ways they actually increased his consciousness of the importance of political institutions, organization, and activities. But to me they account, at least in part, for a certain dogmatism and unreality in his political writings.

His long residence on a rural estate on which he, as owner and manager, had little manual work to do did give him much time for reading, cogitating, and writing. He also had the means necessary to acquire a considerable collection of books. And he had a wide range of interests and a facile, interesting style of writing. He used his time and resources to good effect, producing a number of works in different fields that his contemporaries and their successors in succeeding generations found worthy to be saved. Enough of his writings have been preserved to fill seven small volumes of Greek texts and English translations in the Loeb Classical Library.[13]

It would be better, perhaps, to refer to his *styles* of writing. With the works of others before him, he apparently experimented with imitating various forms of composition such as the narrative, expository, and dialectical. Because of his stylistic versatility, scholars have found it difficult to determine in every instance whether works attributed to him were actually of his composition. Furthermore, there seems to be some evidence that within his writings there are passages copied or paraphrased from the works of others, works that are in some cases no longer extant. In short, not everything he wrote was entirely of his own composition.

Against this background, what can be said about the study and teaching of politics by this "ideal squire and soldier," as Werner Jaeger characterizes him,[14] who was neither a politician nor a professional educator and who lived during much of his active writing career at some distance from the educational and political centers of Greece?

Let us first look at Xenophon as an educator, an amateur educator. He knew his own role in life, and he specifically said, "I am no professor."[15] He conducted no school. Nevertheless, in practical matters like farming, horse training, and hunting where he knew many things at first hand and from experience, he definitely aimed by his writings to educate those interested in the subject who could and would read. Jaeger in fact concludes that "All Xenophon's books are more or less dominated by the desire to educate."[16]

Some brief quotations from his work *On Hunting* will suggest the quality of his thought. He starts this work with some paragraphs in praise of Chiron (Cheiron), one of the Centaurs, the wise and benevolent medicine man and teacher mentioned in the *Iliad*. Xenophon then charges "the young not to despise hunting [which he considers highly educational and wholesome] or any other schooling. For these are the means by which men become good in war and in all things out of which must come excellence in thought and word and deed." After learning hunting in boyhood the young man "should go on to the other branches of education, provided he has means."[17] This may appear to be just a rural squire's view of things, but he finds ways to extol the training men get from learning to hunt well and to show how he thinks this education benefits not only the individual—in improving health, sight, and hearing, and perfecting warlike skills—but also the state.[18] Men hardened and made keen by all that is involved in hunting will be far ahead of the idlers and the dissolute who waste their time in pursuit of bodily pleasures. Those who toil not "do not discover what a good man ought to be, so that they cannot be pious or wise men; and being without education they constantly find fault with the educated."[19] From these homely sentiments Xenophon turns to an attack upon the Sophists, those "masters of the art of deception . . . philosophers I will not call them— because the wisdom they profess consists of words and not of thoughts."[20] They lead men not to virtue but to its opposite. He links them and their followers rather vaguely with those "engaged in robbing private persons of their property, or plundering the state."[21] As for himself he wishes his work (in writing and teaching) "not to seem useful, but to be so."[22] "In fine," he concludes, "the politician whose objects are selfish practices for victory over friends, the huntsman for victory over common foes."[23] Xenophon even contrives to link impiety to those who are misled by the Sophists into being crooked politicians, and piety to those who work at and become skillful in hunting.

It is clear that subjects of government and politics receive some attention in a number of Xenophon's works. The *Hellenica,* next to the longest of his works, which was written by Xenophon to carry forward the history of Athens from the point where Thucydides left off, is largely a military history but it has many passages relating to Athenian politics. As a whole, it is not rated high as history, and as political history is certainly not in the same class as the work of Thucydides.

The longest work of Xenophon, the *Cyropaedia,* or *The Education of Cyrus,* is an idealized biography of the young Cyrus whose attempt to take over the government of Persia by military invasion ended so dismally for him and his followers. One of Xenophon's editors, Walter Miller, says of this book: "We may best call it an historical romance—the western pioneer in that field of literature."[24] To some extent, however, it falls into the class of literature written for or about the education of the prince. Jaeger, who calls the *Cyropaedia* "Xenophon's great educational novel,"[25] shows that the fourth century B.C. saw a number of books produced in Greece that relate to the education of leaders or princes as a means of promoting culture. The generally political motivation of these books is fairly clear, but it is evident also that most of them did not have much real political content. Their thrust was mainly in the direction of morals, manners, and general culture. This is the case even up to Book VII of the *Cyropaedia,* but in Book VIII Xenophon finally reaches the principles of administrative organization and personnel selection and the personal leadership qualities that appealed to Cyrus as best for him and his empire. Here there are a number of points of interest for modern students of government but nothing of real profundity.

A small work, the *Hiero* or *Hieron,* also discusses a question that has political implications, namely, whether a despot or a private citizen has the more joys and sorrows. As we have seen, Isocrates in his *Helen* discusses a similar question.

The short work on the *Constitution of the Lacedaemonians* actually deals with the social and political system and the institutions of Sparta as a whole and reaches the subject that we today call "politics" only in a few passages and these toward the end. The book begins with the training of women for child bearing, Spartan rules on sex relations, the segregation and training of boys for state and military service, hunting as training for men, the public messes, military organization and training, the restrictions on commercial careers and money-making by the citizens, training in obedience to law, the practice of virtue, and so on. Throughout this work Xenophon praises the legislation formulated by Lycurgus, and credits it with having made this "most thinly populated of states . . . the most powerful and most celebrated city in Greece."[26] Lycurgus had, indeed, "reached the utmost limit of wisdom" in his legislation for Sparta.[27] In fact, "the compact made by Lycurgus between King and state" had been so beneficial and enduring that "this is the only government that continues exactly as it was originally established, whereas other constitutions will be found to have undergone and still to be undergoing modifications."[28] When Sparta later suffered defeats his principal explanation was that the people had not maintained their ideal constitution.

To summarize, Xenophon wrote nothing of general philosophical import, and nothing on scientific subjects, or mathematics, or on rhetoric, oratory, or dialectic—that is, if minor detours into several of these subjects be excepted, as when he was denouncing the Sophists. The center of his interests was in human affairs, and in that area he contributed something to morals or practical ethics, history, economics, military affairs, and government and politics.

As a student of and writer on politics his work was marred by several obvious defects. He started with and seems to have held to the end an antidemocratic, pro-oligarchic view (or anti-Athens and pro-Sparta). He seems to have felt that there were, under any and all conditions, certain fundamental political principles, exemplified by the Spartan political system, from which there should never be any deviation. In describing the Persian political system he could give it no higher praise than to equate it with the Spartan. The defeats that came to both Persia and Sparta could be explained in terms of their having departed from their early constitutional principles. The differences between the Spartan and Persian systems did not seem to him to be sufficiently important for elaboration.

He was clearly not a social scientist or a political scientist in the modern sense. He could not tolerate the idea of any change in political systems, or approve any system that did not conform to his rigid pro-Spartan and pro-oligarchic view. He could write encomiums on Spartan and Persian leaders, but not on those of democratic Athens. Furthermore, although the center of his interests was in human affairs, he did not see men as responsible for their own political welfare and decisions. Time and again he has God or the gods intervening in human affairs, and for reasons and with purposes that are not clear. This makes anything approaching a scientific study of politics impossible. Xenophon clearly had no such scientific idea in mind. In this respect he had not advanced to the point that Solon had reached two centuries earlier.

Nevertheless in the decades and centuries that followed, so low did the level of studies in politics and related fields fall that Xenophon's works were highly rated. His elementary and unreliable book on the constitution or polity of the Lacedaemonians apparently was widely read. When later an anonymous similar work on the constitution or polity of the Athenians was published it was also and for a long time credited to Xenophon.[29] This erroneous attribution has since been decisively rejected.

In short, Xenophon with all his dabbling in writing about politics made no outstanding contributions to the study of political theory, public law, comparative government, international relations, political processes, or political behavior. Neither did he do as much as Isocrates and Demosthenes in participating in the discussion of the difficulties and problems of the city-states in his time.

Demosthenes

Demosthenes (385–322 B.C.) was born an Athenian, and he remained one—patriotic, loyal, and public spirited—throughout his life. The span of his life corresponded almost exactly with that of Aristotle (384–322 B.C.) and covered the period of the rise of the Macedonian power over Greece and the whole eastern Mediterranean area under Philip and Alexander. The latter died in 323 B.C., only a year before Aristotle and Demosthenes.

The parents of Demosthenes enjoyed considerable means and a respectable position in Athenian society. When Demosthenes was only seven, however, his father died, and while young Demosthenes was getting his early education, his older brothers and a friend of theirs, as trustees of the family estate, were mismanaging and dissipating it. This disaster hung as a cloud over Demosthenes' early life, but also spurred him to great efforts in preparing himself for his later career. One of his teachers in his late teens and early twenties appears to have been Isaeus, an orator of considerable fame who was also an authority on the law of estates and inheritance. Isaeus is supposed himself to have been a student of Isocrates. If this is true, the chain of studies in law, government, rhetoric, and oratory may have run from Isocrates to Isaeus to Demosthenes. In 368 B.C. when Demosthenes was seventeen and ready to begin his advanced studies, Isocrates was sixty-eight, young for his years, and destined to live for thirty years more. While a direct teacher-pupil relation between the two is not reported, they had common interests in rhetoric, oratory, and politics, and in the defense of Athens and the other Greek city-states against foreign enemies.

Like Plato, Demosthenes early resolved upon a political career, but unlike Plato, Demosthenes persisted in his resolve and succeeded magnificently in realizing his objective. In the meantime, however, to help support himself he had to work as a lawyer and writer of court speeches for others to deliver while he sought to win back his share of his family's estate. This suit was fairly successful, with the result that he was freed thereafter from the necessity of earning a living and could turn to his main interest, namely, participation in the politics of Athens.

For this he needed, among other things, to improve his powers as an orator. Primarily he had to overcome some early weakness of voice and faults in delivery. Skill in organizing his materials and in writing out his thoughts in a persuasive and felicitous style seems to have come more easily, but he persisted tenaciously in oratorical exercises. He did some early speaking in the courts and in the Ecclesia or meeting of the citizens of Athens. In 351 B.C., at the age of thirty-four, he delivered before the Ecclesia the first in a series of great Philippics, or orations against Philip of Macedon, which continued over the next decade. These orations along with others, and a number of letters, are the principal source of information about his career.[30]

All along he was increasing his intellectual mastery of Athenian politics and government, and of the city's problems of international relations and defense. Although himself of aristocratic birth, he came to be accepted as the foremost expounder of the advantages of the democratic institutions of Athens. The city's other leaders frequently called upon him to deliver the principal oration on important state occasions. By modern standards his speeches would be considered rather long, and perhaps unduly repetitive, but he had the power to hold his hearers' attention while he made a thorough factual analysis of some situation that confronted them, and then offered words of consolation and hope that gave them the new courage they so often had need of.

Like Solon long before him, Demosthenes seems to have thought of himself as a teacher of his fellow citizens, but he never was a teacher in the technical and professional sense. Indeed, in the tongue-lashing he gave to Aeschines in the oration *On the Crown,* he shows a certain contempt for teachers, undoubtedly meaning the paid teachers of reading at elementary levels, such as Aeschines had once been.[31] He recognized, nevertheless, that the teaching of the political facts of life to the Athenians, and indeed to all Greeks, was one of his functions. His speeches on public policy must have circulated to some extent in written form, and thus have served the purpose of popular political education as untold numbers of pamphlets and periodical and newspaper articles have in modern times.[32] For better or for worse, his fellow citizens did not always follow his advice, but they showed their appreciation of him several times by conferring on him the city's highest honors.

Demosthenes' true role became that of a statesman or *politicus,* a leader in the government and politics of Athens, and one who was frequently sent abroad on important embassies for the Athenian state. He recognized that as a statesman he had definite responsibilities to the people, and that the latter had a perfect right to investigate his conduct in office. Concerning the statesman's duties he said: "The statesman declares his judgement before the event, and accepts responsibility to his followers, to fortune, to the chances of the hour, to every critic of his policy."[33]

His basic principles of statesmanship, in addition to complete loyalty and honesty, I would summarize as follows: (1) to inform himself as fully as possible before he spoke in public; (2) to recommend only what he deemed to be best for the state; (3) to speak, if at all, only under a sense of responsibility, on the basis of knowledge, and with the idea of informing and educating as well as persuading his hearers to a line of action; and (4) to accept responsibility for any action proposed by him that was adopted by the governing body. To this one might add that even when he was voted down on any proposal, and a different line of action was adopted, he felt he had the duty to continue to try to make the best of things for the welfare of the state. He led no movements to overthrow or even to alter the constitution in any substantial way, but used his abilities to promote higher ethical standards and wiser policies in legislation, public finance, defense, and foreign affairs. These are principles of responsible political leadership under a democratic regime such as few earlier writers had attempted to state.

Pursuing these principles, Demosthenes—at some risk to himself—made frequent appeals against rival politicians directly to the people.[34] He tried to make the people aware of their dangers and their opportunities, and to get them to put pressure for action on dilatory, indecisive, and timid politicians.

Demosthenes certainly had had no formal courses in political science as American scholars would define them today, but in his writings he revealed a broad and thorough grasp of important aspects of government and politics. He knew the political and constitutional history of Athens and other Greek city-states; the public law of Athens; the essential elements of national defense, both by land and by sea; the elements of national welfare and prestige; and the state of funds and finances in Athens. He knew something, too, of political psychology, and what is needed to keep up the courage and the morale of the people.

He wrote little about general political theory, and consequently he receives relatively little attention from the historians of that subject. But that Demosthenes had a general theory of politics, one of a highly intellectual as well as ethical nature, is evident throughout what writings of his remain.

In these writings, Demosthenes made a special theme of the international posture of Athens and the other Greek city-states in the face of the growing power of the Macedonians under Philip. Earlier Isocrates had argued for the principle of strong union among the Greek cities for defense against the Persians. Their weakness in defense, due to their intercity suspicions, jealousies, and mutually destructive wars, and their failure to see the Persian menace in its true dimensions were obvious to him. Demosthenes followed much the same line, but his attacks were directed against that other menace, the Macedonians, and his speeches concerning this threat were mostly *ad hominem,* against Philip, as an unscrupulous and powerful destroyer of the independence of the Greek city-states. Demosthenes led the Athenians in taking prompt and strong measures to defend the city, and continued to deliver his Philippics. But when Philip made peace with Athens on terms that the people approved, Demosthenes accepted the decision of his fellow citizens and the Philippics ended.

It was at this time that the longest and most famous of his *ad hominem* orations came. While the war was being liquidated and peace was being made, an Athenian political leader of Demosthenes' party, one Ctesiphon by name, proposed a state decree to award a crown of honor to Demosthenes for his work in laying plans to defend the city and for other meritorious public services. This proposal aroused the fury of one of his long-standing enemies, Aeschines, a leader of the Macedonian party in the city. Aeschines proceeded to prosecute Ctesiphon for proposing an illegal decree, but the real purpose was to give Aeschines an opportunity to attack Demosthenes and his record. An indictment was drawn up and presented to the chief magistrate of Athens and a jury of some five hundred citizens was empaneled. Others apparently crowded the hall. Because Demosthenes' reputation was what was really at stake, he was allowed to make his own defense, which he did at some length—and successfully.

His speech (oddly entitled *On the Crown*) against Aeschines was replete with abusive language, and full of bitterness and strong charges, most of which were undoubtedly well founded. I mention these points in part because they reveal the mind of a great man deeply hurt by the course of events in Athens and by the actions of his political rivals, led by Aeschines, in rubbing salt into his wounds. But the speech is important to the study of politics for other reasons. It gives one side, at least, of one of the earliest interparty debates in the history of democratic politics. More than that it presents an able though somewhat boastful review of important aspects of Athenian policy during Demosthenes' career in politics, and documents the evidence of his participation therein. With the invectives against Aeschines left out, it is an excellent example of political reporting by one who was a leading participant in the events mentioned. It could well serve as a general survey for those studying the Athenian politics of the period covered. Indeed nearly all his extant orations have this timeless quality.

Going through the works of Demosthenes, I have been impressed time and again by the breadth and depth of his study and knowledge in the field of politics, especially Athenian and Greek. Public law, public finance, international relations, political history, the nature of absolute rule, the principles of democratic freedom and responsibility, the duties and responsibilities of the statesman, the importance of an adequate gathering and marshaling of facts as a basis for political decisions, the need to inform and educate the people in a society where they bear political responsibility, the dangers of the use of bribery by foreign rulers trying to gain ascendancy over free states—all these and more are touched upon in his speeches, here and there.

But with all his knowledge of politics and government, Demosthenes did not rise to the level of insight and vision required by the political changes that were coming in his own time. J. B. Bury, the famous historian of Greece, may be too savage in his appraisal and comments, but he points in the right direction. Demosthenes was like a man in a treadmill, busy from day to day, and from crisis to crisis, but getting nowhere. He had no comprehensive plan for meeting the Macedonian menace. Says Bury, "he did not originate one fertile political idea." He devised no plans for the improvement of the Athenian constitution, or for changing or enlarging Athens' role in the Greek system of city-states. His teaching brought no vision to the Greeks of how to make their world better and more secure.

I would, nevertheless, place Demosthenes in the line of great Athenian leaders from Solon through Pericles and beyond. Like Solon and other

Athenian leaders he did not expect the gods to intervene to save Athens from its internal and foreign perils and enemies. He put the responsibility squarely on the people themselves. His was a secular and humanistic approach to the study of politics: the Athenians and other Greeks had to stand by right principles as they saw them and make the best choices they could from among alternatives in policy in defense of those principles. If they suffered defeat it would be due to the superior force of the enemy. Even in defeat, men could under such circumstances still hold up their heads and remain free in spirit to make their own decisions. As a student and practitioner of politics, Demosthenes was one of the greatest and one of those most worthy of study. While a teacher in one sense, he could not be satisfied as Plato and Isocrates were (with occasional lapses) in a strictly academic environment. In Demosthenes' view the immediate political needs and perils of Athens and the Greek world required that he be active in politics. True, he failed to galvanize the Greek people into timely and effective action to save themselves from conquest by Philip. But he recognized the danger and, unlike men such as Plato and Isocrates, he entered the arena of practical politics on behalf of his convictions. He failed, but grandly.

Chapter 10

⌐ Aristotle

More than any other ancient scholar, Aristotle laid the intellectual foundations for what came to be, many centuries later, the modern study and teaching of political science.[1] Just before him Plato took political studies just about as far from earthly realities as can be conceived. But in Aristotle's work their secular and humanistic character is firmly established and brilliantly developed. That work is best represented—for students of politics—in his study of "158 constitutions." No one before him had undertaken research so magisterial and so comprehensive in scope as this, and it is difficult to think of any to match it even in modern times, over two thousand years after his death.

His Life

Aristotle's father and his mother both apparently came of Ionian Greek stock. Little is known of his mother, Phaestis. His father, Nicomachus, was a physician, a member of the guild of the Asclepiads. At the time of Aristotle's birth, in 384 B.C., Nicomachus was court physician to King Amyntas II of Macedonia, grandfather of Alexander the Great. The birth took place at Stagira (hence the epithet "the Stagirite") on the Chalcidic peninsula in the northwestern region of the Aegean, an area under Macedonian rule. Both of Aristotle's parents died while he was young. A relative named Proxenus served as Aristotle's guardian, and evidently supervised his education up to the age of about seventeen. In 367 B.C., Aristotle was sent, or went of his own accord, to Athens to complete his education. He evidently enrolled first in Isocrates' school of rhetoric, but on Plato's return from his first experiment in making a king into a philosopher at Syracuse, Aristotle entered the Academy.

There can be little doubt that there was a strong mutual attraction between the two from the start, despite the difference in age—when the youth from Stagira entered the Academy, Plato was already nearing sixty-two years and was at the height of his powers. But Aristotle soon gained a reputation for unusual acumen and intellectual power (one nickname for him was "the brain" or "the mind") and Plato quickly came to admire the abilities of his pupil.

For some twenty years Aristotle remained associated with the Academy—first as student, then as tutor or teacher. He made a conscientious effort to absorb and reconcile himself to Plato's philosophical views and to the Platonic educational method. Plato exerted a powerful influence too on his manner of writing. Aristotle prepared dialogues that paralleled in form and subject matter Plato's output. Most of the early dialogues by Aristotle have been lost, but enough fragments have been discovered in the later writings of others to throw some light on what Aristotle was doing. He was honestly trying to model himself on his mentor.

At the same time, even in the early years, he did not surrender his independence of judgment or succumb entirely either to Plato's magnetic charm or to his doctrine of universal ideas or "forms." Jaeger is the authority for the statement that "the young Aristotle was completely independent of Plato in the sphere of logic and methodology." And over a long period he carried out independent research in areas Plato scoffed at or made fun of.

Eventually there developed a serious intellectual breach between the two as Aristotle came to reject outright the philosophical basis of Plato's thought. It is Diogenes Laertius who reports that Aristotle "seceded from the Academy while Plato was still alive." He also reports "the remark attributed" to Plato that " 'Aristotle spurns me, as colts kick out at the mother who bore them.' "[2] However, Aristotle actually left the Academy probably only a very short time before Plato's death, and he apparently would have been willing to succeed Plato as head of the school. But when Speusippus, a nephew of Plato's, received the call, Aristotle's connection with the Academy was finally and irrevocably severed.

Aristotle, with Xenocrates, another member of the Academy staff (who later succeeded Speusippus as head of the Academy), left Athens to join two other former Academy students, Erastus and Coriscus, at

Assos, a small city in the Troad near the Hellespont. To the south of them was a small kingdom whose ruler, Hermeias, a eunuch and former slave, had cultural ambitions. In this area, and to some extent under Hermeias' protection, Aristotle found opportunities to do some lecturing, to discuss with Hermeias the public problems of Hermeias' small state, and to begin studies in biology, especially marine biology, that grew into one of his major scientific interests. (Aristotle's biographers, in searching for influences on his scientific interests, have pointed to his origins in Ionia, land of scientists, and to his father's profession as doctor and scientist; but it must be remembered that Aristotle was still a young boy when his father died and that he left Stagira at the age of seventeen. Of course he may have kept some of his father's books and instruments.) It was during this period of his life that he married a niece of Hermeias'. He also lived for a time on the island of Lesbos where he carried on his scientific studies.

A continuation of this idyllic life was not to be. Philip summoned an apparently willing Aristotle to come to Macedonia, less than 300 miles away, to tutor his thirteen-year-old son Alexander in a manner that would fit him to rule an expanding empire. Plato had tried his hand at the education of a prince with very sorry results. Aristotle's opportunity was a much more promising one, and Aristotle himself far more realistic. The years between 342 and 336 B.C. when Aristotle was at Pella, close to the Macedonian court, gave him opportunities to observe close at hand monarchical government and administration, and probably a great deal of time to pursue his own reading, studies, and writing. It is hard to imagine Aristotle giving full time to the teaching of one boy in what would be essentially secondary school subjects—reading, mathematics, elementary science, history, government, music, and the rest. Aristotle's strong and active intellect must have been at work during these years at Pella preparing for what he would do on the day Alexander came of age and was called by his father into a more active role in Macedonian affairs, both civil and military.

That day came even sooner than expected. Before he was twenty, Alexander had important duties to perform at the imperial Macedonian capital while his father led his military forces in western Asia. By 336 Philip was dead at an assassin's hands, and Alexander succeeded to his place. The formal education of the prince was at an end, and Aristotle was free to go on to other things.

With a liberal endowment from Alexander and under Macedonian protection, Aristotle returned to Athens and set up a school, the Lyceum. (On one side of the building in which the school was housed was a long, columned, and roofed-over walk called the *Peripatos,* where teachers and students could stroll up and down while thinking and conversing. This gave the public a reason for calling it the Peripatetic school, while the name Lyceum came from the surroundings in which the school stood.) For a dozen years Aristotle held a special status in Athens. Antipater, who served the Macedonian throne firmly and intelligently as chief administrator of Macedonia and Greece while Alexander was engaged in his Asiatic campaigns, gave strong personal support to his king's former tutor, which kept in check the grumblings of the anti-Macedonian leaders in the city, Demosthenes among them, against Aristotle. But with Alexander's death in 323, overt hostility increased. Aristotle, remembering the case of another teacher, Socrates, turned his school over to Theophrastus and left the city, remarking that Athens should not be given the opportunity to sin twice against philosophy. He died the following year, at the age of sixty-two.

Aristotle and the Lyceum

When Aristotle established the Lyceum about 335 B.C. he was, at the age of fifty, ready to do the greatest work of his career, in teaching, in research, and in writing. The years had eroded away the influence of Plato on his philosophical, scientific, and social ideas (though vestiges of Platonism remained with him to the end). Aristotle now had developed rather fully the historical and empirical approach to intellectual study that had effectively invalidated for him the Platonic concept of self-subsistent ideas or forms existing separately from, yet with a one-for-one correspondence to, all "sensible" things. Basically this Platonic doctrine reflected a distrust in the ability of mankind to acquire anything but misleading opinions—never true knowledge—by the use of the senses. Aristotle argued cogently (in the *Metaphysics*[3]) against the whole doctrine of ideas: he declared that it posited a doubling of things for no useful purpose; that it contributed nothing to an understanding of the real world, since the ideas were not causes of anything; that it had the essence of a thing existing in complete separation from the thing itself, which he thought impossible; and so on. For these rejected doctrines, Aristotle substituted an acceptance of the sensible world and its manifold phenomena as real and as important for men to study; and he proposed a scientific method of studying phenomena that would enlarge and improve man's knowledge. First it was necessary to examine all that could be learned about what earlier men had thought and written in the struggle for truth in every field of potential knowledge. Then would follow a tentative classification of the fields of knowledge based on their characteristics and differences; an ample gathering of specimens of actual objects in any field to be studied, including written materials like laws and histories in the areas of human affairs; an intensive study and further classification of these; and so on through to the writing of a reasoned account of the phenomena observed, and the providing of answers as far as possible to questions that had arisen.

It was this general philosophy on which the program of the Lyceum was based. The Lyceum was obviously quite different from Plato's Academy, which was still in operation not far away, under the headship of Xenocrates, Aristotle's old associate. Since the great reversal suffered by Plato in the affair of Dion versus Dionysius II of Syracuse, the Academy had been under the shadow of public suspicion. It was officially tolerated, as were many other institutions and practices in Athens, under the rule of Alexander and his regent Antipater, whose policy it was to disturb the Athenians as little as possible in order to win them over. But it seems not to have received any special support from the Macedonian court as Aristotle's school did; and the latter soon forged ahead in popular esteem.

(The later fortunes of the two schools, it should be noted, were reversed. Protected in part by its financial endowment, by its relative obscurity, and by its avoidance of controversial subjects, the Academy outlived the Lyceum by nearly eight hundred years. It followed current trends in philosophy and gave cultural instruction and inspiration to its students, Greeks, Romans, and others. The Lyceum, on the other hand, endured for only sixty-seven years, from 335 to 268 B.C. After Aristotle it enjoyed a vigorous and productive career for thirty-four years under Theophrastus, and then a period of twenty years of relative decline under Strabo.)

The principal difference between the two schools lies in the way knowledge was sought. Aristotle's Lyceum was to a large extent a research institution, a place for gathering, organizing, and interpreting large bodies of empirical data, and for preparing out of them useful compilations of information and scientific handbooks.[4] While Plato had permitted his associates to engage in their own researches even within the walls of the Academy, he had never made empirical research a part of the Academy program—this would have been inconsistent with his view that all learning is merely the recovery or recollection of what mankind had known for ages past, time out of mind. Aristotle took the opposite or empirical view: that there is much left to be learned by the rational use of our senses, and that a thorough stock-taking of past experience and of the facts in the world around us will yield knowledge never before brought together. His was a progressive view of science and of learning—but to realize its possibilities would require great, intelligent, and organized effort.

Aristotle must have discussed his future school at Athens, in principle if not in actual hope of its realization, with a number of the rulers and scholars with whom he associated in the years he was away from that city. But whatever credit may be due to men like Theophrastus, Eudemus, Erastus, and Coriscus, or to Philip, Alexander, and Hermeias, I think it is safe to say that the responsibility for planning the Lyceum's program, for setting its objectives, and for establishing its general nature was primarily Aristotle's. He controlled the expenditure of the endowment from Alexander out of which the purchase of the buildings and the other expenses of the school were evidently paid. He undoubtedly selected the members of the staff who were to be associated with him in the enterprise, some of whom like himself had initially started in the Academy under Plato. He developed the research projects to be carried out.

Among these projects were several compilations of lengthy lists, some of which now seem rather odd. One was a list of the winners of the Pythian games, from earliest times until their discontinuance about 394 B.C. This work may have begun, with Aristotle's nephew Callisthenes assisting him, even before the Lyceum was established. Other lists were compiled to record and date the dramatic performances given at Athens, and the competitions, festivals, and celebrations held several times a year in Athens in honor of the god Dionysus. Another kind of collection brought together claims or pleas of city-states with respect to boundary disputes.[5] This is sometimes referred to as a collection of cases in international law. The compilation of all these lists, which aided in establishing a correct chronology of events, served public purposes and was well received by the authorities. For Aristotle and the Lyceum this kind of work thus resulted in improved public relations; it also enabled the Lyceum's staff to gain access to important archives for historical studies.

Aristotle apparently developed the practice of employing special assistants for these collecting and compiling projects. He also assigned to leading associates on his staff historical projects of another kind. The plans for the school covered a wide range of fields of knowledge, and Aristotle selected men on the basis of their subject-matter interests and special fields of knowledge. One requirement seems to have been made of all these associates, namely, that each prepare a history of the work previously done by scholars in whatever field was being investigated. This was in accordance with Aristotle's belief that one cannot know any scientific field thoroughly without knowing its development from the beginning. Aristotle is reported to have made the following division of responsibilities among his staff: Theophrastus, the history of physical studies and metaphysical systems; Eudemus, the history of arithmetic, geometry, and astronomy; Menon, the history of medicine; Aristotle himself, the history of the study of politics, of ethics, and of general philosophical systems. Aristotle seems not to have written separate works on the histories of these studies, but to have worked his findings into his lectures and texts where appropriate. In the *Politics*, for example, he describes and criticizes the political writings and ideas of such predecessors as Plato and Hippodamus.

The Lyceum was, then, a well-organized research center with a definite program. Primarily for research, but also probably for student use, Aristotle saw to it that a library was collected—"the first considerable collection of books that we know of on European soil . . ."[6] It is evident, too, that there were collections of specimens and perhaps of maps, instruments, and other things useful to research and to studies in the natural sciences and other fields.

But if it was a research institution, it was also a place for teaching. Aristotle himself lectured and so undoubtedly did Theophrastus and others in their respective fields. According to tradition, Aristotle lectured on the more difficult subjects in the morning, on the more popular and less difficult ones in the afternoon. There were also social events, such as meals in common on certain occasions. Presumably the assistants and more advanced students were invited to these.

As to the numbers of students, their maturity, where they came from, how long they stayed, how they studied, and what they did later, the record is very meager. Students came from Athens and from throughout the Alexandrian empire. Aristotle himself was apparently not an outstanding speaker, but Theophrastus evidently was. The latter is reported by Diogenes Laertius to have lectured to as many as two thousand students, but there is no such report for Aristotle. His morning discussions on the more difficult subjects were probably attended by small numbers of advanced students, his more popular afternoon lectures by larger numbers of less advanced students. But I have failed to find any lists of his students, and one of his principal biographers, Werner Jaeger, thought the discovery of a previously unreported but important student of Aristotle's, Diocles of Carystus, to be worthy of an appendix in his biography of Aristotle.[7]

Aristotle as Student and Teacher of Politics

Aristotle's outstanding political studies should not be seen as isolated peaks of his achievements. He was an important originator in various areas: "inventor of the notion of intellectual development in time," "the father of logic," "discoverer of psychophysical relations," "creator of philology," "founder of the history of philosophy and science," "founder of scientific philosophy"[8] are, among others, firsts that have been attributed to him. If the general high level of his achievements would be exceptional in any era, the wide range of his interests was not, for the Greece of his age, unusual. It is well to remind ourselves that the subdivision of knowledge into separate categories was much less elaborate then than now. While Aristotle assigned to his associates at the Lyceum and to himself "specialized" areas of concentration, these were in modern terms very broad indeed. In writing on politics, for example, Aristotle, in line with the common practice of his day, deals with problems of the family (sociology), economics, ethics, even anthropology and psychology, as well as government and "politics" in the narrow sense.

There is even a relation between Aristotle's biological studies and his approach to politics. He saw man as an animal and a part of nature. His observations revealed to him common anatomical features and functional processes in men and other animals, and also similar traits of behavior and organization in the communities of men and the various types of animal groups. He came to consider man as subject to natural

266

law as well as to man-made laws. But he kept one distinction clearly in mind, the possession by men of souls or the faculty of reason, and the ability of men to understand the laws of nature and to transcend them, even to improve upon them, by conscious and deliberate acts of will based on knowledge. Man is a part of nature, but he is able to reshape, to some extent, his own nature and even his natural environment to suit his needs and purposes. It is his special function to seek "the good" for himself and his kind. Aristotle believed that in the world there is a general movement toward the best organization and functioning of things. The *polis* is a natural product of man's striving for the good, and the *polis* in turn becomes a means for further progress toward the good life.

In this progress, general education is an essential. "The whole of a state [i.e., the whole body of its members] has one common end. Evidently, therefore, the system of education in a state must also be one and the same for all, and the provision of this system must be a matter of public action. It cannot be left, as it is at present, to private enterprise, with each parent making provision privately for his own children, and having them privately instructed as he himself thinks fit. . . . We must not regard a citizen as belonging just to himself: we must rather regard each citizen as belonging to the state."[9] So writes Aristotle in the *Politics*. "All would agree that the legislator should make the education of the young his chief and foremost concern. . . . the constitution of a state will suffer if education is neglected. . . . The citizens of a state should always be educated to suit the constitution of their state."[10] (It must be noted, as Professor Barker puts it, that "the constitution, in Aristotle's view, is 'not only an arrangement of offices,' but also 'a way of life.' "[11]) Aristotle goes on: "The type of character appropriate to a constitution is the power which continues to sustain it, as it is also the force which originally creates it. The democratic type of character creates and sustains democracy; the oligarchical type creates and sustains oligarchy; and as the progression ascends each higher type of character will always tend to produce a higher form of constitution. In the second place every capacity, and every form of art, requires as a condition of its exercise some measure of previous training and some amount of preliminary habituation. Men must therefore be trained and habituated before they can do acts of goodness, as members of a state should do."

In these passages Aristotle concedes the right of every state, no matter what the form of its government, to indoctrinate the young in the principles of its governmental system; the government of Sparta was, of course, already doing this, and Plato also approved of the idea. Aristotle clearly believes that only through compulsory education by the state of all the young potential citizens in the principles of its political system could any form of government be assured of long continuance.

It is interesting to note that he places democracy at the bottom of his scale of the forms of government. The good life, in his view, could best be promoted under a "higher form of constitution." But he was always the relativistic scientist in his studies, not the politician trying actively to reform the world. One seeking to increase man's store of knowledge should, he felt, gather large bodies of specimens and data, as comprehensively as possible, without bias, revulsion, or squeamishness. As in biology this meant handling the lowest forms of life as well as the highest, and all the bodily parts and organs with equal care, in order to understand them all in relation to life as a whole,[12] so in politics it required the careful study not only of one's ideal form of government, but of every form. From extreme democracies through various intermediate forms to utter tyranny—all forms must be examined and compared as to their nature, operations, and consequences, logically, carefully, and impartially. If after examination one concluded that a given form of government did not encourage moral virtue, intellectual virtue, justice, friendship, and continence—all of which contribute to the good life— one might point out improvements that should be made. But Aristotle did not take as his province the implementing of them.

In this connection it should perhaps be stressed that Aristotle apparently never seriously entertained an ambition for a political career as Plato did. True, Aristotle associated on a friendly basis with rulers like Philip and Alexander and Hermeias; his relations with the Macedonian regent, Antipater, were also cordial. That he advised these rulers on political matters is well known. That he was privy to some of their plans, and may even have acted as a go-between for Philip and Hermeias when the former was laying plans for a campaign against Persia, seems to be fairly well documented. But Aristotle knew his place as scholar. He did not, like Plato, turn against politicians or try to make over any ruler into his model of a philosopher-king. He did not participate in any conspiracies against existing rulers as Plato seems to have done while Dion was striving first to reform and then to oust Dionysius II of Syracuse.

He was content to be adviser when called upon; otherwise he played the role of scientific observer.

As teacher at the Lyceum Aristotle was one of the earliest, and certainly one of the most scholarly and influential, lecturers on politics. Further, he either wrote out many of his lectures himself or allowed his associates or students to do so. At any rate at least some of them were collected in the *Politics,* no doubt with some revision and additions, to make up the first really important text on the subject to be put together in ancient times. Plato had been forced to write out materials in the dialogues for student use, but he had continued to insist upon the superiority of the spoken word and to condemn the written word as likely to be misleading. He of course was trying to "form souls" not really to convey scientific information, although he did raise and discuss significant scientific questions. But Aristotle, who had devoted himself to collecting data and who believed in the necessity of cumulative growth and persistent refinement of scientific knowledge, recognized the importance of leaving a written record of his findings for future scholars to examine, learn from, and correct as they were able.

(It may be of interest to note that Aristotle's most famous pupil, Alexander, apparently did not approve of writing out for all to read the intellectual mysteries into which Aristotle had initiated him. For when he heard of the publication of some treatises by Aristotle, he wrote: "Alexander to Aristotle, greeting. You have not done well to publish your books of oral doctrine; for what is there now that we [Alexander?] excel others in, if those things which we have been particularly instructed in be laid open to all? For my part, I assure you, I had rather excel others in the knowledge of what is excellent, than in the extent of my power and dominion. Farewell."[13] His letter does indicate that he clearly valued highly Aristotle's instruction, as Dionysius II at one stage had valued Plato's.)

In the writing Plato did do it must be admitted that he had one advantage over Aristotle. The latter wrote his lectures and treatises as a scientist would, in a clear prose style but generally without literary flourishes or embellishments. Plato, on the other hand, was a master of style, and in modern times appears to have many more readers.

But for our purposes here this defect, if such it may be called, in Aristotle's writing is far outweighed by a most significant change he initiates in the handling of political materials. Plato's use of the dialogue form to put forth political and other ideas through the mouths of others made it possible for Plato, at least to a large extent, to avoid coming out flatly as holding or denying certain views. In the dialogues of Plato it was apparently always others who were expressing their views. Where the dialogue was not a patent sham, as it was in some cases, it was difficult if not impossible to pin a certain belief on Plato, and also hard to find out what had actually been decided in the exchange between participants. Aristotle on the other hand made his own position clear, and wrote out his ideas so that he was on record in a way that could not be denied. Later writers could then go on from there and show wherein he was wrong, or how his views could be made more accurate and scientifically defensible. Aristotle's forthright statement of what he had found through investigation and what conclusions he based on those findings marked a point from which progress could be made in building up a science of politics in later times.

Aristotle himself saw politics as a science, the highest of the sciences. He saw it also as closely connected with the study of ethics. Two works on the latter subject are attributed to him. The one entitled the *Nicomachean Ethics* was named after, and was perhaps edited by, his son Nicomachus. The other, which is both shorter and less closely related to the subject of politics, is entitled the *Eudemean Ethics*, after his student and associate, Eudemus of Rhodes. In the *Nicomachean Ethics*, where he endeavors to define "the supreme good," that toward which human actions should be directed, he comments:

Now it would seem that this supreme End must be the object of the most authoritative of the sciences—some science which is pre-eminently a master-craft. But such is manifestly the science of Politics; for it is this that ordains which of the sciences are to exist in states, and what branches of knowledge the different classes of the citizens are to learn and up to what point; and we observe that even the most highly esteemed of the faculties, such as strategy, domestic economy, oratory, are subordinate to the political science.[14]

At the end of this work, after discussing the need for public education as an aid in promoting the good life, Aristotle turns to the necessity for the educator to know the principles of government in a scientific way. Mere practice or experience is not enough. The Sophists, whom he attacks at this point, fall short in both respects, yet they seem to think that anyone can pick out of the laws existing in different places those that will be best for any *polis* to adopt. Aristotle holds that only the experts in an art can judge correctly, and that "Laws are the product, so to speak, of the art of politics . . ." The mere possession of a collection of laws, or of handbooks on the subject, as in medicine, will not make an expert. Practical experience and a trained faculty of judgment are needed. Given these two things, he says,

Very possibly . . . collections of laws and constitutions may be serviceable to students capable of studying them critically, and judging what measures are valuable or the reverse, and what kind of institutions are suited to what national characteristics. . . .

As then the question of legislation has been left uninvestigated by previous thinkers, it will perhaps be well if we consider it for ourselves, together with the whole question of the constitution of the State, in order to complete as far as possible our philosophy of human affairs.

We will begin then by attempting a review of any pronouncements of value contributed by our predecessors in this or that branch of the subject; and then on the basis of our collection of constitutions [at this point the editor of the Loeb Classical Library edition inserted the following note: "Aristotle compiled, or caused to be compiled, descriptions of the constitutions of 158 Greek states: of these the *Constitution of Athens* alone survives"] we will consider what institutions are preservative and what destructive of states in general, and of the different forms of constitution in particular, and what are the reasons which cause some states to be well governed and others the contrary. For after studying these questions we shall perhaps be in a better position to discern what is the best constitution absolutely, and what are the best regulations, laws, and customs for any given form of constitution. Let us then begin our discussion.[15]

Thus in a few sentences this passage outlines briefly the plan of the central books of the *Politics*. In Book II of that work Aristotle examines the ideas of writers who preceded him on the subject of the ideal or best state, with a few important examples of actual constitutions. In Books III–V he summarizes to some extent and analyzes the constitutions and the political experiences of certain states under their constitutions with respect to citizenship (Book III); the types and classes of constitutions and how they were established (Book IV); and the causes of revolutions and other modes of change in established governments (Book V). The closing books of the *Politics* deal with theory, ideals, and education, including the topic of what is the best constitution. Books III–IV present the earliest known extensive and detailed comparative study of actual systems of government. They are based on the empirical data from the "collection of constitutions" referred to in the passage from the *Nicomachean Ethics*—incidentally, the only significant reference to this major data-collecting and research project that I have found in his writings. Of course, the factual knowledge Aristotle displays in the *Politics* came from a variety of sources: he had traveled widely, interviewed many scholars and leaders in government, and read the works of leading authorities in many fields; while the scientific and philosophical principles which underlie the work were the result of association and discussion with many colleagues over many years. The research project, in other words, is not the whole of the *Politics,* but it deserves special emphasis here because it introduces a new dimension to the study of politics.

The "Collection of Constitutions"

First of all in discussing Aristotle's "collection of constitutions" we face a problem of terminology.

To begin with the most elementary and obvious consideration, one does not collect the constitutions of states as physical things like sea shells, pictures, coins, or specimens of ore are collected. A constitution is something intangible and variable; its constituent elements are debatable even in the place in which the constitution is known or supposed to exist. It is a more or less integrated but ever changing group of understandings as to governmental organization, powers, and practices among the people in an independent community. The constitution of Thebes, for example, would have to remain at Thebes as a part of the organized life of its people—it could not be "collected" and brought to Athens; and even the men of Thebes would disagree as to just what it included and how it should be interpreted. In modern times there has developed a widespread practice of writing down the basic constitutional agreements in a single document, like the Constitution of the United States, or, for Canada, the British North America Act. Today such formal written documents are numerous and important. Anyone can acquire copies of them and thus, in a sense, collect "constitutions." But in so doing one does not get the entire constitution; nor can any individual fully understand the entire constitution, no matter how learned he may be.

In ancient Greek city-states some distinction was made between different kinds of laws. Their learned and experienced men, Aristotle among them, as in his comment in the *Nicomachean Ethics* quoted above, recognized that certain sorts of agreements or laws, those that dealt with the organization and powers of the government, the ones that were nearly always changed when, say, democracy replaced tyranny or oligarchy, belonged to a category different from and superior to laws on such matters as marriage, property, and misdemeanors.[16] But they never developed completely the modern idea of a written document called a constitution that stood apart from and above other laws. Hence it was not a number of such documents that Aristotle collected.

What he did assemble in a physical sense was a library composed of a great variety and a large number of books or documents pertaining to the government of the city-states. These were in a manner of speaking the "specimens" that had to be examined as the first stage in the great research project on politics that Aristotle had planned. With this mass of materials at hand he was ready to select out the significant data for his purposes and analyze them. Theodor Gomperz, among others, has suggested that the next stage in the project was the making of a kind of digest; he postulates a volume—now lost—called the *Polities*, which "contained the description, in alphabetical order, of 158 constitutions of single states and confederations."[17] The third and final stage in this view was the preparation of the *Politics*. I regard this as a reasonable and necessary explanation. "Collection of constitutions" may be taken, then, to be a kind of shorthand way of referring to the first two stages of the research project: collecting materials and compiling "constitutions," or summaries of the formal governmental organization and operation of certain places.

The use of the word "constitution" remains somewhat misleading for Americans and other Westerners. It is actually not a Greek word at all, but one of Latin derivation. It originally meant something that is formally enacted or decreed by a higher authority for a lower one to obey, not something that arises naturally or by agreement, although the latter is implied in modern democratic parlance. The basic Greek word that is involved in all the ancient Greek documents and other writings on government is not "constitution" but *politeia* (plural, *politeiai*), which is of course related to *polis*. *Politeia* is sometimes translated as "polity" but since "constitution" is the word more commonly used in connection with Aristotle's phrase, it is the one I will use here.

273

Terminology aside, there are a number of interesting questions about the "collection of constitutions" in its various aspects that have aroused scholarly speculation.

Since Aristotle's library itself has disappeared, we have to make the best guesses we can about its contents. The documents in it were for the most part presumably written on papyrus. The sheets would vary in breadth and height from about fifteen by nineteen inches to much smaller dimensions. For recording lengthy accounts, these sheets would be glued together end to end, so that the typical book became a roll, sometimes as long as thirty-five feet. It seems reasonable to assume that there was a core of "standard" works in the library—the writings of general historians, scientists, philosophers, poets, dramatists, statesmen, and others. References to these appear in the *Politics* as well as in other of Aristotle's books. In addition, especially for the second stage of the project, he must have thought it important to obtain local materials that would yield specific information on the constitutions of the various places. Unquestionably written laws existed in all but the smallest places. Some such laws were posted in public places where they could be copied. But there was another class of local materials that I believe to have been even more readily available. At some time perhaps late in the sixth century B.C., local oral traditions and accounts of historical events in the various city-states began to be written down in prose, and so became increasingly available to the growing numbers of citizens who could read. What scholars in large and well-known cities did in this respect, writers in smaller and more obscure places would be likely to emulate. No doubt many of the earliest writers had little experience in writing chronologies and histories, but as the trend gathered momentum techniques must have improved. By the time of Aristotle, logographers—as these early chroniclers came to be called[18]—must have furnished many compilations of materials about a city-state here and another there. It seems safe to assume that these accounts contained a great deal of information on local governments; indeed, the central theme of municipal histories after the preliminary settlements have been described and the principal citizens and families catalogued is almost bound to be the organization and work of the city's government. At any rate it seems agreed by most recent writers on the fifth and fourth centuries of Greek history that the local chronicles were important sources for Aristotle's digest of constitutions.[19]

Traditionally the number 158 has been associated with Aristotle's collection. Diogenes Laertius, who flourished about five hundred years after Aristotle, was apparently the first to use it ("Constitutions of 158 Cities"), and scholars since his time have generally accepted it.[20] Not all, however, clearly state whether they think Aristotle's collection consisted of 158 separate constitutions (some places being represented by several when their basic constitutional law changed decisively over time—Athens alone apparently had eleven such different constitutions[21]) or the constitutional histories of 158 different cities. Aristotle himself does not mention a number, nor does he say that all the cities were Greek, although the latter assumption is made by a number of distinguished authorities. W. D. Ross, for one, refers to Aristotle's "account of 158 Greek constitutions."[22]

Probably the exact number of constitutions or constitutional histories will never be satisfactorily determined. It may be of some interest, however, that my research assistants were able to compile a list of 116 states, both Greek and non-Greek, mentioned by Aristotle in his writings or by other authors who linked Aristotle with the place in some manner.[23] Of these 116, 77 (including all those of the total list that are definitely not Greek—Babylon, Carthage, Ethiopia, India, Italy, Macedon, Persia, and Spain) are mentioned in the *Politics*. The fact that less than half of 158 states are mentioned in the *Politics* does not, of course, invalidate the statements of Ross and others. Aristotle may well have felt it unnecessary to mention in the *Politics* all the states studied—they were probably listed in his earlier compilation, the *Polities*. But at this point in history it appears unlikely that any final identification is possible.

Whatever the number it is obvious that Aristotle had to have a great deal of help in the first two stages of his great work. To collect the constitutional materials on so many different states, both Greek and non-Greek, was itself a large task. It may be worthwhile to pause briefly and consider how Aristotle may have acquired all these materials. Athens itself, of course, was the center of the Greek book trade, and he would have had an opportunity to buy a variety of materials. He did have fairly substantial financial resources: his endowment from Alexander was perhaps as much as 800 talents (possibly equivalent to $500,000 in present-day money). Undoubtedly he considered investment of part of that sum in a library not only desirable but essential. Then too he had more than monetary support from the Macedonian regime, as we have seen. Antipater had thrown his weight behind Aristotle's school and it is more than likely that he would have given whatever aid he could to one of its major research projects. Alexander himself is said to have supported Aristotle's biological studies by directing all fishers and fowlers to send him unusual specimens. One cannot document a similar order to Macedonian and Greek administrators to help Aristotle with his assembling of documents for the study of politics, but it is certainly within the realm of reason. Students at the Lyceum, who came from all over the Greek and Macedonian worlds and perhaps from other areas, may have been of some help to him as well, for they probably returned to their homes from time to time and could there obtain materials to bring back to Athens.

Some of his students may also have supplied Aristotle with information not available in written documents about their local city-states. But they probably played a larger role as research assistants in the library than as independent collectors of either documents or information. Others besides students must have helped in this second stage of the project too, for it was a large job to select out from the mass of material the pertinent parts and to condense them into one work, the *Polities*. If Aristotle had had to work alone, he certainly would not have been able to produce all the important works that he did during this period.

One of these other works deserves special mention here. In 1890 a papyrus document in four rolls was discovered in Egypt (where the climate was more conducive to the preservation of papyrus than that of Greece) and acquired by the British Museum. It was promptly deciphered and published, with elaborate notes, under the title *Aristotle's Constitution of Athens*.[24] Notice the title: the Greek word *politeia* has again become "constitution" in translation. And again it is misleading. The document is actually a two-part piece of private writing of which the first section is a political and constitutional history of Athens up to Aristotle's own time, while the second section is a descriptive and analytical account of Athenian government and basic law during the time Aristotle was in Athens as the head of the Lyceum. To me it is, for ancient times and even today, the *ne plus ultra* of local governmental and political history and analysis. It is, I think, in quality far ahead of Xenophon's *Constitution of the Lacedaemonians,* the somewhat laudatory and very uneven volume on Sparta, which is probably more typical of the works of the logographers, who had to take care not to offend local personalities and sentiments.

It may be asked why Aristotle, who was not a citizen of Athens and was safe to teach there only while under Macedonian protection, wrote the kind of searching study he did. Aristotle was a devoted student and teacher. He must have wanted to give his students, many of whom were from Athens and were deeply interested and even involved in its government, an example of how local constitutional history and the description of contemporary government of a city should be written. He may have been trying to set a high standard for future textbooks dealing with local governments. That its usefulness as a model was lessened by the decline in importance of the city-state system must be admitted. But it nevertheless remains a great achievement in the history of the study of politics.

Its survival makes us all the more regretful that the work on the *Polities* was not preserved. Werner Jaeger has called the *Constitution of Athens* a sort of canon for the whole, and has commented: ". . . the disappearance of that monument of Peripatetic scholarship, the collection of 158 constitutions, has dealt our knowledge of Greek history and culture an incurable wound."[25] I fully concur in the spirit of this remark, although I find it difficult to picture as a wound to our knowledge the loss of something that our knowledge never contained.

In any case, while regretting the loss of the *Polities* we must be grateful for the survival of Aristotle's other works in this field, the *Constitution of Athens* and the *Politics*. They amply demonstrate how a man of first-rate mind, prodigious energy, and adequate support and assistance could combine theory and a shrewd use of abundant historical evidence in the comparative study of government.

The Importance of Aristotle

In one of the best of the shorter works on the history of political theory, George H. Sabine remarks: "In the history of political philosophy the death of Aristotle in 322 marks the close of an era, as the life of his great pupil [Alexander], who died the year before him, marks the beginning of a new era in politics and the history of European civilization. The failure of the city-state is drawn like a sharp line across the history of political thought, whereas from this date forward its continuity is unbroken down to our own day."[26] While for the history of the study of politics the era after Alexander is marked by a tapering off of ancient developments rather than by new beginnings, Sabine's remark concerning the history of political thought has pertinence for us here.

Aristotle wrote and taught as though the city-states were the only units of government worth considering. Alexander, on the other hand, in his program of empire-building anticipated a change in the whole nature of political organization that was finally accomplished three centuries after his death in the Roman Empire. In carrying out his program Alexander developed a cosmopolitan policy. Unlike Aristotle, who showed the common contempt, even hatred, of the Greek for non-Greeks, who regarded the latter as barbarians without rights against the superior Greeks, Alexander recognized the need of support from all peoples if he was to be successful in making his world into one *polis* living under a single constitution. This meant treating all the people within his empire substantially as equals; it also meant Hellenizing the non-Greek peoples as fully as possible so as to bring them all to the same level of civilization. Aristotle, who believed there were biological differences between Greeks and non-Greeks, would not even have considered this. Alexander died before he could turn his cosmopolitan ideal into reality, but Rome went far toward realizing the objectives Alexander had formulated centuries earlier. Thus Alexander, who wrote no books and taught no classes and hence cannot be regarded as a student and teacher of politics in the usual sense, nevertheless grasped two fundamental political ideas that the great writer and teacher Aristotle failed to comprehend: the need for units of government on a larger scale than the old city-states (if for no other reason than to end the latter's wars of mutual destruction) and the need for recognition of the basic equality of all human beings, without regard to national or ethnic origins, within the area of the enlarged political unit.

Aristotle's failure to understand the importance of the changes in political organization that were taking place in his time and to foresee their implications must be recognized as a shortcoming in his work. There are some others. His doctrine that there is in the world a general purpose moving toward the good did not take sufficient account of the counter-tendency toward degeneration. In paying too little attention to economic affairs and undervaluing the role of economic welfare in the achievement of the good life, he revealed the class bias of an intellectual of the middle or upper class. It should perhaps be noted too that Aristotle's work was qualitative, not quantitative; he apparently made no attempt to tabulate or organize in a systematic point-by-point comparison his findings on the "158 constitutions." But since the tools of statistics had not yet been developed this can hardly be charged as a fault to him.

Since Aristotle himself was critical of some of his predecessors and contemporaries, notably Plato and Isocrates, and justly so, it has seemed only proper to point out his own errors and biases. But on balance, these seem decidedly small when viewed against the background of his truly great intellectual achievements. In comprehensiveness of scientific vision, in architectonic capacity to define and interrelate the fields of knowledge, in capacity to plan, organize, and direct research on a large scale in many fields, in recognition of knowledge as a cumulative thing, developing throughout the ages, in willingness to make direct statements of his own findings and position without evasion, in his recognition that knowledge comes from hard work, observation, experience, and reason guided by logic, in his recognition of human responsibility for human affairs including politics, in his accuracy of observation and in clarity of expression—in all these respects Aristotle was truly outstanding, not only in his own age but in all the centuries since then. He is a fitting progenitor of the science of politics.

Part III

THE DECLINE AFTER ARISTOTLE

✎ Introduction

ARISTOTLE was the last of the ancient scholars who had any opportunity to make a truly comparative study of independent states and their governments—indeed to make any political study of major significance at all. The study and teaching of politics went into a decline which lasted, for all practical purposes, until the Renaissance. The reason lies in the changed political milieu.

There were two factors of overriding importance: the loss of independence and power of the city-states and the corresponding rise of monarchically governed states of imperial size. After Alexander's short-lived empire (which embraced Macedonia, Greece, Egypt, and the Near East to Persia and beyond) broke up at his death in 323 B.C., three large succession states appeared. These were a Macedonian empire that ruled Macedonia and Greece; a Seleucid empire that controlled the main Asiatic parts of Alexander's former empire; and a Ptolemaic empire that ruled over Egypt and adjacent African and Asiatic areas. These carried on wars against each other over disputed areas, with important resultant changes in boundaries.

In the meantime a new world power, Rome, began to rise in the west. After assuring its control of the western Mediterranean by defeating and ultimately destroying Carthage, it proceeded to conquer the succession states to the east, one after another. By 148 B.C., Macedonia had become a Roman province, while Greece was somewhat more leniently dealt with but still subordinated to Rome. By 62 B.C. the Seleucid empire in the Near East and its successors had been conquered by the Romans and made part of the Roman Empire, and by 30 B.C., Egypt, the last of the Hellenistic monarchies, succumbed to Roman rule. The Jews in the meantime had also felt the heavy hand of Rome. Thus before the birth of Christ, Rome had come to dominate the entire Mediterranean and Near Eastern world. The *Pax Romana* was in the making, but for the self-government of peoples, and for the study of politics, it was nearly the peace of death. The formerly self-governing Greek city-states, from the western Mediterranean eastward to Ionia and beyond, were in effect reduced to the status of mere municipalities, and not very prosperous, active, or potent ones at that. Rome came to hold a complete monopoly of political power. There was no other state to compete or to compare with it; no local units could oppose it.

Since politics to the Greeks really meant all the affairs of the *polis* as distinct from purely private affairs, the effect of the decline in the importance of the *polis* under the Macedonian and Roman empires was to make politics itself far less important. No longer could a political writer argue convincingly that the *polis* was the indispensable promoter of the good life and the protector of men's interests and welfare. Men could see that the important decisions on war and peace, on finances, on taxes, on laws, and on major public improvements came from the rulers of the larger and higher units of government, whose powers and actions tran-scended those of the *polis* in every measure of significance.

It took only a few decades of time after Aristotle for well-informed people to grasp the significance of this great change. The mighty had fallen. Greeks and Macedonians of old citizen families that had participated in ruling their states were now no better off than metics had been earlier, if as well off. Theirs became a sick civilization. Pessimism and escapism became common. What was there left for the once proud Greeks to do when a foreign power centered outside their city, as in Rome, for example, controlled all important governmental, military, and foreign affairs, and imposed its laws and taxes without consent upon the hapless subject peoples of the *polis*?[1]

It was not only their political subordination that brought discouragement. The economic conditions of life had also changed for the worse. The soil of many parts of Greece had become infertile through exhaustion. Mineral resources had been largely used up. Where once the Greeks had sent their surplus population out to establish colonies, east, west, north, and south, now those opportunities were very few. Furthermore, science and technology had not advanced sufficiently to provide enough alternative means of employment. In fact the population was so much more than the land could support adequately that the Greeks turned generally to infanticide as their main means of controlling population and preventing starvation.

There were, of course, some remunerative activities for qualified people. Young male Greeks could in some cases serve as mercenary troops for their masters, the Macedonian, Seleucid, or Egyptian rulers, and later for the Romans. Those with education could work as secretaries for the officials of the succession states and later of the Romans, as well as for individuals and families of great wealth. And they could tutor or teach—a thing that many Romans would not deign to do. The Greek language continued to be a principal medium of communication for centuries, and this gave educated Greeks some advantages.

Since long before the final subordination of the Greeks to the Roman power, young Macedonians, Romans, and others had gone to Athens, and to some small extent to other Greek cities, for their education, after learning at home from tutors how to read, write, and do arithmetic. These streams of non-Greek students to Greece must have been interrupted to some extent during the many wars and campaigns, but Athens at least was usually spared from major fighting and destruction. In the fourth century B.C. Athens had many such foreign students in various small schools of more or less collegiate level—the Academy, the Lyceum, Isocrates' school, the schools of the rhetoricians, and others. This continued into later centuries. Greek scholars also traveled about to give their lectures, and some of these got to Rome (when the political climate was favorable) as well as to other cities in Italy and elsewhere.[2]

In short the Romans recognized the value of Greek culture and education. It was a part of the well-to-do young Roman's career to go to Athens for some or all of his higher education. There he learned the Greek language, together with music, rhetoric, literature, mathematics, and other nonpolitical arts and sciences. But at the same time the leading families of the Roman people—the rulers, the military leaders, the great businessmen and bankers, engineers of public works, and the wealthy in general—exhibited a certain condescension toward teachers, which did not contribute to improvement of morale among the Greeks.

In their new status as a subordinate and inferior people, the Greeks found little solace, such as the Christians later did, in religion. Their gods were rather human and secular. Besides that, except for differences in name the major Greek and Roman gods were much the same (e.g.,

Greek Zeus equal or akin to Latin Jupiter). Most Greeks, it seems, did not expect the gods to interfere on their behalf against their Macedonian and later Roman superiors, although there were many references to *tyche* or fortune as being responsible.

The Greek outlook on life during the centuries after Alexander was, then, not a buoyant and hopeful one, and this, it seems to me, is reflected in their philosophies, their studies, their writings, and their teachings. In the absence of adequate and rewarding outlets for the employment of their great natural talents the Greeks at home turned to trivial things like social clubs, festivals, games, and other essentially recreational and unproductive activities, and to new philosophies of individualism that developed as rationalizations of the new mood. Whereas they had once been rather firmly knit together and active in performing political functions, they now turned more and more to individualistic activities and satisfactions, and gave relatively little attention to public matters, including the study and teaching of politics.

For Romans themselves conditions for political studies were even less favorable than for the Greeks. Even under the Republic, which of course was not truly a republic in the modern sense, the Roman ruling classes gave very little encouragement to either study or teaching in this field, and once the Empire, following Caesar's dictatorship, was well established near the end of the last century B.C., the conditions adversely affecting any such study were considerably worsened. Prior to this time, and in imitation of the former Greek models in the field, Polybius in the second century B.C., and Cicero in the following century but before Caesar had overthrown the Republic, could deal in an objective and historical manner and in relative safety with questions about the best form of government, as well as with other political issues. But once Caesar had raised himself up by force, and he and his successors in office had made the Senate less and less important in the government of the Empire, with the popular assemblies also becoming increasingly impotent, questions concerning the form and the powers of the imperial government or the wisdom and justice of major pieces of legislation proposed by the dictators ceased to be debated freely in public assemblies. Men made themselves emperors by destroying their opponents, and once in office they used spies and provocateurs to seek out possible enemies, and resorted to murder along with other drastic measures to dispose of dangerous opponents and so retain their own powers.[3] Those who opposed an emperor had to resort to clandestine and conspiratorial methods, as happened often within the armed forces, and the aim was more to overthrow the emperor and to replace him with another than to change either the form of the government or its policies.

This being true, the old free public discussion of political questions sank to a very low point, and came to be the exception rather than the rule. If it did not entirely disappear, men in general at least kept it more secret and confined it to presumably safe and trusted friends. For centuries under the Empire there was almost no serious public writing on major issues of government and public policy.

As the capital of the Empire, Rome would have been the natural place of resort for scholars and teachers in all subjects, but except under a few emperors more tolerant than the rest, not many such individuals found Rome the most congenial place to be. Any school of higher studies like Aristotle's Lyceum in fourth-century B.C. Athens was out of the question in Rome under the Empire. More could be done at outlying places like Alexandria, but even there the emperor's officials kept a close watch.

Besides official disapprobation, any scholar who might have attempted to make political studies would have found the arrangements for the government of the different parts of the Empire to be extremely varied and complicated. Although the documents and laws for each part of the Empire probably existed in the imperial archives and offices, and the locally appropriate ones in the provincial offices, it is most unlikely that any public library in Rome, Constantinople, or elsewhere contained copies of all of them, and there was no reason to have extra copies in other places of many of them. The Empire had a complicated political structure, and one that was constantly changing, and hard to comprehend.

Even the study of municipal government and local administration lost all interest for the citizens as local powers were progressively transferred to the central government, and the holding of local office was transformed from an honor into a burden to be avoided at almost any cost.[4] And as for the study of political parties, or elections and election methods, or constitutional law and rights—such subjects were either unknown because the subject matter did not exist, or too insignificant to merit study.

One other consideration is perhaps worthy of mention. The place that local politics had formerly occupied in the lives of the people wherever city-state or even tribal forms of government had prevailed was increasingly taken over by the doctrinal disagreements of religious sects. The Christian church came in time to be the most important movement in this respect, but until it became dominant there were a number of other important ones. Eventually the doctrinal strife that developed within the Christian church tended to absorb a large part of the people's attention, and to help fill the void caused by their exclusion from meaningful political activity.

But these conditions and developments represent primarily negative factors, discouragements to men of intellect and good will to undertake any serious studies of politics. There was on the other hand an important positive force that was absorbing and directing the thoughts and the energies of men and deflecting them away from any independent studies of political, economic, or other similar subjects. I refer, of course, to the emperors themselves and the very nature and interests of the imperial institution.

The emperors were in general interested in protecting if not always in extending the area of the Empire, in maintaining its internal strength and unity, and in preserving the one-man system of rule that characterized its government. For these purposes they tried to keep in their own hands all military power, all legislative policy-making, and the entire direction and control of the administrative and judicial machinery of government, ultimately down to the government of the cities. These objectives could not be achieved without making the regime palatable to the great majority of the population, as well as rendering it difficult if not outright dangerous for dissenters to raise hands and voices against the regime. To achieve these ends the emperors in time established laws and policies that (1) gave substantially equal citizenship rights to all the people, of whatever original nationality, and whether former slaves, or freedmen, or persons of higher social classes; (2) recognized the rights to their own religious beliefs and practices of the increasingly numerous and powerful sect called the Christians; (3) provided "bread and circuses" for the poor; (4) beautified the cities; (5) improved the laws and the courts; (6) maintained security and peace as far as that was possible, or at least, until fairly late, kept the military operations against the ever-threatening barbarians far from the centers of population; (7) laid the main burdens of taxation upon the well-to-do; and (8) allowed themselves to be deified and so placed somewhat above popular criticism. As a result of these and various related actions the emperors contrived, on the whole, to keep public opinion, such as it was in those times, on their own side. The loss of political power and activity seems not to have disturbed men noticeably. For many there had been no loss at all.

These several purposes could not be attained without great attention to effective military defense, improvements in the laws and the courts, and especially the strengthening of the imperial administrative organization, personnel, and methods of work. The abler and more energetic emperors reached out for, took control of, and directed the training and work of various vocational and professional classes needed for the administration of the Empire. In doing this they so monopolized the time, thought, studies, and teaching of these classes, and so increased their public importance and prestige as to exclude the possibility of their becoming free and independent students or professionals in their respective fields. These groups or classes included the military, the rhetoricians, the public administrators, the lawyers, and finally, for a time, even the Christian clergy. These all tended to become cogs in the government of the Empire. The idea of free and self-directing professions, made up of men who carried on their own professional practices and studies, even at times against the government, had very little if any standing in the Roman Empire.

While the records of the centuries from Aristotle to about 600 A.D., where this volume will conclude, leave much to be desired, they are sufficient to document a great decline from the standards set by the Greeks in the fourth century B.C. in practically all secular studies, including the study of politics. On the positive side, however, the records are valuable for indicating some of the major factors that apparently brought on the general decline of secular studies, as well as those special conditions that affected adversely the study of politics. The first of the two chapters in this section will cover the Hellenistic, or Greek and Roman, period down to the Christian era, while the second chapter will begin when the Christians appear and become active among the peoples of the region, and will end as the Roman Empire reaches the zenith of its powers, then divides into eastern and western empires, and finally disappears as a force in the West, leaving only the East Roman Empire or Byzantium to carry on the old imperial tradition in the centuries that followed.

Chapter 11

⌐ The Hellenistic Period

THE general changes in Greek attitudes and interests described in the introduction to this part did not take place overnight.[1] In the first hundred years or so after Alexander and Aristotle, despite the almost continuous wars and disorder throughout the region, some of the old spirit of independence, self-government, and inquiry lingered on in the city-states, especially in Athens. Men educated under Plato, Aristotle, Isocrates, and the rhetoricians still carried on their old schools for a time. Then, too, new philosophical schools were established. Zeno came to Athens from Cyprus in about 314 B.C., and by 301 he was teaching his Stoic doctrines in the porch or Stoa. Epicurus opened a school to expound his philosophical ideas in Athens in about 306 B.C. Not long after this, say about 290 B.C., at Alexandria, a great library and study center were begun. But politics as a subject of study presently disappeared from the older Athenian schools and was not taken up formally in the new. The young Greek, Roman, and other students who came to Athens for what would conceivably be called a college education in our day were offered instruction in cultural studies but not formally at least in the field of politics and government.

This does not mean that politics ceased to be of any interest to people, or that no one engaged in studying the subject. Actually, of course, the nature of the subject and the problems that it presented had significantly changed. The new schools of philosophy that sprang up reflect to some extent these changes. On the other hand various statesmen and historians who had read the political writings of Aristotle, Plato, and earlier Greek authors kept up some interest in politics and did some thinking, inquiring, and writing on the subject. The work of both groups will be considered in the pages that follow.

Cynics and Skeptics

Diogenes of Sinope, a contemporary of Plato's, who was born in 412 B.C., is credited by some with being the founder of the Cynic sect or school of philosophers.[2] Actually he got some of his ideas from, and may have studied under, Antisthenes of Athens (c. 455–c. 360 B.C.). The latter may be the real originator of the Cynic doctrines, for after the death of Socrates, whose disciple he had been, he gave up his life of philosophy and relative comfort to live with working men and to preach a program of return to nature and the abolition of government, religion, marriage, and property. Simple personal virtue, he thought, was all that man required for right living and happiness. Diogenes carried Antisthenes' doctrines to the point of revolt against all social conventions. He came to be known as "the dog" or "cynic," meaning canine, for in some ways he lived like one. His return to nature went far beyond that of Antisthenes. At the same time he professed a strong desire to live virtuously and in freedom, as a friend of beasts as well as men, and equally as unburdened with property and responsibilities as animals are. Why should anyone do anything for his country, or feel any affection for it?

From philosophers, if such they were, professing this kind of doctrine, one would hardly expect any serious or unbiased study of politics or government, and apparently they produced no such studies of any kind.

Another school or group of philosophers who had little to contribute to the study of politics, or who chose not to do so, were those called the Skeptics. They included Pyrrho of Elis (c. 360–270 B.C.), Timon of Phlius, near Corinth (c. 320–230 B.C.), Arcesilaus of Aeolia (c. 315–240 B.C.) who was a member of the Academy and later head of that school, and Carneades of Cyrene in northern Africa (c. 214–128 B.C.).

The doctrines of skepticism went through various changes, but in general this school systematized and rationalized the view that neither through their senses nor by reason can men establish any firm basis for knowledge or beliefs. Therefore, it made little difference what a man believed, and he could with a clear conscience go along with any prevailing set of beliefs or course of action. These skeptics became skilled in presenting equally cogent arguments on opposite sides of the same question, in somewhat the same way as Socrates had demonstrated. It was only natural that they should be classed as unbelievers in matters of religion as well as in other fields. That they knew something, in fact a great deal, about politics was demonstrated by Carneades when, in 156 B.C., he, as one of a group of three philosophers sent by Athens to Rome on a diplomatic mission, took it on himself to deliver a lecture on justice as seen by Plato and Aristotle, and then to deliver another denying all that he had argued in the first. His young Roman listeners evidently applauded this feat of ridiculing learning, but the elder Cato, for one, did not. Further, in the course of his remarks Carneades had pointed out that great states like Rome had achieved greatness "by unjust aggressions against their weaker neighbors." Rome was not the place to make a speech on that subject, and the three Athenian ambassadors were sent packing back to Athens.[3]

Unlike Plato and Aristotle, then, some contemporary and later philosophers generally stayed off the subject of politics. It was too sensitive a matter at that time, and one about which learned men could then do very little except to get themselves into trouble by discussing it.

Epicurus and the Epicureans

Epicurus, who was born in Attica about 342 B.C., and lived to about 270 B.C., developed a philosophy that was designed as a rational guide for individual living in the period of the collapse of the Greek city-states after Plato and Aristotle.[4] He was one of the most famous philosophers of ancient Greece and had many followers, for centuries after his death, both in Greece and in various other countries in that region.[5] He had reasons like those of Plato for being shocked and revolted by Athenian politics, but his reaction was quite different. Plato clung to the nauseating mess that he thought politics to be, and to the city-state, because he saw ethics and politics as being almost indissolubly united. Man could not be a truly moral being without the *polis*. He hoped to reform it by getting philosophers who held his own philosophical and ethical views to be kings in the city-states.

Epicurus studied Plato's works, but in general turned against his views. He wanted to divorce ethics from politics completely. The *polis* or city-state which had given rise to politics was already practically emasculated; what little self-government remained to the city-states apparently did not seem important enough to Epicurus for the Greeks to concern themselves with. Epicurus sought, therefore, for a simple, individualistic sort of ethics in accordance with nature, as he understood it, by which a man could live in freedom, happily and morally, without troubling himself with the state and public affairs. He recognized that some sort of government was probably necessary or at least unavoidable. Men should, therefore, do what is necessary to obey the law, but avoid participating in politics.[6] Whether in democracies or monarchies, politics involves competition of man with man, and this limits a man's ability to attain and keep the quiet and happiness that ought to be his first objectives in life. The development of individual friendships was a major part of Epicurus' program.

There are many other things of outstanding interest in Epicurus' philosophy, but enough has been said, I believe, to show why he can hardly be accounted a student of politics. He made some shrewd observations about the field, but his main recommendation to his followers was to avoid it. No great work of political analysis came from him. His was a comforting philosophy for the nonpolitical, for those who desired "a quiet life and . . . retirement from the world."[7]

The Epicurean philosophy attracted many followers and endured for a number of centuries, but with waning importance. Its doctrines did not change significantly, in part perhaps because Epicurus wrote them down so precisely, and was so strongly opposed to any alterations of his views. Diogenes Laertius reports that Epicurus wrote many books, but of all that he wrote only a small fraction remains. A catechism consisting of some forty "principal doctrines" is extant, plus a few letters and some dozen pages of fragments from his reportedly great work *On Nature*.

Over two hundred years after Epicurus a Roman poet, Lucretius, put the Epicurean philosophy into beautiful verse and thus helped to preserve it for posterity. But he was the only important writer of Epicurean philosophy after Epicurus himself.

In time Epicureanism gave way to Stoicism on the one hand and to Christianity on the other. No great political studies, either historical or analytical, came from the Epicurean school. Within the confines of their own philosophy the Epicureans already had answers satisfactory to themselves with respect to the direction of their individual lives and conduct. It was not for them to carry on studies to improve their knowledge of politics, or to enlarge the sphere of their philosophy to cover the public life.

The Early Stoics

The most important of the pre-Christian schools of philosophy in the region of the Greeks' greatest influence was that of the Stoics. They took a broader, a more public and more responsible view of man's life on earth than the Epicureans, and partly because they did so they discovered new ideas. The fact that many non-Greeks contributed to this school does not deprive the Greeks of primary credit for what the Stoics achieved. Unfortunately, although much is known about the Stoic doctrines of the pre-Christian era, very little of what the philosophical leaders of the school of that time wrote down has survived. An exception must be made of the writings of the Roman statesman Cicero (106–43 B.C.), who, though not usually classed as a philosopher, was "more or less of a Stoic,"[8] and I believe more Stoic than anything else.

The man who is generally credited with being the founder of Stoicism is Zeno of Citium (c. 336–c. 264 B.C.) on the island of Cyprus. He may have had some Greek blood, but he is usually described as a Phoenician, that is, a Semite. He was born the year before Aristotle returned to Athens to set up the Lyceum, and he would have been about thirteen when Aristotle left Athens for the last time. Zeno himself went to Athens as a young man, about 300 B.C. Whatever the business that brought him there, he sought out the schools of philosophy, attended several of them (e.g., the Cynic school and the Academy of Plato), and then proceeded to think out his own philosophical system. He built up a personal following, also, and soon organized a school in a building with a porch (Stoa) from which came the name Stoics. In the realm of ethics his ideal became the martyred Socrates whose principles of "virtue, endurance and self-sufficiency" became basic to his teaching.[9] As he saw it, the physical universe was predetermined, solid and reliable. He "had no patience with metaphysical subtleties."[10] Things did not happen in the world just as a matter of chance, but as the result of the operation of natural laws. Whoever designed and made this universe, God or Providence, made it real and solid and enduring. God also provided a definite place in it for mankind to make its own way in accordance with the laws built into nature. And Zeno did not think in terms of Greeks versus barbarians; he thought of mankind as a whole—an important fact in his views on ethics and politics. A man could make his career in the world with assurance and live a rewarding and virtuous life, if he learned the ways of nature and willed to live in accordance with them. There was a place in the world for human knowledge, decision, and action. This was not a teaching of fear and avoidance, but of acceptance of the world as it was, and of doing with courage and even self-sacrifice what was necessary to a good life.

It would be a great boon to modern understanding of Zeno's ideas to have his own words to study, but this is not possible. Later writers who followed more or less in his footsteps undoubtedly present most of his basic ideas, but he left no fixed catechism as Epicurus did. Down to the Christian era some of his leading followers were Cleanthes, a Greek of Assos (c. 331–232 B.C.), Chrysippus (c. 280–207 B.C.), a native of Cilicia (these two being successors to Zeno as head of the Stoa); Panaetius (c. 185–109 B.C.), a Greek from Rhodes, who lived for a time in Rome, but ended his career at Athens as head of the Stoa; and Posidonius (c. 135–c. 51 B.C.), a part-Greek from the region of Syria, who studied philosophy at Athens and then taught at Rhodes, where Cicero was one of his pupils. Posidonius had scientific as well as philosophical interests and also wrote history. Other Stoic thinkers back to Zeno himself were men of wide interests too. Like Aristotle a number of them had contacts with leading statesmen of their time, and were evidently called upon for political advice.

Zeno is reported by Plutarch, Diogenes Laertius, and other ancient writers to have written a work on politics, or on public affairs, or on the Republic—the words used depending on whose work and whose translation one uses.[11] Thus in the Dryden translation of *Plutarch's Lives*, in the article on Lycurgus, one reads: "And therefore all those who have written well on politics, as Plato, Diogenes, and Zeno, have taken Lycurgus for their model . . ."[12] As to the wisdom of going into politics, Seneca reports as follows: "Zeno says: the wise man will go into politics . . . unless something stops him from doing so. . . . I [Seneca] follow Zeno and his disciples promptly and readily; but none of them actually went into politics, though none of them failed to send some pupil into politics."[13]

The body of Stoic writings from the period before Christ that are still extant is too small to support any full and reliable account of the changes that took place in Stoic ideas. Posidonius, for example, is generally rated as one of the ablest and most productive of the Stoics, yet little of his writing remains, excepting some extracts from his *Histories.* Just before him there had been a much more important writer and student in the fields of history and politics, Polybius. Fortunately more of his writing has survived.

Polybius

Polybius, the Greek who wrote a great history of ancient Rome, has considerable importance as a student of politics and, through some parts of his *Histories,* even as a teacher of politics. Born at Megalopolis in southern Arcadia near Sparta toward the end of the third century (c. 203 B.C.), and provided with a good liberal education, he lived until about 120 B.C. He was an active leader in Megalopolitan politics in his early adult life. Although he was not unfriendly to the Romans, he was deported to Rome with about a thousand other hostages after the Romans had defeated the Achaeans at Pydna in 168 B.C.

Then about thirty-five years of age and a man of much military and political experience as well as of good mind and education, he was even though a hostage taken into Roman high society where he evidently made a fine impression. He developed great admiration for the Romans and their military and political accomplishments at that time. By interviewing and observing during his extensive travels with leading Roman civil and military officers throughout the expanding empire, and by reading widely and gathering many documents, he gained a remarkable fund of knowledge about history and government in the entire Mediterranean world. He looked into the histories, constitutions, and governments of Athens, Achaea, Sparta, Carthage, and many other places. Using all these sources he wrote what he considered to be a universal history, although Rome and its achievements provided the central and guiding thread. His work covered the period from the beginning of the first Punic War (c. 264 B.C.) down to nearly his own times.[14]

It is clear from his own statements that Polybius wrote for the purpose of instructing others about Rome and its remarkable world and that he looked on himself as a teacher. This is so despite the fact that he did not organize a school or teach in one. At the very outset of Book I he starts out as if he were writing a textbook. He speaks there "in praise of History" and its educational value "since there is no more ready corrective of conduct than knowledge of the past," and he goes on to argue "that the soundest education and training for a life of active politics is the study of History . . ."[15] Frequently thereafter he makes statements such as that he will arrange his materials so as to "render the approach to what follows intelligible and easy for students";[16] that he will present a brief prefatory survey of his work, "For I believe this will be the best means of giving students an adequate idea of my whole plan";[17] and that in discussing, as he does, other writers on his subject, "my object has not been to censure previous writers, but to rectify the ideas of students."[18] It is evident that in these passages he, as a writer and teacher, is arguing for a training in political history as the best education for men who desire to go into politics and to become statesmen.

As a historian, Polybius also developed concepts and rules of historical method that still merit the praise of historiographers today. Others had written history (or accounts of events) in order to entertain people, or to promote patriotism, or, as in Herodotus' case, so that people coming after him would know what had happened before them. Polybius had in mind to help produce effective, farseeing, and wise political leaders by teaching them how cause leads to effect in human affairs. He was not the first to do so, but still he was somewhat original in setting forth definite standards of truth in history and reliable ways of tracing political events back to their true causes. Thucydides, for example, had certainly preceded Polybius in setting forth such standards, but Polybius does not seem to have learned his standards from Thucydides.[19]

It is not my intention to analyze in any detail his ideas of historical method, but a few points need to be made to show how his principles of method had a bearing on education for politics. He felt his work had to be factually in accord with the best evidence in the documents that he assembled and that he tested as far as possible by interviews with persons who had knowledge of what happened. It also had to be chronologically correct, and to this end he used not only the chronology of the Olympiads but also that of the Roman consuls, his being a history that put Rome at the center of events. It must also be comprehensive, or even "universal," just as Roman power was coming to be; and he was very critical of the value of special histories that dealt with single places or limited series of events and that covered only short periods of time. Living in the age of the rise of Rome, he saw more clearly than some earlier writers had the interdependence of events throughout the Mediterranean world.

He also came to believe that history is a subject relating to human beings and that it should be dealt with secularly. But here we must recognize some confusion in his writing, and a certain amount of change in his thinking as the years went by. Putting aside the effects on men of disease, storms, earthquakes, and other such nonhuman natural phenomena, he seems to have thought the primary or controlling causes in human affairs to be human decisions and actions. This is the line that Solon had taken some centuries earlier. But Polybius was not wholly consistent in this matter of causes. He did not bring in the ordinary Roman gods as interferers in human affairs, but he refers frequently to *tyche* (chance) or fortune as determining the course of events. Thus almost at the beginning of Book I of his *Histories* he writes: "For what gives my work its peculiar quality, and what is most remarkable in the present age, is this. Fortune having guided almost all the affairs of the world in one direction and having forced them to incline towards one and the same end [i.e., toward domination by Rome], a historian [e.g., Polybius himself] should bring before his readers under one synoptical view the operations by which she has accomplished her general purpose."[20]

This statement and another that immediately follows it are broader and stronger statements about the influence of fortune in human affairs than Polybius usually makes, but their purport is unmistakable. Polybius is writing a history of not only the rise of Roman power in the world but also the ways and works of fortune in the affairs of men; and fortune is, as it were, personified as a sort of goddess who rules in many human affairs. Various other references to *tyche* or to this personified "Fortune" and her influence and actions in human affairs are to be found in the *Histories*. In this respect, he was not as far advanced in his thinking as Solon was some three centuries earlier.

Polybius' main line of argument was, however, that these unexplainable interventions of fortune in Roman and other affairs had in the long run little or no effect on Roman success in achieving dominance over the known world. That eventual and very great success, he argued, was achieved by Rome because her republican political system was superior to that of her neighbors and rivals, and gave her the strength and the drive and the leadership that could result eventually only in victorious achievement and in the subjugation of her neighbors and rivals. His purpose was, therefore, to show "by what means and under what system of polity the Romans in less than fifty-three years have succeeded in subjecting nearly the whole inhabited world to their sole government—a thing unique in history . . ."[21]

Since the Roman system of government became the key issue with Polybius, he felt called upon to describe it and to compare it with the systems of other states—Carthage, Sparta, Athens, Persia, and others. For the purpose of making this comparison more systematic, he also devised a classification of types of constitutions; there were three good types, with each one set over against a corresponding bad one, and a seventh or mixed type exemplified by the Roman system, which he considered to be truly superior to the others.

Along with this analysis and comparison of constitutional types, Polybius' studies led him to consider and to describe the changes that occur within each type largely from internal causes and that lead to its being transformed into another type. Looking at these dynamic processes of change in the large, he saw also a general cyclical movement composed of changes from type to type and capable of repeating itself. The Roman type of "mixed" or balanced constitution seemed to him to offer the greatest resistance to such internal changes and, therefore, the best available protection of constitutional stability. In time, however, his studies led him to see that even the Roman mixed republican constitution offered no final insurance against change.

Several criticisms of Polybius' methods and of his standards of historical work seem to be warranted. He was not entirely fair and objective. His admiration for the Romans and Spartans stands in clear contrast to his dislike for Athenian politics and institutions and for those of some other places. His frequent attribution of the turn in events to a personified force called chance or fortune was a step backwards. Also, in spite of the fact that he saw Rome as dominating the known world in his time, and subordinating the former city-states to its rule, he did not clearly see the Roman Empire as a new political unit. But he was both a student and a teacher of government and politics, and an important one.

Cicero

The time intervals between important writers on politics in post-Aristotelian times are illustrated by the gap between Polybius and Cicero. The former died about 120 B.C., and the latter was not born until 106 B.C.

Cicero claimed to have translated Xenophon's *Oeconomicus* at the age of nineteen. Assuming this to have been his first writing, it came thirty-three years after Polybius' death, and his first "original" work in politics, though it was not wholly original, *The Republic*, did not come out until about 51 B.C., or about seventy years after Polybius' death. What would the literature of politics in the West since, say, the eighteenth century be like if such time intervals stood between one major publication in the field and another? And yet after Cicero's time the intervals between important writings on politics became even greater.

In his own time, Cicero had no outstanding contemporary in political writing to compete with. However, there was one important contemporary writer with whom he may be contrasted rather than compared. This was the philosophical Epicurean poet Lucretius. Cicero was born seven years before Lucretius and died twelve years after him, in 43 B.C. Between 99 and 55 B.C., the whole span of Lucretius' life, the two men both lived in Rome, and there is evidence that they knew each other. But they lived by different philosophies and pursued entirely different careers and modes of life. The contrast between their respective ideals, careers, and accomplishments is a striking one.

About the life of Lucretius very little is known. His recorded accomplishments consist almost entirely of the writing of one great philosophical poem, *On the Nature of Things*, in which he sets forth his version of much of the Epicurean doctrine. From this work he is known as an important poet and philosopher, although in his lifetime the poem received little attention. The obscurity that veils the facts of his life suggests that he observed well the Epicurean principle of avoiding politics and public activity. He is reported to have committed suicide at the age of forty-four.

In the fifth "book" of his poem Lucretius discusses early men and women, their learning of speech, their mating, their getting of fire, learning to cook, and so on, and their increase in knowledge which led to their exchanging "their former way of living for new methods. Kings began to build towns," etc.[22] Then follows an elementary and essentially imaginary brief general history of early civilization, in accordance with Epicurean theories. Instead of being satisfied with "a frugal subsistence joined to a contented mind" men sought fame and political power.[23] Instead of peace and quiet mankind began to experience struggle and turmoil. Kings were slain and the rabble seized power. But men got tired of this disorderly condition of rule by brute force and so moved back toward effective government, with election of officers, and the making and enforcement of laws. There is more, but this is enough to show the elementary level of Lucretius' brief discussion of the history and problems of government from the most ancient times down to his own time in Rome. This hardly deserves to be called a study of politics or government, especially as it came more than two centuries after Aristotle, Thucydides, and other such observers of the actual political scene. The anti-political though not anarchistic prejudice of the Epicureans obviously precluded them from becoming real students of politics even (or especially?) in a politics-ridden city like Rome in the last century before Christ. Lucretius was simply one of the last and more articulate spokesmen of an essentially decadent anti-political sect.

Cicero, on the other hand, accepted the Stoic doctrines in ethics and politics, and lived up to them in the main until compelled by his convictions and his opposition to the Pompey-Caesar-Crassus triumvirate to retire in 59 B.C. from an active political career.[24] Up to this time he had been deeply involved in the government and politics of Rome, through a period of important constitutional changes and forebodings of more to come. Controversy and turmoil were almost constant. As a statesman, politician, orator and lawyer, Cicero was continuously in the public eye.

During his quarter century or more of active public life Cicero dared much, as he showed in standing up against powerful men like Pompey and Caesar, and he actually accomplished much. Unlike the withdrawn and obscure Lucretius, he left behind him an extensive record of public service, as well as important writings on politics, law, rhetoric, and philosophical and other subjects done during his fourteen or fifteen years of semiretirement.

Cicero's general attitude toward investigations in politics and law and toward the teaching of politics is revealed most fully in two of the major works of his last ten years of life, his *De Re Publica* (*The Republic*, also translated as *The Commonwealth*), issued in 51 B.C., and his *De Legibus* (*The Laws*), issued after his death in 43 B.C. Despite some lacunae, these works exist in fairly complete form, and are very revealing of a mind confused if not tortured by the turn of events that drove him from public office. The titles of these two main political works show how deeply indebted Cicero was to Plato.

Cicero made no secret in his later years of his admiration for and dependence on Plato's ideas and works. Whether this was a case of taking on protective coloration in view of his own danger in the current situation in Rome, I would not venture to say. In any event, the practical politician and statesman, out of office and power, turned to Plato's well-known theoretical works on politics for solace and support. He patterned his works definitely after those of Plato, not only in titles but also in contents and in the dialogue form, although he differed from Plato in a number of ways, as shown by his apparent insistence on the direct teaching of politics and on having men experienced in politics instead of philosophers as rulers. Cicero's indebtedness to Plato is most succinctly set forth in the following bit of dialogue at the beginning of *The Laws,* where Cicero himself is the interlocutor:

M. [*Marcus Tullius Cicero*]. I will follow again, then, as I did before, the example of that divine personage, whom I praise oftener, perhaps, than I should, such is the admiration I feel for him.
A. [*Atticus*]. Of course you mean Plato.
M. None other, Atticus.
A. Surely you can never praise him too highly or too often . . .[25]

In *The Republic,* Scipio carries the burden of the discussion for Cicero (as Socrates had done for Plato in numerous of the dialogues) while others put in questions, comments, and occasional minor objections. What Scipio says may, I suppose, be taken as being just about what Cicero believed. The Roman Republic is the center of interest, and the presentation is both historical and analytical. Brief and incisive comparisons and contrasts with other governments, such as those of Sparta and Athens, are given at various points. In this respect the work attains at some points the level of a study in comparative government. But note that Cicero is writing at about the middle of the first century B.C., when the city-states are nearly all passé as independent units of government. Cicero, who unlike Polybius had not traveled extensively, obviously had had to rely on old published accounts of these city-states. His discussion of the "mixed" or "balanced" type of constitution that had developed in Rome, and which he considered so advantageous to the stability of the government and to the welfare of the people, had obvious implications for the then current situation in Rome, where powerful leaders and factions were struggling to change the constitution, each to his or its advantage. The displaced politician turned student of and writer on poli-

tics could not refrain from trying to influence current political developments. Other parts of his discussion are more valuable, such as his treatment of ethical questions like the nature of justice and whether any
government can be carried on without injustice.

I shall not attempt to analyze all parts of Cicero's work on *The Republic*. Instead I shall examine some of his views on the study and teaching of politics in relation to actual participation in the political process.

In Chapter I Cicero attacks the Epicurean philosophy for its negative
stand concerning participation in politics, and also proclaims the superiority of an active political career over any that involves mere studying and teaching. Whether he had Lucretius especially in mind is uncertain, but this is rather questionable. With respect to the Epicurean
defeatist attitude, that a man gets into great trouble when he goes into
politics, and that in any case nothing can really be done through politics
to improve the state and government, Cicero takes the high ground of
courage and moral duty. The country that has given a man his birth
and education has high claims on his services. Personal safety, quiet,
and peace of mind are not the noblest of ends. Virtue is as virtue does.
Yes, "the existence of virtue depends entirely upon its use; and its noblest
use is the government of the State, and the realization in fact, not in
words, of those very things that the philosophers, in their corners, are
continually dinning in our ears."[26] And what is worth more to a man
than risking his life, if need be, to keep wicked men from gaining control of the state, even if little more can be accomplished?[27]

To achieve this desirable end, and to give the state good laws, good
customs, and good administration, it is necessary not only to forego one's
desire for leisure and quiet, and to risk one's own safety. It is also important to gain the knowledge of what is needed for good government,
so as to be equipped to act when the occasion comes. Even the philosopher "ought by no means to neglect this science of politics, because it
is his duty to acquire in advance all the knowledge that, for aught he
knows, it may be necessary for him to use at some future time."[28] How
absurd it is of the Epicureans, he argues, to say that even though they
generally avoid taking part in politics, in cases of urgent need in emergencies they will step into the political arena and take action! To know
what to do and how to do it in emergencies requires not only knowledge
gained from study but also experience. "It has always seemed to me that
the most amazing of the teachings of [these?] learned men is that they

deny their own ability to steer when the sea is calm, having never learned the art nor cared to know it, while at the same time they assure us that, when the waves dash highest, they will take the helm."[29]

About the negative attitude of the Epicurean philosophers toward the study of government Cicero says "that they have neither learned nor do they teach anything about the principles of the State . . . and that they consider the knowledge of such things unsuited to learned or wise men, but better to be left to those who have trained themselves in that business."[30] This was evidently their usual attitude, but not their plan for emergencies.

How fair Cicero was in these criticisms of the Epicurean philosophers I would not venture to say. I suspect that there may be some exaggeration and not a little bias against Epicureans in what he wrote. It is interesting to note, also, that in exalting the role and the services of the active politicians like himself, and expressly including himself among them, he reveals a considerable prejudice against men who are primarily scholars (or, as he usually says, philosophers), and also against teachers. Men of action are superior to mere philosophers. Legislators who by law compel men to be virtuous are superior to those who merely teach them to be so. Those who "rule . . . cities by wise counsel and authority are to be deemed far superior, even in wisdom, to those who take no part at all in the business of government."[31] While asserting his "enthusiasm for learning and teaching,"[32] Cicero says he tried to avoid preparing and presenting his materials "as a schoolmaster might," which is a phrase put into Scipio's mouth by Cicero.[33] In fact he was at this very time emulating that great teacher of more advanced students, Plato, by putting out textbooks on government and law, and trying to promote the study of politics as a necessary training for engaging in politics and public service. Had there been strong and free universities in his day as in modern times to invite out-of-office political leaders to join their faculties as lecturers or professors, I feel confident that he would have welcomed and accepted such an invitation, and that his apparent or feigned superiority over teachers would have melted away. Instead he was forced to employ his mind and energies in writing books, as he did at a feverish pace, on government, law, rhetoric, and philosophical subjects.

Cicero was not a man of great originality or of searching mind. He took ideas from Plato, Polybius, and others, and made good use of them, but he also rejected some ideas. It seems to me that he never raised his sights high enough to see the possibility of increasing and improving mankind's knowledge of politics through research. Having read Plato, Polybius, and other Greek authors, and having gained from his own experiences and observations in Rome a set of views on politics, he wrote as if the book of knowledge about politics had been completed, and nothing more could be added. I have found no questions raised by him concerning the need for further study of any question in the field. In this respect he conformed to a broader statement about the Romans of his day made by one of his more thorough and conscientious critics: "In the Roman Republic the very notion that there was anything to be measured, or that study will bring any help in controlling the fate of social groups and classes, seems to have been wanting."[34]

This deficiency in both his thinking and his writing, coupled with evidences of his vanity, his boastfulness, and even a willingness to have the truth doctored in his own favor,[35] tends to lower one's evaluation of his work. And other points can be charged against him. For example, although he seems to urge that men make a real study of political science, he also says in *The Laws*: "So in the very beginning we must persuade our citizens that the gods are the lords and rulers of all things, and that what is done, is done by their will and authority; that they are likewise great benefactors of man, observing the character of every individual, what he does, of what wrong he is guilty . . . For surely minds which are imbued with such ideas will not fail to form true and useful opinions."[36]

In passages like this, Cicero clearly shows that he has not reached the level of thought of such an ancient thinker as Solon. Indeed his book on *The Laws* is a most disappointing one, except as it reveals Cicero's mind in the period of his defeat and disillusionment. Book I wanders over many subjects without coming to any definite focus. Book II is given over almost entirely to religious laws and rituals. Everything good must be credited to the gods, and their punishment can be avoided by men only by strict observance of a code of religious ritual, including correct burial practices. Hardly any modern problem of public law—constitutional, administrative, or international—receives significant attention. In Book III Cicero reaches some problems of the law of legislative bodies (the Senate) and administrative law, but these are limited to Roman practices and rules and would have little application elsewhere. Cicero did not, like Polybius, make any significant contribution to the study of comparative government. What was there in his day and experience worth comparing with Rome?

Nevertheless I think the students and teachers of political science owe some measure of credit to Cicero. It is in my opinion fortunate that we are able to find any outstanding Roman at all in his time who was interested in the analysis of a governmental system and how it operates; who pleaded for the study of politics even though it was only with a view to current political action and not also for the advancement of the science of politics; and who wrote as persuasively and interestingly as he did, at least in some of his works.

In the three hundred years between the death of Aristotle and the birth of Christ, on the basis of existing records, Polybius and Cicero, one a Greek, the other a Roman, stand out as the two most important students of politics in the West. Without them these three centuries would be barren indeed in the study of politics—as barren, perhaps, as many following centuries were destined to be. It is interesting to notice, however, that it was Greek thought and writings in politics, and even Greek political experience, that largely dominated the political writings of both these men. Their interest was in Rome and its rising empire, but their mentors were Plato and other Greek writers and their illustrations for comparison with Rome were Greek city-states such as Athens and Sparta, which were much smaller than the Roman Republic that they knew and which were already practically defunct.

Chapter 12

⌣ The Era of the Roman Empire

This chapter covers a period of about six hundred years, from the reign of Augustus beginning in 31 B.C. until after the death of Justinian in 565 A.D. At the beginning of these centuries the Empire dominated the entire Mediterranean basin and much of the adjoining hinterland. By the third century a combination of internal crises, misgovernment, and decay, accompanied by the invasion of hordes of barbarians from the north and Persians from the east, led to a division of the Empire for administration and defense into two parts, western and eastern. The western part crumbled and succumbed under barbarian attacks. The eastern half continued to hold out for another thousand years but finally disappeared under the attacks and invasions of the Turks.

We shall deal here with certain matters related to the study and teaching of politics in the Empire as a whole down to the demise of Roman rule in the West and consider briefly a few developments in the eastern half of the Empire, also called Byzantium, through the reign of Justinian. The main story of Byzantium in connection with the central theme of this book will be dealt with in a later volume on medieval and modern times.

The study and teaching of politics were conspicuously absent from the curricula of even such institutions of higher education as were functioning during the second-century heyday of the Roman Empire.[1] "Universities" of one sort or another there were. In Rome in about 135 A.D. the emperor Hadrian built the Athenaeum, which has been called "the first public educational institution" in that city, and again "the first known public institution for higher education with salaried teachers."[2] "There rhetoricians and poets held their recitations, and salaried profes-

sors gave their lectures in the various branches of general liberal education, philosophy and rhetoric, as well as grammar and jurisprudence."[3]
But, be it noted, *not* in politics. Other cities in the Empire besides Rome
that are said by one writer or another to have had a "university" in ancient times are Alexandria (whose institution is often referred to as a
"museum and library"), Athens, Bordeaux, Constantinople, Pergamum,
and Rhodes.[4] In general I think it is safe to assume that most of these
ancient institutions were more like guilds of teachers using a building
in common than truly corporate universities in the modern sense. Their
exact nature is, however, beyond my scope here. What is of special concern to us is that none of them seem to have developed the study of politics as a distinct subject. We need to examine activities in such areas as
rhetoric and law to find whatever political content there was in Roman
education and writing.

Rhetoric in Roman Higher Education

A recent writer says that higher education "was identified with philosophy in Greek times, rhetoric and law in Roman times, and theology in
medieval times."[5] The general trends in ancient higher education could
hardly be more succinctly stated, although it must be remembered that
the Roman emphasis on rhetoric had, of course, Greek precedents.

In the time of the Empire, every large Roman city seems to have had
its teachers of rhetoric, some of them Greek, and Rome apparently had
many. The ability to formulate and deliver agreeable and persuasive
speeches was a highly rated achievement. But in the face of the monolithic political structure of the Empire, and of the repression from above
of all political dissent, there were severe limitations on the content of
orations.

Long before the Roman Empire came into being, the Greek teachers
of rhetoric, including Aristotle, had recognized that the practice of oratory, to which the knowledge of rhetoric made a principal contribution,
fell into three main divisions: deliberative oratory, which was designed
to sway legislative bodies to enact certain laws; forensic oratory, intended to influence courts and juries to decide for one side or the other
in court cases, whether civil or criminal; and epideictic oratory, prepared to mark patriotic, festive, or memorial occasions. Cicero along
with other Romans made significant contributions to the studies of both
rhetoric and oratory.[6]

Before the days of the Empire, the Romans, like the Greeks, had a period when political oratory stood high.[7] Cato was a political orator, as were the Gracchi brothers, Tiberius and Gaius, as well as Cicero, Brutus, and Caesar. But with Caesar's overthrow of the republican constitution "the occasions and materials for [political] oratory also disappeared . . . and the hindrances and limitations to its public exercise increased in the same proportion."[8] Deliberative oratory was abandoned almost entirely under the Empire. The decline and ultimate practical extinction of the legislative functions of the Senate and popular assemblies made this type of oratory practically useless. Forensic or courtroom oratory continued to be engaged in, and was a sort of prerequisite for the study of law. But it was the epideictic or display oratory that was most prominent among the Romans.

To protect and in a sense to "sell" to the people their own policies through appropriate spokesmen, the emperors took to licensing and paying out of their "personal-public" funds a number of rhetoricians whose functions included the entertainment of the people and their instruction in affairs suitable for the people to know.[9] It became unsafe for any unlicensed person to put himself forward as a teacher of rhetoric. Those licensed by the emperors who did well in their work of propagandizing for the ruler, and in pleasing the public, were in line for careers in the law and for important positions in the Empire. Understandably, whatever political matter entered into the rhetoricians' work, including their teaching, was unlikely to involve serious discussions or analysis of policy. A rhetorician could not risk incurring the emperor's displeasure, and thus jeopardizing his future. Brilliance of style, skillfulness in persuasion, and successful imitation of the best and safest orators of the past were what they aimed at, not deep study or original thought.

The Study of Law

In the Roman Empire teachers and writers in the field of law probably had a closer relationship to the emperors than the members of any other profession. Students of the history of political theory under the Roman Empire have found that writings of the great lawyers provide them with the best clues to the political thought of the time.[10] It is likewise necessary for us here to pay considerable attention to lawyers and their writings in this field; but the question still remains whether these reveal much about the study and teaching of politics.

We should recall that in early times in Rome, before about 450 B.C., the laws were not in written form at all. Rome was ruled by an aristocracy and the laws were the preserve of a College of Pontiffs representing this ruling class. These pontiffs memorized the laws and handed on their knowledge of them orally to new members of their group as they were recruited. Finally, the poorer people rebelled against being at the mercy of these pontiffs and demanded to have the laws put into writing. This was done in the form of the Twelve Tables, the earliest codification of Roman law. This was an essential and major step toward real due process. From then on the people had more and more access to and knowledge of the law. It is reported that one Tiberius Coruncanius (consul about 280 B.C. and *pontifex maximus* in about 253 B.C.) was a jurist who admitted law students and probably others to his consultations on legal subjects.[11] Thus public knowledge of the law began to spread.

Even to a people far from being entirely literate, the right to have the laws written out and posted up in public places was an advantage so great that they never willingly gave it up. When Caesar overthrew the Republic he made no effort to abolish this right. Instead he and his successors in office proceeded to utilize the legal system to strengthen their hold on the entire people.

As Republican Rome changed from being a single city-state into a conquering and expanding power, and then into the head of an Empire with a number of adjacent cities, peoples, and areas under its control, the body of laws became ever larger and more complex.[12] The accumulations of new laws issued by the emperors necessitated codifications and revisions from time to time. Besides that, it became increasingly more difficult for beginners to learn the laws, and yet a constantly increasing number of men learned in the laws was necessary to do the legal work of the courts and the government.

To meet the needs of the people and of the state for proper legal guidance and assistance, the emperors, no doubt with much assistance from the leading jurists, worked out a scheme of legal education and legal services to the public. Its essential elements were as follows. On the basis of some proof of competence, lawyers were licensed by the emperors, and unlicensed persons were forbidden to perform legal services. The Empire provided salaries for the licensed lawyers, but did not forbid them from earning additional remuneration, whether through teaching or the service of clients. Legal training became an important qualification for many appointive positions under the Empire, both in the courts and in the administration, including the very highest. The training of new lawyers was left to the private initiative of lawyers already licensed. There was some competition among law teachers, and their remuneration from their students was left to private arrangement between teacher and pupil. It was the duty of state-paid lawyers, at least in Rome itself and probably in other centers, to give legal aid and advice to the people generally, and apparently without charge. This service was evidently given at set times in designated rooms in public buildings, with the doors open to all.

These sessions are worth a little further attention. They were of two kinds, which were held at different times. First, there were systematic lectures summarizing the main points of law, from which resulted short written summaries of the law called *Institutes*. Once these books became available for student and public use, they were accepted as good teaching materials. Second, there were question-and-answer periods (*responsa*) in which a variety of questions were posed by those in the audience, or, failing that, by the lawyer-teacher in charge, who also provided the answers with explanations. Many of the responses were put into the digests and codes as acceptable statements of the law on various points.[13] These public sessions served several purposes. They were in a sense legal-aid clinics for the benefit of all the people. It is likely that the answers given often served as free legal advice to persons really interested and even helped to ward off litigation. They were also elementary law courses for young men planning to enter upon careers as lawyers. By sampling the lecture courses and the *responsa* sessions of several teachers, young men aspiring to become lawyers could select their teachers for more intensive study later. At the same time the teachers planning to write short works of *Institutes* or even longer treatises on law could in these sessions try out their materials on various audiences.

There were apparently no large law schools with numerous faculty members, but a number of small ones, many possibly with one teacher in each. These teachers divided, however, into two groups or societies, the Sabinians and the Proculians. The legal principles, if any, that separated them are not known, and it may be that they were simply two separate clubs or societies of lawyers.

It has been questioned whether the lawyers of highest rank known as jurisconsults deigned to teach law; was not this sort of teaching, like that done by the grammar school teacher, looked down upon by the ablest and most famous of jurists?[14] The attempt of an able German scholar in the latter part of the past century to answer this and certain related questions led to his writing one of the most complete accounts of the law schools and law teachers of the Roman Empire there is in print.[15] His well-documented conclusion was that law teaching was a respected calling and that leading jurists not only taught law but also wrote books to support their oral teaching. The emperors evidently made no protest against any of their principal legal advisers engaging in teaching to supplement their official salaries.

The freedom of the jurists to do this was clearly a part of the general understanding they had with the emperors who licensed and employed them. In return all lawyers holding an imperial license and receiving an imperial salary were not to question the emperor's absolute authority to head the Empire, to make and change the laws, and to conduct the government as he saw fit. They were to understand that they were like members of his own household, servants of his desires, and at his beck and call for any service. They were not like the members of the bar in a modern, free, democratic society, entitled to criticize and oppose the regime in court or otherwise, or to question its ethical or constitutional right to do certain things. They were in a true sense "kept professors," and legally incapable of opposing the emperor in anything he decided to do. They owed him counsel and assistance. They had no right or duty to try to protect the public or any individual against him.

This is, I confess, my own interpretation, but it helps to explain what I have found and failed to find out about the teaching of law in the Roman Empire. The law that was being taught then was almost entirely the law of private legal relations with respect to property rights of A against B, private contracts, marriage relations, wills and estates, private wrongs or torts, slavery and the freeing of slaves, and so on. No truly constitutional questions could be or were considered. Everything of any important public-law nature was practically ruled out of court by the simple proposition that the people (undefined) had by passing a *lex regia* (method of passage and contents undefined) irrevocably relinquished all their former law-making power, and by the same act delegated all this power to the emperor. In the words of Ulpian, the famous jurist of the late second and early third century A.D., "The will of the Emperor has the force of law, because by the passage of the *lex regia* the people transfers to him and vests in him all its own power and authority."[16]

In studying and teaching law under the Empire, therefore, there was no legal basis for questioning any action of the emperor, no matter how irrational, how violent, how destructive of life or anything else it might be. There was no limit on the emperor's powers, no question of due process, or of equal protection, or of adequate compensation for property seized by the emperor's orders. If the action taken by any officer of the government adversely affecting an individual was authorized by anything coming from the emperor, in any form—a letter, a decree, an imperial "constitution," or anything else—there was no case that any court could adjudicate. I have found one reference to a case under the Empire where a court asserted its power to decide which one of two relatively low-level administrative officials had jurisdiction over a certain matter, but this was a question of statutory interpretation.

There was, then, nothing of any political consequence to be dealt with in the law books—the codes, the digests, or the *Institutes*. In a technical legal sense these works are very impressive, but they are not political science or studies in politics.

In the *responsa* or question-and-answer sessions, embarrassing questions about the emperor and his government may have arisen at times. Relatively uninformed persons might not have realized how dangerously thin was the ice on which they stepped in asking any such questions. But an adroit teacher could certainly parry any questions relating to the powers of the emperor, the justness of his taxes, or the fairness of any law or decree, and thus protect his questioners—and himself—from prosecution for seditious or otherwise dangerous political utterances. As a matter of fact, it seems likely that the teacher often came to the *responsa* sessions prepared to fill the time with questions of his own in the form of hypothetical cases so that there would be no opportunity for the discussion of politically controversial matters. Franz Bremer, whose *Teachers of Law and Schools of Law in the Roman Empire* is my principal source of information on the Roman law schools, provides many examples of hypothetical cases in law, some of them ludicrously complicated, that were brought up in the question periods. These included questions on dowries, wills, property in slaves, abortion, the marriage relation, the wrongful conversion of personal property left as security, creditors' rights against estates, rents, sales, the freeing of slaves, and other private law issues. Public-law questions, even such as concerned the powers and problems of municipalities, were conspicuously lacking.

In short I submit that the teaching of public law in any deep or searching sense was not a part of the work of the Roman law teachers in imperial times.

The Study of Public Administration

Problems of public administration were faced by the emperors as early as the reign of Augustus and continued to receive attention from them and their leading officials down through the centuries. It is hard if not impossible to set either a beginning or a terminal date for this study because there are no records of specific studies but only of changes made and things done, and even these reports are not many. We may surmise that when people within the administrative hierarchy met with problems and difficulties, they put their minds to work on them, discussed them with fellow officials and, at the top level, with the emperor himself, and finally agreed upon certain changes in administrative organization, procedures, and personnel, which the emperor then would order into effect.[17]

From a modern viewpoint one of the most significant features of this procedure in Roman times is that, as far as I have been able to ascertain, it was carried through entirely within the government. There were no outside institutions or individuals engaged in studying or in teaching about administrative problems. In modern democratic societies, especially in North America and in Europe, men in institutions of higher education, professional societies, special research agencies, and foundations are constantly probing into matters affecting government and public administration and publishing reports containing recommendations for improvements. In addition legislative committees, government departments, and governmentally sponsored and financed commissions of inquiry, national, state, and local, are frequently engaged in similar investigations. We even have state commissions to study and to recommend state constitutional revisions, and city charter commissions to revise city charters or to propose revisions. The results of such inquiries are usually published for all citizens to read. In the Roman Empire the attitude was just the reverse. The emperors discouraged the people in all possible ways from inquiring into the inner operations of the government. The fear that factions might be formed to overthrow the regime was so strong in imperial circles that even the organization of social clubs was restricted and required a license from the authorities. Only innocuous groups like burial societies were likely to obtain licenses. Furthermore, there was no provision for any publication of internal changes in the government. Such matters were considered to be essentially the private affairs of the emperor. In a number of cases he used his private slaves and other employees to handle public business, and no one really dared to inquire about the line between his private funds and the public revenues.

I would hazard a guess that somewhere in the masterworks on Roman history and in the voluminous periodical literature on that subject some material will be found that throws more light on Roman Empire studies in public administration than I have presented here. The time limitations under which I have labored, in this matter as in others, have prevented me from attempting to exhaust all the resources open to scholarship. From what I have been able to read my conclusions are that, under the emperors, a number of studies were made into the subjects of central, regional, and local administration; that they were made within the administrative services themselves, both at Rome and in outlying parts of the Empire; that they resulted in changes in organization, personnel, powers, and procedures; and that the emperors in approving such changes tried to see to it that their own powers and perquisites were no way seriously impaired. If they happened to benefit the public, so much the better for the emperor's public relations.

As to the teaching of public administration generally to young men of, say, college age, a field of instruction that has developed very fully in the West in recent times, I find no trace of that in what I have been able to learn about the Roman Empire. Even within the Roman imperial administration I suspect that the teaching (i.e., in-service training) went little farther than was necessary to prepare each man to perform his own duties.

Philosophy and Ethics

Among the Greeks of the fourth century B.C., it was certain philosophers, notably Plato and Aristotle, who took the lead in studying and writing about the problems of the city-states and the best forms of government. With all its great extent and large population, the entire Roman Empire in the first three centuries A.D. produced no philosophers to compare with these. But there were some respectable ones who should be mentioned: the Greek Epictetus (A.D. 55–175); Marcus Aurelius, the Roman emperor and philosopher (A.D. 121–180); Plotinus, the Greek Neoplatonist (A.D. 204–270), and a number of lesser lights including Diogenes Laertius, who flourished about 150 A.D. and was a compiler of other men's philosophical works, and Philostratus (A.D. c. 170–245), a mystic and philosopher of sorts.

These men surely knew much about politics, from reading, observing, and experience. The case of the Emperor Marcus Aurelius is obvious. Plotinus, who has been called "the last of the great philosophers of antiquity,"[18] late in life toyed with the idea of establishing an ideal city in Campania, where people would live in accordance with Plato's *Laws*.[19] The Emperor Gallienus scotched this idea. In general Plotinus' ideas were rather ethereal and introspective and not concerned with the actual world of human affairs and politics. Barker says of him that "He is non-social as well as non-political; he has no feeling for community, and no feeling for any association or voluntary society, any more than for the State and its political organization."[20] Epictetus wrote some sage words of caution to men not to communicate their political thoughts lightly for fear of the spies who tried to trap the unwary into disclosing their thoughts against the regime. Others, too, touch upon politics in their writings, but none of them made any significant study of the subject.

History and Biography

Specialized histories in religion, science, art, or literature, to name a few examples, can be written with little or no attention to politics and government. General histories of any place or people, on the other hand, can hardly be written at all without considerable discussion of these twin subjects. The social, economic, political, and other phases of a people's life are distinguishable but hardly separable. Time divisions or annals and place or geography, along with population and resources, provide a framework for history; but it is the life, ideas, activities, and experiences of the people, especially in the fields of politics and government, that supply most of the stuff of history.

When compared with the student of contemporary government and politics, the historian who by definition deals with past rather than current affairs has some advantages—primarily in perspective and objectivity. For scholars in the Roman Empire there was of course an additional practical advantage in restricting their accounts to earlier regimes: they would not have to fear reprisal from the emperor in power should he object to an account of his government and policies.

In any case the historians of the Empire period did not deal at all critically with rulers living at the time they wrote, nor did they even produce any very controversial studies of earlier rulers and their governments. Tacitus (c. 55–118 A.D.) was somewhat exceptional. He took advantage of the fact that he was living at a time when there were emperors whose policies he could praise (Nerva, 96–98 A.D., and his son Trajan, 98–117 A.D.), and, balancing his criticisms of former emperors to some extent with defense and praise of the current rulers and their policies, he wrote with rather more frankness than was generally attempted.[21] Tacitus also made a study of a foreign and relatively unspoiled people, the Germans, which by implication at least showed a striking contrast between them and the somewhat decadent Romans.

Tacitus had several contemporaries who, though not all really historians, also seized the opportunity afforded by the rule of some liberal-minded emperors to discuss politicians, rulers, and government with the evident serious purpose of giving instruction to princes and the rulers of the people. Plutarch (46–120 A.D.) wrote many paired biographies of famous men which included accounts of a number of political leaders and rulers. Suetonius (69–140 A.D.) also wrote political biographies, while Dio Cocceianus, sometimes called Dion Chrysostom (40–c. 112 A.D.), an orator and philosopher, directed much of his writing to the Emperor Trajan, to whom he addressed some laudatory speeches "on the duty of a prince." Arrian (c. 95–c. 170 A.D.), a Greek, who had some importance as a philosopher and disciple of Epictetus, was also an able historian. He wrote historical accounts of Parthia and India and a historical biography of Alexander the Great. These writers unavoidably had to study politics in a certain sense, but no more than other historians have done, and they did not hold themselves forth as teachers of politics, or write any significant works on the Roman political system.

Kingship and the Education of the Prince

The entire age from Alexander through the era of the Roman Empire was one in which kings under various titles, and in practice only slightly checked by aristocratic or popular controls, dominated most of the governments from the borders of India on the east to the Atlantic Ocean on the west. Rome was one of the last places to give up republican government, but after Caesar had defeated the republican forces there his successors went on to solidify their power and extend their control throughout the entire area. As a result, from east to west, throughout the Mediterranean basin, there was in effect only one real monarch, the emperor. Small wonder then that kingship or emperorship came to be a dominant, almost a monopolistic, concept in men's thoughts about government and politics. An emperor seemed to be almost a natural phenomenon, an indispensable and ever present means for directing the government and providing for the defense and welfare of the people. So high and remote did the emperor seem that deification of each incumbent of the office came to be accepted as a normal arrangement.

It is not my intention to try to summarize or to explain the different theories of kingship that were prevalent. Ernest Barker has written a valuable volume that provides much material and a number of leads to the writings available on the various concepts.[22] But I should like to comment briefly on one aspect of this subject that might be assumed to have some bearing on developments in the study and teaching of politics, that of education for the princes.

Considering the fact that each emperor usually wanted a son to succeed him, and would adopt one if necessary, it is not surprising that the education of the prince became an important matter. We have seen how Philip of Macedon called in Aristotle and paid him well to tutor Alexander. The idea of a special education for the heir-apparent is an ancient one. Such education undoubtedly included at all times and everywhere some instruction in government, from the viewpoint of the powers, rights, and duties of the king that the prince was expected some day to become, but it also covered much more. When started early, as it usually was, it included instruction in language, Latin or Greek, or both; rhetoric (always rhetoric!) or the ability to speak well; sometimes philosophy, music, and other cultural subjects. How much political content was included for the more mature princes it is hard to say. Probably no teaching of princes in the Empire period even approached in difficulty and political content the instruction that Aristotle gave Alexander. We may assume, of course, that if any politics were to be taught to the prince, the tutor appointed to give the instruction would have been selected with great care to get one of approved and safe views.

I have made no special effort to ascertain how many and what princes were given education for kingship, or to find out who were the tutors appointed for the several princes. Mentioned in the literature are Seneca the Younger, the philosopher and rhetorician in the first century A.D., appointed by Claudius to tutor Nero; Fronto the rhetorician in the second century chosen by the joint emperors Hadrian and Antoninus Pius to educate the princes Marcus Aurelius and Lucius Verus; and Ausonius, the fourth-century poet and professor of grammar and rhetoric, entrusted by Valentinian to educate his son Gratian.

It seems to me that the writings on kingship and the education of princes reveal no clear and decisive efforts in the Empire to study and teach politics as such, not even to princes. Grammar, rhetoric, and oratory stand out most clearly as subjects to be mastered by the princes, and whatever was taught to them on politics was kept more or less unreported. The essays on kingship are primarily theoretical and ethical—what ought to be—and are not such as to suggest much study of the actual institution and how it operated.

The Christians and the Empire

I have put off to the end of this chapter any consideration of political studies and teaching that may have emanated from the rising Christian religion and its church. The year of Jesus' birth is now believed to have been between 8 and 4 B.C., and his death came by crucifixion in about 30 A.D., when he was about 35 years old.[23] Inspired by his life, his works, and his sayings, men founded the several branches of the Christian religion that together dominate (at least numerically) the Western world, and account for well over a fourth of the world's population.[24] Historically it is in the area of Christian numerical supremacy that the study and teaching of politics have made their greatest advances. And because church and state have been closely associated in developing Western ideas, education, and political institutions, much attention needs to be paid to the interrelations and the influences upon each other of religious and political institutions and of both these upon the special historical development that I am here trying to outline. For the ancient period, however, there is very little to report that bears directly on the study and teaching of politics.

It would be an easy thing to dismiss the meager Christian beginnings in the study of politics by saying that the non-Christians did not study and teach politics seriously because they did not dare, while the Christians did not do so because they did not care. Such a contrast points in the right direction perhaps, but it is not a sufficient explanation. For example, the Christians too might not have dared even if they had cared. Moreover it assumes something about Christians that is not necessarily true of all of them. We need to look at the record, slight as it is.

The world into which the Christian religion was born and in which it grew to considerable strength was that of the Roman Empire, which in welding the one great political unit had leveled classes, mixed and equalized various tribes and nationalities, and opened the doors to travel by all throughout its entire area. The Christian religion found the waterways and the roads by land open in all directions to its missionaries. Communication with potential converts in all parts of the Empire was made reasonably easy by the widespread knowledge of Greek and Latin. The church took full advantage of the benefits the Empire offered and spread its arms widely. Its very success brought troubles. It claimed to represent the one and only true God and his crucified Son—but this God by definition could not be and was not among the pantheon of the gods of the Empire whom the emperor represented before all the people. Believers in other gods attacked these upstart Christians who condemned the pagan gods and the graven images. The emperors, too, found the new sect to be a trial, and alternately persecuted them and were more lenient. But attacked in one place the church grew in another, and every respite from persecution led to further growth. In time the Christians became the largest single sect in the Empire, and the emperors had to make peace with them. Partly if not mainly because Rome was the political capital it also became the center for church activities. Its bishop came to outrank others. Political power *within* the church began to center in him almost by force of circumstances, because he was the one nearest to the emperor and some of the main problems of the church were essentially political, namely, the relations of the church to the state or Empire.

The ways in which an accommodation was worked out between the church and the Empire do not concern me here. Simply stated, the church leaders reached a stage in which they needed the respectability and security that might go with recognition by the emperors. They even needed the emperor's support to suppress dissident movements and doctrinal schisms, so that a single ecumenical church could stand up alongside the universal Empire. On the other hand the emperors at times needed the support of the church. In order to get the help of the emperors the church had to accept control by the emperors. For a time in the later years of the Empire, the emperor was at the head of the Christian church, especially in the eastern half of the Empire, and actually controlled the appointments to bishoprics and other offices within it. Later the church reasserted its independence, but this is a story well beyond the time limits of this volume.

For doctrinal clues to the Christian attitude toward government and politics one must look into both the Hebrew backgrounds of the Christian church as revealed in the Old Testament, and the changes introduced by the New Testament books. (It should be noted that the earliest Christians undoubtedly had some documents concerning the life and teachings of Jesus, written in Hebrew or Aramaic, but the books accepted as making up the New Testament are not from the time of Christ's life but later, and were originally in Greek. Paul's writings are probably the earliest; he died in 64 A.D., at about the time of the Emperor Nero. The synoptic gospels of Matthew, Mark, and Luke came still later, after the Roman destruction of Jerusalem in 70 A.D.)

Briefly stated, the old doctrine was that God was the source of all law and government. Moses received the law from God on Mount Sinai. All Hebrew secular and religious authority was subject to and bound by the laws laid down by God. The priests and prophets who knew and expounded God's laws stood above kings and other worldly rulers. They alone had the right to interpret the laws of God and to lay down rules of right conduct for kings and other secular officials. Coming into a world dominated by the emperors at Rome, and finding himself goaded by opponents who wished to get him into trouble with the Roman rulers in Judea, Jesus was forced to find a new formula concerning the relations between the secular authorities and the God whom he preached. As reported in Matthew (22:17–22) and with slight variations in Mark and Luke, we find him in Jerusalem telling parables to a crowd when some Pharisees decide to bait him: " 'Tell us, then, what you think. Is it lawful to pay taxes to Caesar, or not?' But Jesus, aware of their malice, said, 'Why put me to the test, you hypocrites? Show me the money for the tax.' And they brought him a coin. And Jesus said to them, 'Whose likeness and inscription is this?' They said, 'Caesar's.' Then he said to them, 'Render therefore to Caesar the things that are Caesar's, and to God the things that are God's.' When they heard it, they marveled; and they left him and went away."

This parable raises a number of questions, in fact more than it answers. It ignores the fact that the emperor ("Caesar") was the religious as well as the secular head of the Empire—there being no distinction in Roman practice between the two—and that he represented in person, whether deified or not, the whole pantheon of Roman gods. It overlooks the facts that the emperor did not own all the money on which his face appeared, and that the same coins were being used constantly for contributions to the gods—and even to Jesus' own God. It blandly assumes what the Pharisees might have accepted but not the Romans—that there was but a single God who stood over against Caesar, and that all the Roman gods were nothing. Moreover, the advice given in the parable, to "Render therefore to Caesar the things that are Caesar's, and to God the things that are God's," provides no clue to which things belong to each. By the old Hebrew standard all things really belonged to God, who created not only the world but also man, and made all the laws for him. By the Roman standard of Jesus' time both religious and secular affairs were completely under the emperor's sole control, albeit his power was by delegation from the people; and the emperor was himself a god, a deified person, a sort of embodiment of all the Roman gods.

Despite these and other difficulties inherent in the parable, it points toward a major issue, or cluster of issues, that plagued the church throughout its early history, many of which are still unresolved today—church-state relations. The parable undoubtedly had much effect in creating the impression that there are two distinct and separate spheres of human interest and activity, and that each should be allowed by the other to co-exist and to function freely in its own sphere, without interference by the other. One result of this was to turn the minds of most churchmen toward studying and teaching about the things of God, thus leaving in general the study of political, economic, military, and other mundane matters to those who are not of the clergy. This line has never been rigidly drawn, nor has any line ever been fully observed by either side. Powerful churchmen and church groups have brought their influence to bear against governments and their rulers, and powerful political leaders and political parties have moved governments to take away long-vested church rights, have disestablished the established, and have even, as in the U.S.S.R. in this century, thrown their weight against all religions and religious observances. There is much evidence that the church leaders in the Roman Empire gave extended thought to problems of church-state relations but they did so generally as special pleaders for the church's interests and viewpoint, not as philosophers or political scientists trying to view the problems broadly and impartially.

In a valuable work that has helped me greatly, *From Alexander to Constantine,* Ernest Barker has brought together some excellent examples of the political thought and speculations of Jewish forerunners of the Christian church fathers and leaders, and also of some of the church's own most famous apologists for the centuries just after the death of Christ. I must emphasize that Barker's aim was to present a "history of social and political ideas" during the centuries that he covers, and that many people may have interesting speculations and ideas on political matters without being careful students of the field and certainly without concentrating on politics, writing significantly about it, or teaching it. I therefore shall draw on Barker's material very selectively.

Barker's collection of Jewish documents begins with some passages from later chapters of the book of Daniel.[25] These set forth the writer's visions in the second century B.C. of the fall of four great kingdoms—Babylonian, Median, Persian, and Alexandrian. They are depicted as four great beasts, and their destruction as the work of a deliverer coming to save mankind from such beasts. This deliverer is to be a sort of Messiah or savior, in human likeness, and his kingdom will not be destroyed. Following these visions Barker presents extracts from a letter of about 100 B.C. written by a Jew named Aristeas who, under Hellenistic influences, discusses in dialogue form his ideal of a king—one who keeps the law, preserves peace, and does justice.[26] Next from the book of Ecclesiastes (about 200 B.C.), Barker gives an excerpt of warning to beware of royal spies (under Ptolemaic or Seleucid kings)—"Curse not the king . . . for a bird of the air shall carry the voice."[27] From *Ecclesiasticus* comes a piece on meditating and finding wisdom "in the law of the Most High," and so becoming wise and being called in to advise rulers (an early example of training for the public service?).[28]

But enough of these examples from pre-Christian times. They reveal mainly the speculations of men whose thoughts are really on God and who have little to say about the problems of actual government and politics. Let me consider in conclusion three fairly outstanding writers, not teachers of politics, of whom there were few if any in their time, and yet men who obviously studied politics to some extent while devoting their minds and time mainly to other things.

Philo Judaeus (c. 30 B.C.–45 A.D., or c. 20 B.C.–50 A.D.) was a learned Jew who lived at Alexandria in a momentous period, and he combined Jewish with Greek learning.[29] Primarily a philosopher and an apologist for Jewish thought and religion, he was drawn into political activity in diplomatic missions and other work in defense of the Jewish sub-community of his home city, Alexandria. He thus had a close-up look at politics at an important place at a crucial time in the early Empire. His main political work is *De Josepho*, subtitled *The Statesman*.

Origen (c. 185–254 A.D.) was born in Alexandria of Christian parents. He devoted a lifetime to scholarship and the work of the church. Probably few men of his time were as well and broadly educated as he. Of vigorous, original, and independent mind, he produced much learned writing, mostly about the Christian faith and biblical literature. One of his works is a little different from the rest.[30] Some ten years before he was born, a Roman named Celsus had written a book attacking the Christian religion and its monotheism, and arguing that the Christian doctrines about not serving two masters were making Christians disloyal to the emperor. In replying to Celsus in *Contra Celsum*, Origen gives evidence that he had made a careful study of the problems involved in obeying God on the one hand and the laws of the state on the other. If he had dealt with other and broader problems of government as ably as he did this one, he would have made a considerable contribution to the study of politics. It happened, however, that his real interest was in the church and religion.

St. Augustine, born in 354 A.D., is the last of the ancient Christian writers to be considered here. For a century or more after him there is little to relate about either Christian or pagan writings that have any importance for the study of politics. He was born in North Africa, educated mainly there, and spent most of his life there also, though he did live for a short time in Rome and taught rhetoric for a year or more at Milan. He became a priest and finally a bishop. He gathered a considerable library, and spent much time in reading and writing.

His book of *Confessions* is famous and has been widely read. It betrays an almost morbid interest in his sinful youth and relates how he found God and so came to be a Christian. He evidently did not take enough interest in politics to make any specific inquiries in that field that were worthy of more than a mention in the *Confessions*. Another major work of his is *The City of God* (*De Civitate Dei*). It is a protracted contrast between an imaginary City of God and the city of man, Rome, with all the praise going to the former. Based upon his reading (and he cites many works relevant to politics among human beings), he finds much that is evil in the city of man—the lust for power, corruption, violence—while the City of God is always righteous and resplendent. The one God of Christianity is in all ways superior to the many gods of Rome. This work reminds one of Plato's genuine aversion to politics— and like Plato's writings it provides no careful study of political constitutions, practices, procedures, or behavior. It is the work of a man whose entire thought is God-centered and who sees little use in studying the actualities of human politics with a view to improving them. It is so much more easy to describe in glowing terms a wished-for City of God to which Christians can look forward as their future heavenly home.

St. Augustine died in 430 A.D., while Gaiseric and his Vandals were already engaged in conquering northern Africa. The Roman Empire in the West was fast disintegrating and in 476 the last emperor in the West gave up his position and his title. In theory the Roman Empire still existed as a single entity, and Justinian, who was emperor of the eastern part from 527 to 565 A.D., made a brilliant effort to reconquer the lost western and African portions so as to reunite them with the eastern part. His success, which was achieved at high cost, was only partial and ephemeral. Within a short time after his death, further efforts to reunite and revivify the Empire as a whole were abandoned. Indeed the emperors of the eastern half, or Byzantium, were soon finding it difficult to hold together any considerable part of the eastern moiety. By 600 A.D., it is safe to say, the age of the Roman Empire had reached its end. The so-called Dark Ages had set in.

Of the foregoing three writers, Philo Judaeus, Origen, and St. Augustine, I think it is fair to say that none of their extant works would be classified today as studies in government or politics. Their interests were primarily in theology. What they contributed to political science was minor and marginal.

EPILOGUE
CONDITIONS FAVORING POLITICAL STUDIES

↰ Conditions Favoring Political Studies

WHILE government in some form, however crude and limited among primitive peoples, has probably been continuous in the history of mankind, time out of mind, the study and teaching of politics—of the formal and informal activities connected with the governing of human communities—have had a strictly limited and partly broken career. It seems obvious that certain minimum conditions are necessary to make such study possible at all, and that the optimum conditions for a true flourishing of this endeavor go far beyond the minimum. By placing into historical context the developments in political study and teaching during ancient times, I have tried in this volume to cast light on the conditions that are fundamental to its rise and growth and on those that are essentially inimical to it.

I have throughout my investigation asked such questions as these: In what geographic areas and under what economic and political conditions did the study of politics make its greatest progress? How did religious beliefs and the relationships between religion and politics seem to affect the study? Where the study developed, what other studies of human problems developed along with it and how if at all did they influence it? What related studies that we know today were lacking and how did these lacunae in knowledge influence such studies of politics as were made? Where the study of politics did develop into something important, what aspects or branches of the study as we know them today were neglected and what ones were emphasized? And, finally, the central question: How can we explain the relative precocity in political studies that the Greeks demonstrated in contrast to the backwardness of other early peoples?

329

A brief summary of the material explored in the earlier chapters may serve to bring into sharp focus the important findings on which I base my general conclusions concerning the conditions that must be present if effective political studies are to take place. I realize full well that the inferences I have drawn must be tentative and provisional. Later students will no doubt reach somewhat different conclusions. This is the way of progress in scholarship, and I gladly accept it.

The lack of writing and records among ancient primitive peoples goes far to explain why we have practically no knowledge of any political studies by them. The ancient Babylonians, Mesopotamians, and Egyptians, on the other hand, had and used systems of writing, and they left administrative and judicial records. However, these people were generally so organized under one-man rule that whatever studies were made took place primarily within the government, and there was little attempt by men outside the government to study and teach politics. From the documents that have survived and been recovered it is evident that within governmental circles studies were made on questions of administrative organization, public finance, and foreign relations. Law codes were written down also, but these dealt almost entirely with the legal relations of private persons. No attempts appear to have been made in these ancient states to teach the people about government and it is likely that any private citizen who was indiscreet enough to publicize studies of his own would have been looked upon by the ruler and his officials as an impious and dangerous person—impious because the ruler was viewed, especially in Egypt, as being in a real sense divine. As a result, practically no writings about politics have come down to us from the most ancient times in Egypt and the Near East.

To the Israelites and the Jews, who for long stretches of time were not self-governing, only God—Yahweh or Jehovah—and his law were worthy of study. Man and his affairs stood low on the scale. What the kings on earth plotted and did was misguided and futile if it did not lead them and their peoples to the worship of God, the true King. Except in certain historical accounts, the Old Testament books pay little attention to the study of politics.

It was the Greeks who first thought politics really important enough to study and who first grappled firmly with the subject. Earlier descriptive and historical works about individual city-states were followed in the fifth and fourth centuries B.C. by more comprehensive historical, descriptive, and even theoretical works, culminating near the end of the fourth century in Aristotle's great work on *Politics,* on the governments of the city-states, which includes also some references to non-Greek states. In these two centuries there were over a hundred Greek city-states, all independent self-governing units, which had different forms of government and went through diverse changes of constitution. Hence the question arose in some minds among these inquisitive people, What is the best form of government?

In seeking the answer to this question, the Greek political writers had certain distinct advantages. The Greeks were one people, using substantially the same language. The Greek attitude toward life was essentially secular. Each *polis* had gods of its own and the people showed much respect for the leading gods in the nation's pantheon; but these gods were not "God." Unlike the priestly teachers of the Jews, who stressed God at all times, the Greeks taught and studied a great number of things of human interest—language, rhetoric, mathematics, science, and whatnot—and at least elementary education was fairly widespread. This general secular attitude opened the door to inquiries into a variety of human, literary, and scientific problems, not the least of which concerned the institutions of the cities in which they lived. Furthermore, distances were short and travel was relatively common and easy, so that opportunities for men from different cities to compare experiences in politics as in other fields were considerable. The Greeks were in addition keen observers, and sensitive to differences between one place and another. Since each city-state was small, information about its government and leaders would be fairly common knowledge among the citizens.

We should remind ourselves here of certain facts about the population and geographic size of ancient political units. A glance at the map of the eastern Mediterranean will help to make my point. Babylonia was the small tract of land between the Euphrates and Tigris rivers at the head of the Persian Gulf, which had as its center a city-state, Babylon. Mesopotamia, farther up these rivers, was not much larger. Egypt was a narrow strip of arable land on both sides of the Nile lying to the north of the first cataract at Khartoum. Greece including the islands then as now had an area of about 52,000 square miles. An average city-state in ancient Greece might have covered an area of about 520 square miles, and would have had a population numbered in the thousands, or at most tens of thousands. States in the world today range in population from Communist China (nearly 700 millions) down through India (over 450 millions), the U.S.S.R. (over 200 millions), and the U.S.A. (over 185 millions), to some of less than a million. It may be of interest that the average population of the more than one hundred member states in the United Nations today is in the neighborhood of 22 millions, more than four times the combined populations of all the Greek city-states. Just to mention these contrasts in population figures for states then and now is to call attention to an influential factor in determining the nature of political studies then and now. In terms of geographic area the contrast is equally striking, for the modern student of politics has to take all the governments of the world into his considerations whereas Greek political writers dealt almost exclusively with a small area occupied by the Greeks at the northeastern corner of the Mediterranean Sea, which amounts to less than one-tenth of one per cent of the world's land area. Aristotle's political studies, important as they were, were based mainly upon the recorded experiences of one people of small population occupying a relatively small land area.

Because the governments of the city-states were on such a small scale, certain problems and aspects of government that came to light under the Romans were not apparent to the Greeks. The city-states had no need for large-scale administrative departments composed of many civil servants with appropriate training and division of labor. The taxing systems and methods of financial administration of the city-states were proportionately simple if not crude. It is understandable that Greek political writers including Aristotle would give relatively little attention to public administration and public finance. Economics, which has been so important a partner of the study of politics in modern times, also was but little developed under the Greeks, and partly because of the smallness of the size of their city-states.

The study of the law, which received such great attention under the Romans, also suffered considerable neglect under the Greeks. It must be admitted that while Rome was still only a city-state, it too developed very little study of law. Only as it conquered, and in effect annexed, neighboring cities and peoples did the Romans make both extensive and intensive studies of the law. For the Greeks with their many little city-states, each with its own legal system, it would have been an almost impossible and largely useless task to collate and study the many little legal systems. Anything like comprehensive and intensive legal scholarship would not have found a broad enough base or have been in sufficient demand among the Greek city-states to warrant the effort. Constitutional law in the modern American sense hardly existed in the Greek city-states. International law and relations received a little attention from the Greeks, but in general the relations among the city-states turned in the direction of either war and destruction, or confederation to avoid destruction. Confederation was an arrangement of convenience and was not looked upon as a way of making larger political units that would supplant the city-states. The Greeks clung stubbornly to the city-state as the only true political unit. This shortsightedness among the Greeks generally was reflected even by Aristotle and was a limitation on the study and teaching of politics done in this era.

Nevertheless, whatever their shortcomings, the Greek works represent the crest of political studies during ancient times—and they reached an impressive height. After the Greeks came a rapid deterioration.

The Romans, of course, never showed any such interest as the Greeks did in studies of politics, or for that matter in the study of other subjects except military matters and later law. The oligarchy that controlled the Senate under the Republic and that through the Senate and the high appointed officials ruled Rome and all the lands and peoples that the Republic conquered, had no taste for political studies. They held the power of the state in their hands and could see no reason to encourage studies that might be unsettling to their political authority. The writings of a Polybius who praised the Roman system could be tolerated, and so could the later writings of a Cicero who had served the Roman state well. But even Cicero fell under suspicion and suffered for his views. In short the atmosphere in Rome under the Republic was one of deep suspicion toward intellectuals who dabbled in political discussion.

As the Republic was transformed into an Empire by conquests abroad and by overthrow of the oligarchy at home, and a giant monolithic state ruled by one man and his advisers was created, there was still less incentive for any study of politics. No other states existed in reasonably close proximity to permit comparative governmental studies or to encourage some analysis of international relations; while at home the government became in effect the private preserve of the emperors. There was nothing connected with government that citizens could study with any hope of action by them that would ameliorate their situation. Under a few of the better emperors there was some encouragement to leading citizens to take part in municipal affairs, but even this became such an unrewarding burden that men tried to escape such responsibilities and even the study of the government of cities died out.

Within the imperial administration there was undoubtedly much study of military problems, the relations of the Empire with the tribes that impinged on it at many points, and the establishment, the administration, and the financing of public services. The results of some of these studies are written in the defensive walls set up in northern Britain and Scotland, in the network of imperial highways, in the architecture of Rome and other cities, as well as in public records of the doles and the circuses provided for the people. But there was no attempt to instruct the people in the affairs of government. There was no general public school system for the Empire, and little or no imperial support for higher education. Law had a high standing in the Empire but it was private law that was studied, not public or constitutional law.

As the Empire began to wane in strength from the third century A.D. on, the Christian church became an increasingly important force in the lives of the people. But whatever individual churchmen like Origen or St. Augustine might do in speculating about government, and whatever the church leaders might do more practically to get the support of the emperors, the church itself engaged in and encouraged no studies or teaching in the fields of government and politics. Following the formula stated by Jesus himself, to "Render therefore to Caesar the things that are Caesar's, and to God the things that are God's," Christians generally felt justified in leaving worldly affairs like politics to the emperor and his government while they prepared themselves for the Kingdom of God, whether on earth or in heaven.

We now come back to the question, How can we explain the relative precocity in political studies that the Greeks demonstrated in contrast to the backwardness of other early peoples—both those who preceded them in time and the Romans who came after? Certain conditions can, I think, be isolated that existed among the Greek city-states but that did not exist, or did not all exist, for any of the other peoples:

1. *A multiplicity of states within easy reach.* The existence of a number of independent or self-governing states within the ken and reach of men who wished to study government and politics was a striking characteristic of the area dominated by the Greek people for several cen-

turies up to Aristotle's time. In using the phrase "ken and reach" I have in mind ease of travel and communication; the use of the same language, Greek, which included a definite word, *polis*, for the political unit, city-state, and hence for politics; and a certain openness with respect to information. For the Greeks the shortness of distances involved made up in part for the lack of the means of transportation and communication that men possess today. The fact that some states like Sparta then and the U.S.S.R. and certain other Communist-dominated countries today have been so afflicted with xenophobia as to make direct observation of their governmental systems by outsiders very difficult does not entirely prevent studies of them—there are many ways of obtaining some reliable information through, over, or around an apparently impenetrable wall, as the cases of Sparta and the U.S.S.R. confirm. In any case during the Greek era there were enough states open to observation to fulfill this condition; the same is true today.

2. *Variety and change in state governments.* A considerable degree of freedom in changing laws and constitutions was revealed by the Greek city-states. The local accounts or "histories" of such changes that Aristotle collected provided some of his best material for appraising the operation of political institutions and for revealing certain trends in constitutions. It is not enough to know the statics of a political situation. The dynamics, and reasons for the changes being made, are usually more revealing.

3. *Freedom of speech and inquiry about political matters.* The Greeks had a long and on the whole valuable experience in the open discussion of their governments, officials, and problems, and in the investigation of city-state affairs. In the election campaigns and in the meetings of local assemblies there was evidently a great deal of free speech and candid criticism. There was always some danger that speakers would be attacked, but the Greeks of the fifth and fourth centuries B.C. apparently took this risk in stride. The local histories that Aristotle used were themselves evidence of widespread free inquiry. Except for the lack of printed books and newspapers, the Greeks were about as well situated with respect to free discussion of political questions as the colonists in America in the seventeenth and eighteenth centuries, and much better off than most Europeans in medieval times when the areas of the states were larger, communications were relatively poor, languages differed, and most people were rather far removed from the seats of power.

4. *Written records and accounts.* Though they lacked printing, the Greeks had many written records, written laws, and various forms of literature in writing. As numerous slaves, among others, learned how to write, it was possible to have handwritten copies of the items most in demand made available to the public at small cost. The writers of the local histories must have made considerable use of such written materials, just as Aristotle in turn made use of their writings.

5. *Financial resources and educational institutions.* Besides the schools of the Sophists and rhetoricians, Athens had the well-endowed Academy, founded by Plato, and Aristotle's Lyceum, which also had substantial financial support. Such institutions provided the facilities and staff for scientific research as well as for teaching. Out of the work at the Lyceum particularly came major political studies. The great research project on city-state constitutions that preceded the *Politics* would have been impossible without the resources of a great research center.

These five conditions are, I believe, essential if the scientific study of politics is to develop. But still something more is needed. This "something" is what one might call *a social science attitude.* By this I mean a secular, man-respecting, and scientific approach to the study of human affairs. Such an approach involves primarily a willingness, indeed eagerness, to observe the propensities, activities, and institutions of men, and an attempt through the gathering and analysis of data to find uniformities in what they do and to develop defensible explanations thereof that fit the facts. The evidence can be only such as comes to the minds of men through their eyes, their ears, and their other natural faculties; there can be no injection into the findings and explanations of any unevidenced and unprovable assumptions concerning the acts of demons, gods, or God as causal factors in the realm of human affairs.

In their several and different ways the Delphic Oracle, Plato, the priests of the various Greek gods, the Jewish priests, and the "fathers" of the early Christian church brought supernatural beings and forces into their explanations of human events. God or the gods punished men when things went wrong with their plans, and when things went well God or the gods were to get the credit—although men might incidentally garner some share of credit for success on the grounds that they had acted according to the wish of God or the gods. Greek scientists, on the other hand, had a naturalistic approach to phenomena and did not resort to the gods in seeking to discover and explain the laws of nature. Aristotle took substantially this same position in his biological studies and maintained it in his studies in politics. This was an exceedingly important step for the study of politics even though the city-states he studied were only miniature prototypes of modern states, and his research and teaching center, the Lyceum, was only a miniature prototype of the modern university or great research center.

Given the conditions affecting the study of politics that prevailed in his lifetime, it seems to me that Aristotle was more successful than any other Greek student of his era in turning them to good use. He was handicapped by not being able to study each city-state personally, but he took full advantage of many locally written works about them. In clinging stubbornly to the city-states as the subjects of his great work even after they had been partly emasculated by the Macedonian rulers, and in practically excluding all "barbarians" from consideration in his work, he showed himself a man of somewhat limited vision. But he found ways to exploit the materials available and to rise above the prevailing conditions better than any other student of his time in Greece. For this Aristotle deserves the highest praise.

NOTES

∿ Notes

The Background and the Book

[1] Anna Haddow's *Political Science in American Colleges and Universities, 1636–1900*, William Anderson, ed. (New York, London: D. Appleton-Century, 1939), is very useful for the early development of political science as a college and university study in the British colonies in America and in the United States to 1900.

[2] See Dwight Waldo, "Values in the Political Science Curriculum," in Roland Young, ed., *Approaches to the Study of Politics* (Evanston, Ill.: Northwestern University Press, 1962), pp. 96–111.

[3] Whether this book is actually the first in its field I do not wish to argue. There are works with similar titles; but Sir Frederick Pollock's *An Introduction to the History of the Science of Politics*, rev. ed. (London: Macmillan, 1911), is in fact only a brief account of certain political theories from ancient to modern times, and Paul Janet's *Histoire de la Science Politique, dans ses Rapports avec la Morale*, 3rd ed. (Paris: F. Alcan, 1887), is really a history of political theories in relation to theories of ethics. I have found no work that covers the same ground as I have in mind here.

[4] Aristotle, *Politics*, trans. by H. Rackham (Loeb Classical Library; Cambridge, Mass.: Harvard University Press, 1959), p. 5 (I.i.1252a).

[5] José Ortega y Gasset, *Toward a Philosophy of History*, trans. by Helen Weyl (New York: Norton, 1941), p. 214.

[6] Harald Höffding, *A History of Modern Philosophy*, trans. by B. E. Meyer (2 vols.; New York: Humanities Press, 1950), I, [xiii].

[7] W. P. D. Wightman, *The Growth of Scientific Ideas* (New Haven, Conn.: Yale University Press, 1951), pp. v, vi.

[8] George Sarton, *The History of Science and the New Humanism* (New York: Braziller, 1956). See also his *A History of Science: Ancient Science through the Golden Age of Greece* (Cambridge, Mass.: Harvard University Press, 1952).

[9] Aristotle called politics the master art or *techné* because it used the other arts and sciences and even determined which ones of the others should be taught and to whom; see *Nicomachean Ethics*, trans. by D. P. Chase (Everyman's Library; London: Dent and New York: Dutton, 1934), p. 2 (I.ii.1094a–b). Arnold J. Toynbee, in *A Study of History* (12 vols.; London, New York: Oxford University Press, 1948–1961), XII, 658–663, considers the question, Is there a master activity in human affairs? Among the possibilities he mentions technology, economics, politics, art, religion, recreation, and education—a list with obvious overlappings. Arguing that "man doth not live by bread alone," he concludes that religion, not politics, deserves to be called man's master activity. I do not propose to enter this arena of de-

341

bate, but it perhaps should be pointed out that Toynbee admits (pp. 598–599) that his studies concentrated mainly on changes in social structure and in religious attitudes.

Introduction to Part I

[1] Henri Frankfort, *Kingship and the Gods* (Chicago: University of Chicago Press, 1948), pp. 215ff.

Chapter 1. Mesopotamia

[1] See Samuel Noah Kramer, *History Begins at Sumer* (Garden City, N.Y.: Doubleday, 1959); Edward Chiera, *They Wrote on Clay* (Phoenix Books; Chicago: University of Chicago Press, 1956).

[2] Henri Frankfort, *The Birth of Civilization in the Near East* (Anchor Books; Garden City, N.Y.: Doubleday, 1956), pp. 121–138.

[3] Henri Frankfort, *Kingship and the Gods* (Chicago: University of Chicago Press, 1948), pp. 215–221; Tom B. Jones, *Ancient Civilization* (Chicago: Rand McNally, 1960), p. 45; Thorkild Jacobson, "Mesopotamia," in Henri Frankfort *et al.*, *The Intellectual Adventure of Ancient Man* (Chicago: University of Chicago Press, 1946), pp. 125–129.

[4] Frankfort, *Kingship and the Gods*, pp. 237–240.

[5] *Ibid.*, pp. 221–223; Thorkild Jacobson, "Mesopotamia," pp. 185–191. There is, however, some difference of opinion about the temple economy in its relation to the state in the Sumerian period. See Jones, *Ancient Civilization*, pp. 45–49.

[6] Kramer, *History Begins at Sumer*, Introduction; Chiera, *They Wrote on Clay*, passim; Frankfort, *Birth of Civilization*, pp. 58–61.

[7] Kramer, *History Begins at Sumer*, pp. 1–7. See also Chiera, *They Wrote on Clay*, Chaps. 5–9.

[8] Jones, *Ancient Civilization*, pp. 41–42.

[9] *Ibid.*, pp. 40–59 passim.

[10] See *Larousse Encyclopedia of Mythology*, trans. by Richard Aldington and Delano Ames (New York: Prometheus Press, 1959), pp. 49–72, especially pp. 54–56; James B. Pritchard, ed., *Ancient Near Eastern Texts Relating to the Old Testament*, 2nd ed. (Princeton, N.J.: Princeton University Press, 1955), pp. 60–67; Frankfort, *Kingship and the Gods*, pp. 220–221.

[11] Pritchard, *Ancient Near Eastern Texts*, p. 64. (Italics, used in Pritchard to indicate technical information about the translation, have been omitted.)

[12] *Ibid.*

[13] *Larousse Encyclopedia*, pp. 54–55.

[14] Frankfort, *Kingship and the Gods*, p. 237.

[15] *Ibid.*, p. 239.

[16] See *ibid.*, pp. 215–274.

[17] Kramer, *History Begins at Sumer*, p. 126.

[18] Frankfort, *Kingship and the Gods*, pp. 240–243.

[19] Kramer, *History Begins at Sumer*, p. 125.

[20] Pritchard, *Ancient Near Eastern Texts*, pp. 44–52; Kramer, *History Begins at Sumer*, pp. 29–34.

[21] Kramer, *History Begins at Sumer*, p. 29.

[22] *Ibid.*, pp. 35–44.

[23] *Ibid.*, pp. 45–50.

[24] Chiera, *They Wrote on Clay*, p. 217; see also O. R. Gurney, *The Hittites* (Harmondsworth, England: Penguin Books, 1952), pp. 24–26.

[25] Kramer, *History Begins at Sumer*, p. 51; G. R. Driver and John C. Miles, *The Babylonian Laws* (2 vols.; Oxford: Clarendon Press, 1952, 1955), I, xxiv–xxv, 34–36.

[26] For the sequence of the ancient Mesopotamian law codes, see Kramer, *History*

Begins at Sumer, pp. 51–55; for the texts, see Pritchard, *Ancient Near Eastern Texts,* pp. 159–198; and for a complete and authoritative analysis and discussion, see Driver and Miles, *The Babylonian Laws.* The second volume of the latter includes all the principal codes (except that of Ur-Nammu), with elaborate notes. See also Theophile James Meek, *Hebrew Origins* (Torchbooks; New York: Harper, 1960), pp. 49–81.

²⁷ Kramer, *History Begins at Sumer,* p. 53.
²⁸ Driver and Miles, *The Babylonian Laws,* I, 54–503.
²⁹ *Ibid.,* II, 21, 83.
³⁰ *Ibid.,* I, 13–15. See also Kramer, *History Begins at Sumer,* pp. xix–xxii, 1–7; Chiera, *They Wrote on Clay, passim.*
³¹ Kramer, *History Begins at Sumer,* pp. 1–7.
³² See Driver and Miles, *The Babylonian Laws,* I, 28–29; Pritchard, *Ancient Near Eastern Texts,* pp. 163–180.
³³ Pritchard, *Ancient Near Eastern Texts,* pp. 164, 177–178.
³⁴ For these codes, see *ibid.,* pp. 180–198.
³⁵ See Kramer, *History Begins at Sumer,* pp. 35–37, for a similar view.
³⁶ See, for example, Kramer, *History Begins at Sumer,* pp. x, xviii–xx, 12–59; Chiera, *They Wrote on Clay,* pp. 17–22, 40–105.

Chapter 2. Egypt

¹ See John A. Wilson, *The Culture of Ancient Egypt* (Phoenix Books; Chicago: University of Chicago Press, 1956), pp. 8–17.
² On the prehistory of Egypt, see *ibid.,* pp. 18–42; V. Gordon Childe, *New Light on the Most Ancient Near East* (New York: Grove Press, 1957), pp. 1–101.
³ Adolf Erman, *The Literature of the Ancient Egyptians,* trans. by Aylward M. Blackman (London: Methuen, 1927), pp. 67–72, "The Instruction of Duauf."
⁴ For the Egyptian chronology by dynasties and reigns, see Henri Frankfort, *Kingship and the Gods* (Chicago: University of Chicago Press, 1948), pp. xxiv–xxv; Wilson, *The Culture of Ancient Egypt,* pp. 319–320. For a discussion of Egyptian calendars and chronology, see J. W. S. Sewell, in S. R. K. Glanville, ed., *The Legacy of Egypt* (Oxford: Clarendon Press, 1942), pp. 1–16.
⁵ On the essentially static nature of Egyptian culture, see Henri Frankfort, *Ancient Egyptian Religion* (Torchbooks; New York: Harper, 1961), pp. v–ix, 49ff.
⁶ Frankfort, *Ancient Egyptian Religion,* p. vii.
⁷ The extracts from the prophetic "Admonitions of Ipu-Wer" are taken from James B. Pritchard, ed., *Ancient Near Eastern Texts Relating to the Old Testament* (Princeton, N.J.: Princeton University Press, 1955), pp. 441–442. (Italics and small capitals, used in Pritchard to indicate technical information about the translation, have been omitted.) See also Erman, *The Literature of the Ancient Egyptians,* pp. 92–108.
⁸ The essentials of ancient Egyptian history are given rather briefly in George Steindorff and Keith C. Seele, *When Egypt Ruled the East* (Chicago: Chicago University Press, 1942), pp. 1–114.
⁹ On the Egyptian gods and religion see *Larousse Encyclopedia of Mythology,* trans. by Richard Aldington and Delano Ames (New York: Prometheus Press, 1959), pp. 8–48; Frankfort, *Ancient Egyptian Religion* and *Kingship and the Gods.*
¹⁰ For the full text of this instruction on "The Divine Attributes of Pharaoh" see Pritchard, *Ancient Near Eastern Texts,* p. 431. (Italics omitted.)
¹¹ Frankfort, *Ancient Egyptian Religion,* p. 33.
¹² From "The Instruction of Ani," in Pritchard, *Ancient Near Eastern Texts,* p. 420. (Italics omitted.)
¹³ There is evidence of such appeals. "The Protests of the Eloquent Peasant," from the twenty-first century B.C., derived from a case of open and public robbery in which

343

the poor victim appealed for redress to the chief steward of the kingdom. The latter found the man and his eloquence so interesting that he referred the case to the king. The chief steward actually heard his various appeals, but the king intervened and apparently made the decision to punish the culprit and to help out his victim. See Pritchard, *Ancient Near Eastern Texts*, pp. 407–410.

[14] *Ibid.*, pp. 412–414. (Small capitals omitted.)

[15] *Ibid.*, pp. 414–418. (Small capitals and italics omitted.) See also Erman, *The Literature of the Ancient Egyptians*, pp. 75–84.

[16] See the full-length discussion in James Henry Breasted, *The Dawn of Conscience* (New York: Scribners, 1934).

[17] For a brief account see Frankfort, *Ancient Egyptian Religion*, Chap. 2.

[18] See Pritchard, *Ancient Near Eastern Texts*, pp. 441–444; and Erman, *The Literature of the Ancient Egyptians*, pp. 92–108.

[19] See Frankfort, *Kingship and the Gods* and *Ancient Egyptian Religion*, Chap. 2, and Wilson, *The Culture of Ancient Egypt*, pp. 49, 62, 72–73, and *passim*.

[20] See Wilson, *The Culture of Ancient Egypt*, pp. 261–263; Erman, *The Literature of the Ancient Egyptians*, pp. xxvii–xxviii, xxxv–xliv.

[21] See Pritchard, *Ancient Near Eastern Texts*, pp. 432–434.

[22] *Ibid.*, p. 434. (Small capitals and italics omitted.)

[23] Erman, *The Literature of the Ancient Egyptians*, p. 197.

[24] From "In Praise of Learned Scribes," in Pritchard, *Ancient Near Eastern Texts*, p. 432. (Small capitals omitted.)

[25] See *ibid.*, Contents.

[26] Allan H. Gilbert, *Machiavelli's Prince and Its Forerunners* (Durham, N.C.: Duke University Press, 1938), in his Introduction, "On the History of Books of Advice to Princes," discusses some medieval and early modern works of this type, but does not go all the way back to the ancient Egyptian and Greek examples.

[27] Pritchard, *Ancient Near Eastern Texts*, p. 415. (Small capitals and italics omitted; the dots of ellipsis and brackets are in Pritchard.) See also Erman, *The Literature of the Ancient Egyptians*, pp. 75–84.

[28] Pritchard, *Ancient Near Eastern Texts*, pp. 415–416. (Small capitals and italics omitted; brackets in Pritchard.)

[29] *Ibid.*, p. 418. (Small capitals and italics omitted.) See also Erman, *The Literature of the Ancient Egyptians*, pp. 72–74.

[30] Pritchard, *Ancient Near Eastern Texts*, pp. 412–413. See also Erman, *The Literature of the Ancient Egyptians*, pp. 54–66.

[31] Wilson, *The Culture of Ancient Egypt*, p. 77.

Chapter 3. The Israelites

[1] See Samuel R. Driver, *An Introduction to the Literature of the Old Testament* (New York: Meridian Books, 1956), pp. 308–313.

[2] *Ibid.*, pp. 497–509; *Columbia Encyclopedia*, 2nd ed. (New York: Columbia University Press, 1950), p. 505.

[3] Driver, *An Introduction to the Literature of the Old Testament*, pp. 501–502.

[4] On the history of the Bible as a book, see Stanley Rypins, *The Book of Thirty Centuries* (New York: Macmillan, 1951).

[5] There is already an extensive literature on the so-called Dead Sea Scrolls or Scriptures. See, among others, Millar Burrows, *The Dead Sea Scrolls* (New York: Viking Press, 1956); *The Dead Sea Scriptures*, trans. by Theodor H. Gaster (Garden City, N.Y.: Doubleday, 1956).

[6] See Rypins, *The Book of Thirty Centuries*, pp. 211, 300–306, 314; H. G. G. Herklots, *How Our Bible Came to Us, Its Texts and Versions* (New York: Oxford University Press, 1957).

NOTES

[7] *The Holy Bible, Revised Standard Version* (Toronto, New York, Edinburgh: Thomas Nelson, 1952).

[8] My quotations from the Apocrypha come from a recent edition, *The Apocrypha, An American Translation*, trans. by Edgar J. Goodspeed (Modern Library; New York: Random House, 1959). There are significant differences in wording between this translation and that in an earlier work on which I had long relied—*The Authorized Version of the Apocrypha*, Manuel Komroff, ed. (New York: Tudor, 1933).

[9] See Harry M. Orlinsky, *Ancient Israel* (Ithaca, N.Y.: Cornell University Press, 1958), pp. 16–21; Theophile James Meek, *Hebrew Origins* (Torchbooks; New York: Harper, 1960), Chap. 1, "The Origin of the Hebrew People."

[10] Here I follow the interpretation of Meek, *Hebrew Origins*, Chap. 1, that the Hebrew conquest and occupation of northern, central, and eastern Palestine occurred approximately two centuries earlier than the conquest of southern Palestine by the Hebrews of the Exodus coming up from Egypt through the Sinai wilderness and the Negeb.

[11] *Ibid.*, pp. 37–48.

[12] Orlinsky, *Ancient Israel*, pp. 43–61, 171.

[13] For an illuminating though brief account of this period, see *ibid.*, pp. 58–88.

[14] *Ibid.*, pp. 89–117, 118–141.

[15] Mayer Sulzberger, *The Polity of the Ancient Hebrews* (Philadelphia: Julius H. Greenstone, 1912), p. 9.

[16] *Ibid.*, p. 8.

[17] Sulzberger presents in *The Polity of the Ancient Hebrews* (pp. 5–18) an interesting but now somewhat out-of-date account of the tribal, territorial, and military factors in the ancient Hebrew political organization that followed the Exodus.

[18] See Tobias Danzig, *Number the Language of Science* (Garden City, N.Y.: Doubleday, 1956), pp. 1–19.

[19] Modern research has revealed that many of the secular provisions of the Torah are similar to and may have been drawn from or at least influenced by the laws of the Hurrians, Canaanites, and Babylonians, and to a small extent also from the Hittite and Assyrian codes. The scribes who wrote out the laws of the Torah must have had some knowledge of these contemporary and earlier bodies of law. See Meek, *Hebrew Origins*, Chap. 2, especially p. 81.

[20] Mayer Sulzberger, *The Am Ha-aretz, The Ancient Hebrew Parliament* (Philadelphia: Julius H. Greenstone, 1910), p. 10. See also his *Polity of the Ancient Hebrews*, p. 2.

[21] See Orlinsky, *Ancient Israel*, Chap. 3, "The Period of the Judges"; Max Margolis and Alexander Marx, *History of the Jewish People* (New York: Meridian Books, and Philadelphia: Jewish Publication Society, 1958), Chap. 3; Sulzberger, *The Polity of the Ancient Hebrews, passim*.

[22] Henri Frankfort, *Kingship and the Gods* (Chicago: University of Chicago Press, 1948); Henri Frankfort *et al.*, *The Intellectual Adventure of Ancient Man* (Chicago: University of Chicago Press, 1946). In the latter see especially William A. Irwin on Hebrew ideas of kingship, at pp. 347–358.

[23] See Meek, *Hebrew Origins*, Chap. 4, pp. 119ff.

[24] On the priests and Levites generally, see *ibid.*, Orlinsky, *Ancient Israel*, pp. 35, 37, 50, 75, 105, 111, 123, 130; Max Weber, *Ancient Judaism* (Glencoe, Ill.: Free Press, 1952).

[25] See Meek, *Hebrew Origins*, Chap. 5; Weber, *Ancient Judaism, passim*; Orlinsky, *Ancient Israel*, Chap. 7.

[26] See *Ecclesiasticus, or The Wisdom of Jeshua, the Son of Sirach*, especially Chap. 10, in Goodspeed, *The Apocrypha*, pp. 241ff. *The Wisdom of Solomon*, written about a century later, and not many decades before the birth of Christ, is a work of a different nature, yet it contains many of the ideas of *Ecclesiasticus* on human af-

fairs, including politics (pp. 177ff). See especially its admonitions to kings and other rulers, pp. 187–188.

Introduction to Part II

[1] For brief accounts of these migrations see such works as Ralph E. Turner, *The Great Cultural Traditions* (2 vols.; New York: McGraw-Hill, 1941), Vol. I, *The Ancient Cities*, Chap. 9, especially pp. 439–492; Tom B. Jones, *Ancient Civilization* (Chicago: Rand McNally, 1960), Chaps. 12, 13.

[2] John L. Myres, *Geographical History in Greek Lands* (London: Oxford University Press, 1952), p. 162.

[3] Diogenes Laertius, *Lives of Eminent Philosophers*, trans. by R. D. Hicks (2 vols.; Loeb Classical Library; Cambridge, Mass.: Harvard University Press, 1958–1959), I, 475 (V.27).

[4] See, for example, the "ten times more" of Gustave Glotz, *The Greek City and Its Institutions*, trans. by N. Mallinson (New York: Knopf, 1929), p. 28; the "countless" and "hundreds" of Kathleen Freeman, *Greek City-States* (London: Macdonald, 1950), pp. xv, xvi; and the "countless" of Thomas A. Sinclair, *A History of Greek Political Thought* (London: Routledge and Kegan Paul, 1952), p. 5.

[5] On the Greeks and their gods I have relied almost entirely on standard authorities, including *Larousse Encyclopedia of Mythology*, trans. by Richard Aldington and Delano Ames (New York: Prometheus Press, 1959); W. K. C. Guthrie, *The Greeks and Their Gods* (Boston: Beacon Press, 1955); *The Oxford Classical Dictionary* (Oxford: Clarendon Press, 1957); and Oskar Seyffert, *A Dictionary of Classical Antiquities*, rev. ed. (New York: Meridian Books, 1956). Other works have been consulted on only a few points.

[6] On the early development of the Greek mind I have been helped especially by Bruno Snell, *The Discovery of the Mind*, trans. by T. G. Rosenmeyer (New York: Harper, 1960), with much help on the cultural side from Werner Jaeger, *Paideia: The Ideals of Greek Culture*, trans. by Gilbert Highet, 2nd ed. (3 vols.; New York: Oxford University Press, 1944–1954).

Chapter 4. The Delphic Oracle

[1] On the Amphictyonic Council see Herbert W. Parke and D. E. W. Wormell, *The Delphic Oracle* (2 vols.; Oxford: Blackwell, 1956), I, 100ff and *passim*; brief articles in Oskar Seyffert, *A Dictionary of Classical Antiquities*, rev. ed. (New York: Meridian Books, 1956) and *The Oxford Classical Dictionary* (Oxford: Clarendon Press, 1957); and an older work, Edward A. Freeman's *A History of Federal Government in Greece and Italy*, J. B. Bury, ed., 2nd ed. (New York and London: Macmillan, 1893). The excellent recent work by Parke and Wormell has been my mainstay and indispensable guide for this whole chapter.

[2] Parke and Wormell, *The Delphic Oracle*, I, 3ff.

[3] *Oxford Classical Dictionary*, p. 68.

[4] The best account is undoubtedly that of Parke and Wormell, *The Delphic Oracle*, I, 17–45.

[5] *Ibid.*, pp. 127–140.

[6] Frederik Poulsen, *Delphi* (London: Gyldendal, 1920), p. 26.

[7] Parke and Wormell, *The Delphic Oracle*, I, give many examples.

[8] *Ibid.*, pp. 49–81. For the economic factors and considerations leading to emigration and colonization, see the excellent brief account in Tom B. Jones, *Ancient Civilization* (Chicago: Rand McNally, 1960), pp. 185–189.

[9] Parke and Wormell, *The Delphic Oracle*, I, 165–179.

[10] Poulsen, *Delphi*, p. 159; and see any edition of the play.

NOTES

[11] *Larousse Encyclopedia of Mythology,* trans. by Richard Aldington and Delano Ames (New York: Prometheus Press, 1959), pp. 156–157.

[12] W. K. C. Guthrie, *The Greeks and Their Gods* (Boston: Beacon Press, 1955), p. 183.

[13] *Ibid.,* pp. 184–185.

[14] *Ibid.*

[15] *The Collected Dialogues of Plato, including the Letters,* Edith Hamilton and Huntington Cairns, eds. (New York: Pantheon, 1961), p. 1226 (*Laws,* I.624, trans. by Alfred E. Taylor).

[16] Guthrie, *The Greeks and Their Gods,* holds a different view, p. 185.

[17] Parke and Wormell, *The Delphic Oracle,* I, 89, are the authorities for the statement that Aristotle in a work on the *Spartan Constitution* near the end of the fourth century B.C. gives this oracle.

Chapter 5. Pre-Socratic Writers

[1] Kathleen Freeman, *The Pre-Socratic Philosophers, A Companion to Diels, Fragmente der Vorsokratiker,* 3rd ed. (Oxford: Blackwell, 1953), and *Ancilla to the Pre-Socratic Philosophers; A Complete Translation of the Fragments in Diels, Fragmente der Vorsokratiker* (Cambridge, Mass.: Harvard University Press, 1948); G. S. Kirk and J. E. Raven, *The Presocratic Philosophers* (Cambridge, England: Cambridge University Press, 1960).

[2] See for example George Sarton, *A History of Science: Ancient Science through the Golden Age of Greece* (Cambridge, Mass.: Harvard University Press, 1952), pp. 160–198 and 239ff. Other general histories of science, as well as of specific fields of study like mathematics, also report a number of "firsts."

[3] On Orpheus see, among other sources, Freeman, *Companion to Diels,* pp. 1–18; Freeman, *Ancilla to the Pre-Socratic Philosophers,* pp. 1–7; John Burnet, *Early Greek Philosophy,* 4th ed. (New York: Meridian Books, 1957), pp. 81–82; W. K. C. Guthrie, *The Greeks and Their Gods* (Boston: Beacon Press, 1955), pp. 307–332.

[4] Freeman, *Ancilla to the Pre-Socratic Philosophers,* pp. 7, 9.

[5] For a brief and graceful account of what is known about Homer see Moses Hadas, *Ancilla to Classical Reading* (New York: Columbia University Press, 1961), pp. 137–149. For the probable date of Homer's writings and other pertinent facts see Oskar Seyffert, *A Dictionary of Classical Antiquities,* rev. ed. (New York: Meridian Books, 1956), pp. 301–305.

[6] *The Iliad,* trans. by Andrew Lang, Walter Leaf, and Ernest Meyers (Modern Library; New York: Random House, n.d.), p. 1.

[7] *Ibid.,* p. 9. See p. 22 for the story of the scepter.

[8] According to Thomas A. Sinclair, the king's functions were both military and civil, but the civil apparently did not include the judicial; see *A History of Greek Political Thought* (London: Routledge and Kegan Paul, 1952), pp. 12, 13.

[9] *Ibid.,* pp. 10–18, has a more complete account of what Homer says on government than I present here.

[10] See especially Bks. I–III of *The Odyssey,* trans. by S. H. Butcher and Andrew Lang (Modern Library; New York: Random House, n.d.).

[11] *Iliad,* p. 7.

[12] *Ibid.,* p. 2.

[13] *Ibid.,* p. 4.

[14] *Ibid.,* p. 7.

[15] Seyffert, *Dictionary of Classical Antiquities,* pp. 301–302, 542.

[16] Henri I. Marrou, *A History of Education in Antiquity,* trans. by George Lamb (New York: Sheed and Ward, 1956), pp. 9–13, and Hadas, *Ancilla to Classical Reading,* pp. 37–41, on "the license to teach."

[17] There is a 1914 edition of Hesiod's works, translated by Hugh G. Evelyn-White: *Hesiod, The Homeric Hymns, and Homerics* (London: W. Heinemann, New York: Macmillan, 1914).

[18] Sinclair, *A History of Greek Political Thought*, p. 19.

[19] This brief section from *Works and Days* appears also in W. H. Auden, ed., *The Portable Greek Reader* (New York: Viking, 1948), pp. 55–58.

[20] *Ibid.*, p. 58. See also Sinclair, *A History of Greek Political Thought*, pp. 19–20.

[21] Seyffert, *Dictionary of Classical Antiquities*, pp. 307–308; *Larousse Encyclopedia of Mythology*, trans. by Richard Aldington and Delano Ames (New York: Prometheus Press, 1959), pp. 158–159.

[22] On Terpander I have not gone beyond the encyclopedias: *Encyclopaedia Britannica*, 14th ed., XXI, 950–951; *Columbia Encyclopedia*, 2nd ed. (New York: Columbia University Press, 1950), p. 1959; Seyffert, *Dictionary of Classical Antiquities*, p. 621.

[23] *Columbia Encyclopedia*, 2nd ed., p. 1959.

[24] Hadas, *Ancilla to Classical Reading*, pp. 155–156; Marrou, *A History of Education in Antiquity*, pp. 15, 16, 21, 39, 42, 65; Herbert W. Parke and D. E. W. Wormell, *The Delphic Oracle*, 2 vols. (Oxford: Blackwell, 1956), I, 89–90; Seyffert, *Dictionary of Classical Antiquities*, pp. 663–664; Werner Jaeger, *Paideia: The Ideals of Greek Culture*, trans. by Gilbert Highet, 2nd ed. (3 vols.; New York: Oxford University Press, 1944–1954), I, 87–98.

[25] Jaeger, *Paideia*, I, 96, 99–100.

[26] Freeman, *Companion to Diels*, pp. 36–41; Freeman, *Ancilla to the Pre-Socratic Philosophers*, pp. 13–15.

[27] *The Oxford Classical Dictionary* (Oxford: Clarendon Press, 1957), p. 331.

[28] Freeman, *Companion to Diels*, pp. 26–31; Freeman, *Ancilla to the Pre-Socratic Philosophers*, pp. 9–11.

[29] Tom B. Jones, *Ancient Civilization* (Chicago: Rand McNally, 1960), pp. 194–197, has an excellent brief account of Solon and his reforms. Various writers have raised questions as to how important the constitutional changes attributed to Solon were, and to what extent he was responsible for them. See *ibid.*, p. 196, and Charles Hignett, *A History of the Athenian Constitution to the End of the Fifth Century B.C.* (Oxford: Clarendon Press, 1952), pp. 86–107.

[30] Sinclair, *A History of Greek Political Thought*, pp. 23–24; Kurt von Fritz and Ernst Kapp, *Aristotle's Constitution of Athens and Related Texts* (New York: Hafner, 1950), pp. 69ff.

[31] Kathleen Freeman, *The Work and Life of Solon* (Cardiff: University of Wales Press Board and London: H. Milford, 1926), p. 208.

[32] *Ibid.*, pp. 207–208; Ivan M. Linforth, *Solon the Athenian* (Berkeley: University of California, 1919), p. 141 (a slightly different translation).

[33] Freeman, *The Work and Life of Solon*, p. 210.

[34] Jaeger, *Paideia*, I, 142ff.

[35] *Ibid.*; see also Freeman, *The Work and Life of Solon*, p. 209; Linforth, *Solon the Athenian*, p. 145.

[36] Freeman, *The Work and Life of Solon*, p. 208.

[37] *Ibid.*

[38] Freeman, *Companion to Diels*, pp. 49–55; Sarton, *A History of Science*, pp. 169–173.

[39] Freeman, *Companion to Diels*, p. 54.

[40] Philip Wheelwright, *Heraclitus* (Princeton, N.J.: Princeton University Press, 1959), p. 4. See also Freeman, *Companion to Diels*, pp. 49–55; Sarton, *A History of Science*, I, 169–173; and Burnet, *Early Greek Philosophy*, pp. 39–50.

[41] See Wheelwright, *Heraclitus*, p. 4.

[42] Freeman, *Companion to Diels*, p. 49.

NOTES

[43] Wheelwright, *Heraclitus*, p. 4.

[44] Freeman, *Companion to Diels*, p. 51.

[45] See *ibid.*, pp. 55–72; Freeman, *Ancilla to the Pre-Socratic Philosophers*, pp. 19–24; Sarton, *A History of Science*, pp. 173–178.

[46] Freeman, *Ancilla to the Pre-Socratic Philosophers*, p. 19.

[47] For the nonspecialist in philosophy the brief accounts in the *Encyclopaedia Britannica*, 14th ed., on the Eleatic school of Parmenides, VIII, 132, and on the Ionian school, XII, 576–577, will provide a good brief introduction.

[48] Freeman, *Ancilla to the Pre-Socratic Philosophers*, p. 23.

[49] *Ibid.*, pp. 22, 24.

[50] The best recent work is undoubtedly Wheelwright's *Heraclitus*. This study includes all the known fragments of Heraclitus' writings, with well-considered comments upon them. Kathleen Freeman's *Ancilla to the Pre-Socratic Philosophers*, pp. 24–34, also includes all the fragments, and her other volume, *Companion to Diels*, pp. 104–132, presents her commentary. The translations are not identical, and the numbering of the fragments is not the same, although for my purposes it is not necessary to emphasize the differences. Wheelwright presents a concordance of fragment numbers at p. 112. Since I worked on the Freeman text before that of Wheelwright came to hand, I am using her translations. However, I am citing both.

[51] Freeman, *Ancilla to the Pre-Socratic Philosophers*, p. 24, no. 1.

[52] *Ibid.*, p. 32, no. 114; Wheelwright, *Heraclitus*, p. 83, no. 81.

[53] Freeman, *Ancilla to the Pre-Socratic Philosophers*, p. 27, nos. 33, 44; Wheelwright, *Heraclitus*, p. 83, nos. 82, 83.

[54] Freeman, *Ancilla to the Pre-Socratic Philosophers*, p. 27, no. 33; Wheelwright, *Heraclitus*, p. 83, no. 83.

[55] Freeman, *Ancilla to the Pre-Socratic Philosophers*, p. 33, no. 121; Wheelwright, *Heraclitus*, p. 84, no. 95.

[56] Wheelwright, *Heraclitus*, p. 12.

[57] Freeman, *Companion to Diels*, p. 106.

[58] Wheelwright, *Heraclitus*, p. 12.

[59] Freeman, *Ancilla to the Pre-Socratic Philosophers*, pp. 24–34; Wheelwright, *Heraclitus*, pp. 19–20, 29, 37, 58–59, 68–69, 83–84, 90–91, 102.

[60] Freeman, *Ancilla to the Pre-Socratic Philosophers*, p. 25, no. 8; Wheelwright, *Heraclitus*, p. 90, no. 98.

[61] Freeman, *Ancilla to the Pre-Socratic Philosophers*, p. 28, no. 54; Wheelwright, *Heraclitus*, p. 102, no. 116.

[62] Freeman, *Ancilla to the Pre-Socratic Philosophers*, p. 32, no. 113; Wheelwright, *Heraclitus*, p. 83, no. 80.

[63] Freeman, *Ancilla to the Pre-Socratic Philosophers*, p. 32, no. 116; Wheelwright, *Heraclitus*, p. 19, no. 9.

[64] Freeman, *Ancilla to the Pre-Socratic Philosophers*, p. 24, no. 1; Wheelwright, *Heraclitus*, p. 19, no. 1.

[65] Freeman, *Ancilla to the Pre-Socratic Philosophers*, p. 27, no. 35; Wheelwright, *Heraclitus*, p. 19, no. 3.

[66] Freeman, *Ancilla to the Pre-Socratic Philosophers*, p. 31, nos. 100, 101a; Wheelwright, *Heraclitus*, p. 19, nos. 8, 12.

[67] Freeman, *Ancilla to the Pre-Socratic Philosophers*, p. 32, no. 107; Wheelwright, *Heraclitus*, p. 20, no. 13.

[68] Freeman, *Ancilla to the Pre-Socratic Philosophers*, p. 34, no. 134.

[69] Edwin L. Minar, *Early Pythagorean Politics in Practice and Theory* (Baltimore: Waverly Press, 1922), pp. 7–8, 25–26, 98, 106–107, on Pythagoras' lectures or sermons, his "school," etc.

[70] *Ibid.*, pp. 13–25; Armand Delatte, *Essai sur la politique pythagoricienne* (Liège: H. Vaillant-Carmanne, 1922), pp. 11–21.

[71] Minar, *Early Pythagorean Politics*, pp. 28–33.

[72] On first reading of this distinction between the two classes of members as applied to the students of Pythagoreanism, I thought it might be parallel to the American university distinction between graduate and undergraduate students, or between upper form and lower form students, or some such merely academic distinctions. In the lower divisions only the fundamentals are taught, as a rule, while upper division students go more deeply into their studies and even engage in research. It appears, however, that the Pythagorean distinction was a far more enduring one, and that the teachers really practiced an "economy of truth" toward the novitiates, and tried never to let them in on the deeper secrets of the society.

[73] Minar, *Early Pythagorean Politics*, p. 99.

[74] *Ibid.*, p. 99.

[75] *Ibid.*, p. 100.

[76] *Ibid.*

[77] *Ibid.*, p. 108.

[78] Ernest Barker points out in *Greek Political Theory: Plato and His Predecessors*, 3rd ed. (London: Methuen, 1947), pp. 53–54, that it was not until the latter part of the fifth century that political thought and physical speculation became independent of each other. In the meantime physical nature had provided examples for politics, and politics for physical speculations.

[79] The information concerning the Seven Sages here summarized was drawn from various biographies, some in book form like those on Solon, and some in articles in the *Encyclopaedia Britannica*, 14th ed., and the *Columbia Encyclopedia*, 2nd ed.

[80] *Encyclopaedia Britannica*, 14th ed., III, 498.

[81] For these pages on early Greek education I have used Marrou, *A History of Education in Antiquity*, Chaps. 1–4; Jaeger, *Paideia*, I, Introduction and Bk. I, Chaps. 1–10; Frederick Eby and Charles Flinn Arrowood, *The History and Philosophy of Education, Ancient and Medieval* (New York: Prentice-Hall, 1940), Chap. 6; Bury, *A History of Greece*, pp. 368–373.

[82] Paraphrased from Robert Lowe, Viscount Sherbrooke, 1867, in *The Oxford Dictionary of Quotations*, 2nd ed. (London: Oxford University Press, 1955), p. 499.

[83] Marrou, *A History of Education in Antiquity*, p. 21.

[84] *Ibid.*, pp. 36–42.

Chapter 6. Socrates' Contemporaries

[1] My principal general authorities and sources for this section of Chapter 6 are as follows: John Burnet, *Early Greek Philosophy*, 4th ed. (New York: Meridian Books, 1957); Kathleen Freeman, *The Pre-Socratic Philosophers, A Companion to Diels, Fragmente der Vorsokratiker*, 3rd ed. (Oxford: Blackwell, 1953), and *Ancilla to the Pre-Socratic Philosophers; A Complete Translation of the Fragments in Diels, Fragmente der Vorsokratiker* (Cambridge, Mass.: Harvard University Press, 1948); G. S. Kirk and J. E. Raven, *The Presocratic Philosophers* (Cambridge, England: Cambridge University Press, 1960); George Sarton, *A History of Science: Ancient Science through the Golden Age of Greece* (Cambridge, Mass.: Harvard University Press, 1952); *Encyclopaedia Britannica*, 14th ed.; Oskar Seyffert, *A Dictionary of Classical Antiquities* (New York: Meridian Books, 1957); *The Oxford Classical Dictionary* (Oxford: Clarendon Press, 1957).

[2] See Alfred E. Taylor, article on Socrates in the *Encyclopaedia Britannica*, 14th ed., XX, 918; Freeman, *Companion to Diels*, pp. xi–xii.

[3] On Alcmaeon, see Burnet, *Early Greek Philosophy*, pp. 193–196; Freeman, *Ancilla to the Pre-Socratic Philosophers*, pp. 40–41; Freeman, *Companion to Diels*, pp. 135–139; Kirk and Raven, *The Presocratic Philosophers*, pp. 232–235.

[4] Kirk and Raven, *The Presocratic Philosophers*, p. 232.

[5] Burnet, *Early Greek Philosophy*, p. 194.

[6] On Parmenides, see *ibid.*, pp. 169–193; Kirk and Raven, *The Presocratic Philosophers*, pp. 263–285; Freeman, *Ancilla to the Pre-Socratic Philosophers*, pp. 41–46; Freeman, *Companion to Diels*, pp. 140–152; Plato's *Parmenides* in Benjamin Jowett, ed. and trans., *The Works of Plato* (4 vols. in 1; New York: Dial, n.d.); Francis M. Cornford, *Plato and Parmenides* (New York: Liberal Arts Press, 1957).

[7] Seyffert, *Dictionary of Classical Antiquities*, p. 459.

[8] Kirk and Raven, *The Presocratic Philosophers*, p. 265, no. 341.

[9] On Zeno, see Burnet, *Early Greek Philosophy*, pp. 310–320 and *passim*; Kirk and Raven, *The Presocratic Philosophers*, pp. 264, 286–297; Freeman, *Ancilla to the Pre-Socratic Philosophers*, p. 47; Freeman, *Companion to Diels*, pp. 153–164.

[10] On Melissus, see Burnet, *Early Greek Philosophy*, pp. 320–329; Freeman, *Ancilla to the Pre-Socratic Philosophers*, pp. 48–51; Freeman, *Companion to Diels*, pp. 164–171; Kirk and Raven, *The Presocratic Philosophers*, pp. 298–306.

[11] On Anaxagoras, see Burnet, *Early Greek Philosophy*, pp. 251–275; Freeman, *Ancilla to the Pre-Socratic Philosophers*, pp. 82–86; Freeman, *Companion to Diels*, pp. 261–274; Kirk and Raven, *The Presocratic Philosophers*, pp. 362–394.

[12] Freeman, *Companion to Diels*, p. 263.

[13] Felix M. Cleve, *The Philosophy of Anaxagoras, An Attempt at Reconstruction* (New York: Kings Crown Press, 1949).

[14] Freeman, *Companion to Diels*, p. 273.

[15] *Ibid.*, p. 273; and see also Kirk and Raven, *The Presocratic Philosophers*, pp. 389–394, and footnote translations, nos. 525, 526, 536, 537.

[16] See Cleve, *The Philosophy of Anaxagoras*, pp. 19–27 and *passim*.

[17] On Empedocles, see Freeman, *Companion to Diels*, pp. 172–204; Freeman, *Ancilla to the Pre-Socratic Philosophers*, pp. 51–69; Burnet, *Early Greek Philosophy*, pp. 197–250; Kirk and Raven, *The Presocratic Philosophers*, pp. 320–361.

[18] Alexander J. D. Porteus, in *Oxford Classical Dictionary*, p. 314.

[19] Burnet, *Early Greek Philosophy*, p. 197.

[20] *Ibid.*, p. 200.

[21] Freeman, *Ancilla to the Pre-Socratic Philosophers*, p. 52.

[22] *Ibid.*, pp. 51, 53.

[23] *Ibid.*, p. 63.

[24] On Archelaus, see *ibid.*, p. 86; Freeman, *Companion to Diels*, pp. 275–277; Burnet, *Early Greek Philosophy*, pp. 358–361; Kirk and Raven, *The Presocratic Philosophers*, pp. 395–399.

[25] On Leucippus, see Freeman, *Companion to Diels*, pp. 285–289; Freeman, *Ancilla to the Pre-Socratic Philosophers*, pp. 90–91; Burnet, *Early Greek Philosophy*, pp. 330–349; Kirk and Raven, *The Presocratic Philosophers*, pp. 400–426.

[26] On Democritus, see Freeman, *Companion to Diels*, pp. 289–326; Freeman, *Ancilla to the Pre-Socratic Philosophers*, pp. 91–120; Kirk and Raven, *The Presocratic Philosophers*, pp. 400–426; Thomas A. Sinclair, *A History of Greek Political Thought* (London: Routledge and Kegan Paul, 1952), pp. 64–66.

[27] *Dictionary of Classical Antiquities*, p. 179.

[28] Freeman, *Companion to Diels*, pp. 293–299.

[29] *Ibid.*, p. 299. See also Kirk and Raven, *The Presocratic Philosophers*, pp. 400–427, especially pp. 400–411.

[30] Freeman, *Companion to Diels*, pp. 309–323; Sinclair, *A History of Greek Political Thought*, pp. 64–66.

[31] See the numerous fragments in Freeman, *Ancilla to the Pre-Socratic Philosophers*, pp. 91–120, and the fragments translated in Kirk and Raven, *The Presocratic Philosophers*, pp. 400–427.

[32] Freeman, *Ancilla to the Pre-Socratic Philosophers*, p. 114.

[33] *Ibid.*, p. 116.

[34] *Ibid.*, p. 114.

[35] *Ibid.*, p. 115.

[36] On these three late Pythagoreans, see *ibid.*, pp. 73–81; Freeman, *Companion to Diels*, pp. 220–239; Burnet, *Early Greek Philosophy*, pp. 99–100, 276–296.

[37] Freeman, *Companion to Diels*, p. 234.

[38] *Ibid.*, pp. 238–239.

[39] This is quoted from Freeman's paraphrase of the words of Archytas in *Companion to Diels*, p. 239.

[40] My principal sources for this section on the Sophists are the following: *The Collected Dialogues of Plato, including the Letters*, Edith Hamilton and Huntington Cairns, eds. (New York: Pantheon, 1961); Freeman, *Companion to Diels* and *Ancilla to the Pre-Socratic Philosophers*; Mario Untersteiner, *The Sophists*, trans. by Kathleen Freeman (Oxford: Blackwell, 1954); Werner Jaeger, *Paideia: The Ideals of Greek Culture*, trans. by Gilbert Highet, 2nd ed. (3 vols.; New York: Oxford University Press, 1944–1954), I; Theodor Gomperz, *Greek Thinkers*, trans. by Laurie Magnus (4 vols.; London: J. Murray, 1901–1912), I; B. A. G. Fuller, *History of Greek Philosophy* (3 vols.; New York: Holt, 1923–1931), II; Henri I. Marrou, *A History of Education in Antiquity*, trans. by George Lamb (New York: Sheed and Ward, 1956); Sinclair, *A History of Greek Political Thought*; Ernest Barker, *Greek Political Theory: Plato and His Predecessors*, 3rd ed. (London: Methuen, 1947), pp. 55–85; Sarton, *A History of Science*; *Encyclopaedia Britannica*, 14th ed.; *The Oxford Classical Dictionary*; and Seyffert, *Dictionary of Classical Antiquities.*

[41] Sarton, *A History of Science*, p. 259; Aristophanes, *The Clouds*, trans. by Benjamin Bickley Rogers in Lane Cooper, ed., *Fifteen Greek Plays* (New York: Oxford University Press, 1943); Sinclair, *A History of Greek Political Thought*, p. 84.

[42] See Sarton, *A History of Science*, pp. 260–261.

[43] On the probable dates and facts of Protagoras' life, see Freeman, *Companion to Diels*, pp. 343–346; Fuller, *History of Greek Philosophy*, II, 17–29; Untersteiner, *The Sophists*, pp. 1–8.

[44] Jaeger, *Paideia*, I, 290.

[45] Freeman, *Companion to Diels*, pp. 346–348; Untersteiner, *The Sophists*, pp. 9–18.

[46] Untersteiner, *The Sophists*, p. 10.

[47] Sinclair, *A History of Greek Political Thought*, pp. 52–53.

[48] *Ibid.*, p. 3.

[49] Freeman, *Ancilla to the Pre-Socratic Philosophers*, p. 126; Untersteiner, *The Sophists*, p. 27, gives a somewhat different translation.

[50] Freeman, *Ancilla to the Pre-Socratic Philosophers*, p. 125; Untersteiner, *The Sophists*, p. 42, offers this different translation: "Man is the master of all experiences, in regard to the 'phenomenality' of what is real, and the 'non-phenomenality' of what is not real."

[51] See, for example, Fuller, *History of Greek Philosophy*, II, 20–29.

[52] Freeman, *Ancilla to the Pre-Socratic Philosophers*, pp. 126, 127.

[53] See *Dialogues of Plato*, pp. 308–352 (*Protagoras*, trans. by W. K. C. Guthrie).

[54] *Ibid.*, p. 312 (312c–d).

[55] *Ibid.*, p. 313 (313c).

[56] *Ibid.*, p. 317 (319a–b).

[57] *Ibid.*, p. 317 (319d).

[58] *Ibid.*, p. 318 (320b).

I confess to considerable puzzlement over the translation of this passage, and over whether Socrates meant that *areté* or excellence and skill *in general* cannot be taught, or whether he meant that the special virtue of excellence or skill in politics cannot be taught. If the translation by W. K. C. Guthrie that I have quoted had used an additional "that" and had said "I do not believe that *that* virtue [i.e., skill or excellence in politics] can be taught," its specific reference to political skill and not to other excellences would have been clear enough. Apparently the translator had been warned against the overuse of "that." In this case a double "that" would have made the meaning clearer. As it is, in dialogues that lack a specific political context Socrates does argue whether *areté*, or virtue or excellence in a somewhat general sense, can be taught, and I have assumed that here, too, he is arguing about the more general proposition.

However, when I turn to the translation by Benjamin Jowett (in *The Works of Plato*, p. 149), I find a different translation, as follows:

"[Socrates]. Do I understand you, I said; and is your meaning that you teach the art of politics, and that you promise to make men good citizens?

"[Protagoras]. That, Socrates, is exactly the profession which I make.

"[Socrates]. Then, I said, you do indeed possess a noble art, if there is no mistake about this; for I will freely confess to you, Protagoras, that I have a doubt whether this art is capable of being taught . . ."

The immediately following context in both these translations makes it clear that political *areté* or virtue is what Socrates had uppermost in his mind at that point, since he went on to use the Athenian assemblymen as examples of popular democratic pretensions to knowledge on political subjects that came before them without their having studied the problems involved. Werner Jaeger in *Paideia*, Vol. I, makes it clear that he thinks that *areté* generally means political *areté*. I am in no position to dispute him on this point, although in several dialogues by Plato, and even toward the end of the *Protagoras*, it seems to me that *areté* is used in a more comprehensive sense.

⁵⁹ *Dialogues of Plato*, pp. 319–320 (*Protagoras, 322c–d*). See also Barker, *Greek Political Theory*, p. 63.

⁶⁰ Jaeger, *Paideia*, I, 3–14. For some of the background of this problem see also Bruno Snell, *The Discovery of the Mind* (Torchbooks; New York: Harper, 1960), Chap. 8, especially pp. 164, 165, 174–178.

⁶¹ Jaeger, *Paideia*, I, 286ff.

⁶² *Ibid.*, pp. 288, 290, 291, 292, 293. See also Untersteiner, *The Sophists*, pp. 12–14.

⁶³ On Gorgias, see Untersteiner, *The Sophists*, pp. 92–205; Freeman, *Companion to Diels*, pp. 353–367; Freeman, *Ancilla to the Pre-Socratic Philosophers*, pp. 127–139; Marrou, *A History of Education in Antiquity*, pp. 52–54.

⁶⁴ Freeman, *Companion to Diels*, pp. 358–367; Untersteiner, *The Sophists*, pp. 93–94.

⁶⁵ Freeman, *Ancilla to the Pre-Socratic Philosophers*, pp. 127–129.

⁶⁶ Freeman, *Companion to Diels*, p. 358.

⁶⁷ See especially *ibid.*, pp. 381–391; Freeman, *Ancilla to the Pre-Socratic Philosophers*, pp. 142–144; Untersteiner, *The Sophists*, pp. 272–303.

⁶⁸ *Dialogues of Plato*, p. 314 (*Protagoras, 315c*).

⁶⁹ Untersteiner, *The Sophists*, p. 272.

⁷⁰ Freeman, *Companion to Diels*, pp. 382–391.

⁷¹ *Dialogues of Plato*, pp. 200–214, 1534–1549.

⁷² *Ibid.*, p. 214 (*Lesser Hippias, 376b*, trans. by Benjamin Jowett).

⁷³ *Ibid.*, p. 1558 (*Greater Hippias, 303e–304a*, trans. by Benjamin Jowett).

⁷⁴ *Ibid.* (304a).

⁷⁵ *Ibid.* (304a–b).

⁷⁶ Untersteiner, *The Sophists*, p. 277. See also pp. 273–274.

⁷⁷ Freeman, *Companion to Diels*, p. 405; Untersteiner, *The Sophists*, p. 313, puts his birth later.

⁷⁸ Freeman, *Companion to Diels*, p. 405.

⁷⁹ Untersteiner, *The Sophists*, p. 313.

[80] *Ibid.*, p. 315, quoting Xenophon, *Memorabilia*, I.ɪɪ.31.

[81] Freeman, *Companion to Diels*, pp. 408–413; Untersteiner, *The Sophists*, pp. 317–319.

[82] Freeman, *Companion to Diels*, p. 393; see also *ibid.*, pp. 391–404, and Untersteiner, *The Sophists*, pp. 228–271.

[83] Freeman, *Companion to Diels*, pp. 394–404; Untersteiner, *The Sophists*, pp. 233–271.

[84] Ernest Barker in his *Greek Political Theory*, pp. 67, 83–85, discusses and reprints two fragments from Antiphon's work *On Truth*. In these, among other things, Antiphon's bias in favor of the laws of nature and against man-made laws is clear.

[85] Freeman, *Companion to Diels*, pp. 391–392.

[86] *Ibid.*, pp. 392–393.

[87] *Oxford Classical Dictionary*, p. 62.

[88] Freeman, *Companion to Diels*, pp. 375–381; Freeman, *Ancilla to the Pre-Socratic Philosophers*, pp. 141–142; Untersteiner, *The Sophists*, pp. 311–313, 324–328.

[89] *Dialogues of Plato*, p. 588 (*Republic*, 338c, trans. by Paul Shorey).

[90] Untersteiner, *The Sophists*, pp. 311–312.

[91] Freeman, *Ancilla to the Pre-Socratic Philosophers*, pp. 141–142.

[92] *Ibid.*, p. 142.

[93] *Ibid.*, p. 141.

[94] Freeman, *Companion to Diels*, pp. 370–374; Untersteiner, *The Sophists*, p. 206.

[95] Untersteiner, *The Sophists*, pp. 206–207.

[96] Freeman, *Companion to Diels*, p. 372.

[97] For this section I have relied especially on the following works: John B. Bury, *The Ancient Greek Historians* (New York: Dover, 1958); Sinclair, *A History of Greek Political Thought*; John L. Myres, *Herodotus, Father of History* (Oxford: Clarendon Press, 1953); *The History of Herodotus*, Manuel Komroff, ed., trans. by George Rawlinson (New York: Tudor, 1934); *The Complete Writings of Thucydides, The Peloponnesian War*, trans. by Richard Crawley (Modern Library; New York: Random House, 1934).

[98] Bury, *Ancient Greek Historians*, pp. 1–35; *Oxford Classical Dictionary*, pp. 511–512; Seyffert, *Dictionary of Classical Antiquities*, pp. 361–362.

[99] Bury, *Ancient Greek Historians*, pp. 11–14. Sarton calls Hecataeus "the father of geography" (*A History of Science*, I, 185), while Jaeger characterizes him as "the first ethnologist and geographer" (*Paideia*, I, 155).

[100] Myres, *Herodotus*; Jaeger, *Paideia*, I, 155. Bury calls his *History* "a 'modern' history in the fullest sense of the term," p. 37, but also credits Hecataeus with having "initiated" modern history, p. 12.

[101] Bury, *Ancient Greek Historians*, pp. 36–74; *Oxford Classical Dictionary*, pp. 421–423; Seyffert, *Dictionary of Classical Antiquities*, pp. 289–290; Myres, *Herodotus*, pp. 1–16.

[102] *The History of Herodotus*, pp. 177–179 (usually cited as III.80–82). Although this discussion is supposed to have taken place in 522 B.C., it was probably composed by Herodotus himself from information supplied to him about seventy years later. See Sinclair, *A History of Greek Political Thought*, p. 36.

[103] *The History of Herodotus*, pp. 180–183 (III.89–117).

[104] Seyffert, *Dictionary of Classical Antiquities*, p. 290. See also Gomperz, *Greek Thinkers*, I, 262–269.

[105] *The Complete Writings of Thucydides*, p. 3 (*The Peloponnesian War*, I.ɪ.1).

[106] Bury, *Ancient Greek Historians*, pp. 91–92.

[107] Joseph Gavorse in the Introduction, p. viii, to *The Complete Writings of Thucydides*, quotes an unnamed authority as saying that he was "the first and the greatest of all critical historians," but this probably goes too far. Ferdinand Schevill, in *Six Historians* (Chicago: University of Chicago Press, 1956), p. 1, is the one who

calls him the "father of historical method," a statement that also needs some qualification.

[108] Compare Jaeger, *Paideia*, I, 389; Schevill, *Six Historians*, pp. 27–28.

[109] For a concise summary of the arguments see Sinclair, *A History of Greek Political Thought*, pp. 100–110. See also Bury, *The Ancient Greek Historians*, pp. 116–149 *passim*.

[110] *The Complete Writings of Thucydides*, p. 14.

[111] *Ibid.*, pp. 14–15.

[112] The literature on the ancient Greek drama is so extensive that I make no pretense to having covered even all that is specifically pertinent to its political aspects. I have used a number of the plays, and especially those in Lane Cooper's edition of *Fifteen Greek Plays*, to which the editor contributed a brief but valuable Introduction; Gilbert Murray, *Aeschylus, The Creator of Tragedy* (Oxford: Clarendon Press, 1940); Part Two of John H. Finley, Jr., *Pindar and Aeschylus* (Cambridge, Mass.: Harvard University Press, 1955); Jaeger, *Paideia*, I, Bk. II, Chaps. 1, 2, 4, 5.

[113] Jaeger, *Paideia*, I, 246–248.

[114] In addition to Sinclair and Jaeger, see the articles on the Greek drama and individual dramatists in the *Encyclopaedia Britannica*, 14th ed., *Oxford Classical Dictionary*, and Seyffert, *Dictionary of Classical Antiquities*.

[115] On Aeschylus, see Jaeger, *Paideia*, I, 237–267; Sinclair, *A History of Greek Political Thought*, *passim*; Finley, *Pindar and Aeschylus*, pp. 179–288.

[116] Sinclair, *A History of Greek Political Thought*, p. 39.

[117] Jaeger, *Paideia*, I, 237, 254–255, 259ff, makes much of the similarity between Solon's ideas and some of those of Aeschylus, while recognizing the differences.

[118] For the essential facts see the articles on Sophocles in the encyclopedias and classical dictionaries already cited.

[119] Seyffert, *Dictionary of Classical Antiquities*, p. 597.

[120] I have used the translation by Robert Whitelaw in Lane Cooper, *Fifteen Greek Plays*, pp. 211–248.

[121] *Ibid.*, p. 217.

[122] *Ibid.*, pp. 217–218.

[123] *Ibid.*, p. 218.

[124] *Ibid.*, pp. 220–221.

[125] *Ibid.*, pp. 222–223.

[126] *Ibid.*, p. 225.

[127] *Ibid.*

[128] *Ibid.*, p. 232.

[129] *Ibid.*, p. 231.

[130] The biographical facts come mainly from the usual encyclopedia and dictionary sources.

[131] Cooper, *Fifteen Greek Plays*, p. 706.

[132] *Ibid.*, p. 709.

[133] The biographical data come mainly from the usual encyclopedia and dictionary sources.

[134] *Oxford Classical Dictionary*, p. 217.

[135] Jaeger, *Paideia*, I, 364.

[136] *The Complete Writings of Thucydides*, pp. 78–83 (*The Peloponnesian War*, I.v.139ff).

[137] *Ibid.*, pp. 116–119 (II.vii.60ff).

[138] *Ibid.*, pp. 102–109 (II.vi.35ff).

[139] On Hippodamus, in addition to the usual sources, see John C. Hogan, "Hippodamus and the Best Form of Government and Law," *Western Political Quarterly*, 12:763–783 (September 1959); Sinclair, *A History of Greek Political Thought*, pp. 63–68.

[140] Untersteiner in *The Sophists* mentions Hippodamus, but not as a Sophist (p. 274).

[141] Hogan, in *Western Political Quarterly*, 12:765–766; Lewis Mumford, *The City in History: Its Origins, Its Transformations, and Its Prospects* (New York: Harcourt, Brace, and World, 1961), p. 172.

[142] Aristotle, *Politics*, trans. by Benjamin Jowett (Oxford: Clarendon Press, 1923), pp. 76–77 (II.viii.1267b).

[143] *Ibid.*, pp. 76–80 (1267b–1269).

Chapter 7. Socrates and Political Education

[1] In addition to the works cited in previous chapters by Eby and Arrowood, Marrou, Plato, Sinclair, and Snell, and various encyclopedias and dictionaries also previously cited, I have for the present chapter consulted the following books among others: Anton Hermann Chroust, *Socrates Man and Myth: The Two Socratic Apologies of Xenophon* (London: Routledge and Kegan Paul, 1957); Werner Jaeger, *Paideia: The Ideals of Greek Culture*, trans. by Gilbert Highet, 2nd ed. (3 vols.; New York: Oxford University Press, 1944–1954), II; René Kraus, *The Private and Public Life of Socrates*, trans. by Barrows Mussey (New York: Doubleday, Doran, 1940); Arthur Kenyon Rogers, *The Socratic Problem* (New Haven, Conn.: Yale University Press and London: Oxford University Press, 1933); Alfred E. Taylor, *Socrates* (New York: D. Appleton, 1933); Xenophon, *Memorabilia [and] Oeconomicus*, trans. by E. C. Marchant (Loeb Classical Library; Cambridge, Mass.: Harvard University Press, 1959); and Eduard Zeller, *Socrates and the Socratic Schools* (London: Longmans, Green, 1885).

[2] Taylor, *Socrates*, p. 123. But the cultivation of the soul was not to be at the expense of the body, although the soul came first; see Jaeger, *Paideia*, II, 39–49.

[3] Herbert W. Parke and D. E. W. Wormell, *The Delphic Oracle* (2 vols.; Oxford: Blackwell, 1956), I, 401–405.

[4] *The Oxford Classical Dictionary* (Oxford: Clarendon Press, 1957), p. 183.

[5] See *The Collected Dialogues of Plato, including the Letters*, Edith Hamilton and Huntington Cairns, eds. (New York: Pantheon, 1961), pp. 7–9 (*Apology*, 20e–23c, trans. by Hugh Tredennick).

[6] *Ibid.*, p. 9 (23a).

[7] *Ibid.*

[8] Xenophon, *Memorabilia*, pp. 281–289 (IV.ii.17–29).

[9] *Ibid.*, p. 289 (IV.ii.29).

[10] Moses Hadas, *Ancilla to Classical Reading* (New York: Columbia University Press, 1961), pp. 19–21; Xenophon, *Memorabilia*, pp. 273–287 (IV.ii.8–25), where Socrates advises the ignorant Euthydemus who boasted of his library, "Know thyself" instead of books; but see *Memorabilia*, p. 75 (I.vi.14), where Socrates recognizes his own debt to books rightly used.

[11] Jaeger, *Paideia*, II, 39ff, develops this thought most interestingly.

[12] *Ibid.*, pp. 27–36; Taylor, *Socrates*, pp. 59–60; *Dialogues of Plato*, pp. 6, 19 (*Apology*, 19e–20d, 33b–34b).

[13] Taylor, *Socrates*, pp. 90–93.

[14] Xenophon, *Memorabilia*, p. 35 (I.ii.47–48), where Xenophon says of Alcibiades and Critias, "Politics had brought them to Socrates, and for politics they left him."

[15] *Ibid.*, p. 11 (I.i.16).

[16] *Ibid.*, p. 33 (I.ii.43), Pericles presumably speaking.

[17] *Ibid.*, pp. 344–345 (IV.vi.12), Socrates speaking.

[18] *Ibid.*, p. 345 (IV.vi.13), Socrates speaking.

[19] *Ibid.*, pp. 277–289 (IV.ii.11–29), Socrates speaking.

[20] *Ibid.*, p. 289 (IV.ii.29), Socrates speaking.

NOTES

[21] *Ibid.*, pp. 313–319 (IV.iv.11–18), Socrates speaking.

[22] Jaeger, *Paideia*, II, 49.

[23] Xenophon, *Memorabilia*, p. 75 (I.vi.15); *Dialogues of Plato*, pp. 17–18 (*Apology*, 31c–33a), gives a different and more detailed explanation of why he decided "to leave politics alone."

[24] Hadas, *Ancilla to Classical Reading*, p. 72; Jaeger, *Paideia*, II, 28–29; Taylor, *Socrates*, pp. 93ff.

Chapter 8. Plato and Anti-Politics

[1] For the facts of Plato's life I have relied especially on Alfred E. Taylor, *Plato: The Man and His Work*, 6th ed. (London: Humanities Press, 1949), and on the same author's excellent condensed account of Plato in the *Encyclopaedia Britannica*, 14th ed., XVIII, 48–64. But a number of other writers have supplied additional facts and insights, notably Werner Jaeger. The principal sources that I have used for Plato's writings are Benjamin Jowett, ed. and trans., *The Works of Plato* (4 vols. in 1; New York: Dial, n.d.), and *The Collected Dialogues of Plato, including the Letters*, Edith Hamilton and Huntington Cairns, eds. (New York: Pantheon, 1961).

[2] See the Chronology in Taylor, *Plato*, pp. 519–520.

[3] Robert Browning, "Bishop Blougram's Apology," *Men and Women* (2 vols.; London: Chapman and Hall, 1855), I, 131.

[4] Jaeger's *Paideia: The Ideals of Greek Culture*, trans. by Gilbert Highet, 2nd ed. (3 vols.; New York: Oxford University Press, 1944–1954), is, of course, the great work on this subject, and Volume II is almost entirely given over to Plato's ideas on culture and education.

[5] *Dialogues of Plato*, p. 658 (*The Republic*, III.414b, trans. by Paul Shorey).

[6] *Ibid.*, p. 659 (III.415a–c). This seems to me to be Plato and not Socrates speaking. In either case, the scheme of selection and classification that is proposed presupposes an inspection and a testing of every one of the offspring of the ruling class and of many others, too, presumably based upon the evidence obtained by the eyes, ears, and other sense organs of the rulers. For how else could the metallic components of either the soul or the body of the individual be discovered? And yet this sort of reliance on the evidence of the senses, which is elsewhere put down as most unreliable, is to be the basis for a final and pitiless decision upon everyone's status in life.

[7] *Ibid.*, pp. 1053–1954 (*Statesman*, 285e–286a, trans. by J. B. Skemp).

[8] *Ibid.*, p. 364 (*Meno*, 81c–d, trans. by W. K. C. Guthrie).

[9] *Ibid.*, pp. 364–371 (*Meno*, 82–85).

[10] G. M. A. Grube, *Plato's Thought* (Boston: Beacon Hill Press, 1958), p. 171.

[11] *Dialogues of Plato*, p. 1442 (*Laws*, X.886e, trans. by Alfred E. Taylor), p. 1526 (*Epinomis*, 984d, trans. by Alfred E. Taylor).

[12] *Ibid.*, p. 1526 (*Epinomis*, 984d). See Benjamin Farrington, *Science and Politics in the Ancient World* (London: George Allen and Unwin, 1946), pp. 101–106; and for useful background, Grube, *Plato's Thought*, Chap. 5, pp. 150–178.

[13] Grube, *Plato's Thought*, p. 161.

[14] Thus in classifying constitutions on the usual empirical basis, the numbers who participate in ruling, Plato's Stranger in *The Statesman*, 291a–292a (*Dialogues of Plato*, pp. 1059–1061), questions whether any of these forms is a "true" constitution.

[15] In the light of all that has been discovered and published in recent decades, I feel that a good solid book on the Academy is now possible and that it would be a boon to scholars in many fields. In the absence of such a comprehensive work, I have relied upon and found most useful Jaeger, *Paideia*, especially Vols. II and III; also his *Aristotle: Fundamentals of the History of His Development*, trans. by Richard Robinson, 2nd ed. (Oxford: Clarendon Press, 1948), Part One, Chap. 1, pp. 11–23; Taylor, *Plato*; Grube, *Plato's Thought*; Alexandre Koyré, *Discovering Plato*, trans. by L. C. Rosenfeld (New York: Columbia University Press, 1960);

and Thomas A. Sinclair, *A History of Greek Political Thought* (London: Routledge and Kegan Paul, 1952).

[16] Ulrich von Wilamowitz-Moellendorff, *Platon* (2 vols.; Berlin: Weidmann, 1920), I, 269.

[17] John Burnet, *Early Greek Philosophy*, 4th ed. (New York: Meridian Books, 1957), pp. 223–230.

[18] Taylor, *Plato*, p. 6.

[19] Alfred E. Taylor, *Socrates* (New York: D. Appleton, 1933), p. 17, n. 1.

[20] Koyré, *Discovering Plato*, p. 70.

[21] León Robin, *Platon* (Paris: F. Alcan, 1935), p. 13.

[22] Burnet, *Early Greek Philosophy*, pp. 219–222.

[23] Guy C. Field, *Plato and His Contemporaries* (London: Methuen, 1930), p. 44.

[24] Henri I. Marrou, *A History of Education in Antiquity*, trans. by George Lamb (New York: Sheed and Ward, 1956), p. 64.

[25] George Sarton, *A History of Science: Ancient Science through the Golden Age of Greece* (Cambridge, Mass.: Harvard University Press, 1952), p. 398.

[26] *Encyclopaedia Britannica*, 14th ed., I, 87.

[27] B. A. G. Fuller, *History of Greek Philosophy* (3 vols.; New York: Holt, 1923–1931), II, 461.

[28] Von Wilamowitz-Moellendorff, *Platon*, I, 269.

[29] Sinclair, *A History of Greek Political Thought*, p. 125.

[30] Jaeger, *Paideia*, II, 274.

[31] Paul Friedländer, *Plato*, trans. by Hans Meyerhoff (New York: Pantheon, 1958), p. 90.

[32] See Charles Alvin Roos, "Greek Libraries before Aristotle" (Unpublished M.A. thesis, University of Minnesota, 1940), p. 7; Harold Cherniss, *The Riddle of the Early Academy* (Berkeley: University of California Press, 1945), p. 62; John Bowle, *Western Political Thought* (New York: Oxford University Press, 1948), p. 48n1.

[33] Ernest Barker, *Greek Political Theory: Plato and His Predecessors*, 3rd ed. (London: Methuen, 1947), p. 110.

[34] Cherniss, *The Riddle of the Early Academy*, pp. 1–3, 11, 13, 31, 59.

[35] Marrou, *A History of Education in Antiquity*, pp. 64–65. I have not made an exhaustive search in order to find additional names for this list, or to get every scrap of biographical information about the men named. My principal sources have been the usual ones for this type of information: *Encyclopaedia Britannica*, 14th ed.; *The Columbia Encyclopedia*, 2nd ed. (New York: Columbia University Press, 1950); *The Oxford Classical Dictionary* (Oxford: Clarendon Press, 1957); and Oskar Seyffert, *A Dictionary of Classical Antiquities* (New York: Meridian Books, 1956).

Chapter 9. Plato's Contemporaries

[1] Isocrates' works in the Loeb Classical Library are in three volumes: Vol. I (1928) and Vol. II (1929) translated by George Norlin, published by W. Heinemann of London and Putnam of New York; Vol. III, translated by Larue Van Hook and published (1954) by Harvard University Press and Heinemann. Secondary works on Isocrates from which I have received much help include Werner Jaeger, *Paideia: The Ideals of Greek Culture*, trans. by Gilbert Highet, 2nd ed. (3 vols.; New York: Oxford University Press, 1944–1954), especially Vol. III, Bk. IV, Chaps. 2, 3, 4, and 6, and note 6, pp. 316–323; Henri I. Marrou, *A History of Education in Antiquity*, trans. by George Lamb (New York: Sheed and Ward, 1956), Part One, Chap. 8, pp. 79–91; Thomas A. Sinclair, *A History of Greek Political Thought* (London: Routledge and Kegan Paul, 1952), Chap. 7, pp. 115–142.

[2] The General Introduction to Isocrates' works (I, ix–li) by George Norlin provides very helpful background on Isocrates.

[3] *The Dialogues of Plato,* p. 524 (*Phaedrus,* 279a, trans. by R. Hackforth).

[4] The six extant forensic speeches written by Isocrates are in Vol. III of the Loeb edition, numbered XVI–XXI, pp. 174–363.

[5] See Loeb edition, II, 236–237, 250–251 (*Antidosis,* 93, 94, 116ff).

[6] On Isocrates' works in this area, see Jaeger, *Paideia,* III, 84–105.

[7] *Columbia Encyclopedia,* 2nd ed. (New York: Columbia University Press, 1950), p. 980.

[8] Loeb edition, II, 169 (*Against the Sophists,* 9).

[9] *Ibid.* (10).

[10] See, for example, Marrou, *A History of Education in Antiquity,* especially pp. 79–91, where the differences between Plato's and Isocrates' ideas on education are presented.

[11] Sinclair, *A History of Greek Political Thought,* p. 135.

[12] *Ibid.,* p. 133.

[13] The volumes are not numbered consecutively, as a single series, but appear in three groups, with four different translators, as follows: *Cyropaedia,* 2 vols., translated by Walter Millar (Loeb numbers 51 and 52); *Hellenica, Anabasis, Symposium,* and *Apology,* 3 vols., translated by Carleton L. Brownson, except that the *Symposium* and *Apology* in the third volume (which also includes Bks. IV–VIII of the *Anabasis*) are translated by O. J. Todd (Loeb numbers 88, 89); *Memorabilia* and *Oeconomicus,* in one volume, and *Scripta Minora* (which includes *On Hunting* and *Constitution of the Lacedaemonians*), in one volume, both these latter volumes translated by E. C. Marchant (Loeb numbers 168 and 183).

[14] Jaeger, *Paideia,* III, 156–181.

[15] *Scripta Minora,* p. 451 (*On Hunting,* XIII.4).

[16] Jaeger, *Paideia,* III, 159.

[17] *Scripta Minora,* p. 373 (*On Hunting,* I.18, II.1).

[18] *Ibid.,* pp. 449ff (XIII.1ff).

[19] *Ibid.,* p. 447 (XII.16–17).

[20] *Ibid.,* p. 451 (XIII.5–6).

[21] *Ibid.,* p. 453 (XIII.11).

[22] *Ibid.,* p. 453 (XIII.7).

[23] *Ibid.,* p. 455 (XIII.15).

[24] *Cyropaedia,* I, viii (I.8).

[25] Jaeger, *Paideia,* III, 85.

[26] *Scripta Minora,* p. 137 (*Constitution of the Lacedaemonians,* I.1).

[27] *Ibid.,* p. 137 (I.2).

[28] *Ibid.,* pp. 185, 187 (XV.1).

[29] The most complete study of this work is that of Hartvig Frisch, *The Constitution of the Athenians: A Philological-Historical Analysis of Pseudo-Xenophon's Treatise De Re Publica Atheniensium* (Copenhagen: Gyldendal, 1942).

[30] The Loeb Classical Library includes seven volumes of the orations and letters of Demosthenes. The most important ones for this study have been I, *Philippics, Olynthiacs, Minor Public Orations;* and II, *De Corona, De Falsa Legatione.*

[31] *De Corona,* 258–259. The translations vary. In one he mocks Aeschines by saying, "You taught reading, I went to school" (*The Crown, the Philippics, and Ten Other Orations,* trans. by Charles Rann Kennedy (Everyman's Library; London: Dent and New York: Dutton, 1911), p. 101). In another translation he makes a point of Aeschines' early poverty, saying, "You helped your father in the drudgery of a grammar-school, grinding the ink, sponging the benches, and sweeping the school-room . . ." (Loeb edition, trans. by C. A. and J. H. Vince, II, 189).

[32] Jaeger, *Paideia,* III, 353n21.

[33] Loeb edition, II, 145 (*De Corona,* 189). The Everyman's edition has what seems to be a more free and easy translation, p. 96, as follows: "What are his [the

statesman's] functions? To observe things in the beginning, to foresee and foretell them to others,—this I have done: again; wherever he finds delays, backwardness, ignorance, jealousies, vices inherent and unavoidable in all communities, to contract them into the narrowest compass, and on the other hand, to promote unanimity and friendship and zeal in the discharge of duty." Above all, he must be loyal to his state, and refuse to take bribes from its enemies. (See also this edition, p. 83, and elsewhere for additional details on the functions and duties of the statesman.)

³⁴ Jaeger, *Paideia*, III, 274–278.

Chapter 10. Aristotle and the "Collection of Constitutions"

¹ My principal sources for Aristotle's works have been as follows: Richard Mc-Keon, ed., *The Basic Works of Aristotle* (New York: Random House, 1941); three editions of Aristotle's *Politics*—one trans. by H. Rackham (Loeb Classical Library; Cambridge, Mass.: Harvard University Press, 1959), one trans. by Benjamin Jowett (Oxford: Clarendon Press, 1923), which is reprinted in *The Basic Works*, and one trans. by Ernest Barker (Oxford: Clarendon Press, 1946); *Nicomachean Ethics*, trans. by H. Rackham (London: W. Heinemann, 1926). I have also examined the translation of *Nicomachean Ethics* by D. P. Chase in the Everyman's Library edition (London: Dent and New York: Dutton, 1934), which differs considerably from the translations by Rackham in the Loeb edition and by W. D. Ross in the McKeon volume. I have, in addition, depended heavily upon Werner Jaeger, *Aristotle, Fundamentals of the History of His Development*, trans. by Richard Robinson, 2nd ed. (Oxford: Clarendon Press, 1948); W. D. Ross, *Aristotle*, 5th ed. rev. (London: Methuen, 1949).

² Diogenes Laertius, *Lives of Eminent Philosophers* (2 vols.; Loeb Classical Library; Cambridge, Mass.: Harvard University Press, 1958, 1959), I, 445 (V.2).

³ McKeon, *Basic Works of Aristotle*, pp. 706–711 (*Metaphysics*, I.ix.990b–993a, trans. by W. D. Ross). See also Theodor Gomperz, *Greek Thinkers*, trans. by Laurie Magnus (Vol. I) and G. B. Berry (Vols. II–IV) (4 vols.; London: J. Murray, 1901–1912), IV, 3–4.

⁴ See especially Jaeger, *Aristotle*, pp. 324ff, and compare Barker, *The Politics of Aristotle*, pp. xxxi–xxxiv.

⁵ See Barker, *The Politics of Aristotle*, p. 387.

⁶ Jaeger, *Aristotle*, p. 335.

⁷ *Ibid.*, pp. 407–425.

⁸ *Ibid.*, pp. 468–469.

⁹ Barker, *The Politics of Aristotle*, pp. 332–333 (VII.i.3–4, 1337a). The bracketed insertion is Barker's.

¹⁰ *Ibid.*, p. 332 (1–2). Jowett's translation (p. 300 of his edition, p. 1305 in McKeon, *Basic Works of Aristotle*) of the key sentence is somewhat different, as follows: "The citizen should be moulded to suit the form of government under which he lives."

¹¹ Barker, *The Politics of Aristotle*, p. 332n2.

¹² McKeon, *Basic Works of Aristotle*, pp. 656–658 (*De Partibus Animalium*, I.v. 645a–b, trans. by William Ogle).

¹³ Plutarch, *The Lives of Noble Grecians and Romans*, trans. by John Dryden and rev. by Arthur Clough (Modern Library; New York: Random House, 1932), p. 805.

¹⁴ Rackham, trans., *Nicomachean Ethics*, pp. 5–6 (I.ii.4–7, 1094a–b).

¹⁵ *Ibid.*, pp. 641–643 (X.ix.20–23, 1179b).

¹⁶ For Aristotle's specific recognition of the distinction between ordinary laws and constitutions, see McKeon, *Basic Works of Aristotle*, p. 1175 (*Politics*, II.xii.15–16, 1274b). See also Kurt von Fritz and Ernst Kapp, *Aristotle's Constitution of Athens and Related Texts* (New York: Hafner, 1950), pp. 9–10.

[17] Gomperz, *Greek Thinkers*, IV, 34.

[18] There are articles on the logographers in the *Encyclopaedia Britannica*, 14th ed., and *The Oxford Classical Dictionary* (Oxford: Clarendon Press, 1957). The special class of logographers who wrote somewhat later on Attic and Athenian local history are called Atthidographers. Their works are referred to as Atthis. Some of these writers about Athenian government (and they were not all native Athenians) had partisan biases and motives in writing, but scholars like Aristotle could safely use their products by the exercise of critical historical methods. On the extensive controversy concerning the Atthidographers, see Felix Jacoby, *Atthis: The Local Chronicles of Ancient Athens* (Oxford: Clarendon Press, 1949). This work supplies abundant evidence concerning the political contents of the Atthis. See especially pp. 71–78.

[19] See von Fritz and Kapp, *Aristotle's Constitution of Athens*, pp. 3, 5, 13ff. Also for his own *Constitution of Athens* Aristotle seems to have made use of the works of the local historians of Attica and of Athens.

[20] Diogenes Laertius, *Lives of Eminent Philosophers*, I, 475 (V.27).

[21] Von Fritz and Kapp, *Aristotle's Constitution of Athens*, pp. 113–114 (Chap. 41).

[22] Ross, *Aristotle*, p. 236. Ross's own translation of the appropriate passage in the *Nicomachean Ethics* (X.IX.17–20, 1181b) has Aristotle saying "in the light of the constitutions we have collected . . ." (McKeon, *Basic Works of Aristotle*, p. 1112).

[23] William S. Caldwell did excellent work on this project, using mainly Aristotle's *Politics*. Later Ben Cochenet, whose knowledge of the Greek sources was outstanding, carried the enumeration, analysis, and tabulation still further. My thanks to them both.

[24] Sir John Edwin Sandys, *Aristotle's Constitution of Athens* (London: Macmillan, 1912). See also von Fritz and Kapp, *Aristotle's Constitution of Athens*. Their work is probably the best edition now available. Another recent edition worthy of close study is *The Constitution of the Athenians by the Old Oligarch and by Aristotle*, by Livio C. Stecchini (Glencoe, Ill.: Free Press, 1950). The Loeb edition, translated by H. Rackman, and published in a volume that also includes *The Eudemian Ethics* and *On Virtues and Vices* (Cambridge, Mass.: Harvard University Press, 1938), is also useful.

[25] Jaeger, *Aristotle*, p. 260.

[26] George H. Sabine, *A History of Political Theory*, rev. ed. (New York: Holt, 1950), p. 141.

Introduction to Part III

[1] On the Hellenistic period generally see the works of Sir William W. Tarn and especially his *Hellenistic Civilisation*, 3rd ed. (London: Edward Arnold, 1952).

[2] On education in Hellenistic times, see Henri I. Marrou, *A History of Education in Antiquity*, trans. by George Lamb (New York: Sheed and Ward, 1956), especially Part Two; Frederick Eby and Charles Flinn Arrowood, *The History and Philosophy of Education, Ancient and Medieval* (Englewood Cliffs, N.J.: Prentice-Hall, 1940, 1956), Chaps. 9–12.

[3] Chester G. Starr, Jr., "The Perfect Democracy of the Roman Empire," *American Historical Review*, 58:1–16 (October 1952). Epictetus among others warned against such spies, *Discourses*, trans. by P. E. Matheson, in Whitney J. Oates, ed., *The Stoic and Epicurean Philosophers* (New York: Random House, 1940), Bk. IV, Chap. 13.

[4] On municipal life and government in the Empire, see Samuel Dill, *Roman Society from Nero to Marcus Aurelius* (New York: Meridian Books, 1956), Bk. II, Chap. 2, pp. 196–250. See also William T. Arnold, *The Roman System of Provincial Administration, to the Accession of Constantine the Great* (Oxford: Blackwell, 1914).

Chapter 11. The Hellenistic Period

[1] See Sir William W. Tarn, *Hellenistic Civilisation,* 3rd ed. (London: Edward Arnold, 1952).

[2] For dates, names, and other basic information on the philosophical schools I have relied on the *Encyclopaedia Britannica,* 14th ed., and the classical dictionaries previously cited, and have been much helped by Bertrand Russell, *A History of Western Philosophy* (New York: Simon and Schuster, 1945).

[3] See the brief account of this episode in Russell, *A History of Western Philosophy,* pp. 236–237.

[4] Two works on Epicurus that I have found especially helpful are Cyril Bailey, *Epicurus, The Extant Remains* (Oxford: Clarendon Press, 1926), and Norman Wentworth DeWitt, *Epicurus and His Philosophy* (Minneapolis: University of Minnesota Press, 1954).

[5] DeWitt, *Epicurus and His Philosophy,* pp. 10–11, 183–187.

[6] *Ibid.,* pp. 183–187.

[7] Bailey, *Epicurus, The Extant Remains,* pp. 98–99.

[8] *Columbia Encyclopedia,* 2nd ed. (New York: Columbia University Press, 1950), p. 392.

[9] *Ibid.,* p. 1897.

[10] Russell, *A History of Western Philosophy,* p. 253.

[11] Ernest Barker, *From Alexander to Constantine* (Oxford: Clarendon Press, 1956), pp. 25–26. This author has gathered together several such statements.

[12] Plutarch, *The Lives of the Noble Grecians and Romans,* trans. by John Dryden and rev. by Arthur Hugh Clough (Modern Library; New York: Random House, 1932), p. 73.

[13] Barker, *From Alexander to Constantine,* p. 26, citing J. von Arnim's *Stoicorum Veterum Fragmenta,* I, 271.

[14] His great work called simply *Polybius: The Histories* is published in English in six small volumes in the Loeb Classical Library, trans. by W. R. Paton (London: W. Heinemann, 1922–1927). This is the edition I have used, but there are other translations.

[15] *Ibid.,* I, 3 (I.i.1–2). Compare John B. Bury, *The Ancient Greek Historians* (New York: Dover, 1958), pp. 209ff. Bury says, p. 210: "Thucydides is an artist, Polybius is a teacher."

[16] *The Histories,* I, 33 (I.xiii.9–10).

[17] *Ibid.,* II, 5 (III.i.6–7).

[18] *Ibid.,* II, 19 (III.vii.4–5).

[19] See Bury, *The Ancient Greek Historians,* pp. 209ff.

[20] *The Histories,* I, 9, 11 (I.iv.1–2); see Bury, *The Ancient Greek Historians,* Lecture VI, especially pp. 200–203.

[21] *The Histories,* I, 3, 5 (I.i.5–6).

[22] There are various editions of Lucretius' poem. I have used that edited by Whitney J. Oates, in *The Stoic and Epicurean Philosophers* (New York: Random House, 1940). See pp. 184ff.

[23] *Ibid.,* p. 185.

[24] There are many works that deal with Cicero. See the bibliography in Frank R. Cowell, *Cicero and the Roman Republic* (New York: Chanticleer Press, 1948), pp. 295–298, itself a most useful account. *The Oxford Classical Dictionary* (Oxford: Clarendon Press, 1957), pp. 188–191, supplies a reliable list of his writings, with approximate dates.

[25] Cicero, *De Re Publica [and] De Legibus,* trans. by Clinton Walker Keyes (Loeb Classical Library; Cambridge, Mass.: Harvard University Press, 1943), p. 459 (*The Laws,* III.i.1).

[26] *Ibid.,* p. 15 (*The Republic,* I.ii.2).

[27] *Ibid.,* p. 25 (I.v.9).

[28] *Ibid.,* p. 27 (I.vi.11).

[29] *Ibid.,* pp. 25, 27 (I.vi.11).

[30] *Ibid.,* p. 27 (I.vi.11).

[31] *Ibid.,* p. 17 (I.ii.3).

[32] *Ibid.,* p. 29 (I.viii.13).

[33] *Ibid.,* p. 63 (I.xxiv.38).

[34] Cowell, *Cicero and the Roman Republic,* p. 238.

[35] *Ibid.,* pp. 243–244.

[36] *De Re Publica [and] De Legibus,* p. 389 (*The Laws,* II.vii.1).

Chapter 12. The Age of the Roman Empire

[1] On Roman education, see Henri I. Marrou, *A History of Education in Antiquity,* trans. by George Lamb (New York: Sheed and Ward, 1956), pp. 229–313.

[2] Oskar Seyffert, *A Dictionary of Classical Antiquities* (New York: Meridian Books, 1957), pp. 80, 207.

[3] *Ibid.,* pp. 206–207. See Donald Lemen Clark, *Rhetoric in Greco-Roman Education* (New York: Columbia University Press, 1957), for a general study of the methods and contents of ancient Greek and Roman study and teaching of rhetoric, which sometimes touched on political subjects of a noncontroversial nature. See also Harold Mattingly, *Roman Imperial Civilization* (Garden City, N.Y.: Doubleday, 1959), pp. 299–301. Note too that Edward Gibbon, in *The Decline and Fall of the Roman Empire* (2 vols.; Modern Library; New York: Random House, 1932), II, 177, speaking of the schools at Athens in the second century A.D., says that "The schools of Athens were protected by the wisest and most virtuous of the Roman princes. . . . The public salaries were assigned by the generous spirit of the Antonines; and each professor, of politics, of rhetoric, of the Platonic, the Peripatetic, the Stoic, and the Epicurean philosophy, received an annual stipend . . ." But I have strong doubts that there were publicly supported professors of politics, even under the Antonines, anywhere in the Empire.

[4] References to these so-called universities will be found under Education and under place names in Seyffert, *Dictionary of Classical Antiquities; The Oxford Classical Dictionary* (Oxford: Clarendon Press, 1957); John B. Bury, *History of the Later Roman Empire* (2 vols.; New York: Dover, 1958), I, 231ff; Mattingly, *Roman Imperial Civilization,* p. 85; and other works. Ausonius, a fourth-century writer, spoke of Bordeaux as a great educational center.

[5] Livio C. Stecchini, "On Encyclopedias in Time and Space," *American Behavioral Scientist,* 6:3–4 (September 1962).

[6] For a full and scholarly account, see Clark, *Rhetoric in Greco-Roman Education,* especially Chap. 4, pp. 77–107, 133–143. For briefer discussions see Seyffert, *Dictionary of Classical Antiquities,* pp. 544–546, and *Oxford Classical Dictionary,* pp. 766–768.

[7] Seyffert, *Dictionary of Classical Antiquities,* p. 545.

[8] *Ibid.,* p. 546.

[9] *Ibid.,* p. 546; Ernest Barker, *From Alexander to Constantine* (Oxford: Clarendon Press, 1956), pp. 275–278.

[10] See for example Charles Howard McIlwain, *The Growth of Political Thought in the West* (New York: Macmillan, 1932), pp. 103, 105, 116–146 *passim;* George H. Sabine, *A History of Political Theory,* rev. ed. (New York: Holt, 1950), pp. 167–173.

[11] *Oxford Classical Dictionary,* p. 237 (Coruncanius), pp. 472–473 (Jurisprudence).

[12] One of the most illuminating articles on the nature of the Roman Empire is

Chap. I, "The Roman Conception of Empire," of Ernest Barker's *Church, State and Education* (Ann Arbor: University of Michigan Press, 1957). The problems connected with law receive a brief but illuminating treatment.

[13] Franz Peter Bremer, *Die rechtslehrer und rechtsschulen im römischen kaiserreich* ([*The Teachers of Law and Schools of Law in the Roman Empire*]; Berlin: Verlag von I. Guttentag, 1868), has supplied much of the information for this brief summary, and for the sketch of the Roman study and teaching of law. A complete translation of this work, which is in German and Latin, was prepared for me by Herbert Sommer (the German text) and Mrs. Conrad R. (Santina) Bayerle (the Latin passages). I have, of course, made some small revisions in the translations. Roscoe Pound's *The Lawyer from Antiquity to Modern Times* (St. Paul, Minn.: West Publishing Co., 1953), pp. 35–58, has been of some help as well. See also Mattingly, *Roman Imperial Civilization*, pp. 55–57, 77–78, 147.

[14] A German scholar named George Friedrich Puchta raised this question sometime before 1868, and the work by Bremer cited above was written in order to answer Puchta's question and set the record straight.

[15] Bremer, *The Teachers of Law and Schools of Law*. I have found nothing else as complete and convincing as Bremer's book—but I have no doubt that there are articles and even books in print on the subject that have not come to my attention.

[16] Quoted from *Digest*, 1, 4, 1, by Sabine, *A History of Political Theory*, p. 171.

[17] A number of works contribute to our knowledge of Roman imperial public administration. See, for example, Mattingly, *Roman Imperial Civilization*, pp. 40, 42, 55–57, 77–78, 135–157; Bury, *History of the Later Roman Empire*, I, 25–66; Leon Homo, *Roman Political Institutions* (New York: Knopf, 1930), pp. 299–361.

[18] Bertrand Russell, *A History of Western Philosophy* (New York: Simon and Schuster, 1945), p. 284.

[19] Barker, *From Alexander to Constantine*, p. 333.

[20] *Ibid.*

[21] Barker in *From Alexander to Constantine*, pp. 238–249, prints some well-chosen extracts from Tacitus that illustrate a part of what I say in the text.

[22] *Ibid.*, pp. 204–224, 303–310, 341–386.

[23] The literature on the life of Jesus is overwhelming in its quantity. I have found useful Albert Schweitzer, *The Quest of the Historical Jesus* (New York: Macmillan, 1962); F. C. Conybeare, *The Origins of Christianity* (Evanston and New York: University Books, 1958).

[24] On the early history of the church, see Hans Lietzmann, *A History of the Early Church* (4 vols. in 2; Cleveland and New York: World, 1961); Johannes Weiss, *Earliest Christianity* (2 vols.; New York: Harper, 1959).

[25] Barker, *From Alexander to Constantine*, pp. 104–105, 124–128.

[26] *Ibid.*, pp. 135–138.

[27] *Ibid.*, p. 139.

[28] *Ibid.*, pp. 140ff.

[29] *Ibid.*, pp. 155–163; see also Erwin R. Goodenough, *An Introduction to Philo Judaeus* (New Haven, Conn.: Yale University Press, 1940).

[30] See Barker, *From Alexander to Constantine*, pp. 430–445.

INDEX

ᔙ Index

INDEX

Augustine, St., church father, 324–325, 334

Augustus, first Roman emperor, 307

Ausonius, tutor to Gratian, 319

Babylon, 275, 331

Babylonia, Babylonians, 23, 24, 27, 31, 32, 42, 74, 84, 138, 220, 323, 330, 331

Babylonians, The (Aristophanes), 195

Barker, Ernest, 12: holds that Plato lectured, 232; on Aristotle's view of "constitution," 267; on Plotinus, 316; volume on ancient theories of kingship, 318; collection of Jewish documents, 323

Bedouins, 51

Beersheba, 73

Benjamin, tribe of, 85, 86, 92, 96

Bethel, 70

Bias of Priene, one of Seven Sages, 147

Bible, 64, 66–68, 69. *See also* New Testament, Old Testament

Bicameral congress, idea of in Mesopotamia, 32

Bilalama, king of Eshnunna, law code of, 35

Biographies, political, under Roman Empire, 317

Biology, Aristotle's work in, 261, 266–267, 268, 276, 337

Birds, The (Aristophanes), 195

Bodin, Jean, 12

Boeotians, 109

Boghazköy, 33

Bordeaux, 308

Bremer, Franz Peter, on Roman law teachers and schools, 313, 364n13–15

British North America Act, 272

Browning, Robert, quoted, 217

Brutus, Roman political orator, 309

Burnet, John, lists studies at Plato's Academy, 230

Bury, John B.: calls Hecataeus initiator of modern history writing, 181; on Demosthenes, 257

Byzantium, eastern Roman Empire, 289, 307, 325

Cadmus, Greek historian, 180

Caesar, Julius, Roman statesman, 286, 301, 309, 310, 321–322, 334

Calebites, 72

Callinus of Ephesus, elegist, 131

Callipus, murderer of Dion, 234, 235, 236, 238

Cambridge University, 4

Canaan, Canaanites, 70, 71, 72, 73, 75, 76, 77, 80, 81, 92

Canada, constitution of (British North America Act), 272

Carchemish, 70

Carneades of Cyrene, Skeptic philosopher, 291–292

Carthage, Carthaginians, 114, 275, 283: Polybius on government of, 296, 299

Cato, Roman orator, 292, 309

Celsus, early critic of Christians, 324

Chabrias, Athenian soldier, 234, 236

Chaerephon of Sphettus, disciple of Socrates, 206

Chaeronea, 244, 247

Chalcedon, 178

Chaldeans, 70, 220

Charlemagne, emperor of West, 67

Cherniss, Harold F., on Plato as lecturer, 232

Chiera, Edward, 33

Chilon of Sparta, one of Seven Sages, 147

China, Chinese, 79, 332

Chion, student at Academy, 234, 236

Chios, 122

Chiron, or Cheiron, Centaur, praised by Xenophon, 249

Choëphoroe (Aeschylus), 189

Christ, *see* Jesus

Christians, 66, 68, 69, 87, 336: under Roman emperors, 285, 288, 289, 293, 320–322; early contributions to study of politics minimal, 319, 323, 325, 334; and church-state relations, 322–325

Chronicles, book of, 67

Chryseis, portrayed in *Iliad*, 124–125

Chryses, priest of Apollo, 124–125

Chrysippus of Cilicia and Athens, Stoic philosopher, 295

Church-state relations: in Mesopotamia, 25–26; Christian doctrine of, 321–323; Origen on, 324. *See also* God and gods, Religion, Theology

Cicero, Marcus Tullius, Roman orator and political leader, 12, 13, 286, 295: writings of, 299–300, 301; contrasted with Lucretius, 300–301; debt to Plato, 301–302; views on duty to serve state, 303; on need for "political science," 303–304; Epicureans criticized, 304; on gods as rulers of men, 305; on Roman governmental problems, 305–306; contri-

369